DECONSTRUCTION AND THE POSSIBILITY OF JUSTICE

EDITED BY

DRUCILLA CORNELL

MICHEL ROSENFELD

DAVID GRAY CARLSON

New York •
London

Published in 1992 by

Routledge
An imprint of Routledge, Chapman and Hall, Inc.
29 West 35 Street
New York, NY 10001

Published in Great Britain by
Routledge
11 New Fetter Lane
London EC4P 4EE

Library of Congress Cataloging-in-Publication Data

Deconstruction and the possibility of justice / David Gray Carlson,
  Drucilla Cornell, and Michel Rosenfeld, eds.
      p. cm.
      Most of these papers were presented at a symposium held at the
  Benjamin N. Cardozo School of Law on October 1–2, 1989.
      Includes bibliographical references and index.
      ISBN 0-415-90303-3 (CL).—ISBN 0-415-90304-1 (PB)
      1. Justice 2. Law—Interpretation and construction. 3. Law and
  politics. 4. Derrida, Jacques. I. Carlson, David (David Gray)
  II. Cornell, Drucilla. III. Rosenfeld, Michel.
  IV. Benjamin N. Cardozo School of Law.
  K246.D43   1992
340'.11—dc20   91–34742
                                                                     CIP
British Library Cataloging-in-Publication Data also available.

Contents

Comparative Perspectives on Justice, Law and Politics

Acknowledgments

This volume grows out of a symposium entitled *Deconstruction and the Possibility of Justice,* held at the Benjamin N. Cardozo School of Law on October 1–2, 1989. Most of the papers in this volume were presented at that conference. The proceedings of that conference are published in volume 11 of the *Cardozo Law Review* pp. 919–1726. We gratefully acknowledge the permission of the *Cardozo Law Review* to reprint portions of some of the papers here.

This conference was made possible through the generosity of Jacob Burns, who has founded the Jacob Burns Institute for Advanced Legal Studies. His generosity has made possible a series of ambitious inquiries into philosophies and theories largely unfamiliar in the context of American legal studies, but which promise to have a profound impact on the way law is to be comprehended in the next century. One of these projects has already been published as *Hegel and Legal Theory* (D. Cornell, M. Rosenfeld and D. Carlson eds. 1991).

Introduction

To many, the very title of this book, *Deconstruction and the Possibility of Justice,* would seem to be an oxymoron. At least by its critics, deconstruction has been associated with cynicism toward the very idea of justice. Justice, so the story goes, demands reconstruction, not deconstruction.

Yet even its critics recognize that deconstruction is, in some way, aligned with the marginalized. As we will see in these essays, they are not wrong in that assumption. The question then becomes whether what has been marginalized should remain marginalized. This question indeed constitutes a reconstruction, as well as a deconstruction, of justice.

Within literary studies we hear the same cry: deconstruction has brought in its wake the clamor for the recognition of many voices outside the traditional canon. The writing of people of different cultures, nationalities, races and sexes are now given equal standing to the work of white men. And, deconstruction, so the story goes, is to blame.

This is not to say that all of Derrida's critics are uncritical defenders of the cultural establishment. "What should be" demands an appeal to some criteria of justice. Derrida's more liberal critics have focused on just this problem. They have insisted that even if one can appreciate deconstruction's alliance with the underdog, deconstruction cannot provide an ethical basis for this alliance, let alone argue the necessity of such an alliance.

According to critics, the reason deconstruction cannot help in this enterprise is that it purportedly undermines the social consolidation that must take place if we are even to be able to speak to one another about standards of justice. This group of critics is not concerned with the defense of the established order; they are concerned with justice and, correspondingly, with criteria for justification so we can determine which theory of justice is ethically better. These critics also associate deconstruction with a set of code phrases similar to that of the more conservative defenders of order. For them, deconstruction purportedly undermines public reason, rejects communitarian standards of morality, mocks legality and denies even the possibility of shared reality given to us in language. Deconstruction is also accused of debunking the validity of the very normative, social analysis that could explain oppression as oppression, rather than just harmless differentiation among groups.

The purpose of this volume is to rethink the questions posed by Derrida's writings and his unique philosophical positioning, without reference to the catch-phrases that have supposedly captured deconstruction in a nutshell. Derrida's own essay, *Force of Law: The "Mystical Foundation of Authority,"* clearly expresses his philosophical commitment to justice.

All the contributions in this volume refuse easy answers. As a result, we believe it can play an important role in deepening our understanding of deconstruction and its relation to questions of law and justice. Perhaps, more importantly, we hope with this volume, to widen the horizon of how justice can and should be conceived.

Drucilla Cornell
Michel Rosenfeld
David Gray Carlson
—September 1991

Part One

Law, Violence and Justice

1

Force of Law: The "Mystical Foundation of Authority"

Jacques Derrida

I

C'est ici un devoir, je dois *m'adresser* à vous en anglais.This is an obligation, I must *address* myself to you in English.

The title of this colloquium and the problem that it requires me, as you say transitively in your language, to address, have had me musing for months. Although I've been entrusted with the formidable honor of the "keynote address," I had nothing to do with the invention of this title or with the implicit formulation of the problem. "Deconstruction and the Possibility of Justice": the conjunction "and" brings together words, concepts, perhaps things that don't belong to the same category. A conjunction such as "and" dares to defy order, taxonomy, classificatory logic, no matter how it works: by analogy, distinction or opposition. An ill-tempered speaker might say: I don't see the connection, no rhetoric could bend itself to such an exercise. I'd be glad to try to speak of each of these things or these categories ("deconstruction," "possibility," "justice") and even of these syncategoremes ("and," "the," "of"), but not at all in this order, this *taxis*, this taxonomy or this syntagm.

Translated by Mary Quaintance. The author would like to thank Sam Weber for his help in the final revision of this text. Except for some footnotes added after the fact, this text corresponds to the version distributed at the colloquium on "Deconstruction and the Possibility of Justice" (October 1989, Cardozo Law School), of which Jacques Derrida read only the first part to open the session. For lack of time, Derrida was unable to conclude the elaboration of the work in progress, of which this is only a preliminary version. In addition, the second part of the lecture, the part that precisely was not read but only discussed at the same colloquium, was delivered on April 26, 1990, to open a colloquium organized by Saul Friedlander at the University of California, Los Angeles on *Nazism and the "Final Solution": Probing the Limits of Representation*.

Such a speaker wouldn't merely be in a bad temper, he'd be in bad faith. And even unjust. For one could easily propose an interpretation that would do the title justice. Which is to say in this case an adequate and lucid and so rather suspicious interpretation of the title's intentions or *vouloir-dire*. This title suggests a question that itself takes the form of a suspicion; does deconstruction insure, permit, authorize the possibility of justice? Does it make justice possible, or a discourse of consequence on justice and the conditions of its possibility? Yes, certain people would reply; no, replies the other party. Do the so-called deconstructionists have anything to say about justice, anything to do with it? Why, basically, do they speak of it so little? Does it interest them, in the end? Isn't it because, as certain people suspect, deconstruction doesn't in itself permit any just action, any just discourse on justice but instead constitutes a threat to *droit,* to law or right, and ruins the condition of the very possibility of justice? Yes, certain people would reply, no, replies the other party. In this first fictive exchange one can already find equivocal slippages between law (*droit*) and justice. The "sufferance" of deconstruction, what makes it suffer and what makes those it torments suffer, is perhaps the absence of rules, of norms, and definitive criteria that would allow one to distinguish unequivocally between *droit* and justice.

That is the choice, the "either/or," "yes or no" that I detect in this title. To this extent, the title is rather violent, polemical, inquisitorial. We may fear that it contains some instrument of torture—that is, a manner of interrogation that is not the most just. Needless to say, from this point on I can offer no response, at least no reassuring response, to any questions put in this way ("either/or," "yes or no"), to either party or to either party's expectations formalized in this way.

Je dois, donc, c'est ici un devoir, m'adresser à vous en anglais. So I must, this is an obligation, address myself to you in English. *Je le dois* ... that means several things at once.

1. *Je dois* speak English (how does one translate this *"dois,"* this *devoir*? I must? I should, I ought to, I have to?) because it has been imposed on me as a sort of obligation or condition by a sort of symbolic force or law in a situation I do not control. A sort of *polemos* already concerns the appropriation of language: if, at least, I want to make myself understood, it is necessary that I speak your language, I must.

2. I must speak your language because what I shall say will thus be more *juste,* or deemed more *juste,* and be more justly appreciated, *juste* this time [in the sense of "just right,"] in the sense of an adequation between what is and what is said or thought, between what is said and what is understood, indeed between what is thought and said

or heard and understood by the majority of those who are here and who manifestly lay down the law. "Faire la loi" (laying down the law) is an interesting expression that we shall have more to say about later.

3. I must speak in a language that is not my own because that will be more just, in another sense of the word *juste,* in the sense of justice, a sense which, without worrying about it too much for now, we can call juridico-ethico-political: it is more just to speak the language of the majority, especially when, through hospitality, it grants a foreigner the right to speak. It's hard to say if the law we're referring to here is that of decorum, of politeness, the law of the strongest, or the equitable law of democracy. And whether it depends on justice or law (*droit*). Also, if I am to bend to this law and accept it, a certain number of conditions are necessary: for example, I must respond to an invitation and manifest my desire to speak here, something that no one apparently has constrained me to do; I must be capable, up to a certain point, of understanding the contract and the conditions of the law, that is, of at least minimally adopting, appropriating, your language, which from that point ceases, at least to this extent, to be foreign to me. You and I must understand, in more or less the same way, the translation of my text, initially written in French; this translation, however excellent it may be (and I'll take this moment to thank Mary Quaintance) necessarily remains a translation, that is to say an always possible but always imperfect compromise between two idioms.

This question of language and idiom will doubtless be at the heart of what I would like to propose for discussion tonight.

There are a certain number of idiomatic expressions in your language that have always been rather valuable to me as they have no strict equivalent in French. I'll cite at least *two* of them, before I even begin. They are not unrelated to what I'd like to try to say tonight.

A. The first is "to enforce the law," or "enforceability of the law or contract." When one translates "to enforce the law" into French, by "*appliquer la loi*," for example, one loses this direct or literal allusion to the force that comes from within to remind us that law is always an authorized force, a force that justifies itself or is justified in applying itself, even if this justification may be judged from elsewhere to be unjust or unjustifiable. Applicability, "enforceability," is not an exterior or secondary possibility that may or may not be added as a supplement to law. It is the force essentially implied in the very concept of *justice as law* (*droit*), of justice as it becomes *droit*, of the law as "*droit*" (for I want to insist right away on reserving the possibility of a justice, indeed of a law that not only exceeds or contradicts "law" (*droit*) but also, perhaps, has no relation to law, or maintains such a strange relation to it that it may just as well command the "*droit*" that excludes it). The word "enforceability" reminds us that there is no such thing as law (*droit*) that doesn't imply *in itself, a priori, in the analytic structure of its concept,* the possibility of being "enforced," applied by force. There are, to be sure, laws that are not enforced, but there is no law without enforceability, and no applicability or enforceability of the law without force, whether this force be direct or indirect, physical or symbolic, exterior or interior, brutal or subtly discursive and hermeneutic, coercive or regulative, and so forth.

How are we to distinguish between this force of the law, this "force of law," as one says in English as well as in French, I believe, and the violence that one always deems unjust? What difference is there between, *on the one hand,* the force that can be just, or in any case deemed legitimate (not only an instrument in the service of law but the practice and even the realization, the essence of *droit*), and *on the other hand* the violence that one always deems unjust? What is a just force or a non-violent force? To stay with the question of idiom, let me turn here to a German word that will soon be occupying much of our attention: *Gewalt.* In English, as in French, it is often translated as "violence." The Benjamin text that I will be speaking to you about soon is entitled *"Zur Kritik der Gewalt,"* translated in French as *"Critique de la violence"* and in English as "Critique of Violence." But these two translations, while not altogether *injustes* (and so not altogether violent), are very active interpretations that don't do justice to the fact that *Gewalt* also signifies, for Germans, legitimate power, authority, public force. *Gesetzgebende Gewalt* is legislative power, *geistliche Gewalt* the spiritual power of the church, *Staatsgewalt* the authority or power of the state. *Gewalt,* then, is both violence and legitimate power, justified authority. How are we to distinguish between the force of law of a legitimate power and the supposedly originary violence that must have established this authority and that could not itself have been authorized by any anterior legitimacy, so that, in this initial moment, it is neither legal nor illegal—or, others would quickly say, neither just nor unjust? I gave a lecture in Chicago a few days ago—which I'm deliberately leaving aside here, even though its theme is closely connected—devoted to a certain number of texts by Heidegger in which the words *Walten* and *Gewalt* play a decisive role, as one cannot simply translate them by either force or violence, especially not in a context where Heidegger will attempt to demonstrate his claim that originally, and for example for Heraclitus, *Dikè*—justice, *droit*, trial, penalty or punishment, vengeance, and so forth—is *Eris* (conflict, *Streit*, discord, *polemos* or *Kampf*), that is, it is *adikia,* injustice, as well. We could come back to this, if you wish, during the discussion, but I prefer to hold off on it for now.

Since this colloquium is devoted to deconstruction and the possibility of justice, my first thought is that in the many texts considered "deconstructive", and particularly in certain of those that I've published myself, recourse to the word "force" is quite frequent, and in strategic places I would even say decisive, but at the same time always or almost always accompanied by an explicit reserve, a guardedness. I have often called for vigilance, I have asked myself to keep in mind the risks spread by this word, whether it be the risk of an obscure, substantialist, occulto-mystic concept or the risk of giving authorization to violent, unjust, arbitrary force. I won't cite these texts. That would be self-indulgent and would take too much time, but I ask you to trust me. A first precaution against the risks of substantialism or irrationalism that I just evoked involves the differential character of force. For me, it is always a question of differential force, of difference as difference of force, of force as *différance* (*différance* is a force *diffé-* ?
rée-différante), of the relation between force and form, between force ¡
and signification, performative force, illocutionary or perlocutionary force, of persuasive and rhetorical force, of affirmation by signature, but also and especially of all the paradoxical situations in which the greatest force and the greatest weakness strangely enough exchange places. And that is the whole history. What remains is that I've always been uncomfortable with the word force, which I've often judged to be indispensable, and I thank you for thus forcing me to try and say a little more about it today. And the same thing goes for justice. There are no doubt many reasons why the majority of texts hastily identified as "deconstructionist"—for example, mine—*seem*, I do say *seem*, not to foreground the theme of justice (as theme, precisely), or the theme of ethics or politics. Naturally this is only *apparently so,* if one considers, for example, (I will only mention these) the many texts devoted to Levinas and to the relations between "violence and metaphysics," or to the philosophy of right, Hegel's, with all its posterity in *Glas,* of which it is the principal *motif,* or the texts devoted to the drive for power and to the paradoxes of power in *Spéculer—sur Freud,* to the law, in *Devant la loi* (on Kafka's *Vor dem Gesetz*) or in *Déclaration d'Indépendance,* in *Admiration de Nelson Mandela ou les lois de la réflexion,* and in many other texts. It goes without saying that discourses on double affirmation, the gift beyond exchange and distribution, the undecidable, the incommensurable or the incalculable, or on singularity, difference and heterogeneity are also, through and through, at least obliquely discourses on justice.

Besides, it was normal, foreseeable, desirable that studies of deconstructive style should culminate in the problematic of law (*droit*), of law and justice. (I have elsewhere tried to show that the essence of law ?

is not prohibitive but affirmative.) Such would even be the most proper place for them, if such a thing existed. A deconstructive interrogation that starts, as was the case here, by destabilizing or complicating the opposition between *nomos* and *physis*, between *thésis* and *physis*— that is to say, the opposition between law, convention, the institution on the one hand, and nature on the other, with all the oppositions that they condition; for example, and this is only an example, that between positive law and natural law (the *différance* is the displacement of this oppositional logic), a deconstructive interrogation that starts, as this one did, by destabilizing, complicating, or bringing out the paradoxes of values like those of the proper and of property in all their registers, of the subject, and so of the responsible subject, of the subject of law (*droit*) and the subject of morality, of the juridical or moral person, of intentionality, etc., and of all that follows from these, such a deconstructive line of questioning is through and through a problematization of law and justice. A problematization of the foundations of law, morality and politics. This questioning of foundations is neither foundationalist nor anti-foundationalist. Nor does it pass up opportunities to put into question or even to exceed the possibility or the ultimate necessity of questioning, of the questioning form of thought, interrogating without assurance or prejudice the very history of the question and of its philosophical authority. For there is an authority—and so a legitimate force in the questioning form of which one might ask oneself whence it derives such great force in our tradition.

If, hypothetically, it had a proper place, which is precisely what cannot be the case, such a deconstructive "questioning" or metaquestioning would be more at home in law schools, perhaps also— this sometimes happens—in theology or architecture departments, than in philosophy departments and much more than in the literature departments where it has often been thought to belong. That is why, without knowing them well from the inside, for which I feel I am to blame, without pretending to any familiarity with them, I think that the developments in "critical legal studies" or in work by people like Stanley Fish, Barbara Herrnstein Smith, Drucilla Cornell, Sam Weber and others, which situates itself in relation to the articulation between literature and philosophy, law and politico-institutional problems, are today, from the point of view of a certain deconstruction, among the most fertile and the most necessary. They respond, it seems to me, to the most radical programs of a deconstruction that would like, in order to be consistent with itself, not to remain enclosed in purely speculative, theoretical, academic discourses but rather (with all due respect to Stanley Fish) to aspire to something more consequential, to *change* things and to intervene in an efficient and responsible, though always, of course, very mediated way, not only in the profession but in what one calls the *cité,* the *polis* and more generally the world. Not, doubtless, to change things in the rather naive sense of calculated, deliberate and strategically controlled intervention, but in the sense of maximum intensification of a transformation in progress, in the name of neither a simple symptom nor a simple cause (other categories are required here). In an industrial and hyper-technologized society, academia is less than ever the monadic or monastic ivory tower that in any case it never was. And this is particularly true of "law schools."

I hasten to add here, briefly, the following three points:

1. This conjunction or conjuncture is no doubt inevitable between, on the one hand, a deconstruction of a style more directly philosophical or motivated by literary theory and, on the other hand, juridico-literary reflection and "critical legal studies."

2. It is certainly not by chance that this conjunction has developed in such an interesting way in this country; this is another problem—urgent and compelling—that I must leave aside for lack of time. There are no doubt profound and complicated reasons of global dimensions, I mean geo-political and not merely domestic, for the fact that this development should be first and foremost North American.

3. Above all, if it has seemed urgent to give our attention to this joint or concurrent development and to participate in it, it is just as vital that we do not confound largely heterogeneous and unequal discourses, styles and discursive contexts. The word "deconstruction" could, in certain cases, induce or encourage such a confusion. The word itself gives rise to so many misunderstandings that one wouldn't want to add to them by reducing all the styles of critical legal studies to one or by making them examples or extensions of Deconstruction with a capital "D." However unfamiliar they may be to me, I know that these efforts in critical legal studies have their history, their context, and their proper idiom; in relation to such a philosophico-deconstructive questioning they are often (we shall say for the sake of brevity) uneven, timid, approximating or schematic, not to mention belated, although their specialization and the acuity of their technical competence puts them, on the other hand, very much in advance of whatever state deconstruction finds itself in a more literary or philosophical field. Respect for contextual, academico-institutional, discursive specificities, mistrust for analogies and hasty transpositions, for confused homogenizations, seem to me to be the first imperatives the way things stand today. I hope in any case that this encounter will leave us with the memory of disparities and disputes at least as much as it leaves us with agreements, with coincidences or consensus.

I said a moment ago: it only appears that deconstruction, in its manifestations most recognized as such, hasn't "addressed," as one says in English, the problem of justice. It only appears that way, but one must account for appearances, "keep up appearances" as Aristotle said, and that is how I'd like to employ myself here: to show why and how what is now called Deconstruction, while seeming not to "address" the problem of justice, has done nothing but address it, if only *obliquely*, unable to do so directly. *Obliquely*, as at this very moment, in which I'm preparing to demonstrate that one cannot speak *directly* about justice, thematize or objectivize justice, say "this is just" and even less "I am just," without immediately betraying justice, if not law (*droit*).[1]

But I have not yet begun. I started by saying that I must address myself to you in your language and announced right away that I've always found at least two of your idiomatic expressions invaluable, indeed irreplaceable. One was "to enforce the law," which always reminds us that if justice is not necessarily law (*droit*) or the law, it cannot become justice legitimately or *de jure* except by withholding force or rather by appealing to force from its first moment, from its first word. "At the beginning of justice there was *logos*, speech or language," which is not necessarily in contradiction with another *incipit*, namely, "In the beginning there will have been force."

Pascal says it in a fragment I may return to later, one of his famous "*pensées*," as usual more difficult than it seems. It starts like this: "*Justice, force.—Il est juste que ce qui est juste soit suivi, il est nécessaire que ce qui est le plus fort soit suivi.*" (*Justice, force.*—It is just that what is just be followed, it is necessary that what is strongest be followed" frag. 298, Brunschvicq edition) The beginning of this fragment is already extraordinary, at least in the rigor of its rhetoric. It says that what is just must be *followed* (followed by consequence, followed by effect, applied, *enforced*) and that what is strongest must also be followed (by consequence, effect, and so on). In other words, the common axiom is that the just and the strongest, the most just *as* or *as well as* the strongest, *must* be followed. But this "must be followed," common to the just and the strongest, is "right" ("*juste*") in one case, "necessary" in the other: "It is just that what is just be followed"—in other words, the concept or idea of the just, in the sense of justice, implies analytically and *a priori* that the just be "*suivi*," followed up, enforced, and it is just—also in the sense of "just right"—to think this way. "It is necessary that what is strongest be enforced."

And Pascal continues: "*La justice sans la force est impuissante*" ("Justice without force is impotent")—in other words, justice isn't justice, it is not achieved if it doesn't have the force to be "enforced;" a powerless justice is not justice, in the sense of *droit*—"*la force sans la justice est tyrannique. La justice sans force est contredite, parce qu'il y a toujours des méchants; la force sans la justice est accusée. Il faut donc mettre ensemble la justice et la force; et pour cela faire que ce qui est juste soit fort, ou que ce qui est fort soit juste*" ("force without justice is tyrannical. Justice without force is contradictory, as there are always the wicked; force without justice is accused of wrong. And so it is necessary to put justice and force together; and, for this, to make sure that what is just be strong, or what is strong be just.") It is diffi-cult to decide whether the "it is necessary" in this conclusion ("And so it is necessary to put justice and force together") is an "it is neces-sary" prescribed by what is just in justice or by what is necessary in force. But that is a pointless hesitation since justice demands, as jus-tice, recourse to force. The necessity of force is implied, then, in the "*juste*" in "justice."

This *pensée*, what continues and concludes it ("And so, since it was not possible to make the just strong, the strong have been made just") deserves a longer analysis than I can offer here. The principle of my analysis (or rather of my active and anything but non-violent interpre-tation), of the interpretation at the heart of what I will *indirectly* pro-pose in the course of this lecture, will, notably in the case of this Pascal *pensée*, run counter to tradition and to its most obvious context. This context and the conventional interpretation that it seems to dictate runs, precisely, in a conventionalist direction toward the sort of pes-simistic, relativistic and empiricist skepticism that drove Arnaud to suppress these *pensées* in the Port Royal edition, alleging that Pascal wrote them under the impression of a reading of Montaigne, who thought that laws were not in themselves just but rather were just only because they were laws. It is true that Montaigne used an interesting expression, which Pascal takes up for his own purposes and which I'd also like to reinterpret and to consider apart from its most conven-tional and conventionalist reading. The expression is "*fondement mystique de l'autorité*," "mystical foundation of authority." Pascal cites Montaigne without naming him when he writes in *pensée* 293: "... *l'un dit que l'essence de la justice est l'autorité du législateur, l'autre la commodité du souverain, l'autre la coutume présente; et c'est le plus sûr: rien, suivant la seule raison, n'est juste de soi; tout branle avec le temps. La coutume fait toute l'équité, par cette seule raison qu'elle est reçue; c'est le fondement mystique de son autorité. Qui la ramène à son principe, l'anéantit.*" ("... one man says that the essence of justice is the authority of the legislator, another that it is the convenience of the king, another that it is current custom; and the latter is closest to the truth: simple reason tells us that nothing is just in itself; everything crumbles with time. Custom is the sole basis for equity, for the simple reason that it is received; it is the mystical foundation of its authority. Whoever traces it to its source annihilates it.")

Montaigne was in fact talking about a "mystical foundation" of the authority of laws: "*Or les loix*," he says, "*se maintiennent en crédit, non parce qu'elles sont justes, mais parce qu'elles sont loix: c'est le fondement mystique de leur auctorité, elles n'en ont point d'autre. . . . Quiconque leur obéit parce qu'elles sont justes, ne leur obéit pas justement par où il doibt*" ("And so laws keep up their good standing, not because they are just, but because they are laws: that is the mystical foundation of their authority, they have no other. . . . Anyone who obeys them because they are just is not obeying them the way he ought to.")[2]

Here Montaigne is clearly distinguishing laws, that is to say droit, from justice. The justice of law, justice as law is not justice. Laws are not just as laws. One obeys them not because they are just but because they have authority.

Little by little I shall explain what I understand by this expression "mystical foundation of authority." It is true that Montaigne also wrote the following, which must, again, be interpreted by going beyond its simply conventional and conventionalist surface: "(*notre droit même a, dit-on des fictions légitimes sur lesquelles il fonde la vérité de sa justice*)"; "(even our law, it is said, has legitimate fictions on which it founds the truth of its justice)." I used these words as an epigraph to a text on *Vor dem Gesetz*. What is a legitimate fiction? What does it mean to establish the truth of justice? These are among the questions that await us. It is true that Montaigne proposed an analogy between this supplement of a legitimate fiction, that is, the fiction necessary to establish the truth of justice, and the supplement of artifice called for by a deficiency in nature, as if the absence of natural law called for the supplement of historical or positive, that is to say, fictional, law (*droit*), just as—to use Montaigne's analogy—"*les femmes qui emploient des dents d'ivoire où les leurs naturelles leur manquent, et, au lieu de leur vrai teint, en forgent un de quelque matière étrangère . . .*" (*Livre II*, ch. XII, p. 601 Pléiade); ("women who use ivory teeth when they're missing their real ones, and who, instead of showing their true complexion, forge one with some foreign material . . .").

Perhaps the Pascal *pensée* that, as he says, "puts together" justice and force and makes force an essential predicate of justice (by which he means "*droit*" more than justice) goes beyond a conventionalist or utilitarian relativism, beyond a nihilism, old or new, that would make the law a "masked power," beyond the cynical moral of La Fontaine's "The Wolf and the Sheep," according to which *"La raison du plus fort est toujours la meilleure"* ("Might makes right").

The Pascalian critique, *in its principle*, refers us back to original sin and to the corruption of natural laws by a reason that is itself corrupt. (*"Il y a sans doute des lois naturelles; mais cette belle raison a tout corrompu,"* section IV, 294; "There are, no doubt, natural laws; but this fine thing called reason has corrupted everything," and elsewhere: *"Notre justice s'anéantit devant la justice divine,"* 263; "Our justice comes to nothing before divine justice." I cite these *pensées* to prepare for our reading of Benjamin.)

But if we set aside the functional mechanism of the Pascalian critique, if we dissociate it from Christian pessimism, which is not impossible, then we can find in it, as in Montaigne, the basis for a modern critical philosophy, indeed for a critique of juridical ideology, a desedimentation of the superstructures of law that both hide and reflect the economic and political interests of the dominant forces of society. This would be both possible and always useful.

But beyond its principle and its mechanism, this Pascalian *pensée* perhaps concerns a more intrinsic structure, one that a critique of juridical ideology should never overlook. The very emergence of justice and law, the founding and justifying moment that institutes law implies a performative force, which is always an interpretative force: this time not in the sense of law in the service of force, its docile instrument, servile and thus exterior to the dominant power, but rather in the sense of law that would maintain a more internal, more complex relation with what one calls force, power or violence. Justice—in the sense of *droit* (right or law)—would not simply be put in the service of a social force or power, for example an economic, political, ideological power that would exist outside or before it and which it would have to accommodate or bend to when useful. Its very moment of foundation or institution (which in any case is never a moment inscribed in the homogeneous tissue of a history, since it is ripped apart with one decision), the operation that amounts to founding, inaugurating, justifying law (*droit*), making law, would consist of a *coup de force*, of a performative and therefore interpretative violence that in itself is neither just nor unjust and that no justice and no previous law with its founding anterior moment could guarantee or contradict or invalidate. No justificatory discourse could or should insure the role of metalanguage in relation to the performativity of institutive language or to its dominant interpretation.

Here the discourse comes up against its limit: in itself, in its performative power itself. It is what I here propose to call the mystical. Here a silence is walled up in the violent structure of the founding act. Walled up, walled in because silence is not exterior to language. It is in this sense that I would be tempted to interpret, beyond simple commentary, what Montaigne and Pascal call the mystical foundation of authority. One can always turn what I am doing or saying here back onto —or against—the very thing that I am saying is happening thus at the origin of every institution. I would therefore take the use of the word "mystical" in what I'd venture to call a rather Wittgensteinian direction. These texts by Montaigne and Pascal, along with the texts from the tradition to which they belong and the rather active interpretation of them that I propose, could be brought into Stanley Fish's discussion in "Force" (*Doing What Comes Naturally*) of Hart's *Concept of Law*, and several others, implicitly including Rawls, himself criticized by Hart, as well as into many debates illuminated by certain texts of Sam Weber on the agnostic and not simply intra-institutional or mono-institutional character of certain conflicts in *Institution and Interpretation*.[3]

Since the origin of authority, the foundation or ground, the position of the law can't by definition rest on anything but themselves, they are themselves a violence without ground. Which is not to say that they are in themselves unjust, in the sense of "illegal." They are neither legal nor illegal in their founding moment. They exceed the opposition between founded and unfounded, or between any foundationalism or anti-foundationalism. Even if the success of performatives that found law or right (for example, and this is more than an example, of a state as guarantor of a right) presupposes earlier conditions and conventions (for example in the national or international arena), the same "mystical" limit will reappear at the supposed origin of said conditions, rules or conventions, and at the origin of their dominant interpretation.

The structure I am describing here is a structure in which law (*droit*) is essentially deconstructible, whether because it is founded, constructed on interpretable and transformable textual strata (and that is the history of law [*droit*], its possible and necessary transformation, sometimes its amelioration), or because its ultimate foundation is by definition unfounded. The fact that law is deconstructible is not bad news. We may even see in this a stroke of luck for politics, for all historical progress. But the paradox that I'd like to submit for discussion is the following: it is this deconstructible structure of law (*droit*), or if you prefer of justice as *droit*, that also insures the possibility of deconstruction. Justice in itself, if such a thing exists, outside or beyond law, is not deconstructible. No more than deconstruction itself, if such a thing exists. Deconstruction is justice. It is perhaps because law (*droit*) (which I will consistently try to distinguish from justice) is constructible, in a sense that goes beyond the opposition between convention and nature, it is perhaps insofar as it goes beyond this opposition that it is constructible and so deconstructible and, what's more, that it makes deconstruction possible, or at least the practice of a deconstruction that, fundamentally, always proceeds to questions of *droit* and to the subject of *droit*. (1) The deconstructibility of law (*droit*), of legality, legitimacy or legitimation (for example) makes deconstruction possible. (2) The undeconstructibility of justice also makes deconstruction possible, indeed is inseparable from it. (3) The result: deconstruction takes place in the interval that separates the undeconstructibility of justice from the deconstructibility of *droit* (authority, legitimacy, and so on). It is possible as an experience of the impossible, there where, even if it does not exist (or does not yet exist, or never does exist), *there is* justice. Wherever one can replace, translate, determine the x of justice, one should say: deconstruction is possible, as impossible, to the extent (there) where *there is* (undeconstructible) x, thus to the extent (there) where *there is* (the undeconstructible).

In other words, the hypothesis and propositions toward which I'm tentatively moving here call more for the subtitle: justice as the possibility of deconstruction, the structure of law (*droit*) or of the law, the foundation or the self-authorization of law (*droit*) as the possibility of the exercise of deconstruction. I'm sure this isn't altogether clear; I hope, though I'm not sure of it, that it will become a little clearer in a moment.

I've said, then, that I have not yet begun. Perhaps I'll never begin and perhaps this colloquium will have to do without a "keynote," except that I've already begun. I authorize myself—but by what right?—to multiply protocols and detours. I began by saying that I was in love with at least two of your idioms. One was the word "enforceability," the other was the transitive use of the verb "*to address*." In French, one addresses oneself to someone, one addresses a letter or a word, also a transitive use, without being sure that they will arrive at their destination, but one does not address a problem. Still less does one address someone. Tonight I have agreed by contract to address, in English, a problem, that is to go straight toward it and straight toward you, thematically and without detour, in addressing myself to you in your language. Between law or right, the rectitude of address, direction and uprightness, we should be able to find a direct line of communication and to find ourselves on the right track. Why does deconstruction have the reputation, justified or not, of treating things obliquely, indirectly, with "quotation marks," and of always asking whether things arrive at the indicated address? Is this reputation deserved? And, deserved or not, how does one explain it?

And so we have already, in the fact that I speak another's language and break with my own, in the fact that I give myself up to the other, a singular mixture of force, *justesse* and justice.

And I am obliged, it is an obligation, to "address" in English, as you say in your language, infinite problems, infinite in their number, infinite in their history, infinite in their structure, covered by the title *Deconstruction and the Possibility of Justice*. But we already know that these problems are not infinite simply because they are infinitely numerous, nor because they are rooted in the infinity of memories and cultures (religious, philosophical, juridical, and so forth) that we shall never master. They are infinite, if we may say so, in themselves, because they require the very experience of the aporia that is not unrelated to what I just called the "mystical." When I say that they require the very experience of aporia, I mean two things. (1) As its name indicates, an experience is a traversal, something that *traverses* and travels toward a destination for which it finds the appropriate passage. The experience finds its way, its passage, it is possible. And in this sense it is impossible to have a full experience of aporia, that is, of something that does not allow passage. An aporia is a non-road. From this point of view, justice would be the experience that we are not able to experience. We shall soon encounter more than one aporia that we shall not be able to pass. But (2) I think that there is no justice without this experience, however impossible it may be, of aporia. Justice is an experience of the impossible. A will, a desire, a demand for justice whose structure wouldn't be an experience of aporia would have no chance to be what it is, namely, a call for justice. Every time that something comes to pass or turns out well, every time that we placidly apply a good rule to a particular case, to a correctly subsumed example, according to a determinant judgment, we can be sure that law (*droit*) may find itself accounted for, but certainly not justice. Law (*droit*) is not justice. Law is the element of calculation, and it is just that there be law, but justice is incalculable, it requires us to calculate with the incalculable; and aporetic experiences are the experiences, as improbable as they are necessary, of justice, that is to say of moments in which the decision between just and unjust is never insured by a rule.

And so I must *address* myself to you and "address" problems, I must do it briefly and in a foreign language. To do it briefly, I ought to do it as directly as possible, going straight ahead, without detour, without historical alibi, without obliqueness, toward you, supposedly the primary addressees of this discourse, but at the same time toward the place of essential decision for said problems. Address—as direction, as *rectitude*—says something about *droit* (law or right); and what we must not forget when we want justice, when we want to be just, is the *rectitude* of address. *Il ne faut pas manquer d'adresse*, I might say in French, but above all *il ne faut pas manquer l'adresse*, one mustn't miss the address, one mustn't mistake the address and the address always turns out to be singular. An address is always singular, idiomatic, and justice, as law (*droit*), seems always to suppose the generality of a rule, a norm or a universal imperative. How are we to reconcile the act of justice that must always concern singularity, individuals, irreplaceable groups and lives, the other or myself *as* other, in a unique situation, with rule, norm, value or the imperative of justice which necessarily have a general form, even if this generality prescribes a singular application in each case? If I were content to apply a just rule, without a spirit of justice and without in some way inventing the rule and the example for each case, I might be protected by law (*droit*), my action corresponding to objective law, but I would not be just. I would act, Kant would say, *in conformity* with duty, but not *through* duty or *out of respect* for the law. Is it ever possible to say: an action is not only legal, but also just? A person is not only within his rights but also within justice? Such a man or woman is just, a decision is just? Is it ever possible to say: I know that I am just? Allow me another detour.

To address oneself to the other in the language of the other is, it seems, the condition of all possible justice, but apparently, in all rigor, it is not only impossible (since I cannot speak the language of the other except to the extent that I appropriate it and assimilate it according to the law of an implicit third) but even excluded by justice as law (*droit*), inasmuch as justice as right seems to imply an element of universality, the appeal to a third party who suspends the unilaterality or singularity of the idioms.

When I address myself to someone in English, it is always an ordeal for me. For my addressee, for you as well, I imagine. Rather than explain why and lose time in doing so, I begin *in medias res*, with several remarks that for me tie the agonizing gravity of this problem of language to the question of justice, of the possibility of justice.

First remark: On the one hand, for fundamental reasons, it seems just to *us* to "*rendre la justice*," as one says in French, in a given idiom, in a language in which all the "subjects" concerned are supposedly competent, that is, capable of understanding and interpreting—all the "subjects," that is, those who establish the laws, those who judge and those who are judged, witnesses in both the broad and narrow sense, all those who are guarantors of the exercise of justice, or rather of *droit*. It is unjust to judge someone who does not understand the language in which the law is inscribed or the judgment pronounced, etc. We could give multiple dramatic examples of violent situations in which a person or group of persons is judged in an idiom they do not understand very well or at all. And however slight or subtle the difference of competence in the mastery of the idiom is here, the violence of an injustice has begun when all the members of a community do not share the same idiom throughout. Since in all rigor this ideal situation is never possible, we can perhaps already draw some inferences about what the title of our conference calls "the possibility of justice." The violence of this injustice that consists of judging those who don't understand the idiom in which one claims, as one says in French, that *"justice est faite,"* ("justice is done," "made") is not just any violence, any injustice. This injustice supposes that the other, the victim of the language's injustice, is capable of a language in general, is man as a speaking animal, in the sense that we, men, give to this word language. Moreover, there was a time, not long ago and not yet over, in which "we, men" meant "we adult white male Europeans, carnivorous and capable of sacrifice."

In the space in which I'm situating these remarks or reconstituting this discourse one would not speak of injustice or violence toward an animal, even less toward a vegetable or a stone. An animal can be made to suffer, but we would never say, in a sense considered proper, that it is a wronged subject, the victim of a crime, of a murder, of a rape or a theft, of a perjury—and this is true *a fortiori*, we think, for what we call vegetable or mineral or intermediate species like the sponge. There have been, there are still, many "subjects" among mankind who are not recognized as subjects and who receive this animal treatment (this is the whole unfinished history I briefly alluded to a moment ago). What we confusedly call "animal," the living thing as living and nothing else, is not a subject of the law or of law (*droit*). The opposition between just and unjust has no meaning in this case. As for trials for animals (there have been some) or lawsuits against those who inflict certain kinds of suffering on animals (legislation in certain Western countries provides for this and speaks not only of the rights of man but also of the rights of animals in general), these are considered to be either archaisms or still marginal and rare phenomena not constitutive of our culture. In our culture, carnivorous sacrifice is fundamental, dominant, regulated by the highest industrial technology, as is biological experimentation on animals—so vital to our modernity. As I have tried to show elsewhere,[4] carnivorous sacrifice is essential to the structure of subjectivity, which is also to say to the founding of the intentional subject and to the founding, if not of the law, at least of law (*droit*), the difference between the law and law (*droit*), justice and law (*droit*), justice and the law here remaining open over an abyss. I will leave these problems aside for the moment, along with the affinity between carnivorous sacrifice, at the basis of our culture and our law, and all the cannibalisms, symbolic or not, that structure intersubjectivity in nursing, love, mourning and, in truth, in all symbolic or linguistic appropriations.

If we wish to speak of injustice, of violence or of a lack of respect toward what we still so confusedly call animals—the question is more topical than ever, and so I include in it, in the name of deconstruction, a set of questions on carno-phallogocentrism—we must reconsider in its totality the metaphysico-anthropocentric axiomatic that dominates, in the West, the thought of just and unjust.

From this very first step we can already glimpse the first of its consequences, namely, that a deconstructionist approach to the boundaries that institute the human subject (preferably and paradigmatically the adult male, rather than the woman, child or animal) as the measure of the just and the unjust, does not necessarily lead to injustice, nor to the effacement of an opposition between just and unjust but may, in the name of a demand more insatiable than justice, lead to a reinterpretation of the whole apparatus of boundaries within which a history and a culture have been able to confine their criteriology. Under the hypothesis that I shall only touch lightly upon for the moment, what is currently called deconstruction would not correspond (though certain people have an interest in spreading this confusion) to a quasi-nihilistic abdication before the ethico-politico-juridical question of justice and before the opposition between just and unjust, but rather to a double movement that I will schematize as follows:

1. The sense of a responsibility without limits, and so necessarily excessive, incalculable, before memory; and so the task of recalling the history, the origin and subsequent direction, thus the limits, of concepts of justice, the law and right, of values, norms, prescriptions that have been imposed and sedimented there, from then on remaining more or less readable or presupposed. As to the legacy we have received under the name of justice, and in more than one language, the task of a historical and interpretative memory is at the heart of deconstruction, not only as philologico-etymological task or the historian's task but as responsibility in face of a heritage that is at the same time the heritage of an imperative or of a sheaf of injunctions. Deconstruction is already engaged by this infinite demand of justice, for justice,

which can take the aspect of this "mystique" I spoke of earlier. One must be *juste* with justice, and the first way to do it justice is to hear, read, interpret it, to try to understand where it comes from, what it wants of us, knowing that it does so through singular idioms (*Diké, Jus, justitia, justice, Gerechtigkeit,* to limit ourselves to European idioms which it may also be necessary to delimit in relation to others: we shall come back to this later) and also knowing that this justice always addresses itself to singularity, to the singularity of the other, despite or even because it pretends to universality. Consequently, never to yield on this point, constantly to maintain an interrogation of the origin, grounds and limits of our conceptual, theoretical or normative apparatus surrounding justice is on deconstruction's part anything but a neutralization of interest in justice, an insensitivity toward injustice. On the contrary, it hyperbolically raises the stakes of exacting justice; it is sensitivity to a sort of essential disproportion that must inscribe excess and inadequation in itself and that strives to denounce not only theoretical limits but also concrete injustices, with the most palpable effects, in the good conscience that dogmatically stops before any inherited determination of justice.

2. This responsibility toward memory is a responsibility before the very concept of responsibility that regulates the justice and appropriateness (*justesse*) of our behavior, of our theoretical, practical, ethico-political decisions. This concept of responsibility is inseparable from a whole network of connected concepts (property, intentionality, will, freedom, conscience, consciousness, self-consciousness, subject, self, person, community, decision, and so forth) and any deconstruction of this network of concepts in their given or dominant state may seem like a move toward irresponsibility at the very moment that, on the contrary, deconstruction calls for an increase in responsibility. But in the moment that an axiom's credibility (*crédit*) is suspended by deconstruction, in this structurally necessary moment, one can always believe that there is no more room for justice, neither for justice itself nor for theoretical interest directed toward the problems of justice. This moment of suspense, this period of *épochè*, without which, in fact, deconstruction is not possible, is always full of anxiety, but who will claim to be just by economizing on anxiety? And this anxiety-ridden moment of suspense—which is also the interval of spacing in which transformations, indeed juridico-political revolutions take place—cannot be motivated, cannot find its movement and its impulse (an impulse which itself cannot be suspended) except in the demand for an increase in or supplement to justice, and so in the experience of an inadequation or an incalculable disproportion. For in the end, where will deconstruction find its force, its movement or its motiva-

tion if not in this always unsatisfied appeal, beyond the given determinations of what we call, in determined contexts, justice, the possibility of justice? But it is still necessary to interpret this disproportion. If I were to say that I know nothing more just than what I today call deconstruction (nothing more just, I'm not saying nothing more legal or more legitimate), I know that I wouldn't fail to surprise or shock not only the determined adversaries of said deconstruction or of what they imagine under this name but also the very people who pass for or take themselves to be its partisans or its practitioners. And so I will not say it, at least not directly and not without the precaution of several detours.

As you know, in many countries, in the past and in the present, one founding violence of the law or of the imposition of state law has consisted in imposing a language on national or ethnic minorities regrouped by the state. This was the case in France on at least two occasions, first when the Villers-Cotteret decree consolidated the unity of the monarchic state by imposing French as the juridico-administrative language and by forbidding that Latin, the language of law and of the Church, allow all the inhabitants of the kingdom to be represented in a common language, by a lawyer-interpreter, without the imposition of the particular language that French still was. It is true that Latin was already a violent imposition and that from this point of view the passage from Latin to French was only the passage from one violence to another. The second major moment of imposition was that of the French Revolution, when linguistic unification sometimes took the most repressive pedagogical turns, or in any case the most authoritarian ones. I'm not going to engage in the history of these examples. We could also find them in this country, today, where this linguistic problem is still acute and will be for a long time, precisely in this place where questions of politics, education and law (*droit*) are inseparable (and where a debate has been recently begun on "national standards" of education).

Now I am moving right along, without the least detour through historical memory toward the formal, abstract statement of several aporias, those in which, between law and justice, deconstruction finds its privileged site—or rather its privileged instability. Deconstruction is generally practiced in two ways or two styles, although it most often grafts one on to the other. One takes on the demonstrative and apparently ahistorical allure of logico-formal paradoxes. The other, more historical or more anamnesic, seems to proceed through readings of texts, meticulous interpretations and genealogies. I will devote my attention to these two practices in turn.

First I will drily, directly state, I will "address" the following aporias. In fact there is only one aporia, only one potential aporetic that infinitely distributes itself. I shall only propose a few examples that will suppose, make explicit or perhaps produce a difficult and unstable distinction between justice and *droit,* between justice (infinite, incalculable, rebellious to rule and foreign to symmetry, heterogeneous and heterotropic) and the exercise of justice as law or right, legitimacy or legality, stabilizable and statutory, calculable, a system of regulated and coded prescriptions. I would be tempted, up to a certain point, to compare the concept of justice—which I'm here trying to distinguish from law—to Levinas's, just because of this infinity and because of the heteronomic relation to others, to the faces of otherness that govern me, whose infinity I cannot thematize and whose hostage I remain. In *Totalité and Infini* ("Verité et Justice," p. 62), Levinas writes: ". . . *la relation avec autrui—c'est à dire la justice*" (". . . the relation to others—that is to say, justice")—which he defines, moreover, as *"droiture de l'accueil fait au visage"* (p. 54) ("equitable honoring of faces"). Equity (*la droiture*) is not reducible to right or law (*le droit*), of course, but the two values are not unrelated.

Levinas speaks of an infinite right: in what he calls "Jewish humanism," whose basis is not "the concept of man," but rather the other; "the extent of the right of the other" is that of "a practically infinite right"; *"l'étendue du droit d'autrui [est] un droit pratiquement infini"* (*"Un droit infini,"* in *Du Sacré au Saint, Cinq Nouvelles Lectures Talmudiques, pp. 17–18*). Here equity is not equality, calculated proportion, equitable distribution or distributive justice but rather absolute dissymmetry. And Levinas's notion of justice might sooner be compared to the Hebrew equivalent of what we would perhaps translate as "sanctity." But since Levinas's difficult discourse would give rise to other difficult questions, I cannot be content to borrow conceptual moves without risking confusions or analogies. And so I will go no further in this direction. Everything would still be simple if this distinction between justice and *droit* were a true distinction, an opposition whose functioning was logically regulated and permitted mastery. But it turns out that *droit* claims to exercise itself in the name of justice and that justice is required to establish itself in the name of a law that must be "enforced." Deconstruction always finds itself between these two poles. Here, then, are some examples of aporias.

1. *First aporia:* épokhè *of the rule.*

Our common axiom is that to be just or unjust and to exercise justice, I must be free and responsible for my actions, my behavior, my thought, my decisions. We would not say of a being without freedom, or at least of one without freedom in a given act, that its decision is just or unjust. But this freedom or this decision of the just, if it is one, must follow a law or a prescription, a rule. In this sense, in its very autonomy, in its freedom to follow or to give itself laws, it must have the power to be of the calculable or programmable order, for example as an act of fairness. But if the act simply consists of applying a rule, of enacting a program or effecting a calculation, we might say that it is legal, that it conforms to law, and perhaps, by metaphor, that it is just, but we would be wrong to say that the decision was just.

To be just, the decision of a judge, for example, must not only follow a rule of law or a general law but must also assume it, approve it, confirm its value, by a reinstituting act of interpretation, as if ultimately nothing previously existed of the law, as if the judge himself invented the law in every case. No exercise of justice as law can be just unless there is a "fresh judgment" (I borrow this English expression from Stanley Fish's article, "Force," in *Doing What Comes Naturally*). This "fresh judgment" can very well—*must* very well—conform to a preexisting law, but the reinstituting, reinventive and freely decisive interpretation, the responsible interpretation of the judge requires that his "justice" not just consist in conformity, in the conservative and reproductive activity of judgment. In short, for a decision to be just and responsible, it must, in its proper moment if there is one, be both regulated and without regulation: it must conserve the law and also destroy it or suspend it enough to have to reinvent it in each case, rejustify it, at least reinvent it in the reaffirmation and the new and free confirmation of its principle. Each case is other, each decision is different and requires an absolutely unique interpretation, which no existing, coded rule can or ought to guarantee absolutely. At least, if the rule guarantees it in no uncertain terms, so that the judge is a calculating machine, which happens, and we will not say that he is just, free and responsible. But we also won't say it if he doesn't refer to any law, to any rule or if, because he doesn't take any rule for granted beyond his own interpretation, he suspends his decision, stops short before the undecidable or if he improvises and leaves aside all rules, all principles. It follows from this paradox that there is never a moment that we can say *in the present* that a decision *is* just (that is, free and responsible), or that someone *is* a just man—even less, "*I am* just." Instead of "just," we could say legal or legitimate, in conformity with a state of law, with the rules and conventions that authorize calculation but whose founding origin only defers the problem of justice. For in the founding of law or in its institution, the same problem of justice will have been posed and violently resolved, that is to say buried, dissimulated, repressed. Here the best paradigm is the founding

of the nation-states or the institutive act of a constitution that establishes what one calls in French *l'état de droit.*

2. *Second aporia: the ghost of the undecidable.*

Justice, as law, is never exercised without a decision that *cuts,* that
divides. This decision does not simply consist in its final form, for
example a penal sanction, equitable or not, in the order of proportional or distributive justice. It begins, it ought to begin, by right or in
principle, with the initiative of learning, reading, understanding, interpreting the rule, and even in calculating. For if calculation is calculation, the decision to calculate is not of the order of the calculable,
and must not be.

The undecidable, a theme often associated with deconstruction, is
not merely the oscillation between two significations or two contradictory and very determinate rules, each equally imperative (for example respect for equity and universal right but also for the always
heterogeneous and unique singularity of the unsubsumable example).
The undecidable is not merely the oscillation or the tension between
two decisions; it is the experience of that which, though heterogeneous, foreign to the order of the calculable and the rule, is still obliged—it is of obligation that we must speak—to give itself up to the
impossible decision, while taking account of law and rules. A decision
that didn't go through the ordeal of the undecidable would not be a
free decision, it would only be the programmable application or unfolding of a calculable process. It might be legal; it would not be just.
But in the moment of suspense of the undecidable, it is not just either,
for only a decision is just (in order to maintain the proposition "only
a decision is just," one need not refer decision to the structure of a
subject or to the propositional form of a judgment). And once the
ordeal of the undecidable is past (if that is possible), the decision has
again followed a rule or given itself a rule, invented it or reinvented,
reaffirmed it, it is no longer *presently* just, fully just. There is apparently no moment in which a decision can be called presently and fully
just: either it has not yet been made according to a rule, and nothing
allows us to call it just, or it has already followed a rule—whether
received, confirmed, conserved or reinvented—which in its turn is not
absolutely guaranteed by anything; and, moreover, if it were guaranteed, the decision would be reduced to calculation and we couldn't
call it just. That is why the ordeal of the undecidable that I just said
must be gone through by any decision worthy of the name is never
past or passed, it is not a surmounted or sublated (*aufgehoben*) moment in the decision. The undecidable remains caught, lodged, at least
as a ghost—but an essential ghost—in every decision, in every event
of decision. Its ghostliness deconstructs from within any assurance of

presence, any certitude or any supposed criteriology that would assure us of the justice of a decision, in truth of the very event of a decision. Who will ever be able to assure us that a decision as such has taken place? That it has not, through such and such a detour, followed a cause, a calculation, a rule, without even that imperceptible suspense that marks any free decision, at the moment that a rule is, or is not, applied?

The whole subjectal axiomatic of responsibility, of conscience, of intentionality, of property that governs today's dominant juridical discourse and the category of decision right down to its appeals to medical expertise is so theoretically weak and crude that I need not emphasize it here. And the effects of these limitations are massive and concrete enough that I don't have to give examples.

We can already see from this second aporia or this second form of the same aporia that the deconstruction of all presumption of a determinant certitude of a present justice itself operates on the basis of an infinite "idea of justice," infinite because it is irreducible, irreducible because owed to the other, owed to the other, before any contract, because it has come, the other's coming as the singularity that is always other. This "idea of justice" seems to be irreducible in its affirmative character, in its demand of gift without exchange, without circulation, without recognition or gratitude, without economic circularity, without calculation and without rules, without reason and without rationality. And so we can recognize in it, indeed accuse, identify a madness. And perhaps another sort of mystique. And deconstruction is mad about this kind of justice. Mad about this desire for justice. This kind of justice, which isn't law, is the very movement of deconstruction at work in law and the history of law, in political history and history itself, before it even presents itself as the discourse that the academy or modern culture labels "deconstructionism."

I would hesitate to assimilate too quickly this "idea of justice" to a regulative idea (in the Kantian sense), to a messianic promise or to other horizons *of the same type*. I am only speaking of a *type*, of this *type* of horizon that would have numerous competing versions. By competing I mean similar enough in appearance and always pretending to absolute privilege and irreducible singularity. The singularity of the historical place—perhaps our own, which in any case is the one I'm obscurely referring to here—allows us a glimpse of the type itself, as the origin, condition, possibility or promise of all its exemplifications (messianism of the Jewish, Christian or Islamic type, idea in the Kantian sense, eschato-teleology of the neo-Hegelian, Marxist or post-Marxist type, etc.). It also allows us to perceive and conceive the law of irreducible competition (*concurrence*), but from a brink where vertigo threatens to seize us the moment we see nothing but examples and some of us no longer feel engaged in it; another way of saying that from this point on we always run the risk (speaking for myself, at least) of no longer being, as they say, "in the running" (*dans la course*). But not to be "in the running" on the inside track, does not mean that we can stay at the starting-line or simply be spectators—far from it. It may be the very thing that "keeps us moving," (*fait courir*) with renewed strength and speed, for example, deconstruction.

3. *Third aporia: the urgency that obstructs the horizon of knowledge.*

One of the reasons I'm keeping such a distance from all these horizons—from the Kantian regulative idea or from the messianic advent, for example, or at least from their conventional interpretation—is that they are, precisely, *horizons*. As its Greek name suggests, a horizon is both the opening and the limit that defines an infinite progress or a period of waiting.

But justice, however unpresentable it may be, doesn't wait. It is that which must not wait. To be direct, simple and brief, let us say this: a just decision is always required *immediately*, "right away." It cannot furnish itself with infinite information and the unlimited knowledge of conditions, rules or hypothetical imperatives that could justify it. And even if it did have all that at its disposal, even if it did give itself the time, all the time and the necessary facts about the matter, the moment of *decision, as such,* always remains a finite moment of urgency and precipitation, since it must not be the consequence or the effect of this theoretical or historical knowledge, of this reflection or this deliberation, since it always marks the interruption of the juridico- or ethico- or politico-cognitive deliberation that precedes it, that *must* precede it. The instant of decision is a madness, says Kierkegaard. This is particularly true of the instant of the just decision that must rend time and defy dialectics. It is a madness. Even if time and prudence, the patience of knowledge and the mastery of conditions were hypothetically unlimited, the decision would be structurally finite, however late it came, a decision of urgency and precipitation, acting in the night of non-knowledge and non-rule. Not of the absence of rules and knowledge but of a reinstitution of rules which by definition is not preceded by any knowledge or by any guarantee as such. If we were to trust in a massive and decisive distinction between performative and constative—a problem I can't get involved in here—we would have to attribute this irreducibility of precipitate urgency, at bottom this irreducibility of thoughtlessness and unconsciousness, however intelligent it may be, to the performative structure of speech act and acts in general as acts of justice or law, whether they be performatives that institute something or derived performatives supposing anterior conventions. A constative can be *juste* (right), in the sense of *justesse*, never in the sense of justice. But as a performative cannot be just, in the sense of justice, except by founding itself on conventions and so on other anterior performatives, buried or not, it always maintains within itself some irruptive violence, it no longer responds to the demands of theoretical rationality. Since every constative utterance itself relies, at least implicitly, on a performative structure ("I tell you that, I speak to you, I address myself to you to tell you that this is true, that things are like this, I promise you or renew my promise to you to make a sentence and to sign what I say when I say that, tell you, or try to tell you the truth," and so forth), the dimension of *justesse* or truth of the theoretico-constatie utterances (in all domains, particularly in the domain of the theory of law) always thus presupposes the dimension of justice of the performative utterances, that is to say their essential precipitation, which never proceeds without a certain dissymmetry and some quality of violence. That's how I would be tempted to understand the proposition of Levinas, who, in a whole other language and following an entirely different discursive procedure, declares that "La vérité suppose la justice" ("Truth supposes justice") (*"Vérité et justice,"* in *Totalité et infini* 3, p. 62). Dangerously parodying the French idiom, we could end up saying: *"La justice, y a qu'ça de vrai."* This is not without consequence, needless to say, for the status, if we still can call it that, of truth.[5]

Paradoxically, it is because of this overflowing of the performative, because of this always excessive haste of interpretation getting ahead of itself, because of this structural urgency and precipitation of justice that the latter has no horizon of expectation (regulative or messianic). But for this very reason, it *may have an avenir*, a "to-come," which I rigorously distinguish from the future that can always reproduce the present. Justice remains, is yet, to come, *à venir*, it has an, it is *à-venir*, the very dimension of events irreducibly to come. It will always have it, this *à-venir*, and always has. Perhaps it is for this reason that justice, insofar as it is not only a juridical or political concept, opens up for *l'avenir* the transformation, the recasting or refounding of law and politics. "Perhaps," one must always say perhaps for justice. There is an *avenir* for justice and there is no justice except to the degree that some event is possible which, as event, exceeds calculation, rules, programs, anticipations and so forth. Justice as the experience of absolute alterity is unpresentable, but it is the chance of the event and the condition of history. No doubt an unrecognizable history, of course, for those who believe they know what they're talking about when they use this word, whether it's a matter of social, ideological, political, juridical or some other history.

That justice exceeds law and calculation, that the unpresentable exceeds the determinable cannot and should not serve as an alibi for staying out of juridico-political battles, within an institution or a state or between institutions or states and others. Left to itself, the incalculable and giving (*donatrice*) idea of justice is always very close to the bad, even to the worst for it can always be reappropriated by the most perverse calculation. It's always possible. And so incalculable justice *requires* us to calculate. And first, closest to what we associate with justice, namely, law, the juridical field that one cannot isolate within sure frontiers, but also in all the fields from which we cannot separate it, which intervene in it and are no longer simply fields: ethics, politics, economics, psycho-sociology, philosophy, literature, etc. Not only *must* we calculate, negotiate the relation between the calculable and the incalculable, and negotiate without the sort of rule that wouldn't have to be reinvented there where we are cast, there where we find ourselves; but we *must* take it as far as possible, beyond the place we find ourselves and beyond the already identifiable zones of morality or politics or law, beyond the distinction between national and international, public and private, and so on. This requirement does not properly belong either to justice or law. It only belongs to either of these two domains by exceeding each one in the direction of the other. Politicization, for example, is interminable even if it cannot and should not ever be total. To keep this from being a truism or a triviality, we must recognize in it the following consequence: each advance in politicization obliges one to reconsider, and so to reinterpret the very foundations of law such as they had previously been calculated or delimited. This was true for example in the Declaration of the Rights of Man, in the abolition of slavery, in all the emancipatory battles that remain and will have to remain in progress, everywhere in the world, for men and for women. Nothing seems to me less outdated than the classical emancipatory ideal. We cannot attempt to disqualify it today, whether crudely or with sophistication, at least not without treating it too lightly and forming the worst complicities. But beyond these identified territories of juridico-politicization on the grand geopolitical scale, beyond all self-serving interpretations, beyond all determined and particular reappropriations of international law, other areas must constantly open up that at first can seem like secondary or marginal areas. This marginality also signifies that a violence, indeed a terrorism and other forms of hostage-taking are at work (the examples closest to us would be found in the area of laws on the teaching and practice of languages, the legitimization of canons, the military use of scientific research, abortion, euthanasia, problems of organ transplant, extra-uterine conception, bio-engineering, medical experimentation, the social treatment of AIDS, the macro- or micro-politics of drugs, the homeless, and so on, without forgetting, of course, the treatment of what we call animal life, animality. On this last problem, the Benjamin text that I'm coming to now shows that its author was not deaf or insensitive to it, even if his propositions on this subject remain quite obscure, if not quite traditional).

II[6]

If I have not exhausted your patience, let us now approach, in another style, the promised reading of a brief and disconcerting Benjamin text. I am speaking of *Zur Kritik der Gewalt* (1921), translated as *Critique of Violence*. I will not presume to call this text *exemplary*. We are in a realm where, in the end, there are only singular examples. Nothing is absolutely exemplary. I will not attempt to justify absolutely the choice of this text. But I could say why it is not the worst example of what might be exemplary in a relatively determined context such as ours.

1. Benjamin's analysis reflects the crisis in the European model of bourgeois, liberal, parliamentary democracy, and so the crisis in the concept of *droit* that is inseparable from it. Germany in defeat is at this time a place in which this crisis is extremely sharp, a crisis whose originality also comes from certain modern features like the right to strike, the concept of the general strike (with or without reference to Sorel). It is also the aftermath of a war and a pre-war that saw the European development and failure of pacifist discourse, antimilitarism, the critique of violence, including juridico-police violence, which will soon be repeated in the years to follow. It is also the moment in which questions of the death penalty and of the right to punish in general are painfully current. Change in the structures of public opinion, thanks to the appearance of new media powers such as radio, begins to put into question this liberal model of parliamentary discussion or deliberation in the production of laws and so forth. Such conditions motivated the thoughts of German jurists like Carl Schmitt, to mention only him. And so I was also interested by several historical indices. For example, this text, at once "mystical" (in the overdetermined sense that interests us here) and hypercritical, this text which, in certain respects, can be read as neo-messianical Jewish mysticism (*mystique*) grafted onto post-Sorelian neo-Marxism (or the reverse), upon its publication won Benjamin a letter of congratulations from

Carl Schmitt, that great conservative Catholic jurist, still a constitutionalist at the time; but you are already familiar with his strange conversion to Hitlerism in 1933 and his correspondence with Benjamin. But also with Heidegger. As for analogies between *Zur Kritik der Gewalt* and certain turns of Heideggerian thought, they are impossible to miss, especially those surrounding the motifs of *Walten* and *Gewalt*. *Zur Kritik der Gewalt* concludes with divine violence (*göttliche Gewalt*) and in the end Walter says of divine violence that we might call it *die waltende (Die göttliche Gewalt . . . mag die waltende heißen)*: "Divine violence . . . may be called sovereign violence." ". . . *die waltende heißen*" are the last words of the text. It is this historical network of equivocal contracts that interests me in its necessity and in its very dangers. In the Western democracies of 1989, with work and a certain number of precautions, lessons can still be drawn from it.

2. Keeping in mind the thematic of our colloquium, this text seemed exemplary to me, up to a point, to the degree that it lends itself to an exercise in deconstructive reading, as I shall try to show.

3. But this deconstruction is in some way the operation or rather the very experience that this text, it seems to me, first does itself, by itself, on itself. What does this mean? Is it possible? What remains, then, of such an event? Of its auto-hetero-deconstruction? Of its just and unjust incompletion? What is the ruin of such an event or the open wound of such a signature? And also, in what does its strength consist, strength precisely in the sense of *Gewalt,* that is, its violence, authority and legitimacy? That is one of my questions. It is a question about the possibility of deconstruction. If you will allow me to cite myself, I happened to write that "the most rigorous deconstructions have never claimed to be . . . possible. And I would say that deconstruction loses nothing from admitting that it is impossible; and also that those who would rush to delight in that admission lose nothing from having to wait. For a deconstructive operation *possibility* would rather be the danger, the danger of becoming an available set of rule-governed procedures, methods, accessible approaches. The interest of deconstruction, of such force and desire as it may have, is a certain experience of the impossible."[7]

Benjamin's demonstration concerns the question of *droit, recht,* right or law. It even means to inaugurate, we shall be able to say it more rigorously in a moment, a "philosophy of *droit.*" And this philosophy seems to be organized around a series of distinctions that all seem interesting, provocative, necessary up to a certain point but that all, it seems to me, remain radically problematic.

First, there is the distinction between two kinds of violence in law, in relation to law (*droit*): the founding violence, the one that institutes and positions law (*die rechtsetzende Gewalt*, "law making violence") and the violence that conserves, the one that maintains, confirms, insures the permanence and enforceability of law (*die rechtserhaltende Gewalt*, "law preserving violence"). For the sake of convenience, let us continue to translate *Gewalt* as violence, but I have already mentioned the precautions this calls for. As for translating *Recht* as "law" rather than "right," as in the published version I'm using here, that is another problem that I'll leave aside for now.

Next there is the distinction between the founding violence of law termed "mythic" (implicit meaning: Greek, it seems to me) and the annihilating violence of destructive law (*Rechtsvernichtend*), which is termed "divine" (implicit meaning: Jewish, it seems to me).

Finally, there is the distinction between justice (*Gerechtigkeit*) as the principle of all divine positioning of the end (*das Prinzip aller göttlichen Zwecksetzung*, p. 198, "principle of all divine end making," p. 295) and power (*Macht*) as principle of mythical positioning of *droit* (*aller mythischen Rechtsetzung*, "of all mythical law making, ibid.).

In the title "*Zur Kritik der Gewalt*," "critique" doesn't simply mean negative evaluation, legitimate rejection or condemnation of violence, but judgment, evaluation, examination that provides itself with the means to judge violence. The concept of "critique," insofar as it implies decision in the form of judgment and question with regard to the right to judge, thus has an essential relation, in itself, to the sphere of law or right. Fundamentally, something like the Kantian tradition of the concept of critique. The concept of violence (*Gewalt*) permits an evaluative critique only in the sphere of law and justice (*Recht, Gerechtigkeit*) or the sphere of moral relations (*sittliche Verhältnisse*). There is no natural or physical violence. We can speak figuratively of violence with regard to an earthquake or even to a physical ailment. But we know that these aren't cases of a *Gewalt* able to give rise to a judgment, before some instrument of justice. The concept of violence belongs to the symbolic order of law, politics and morals. And it is only to this extent that it can give rise to a critique. Up to this point this critique was always inscribed in the space of the distinction between means and end. But, objects Benjamin, to ask ourselves if violence can be a means *with a view* toward ends (just or unjust) is to prohibit ourselves from judging violence *itself*. The criteriology would then concern only the application of violence, not violence itself. We would not be able to tell if the latter, as means, is in *itself* just or not, moral or not. The critical question remains open, the question of an evaluation and a justification of violence in itself, whether it be a simple means and whatever its end may be. This critical dimension would have been foreclosed by the jusnaturalist tradition. For defenders of natural *droit*, recourse to violent means poses no problems, since natural ends are just. Recourse to violent means is as justified, as normal as man's "right" to move his body to reach a given goal. Violence (*Gewalt*) is from this point of view a "natural product" (*Naturprodukt*). Benjamin gives several examples of this naturalization of violence by jusnaturalism:

(a) the state founded on natural law, which Spinoza talks about in the *Theological-Political Treatise* in which the citizen, before a contract is formed by reason, exercises *de jure* a violence he disposes of *de facto*,

(b) the ideological foundation of the Terror under the French Revolution,

(c) the exploitations of a certain Darwinism (and this could later be applied to Nazism), etc.

But if, in opposition to jusnaturalism, the tradition of positive law is more attentive to the historical evolution of law, it also falls short of the critical questioning called for by Benjamin. Doubtless it can only consider all means to be good once they conform to a natural and ahistorical end. It prescribes that we judge means, that is to say judge their conformity to a *droit* that is in the process of being instituted, to a new (not natural) *droit* that it evaluates in terms of means, and so by the critique of means. But the two traditions share the same dogmatic presupposition, namely, that just ends can be attained by just means. "Natural law attempts, by the justness of ends (*durch die Gerechtigkeit der Zwecke*), to 'justify' (*rechtfertigen*) the means, positive law to 'guarantee' (*garantieren*) the justness of the ends through the justification (*Gerechtigkeit*) of the means." The two traditions would turn in the same circle of dogmatic presuppositions. And there is no solution for the antinomy when a contradiction emerges between just ends and justified means. Positive law would remain blind to the unconditionality of ends, natural right to the conditionality of means. Nevertheless, although he seems to dismiss both cases symmetrically, from the tradition of positive law Benjamin retains the sense of the historicity of law. Inversely, it is true that what he says further on about divine justice is not always incompatible with the theological basis of all jusnaturalisms. In any case, the Benjaminian critique of violence claims to exceed the two traditions and no longer to arise simply from the sphere of law and the internal interpretation of the juridical institution. It belongs to what he calls in a rather singular sense a "philosophy of history" and is expressly limited to European particulars.

At its most fundamental level, European law tends to prohibit individual violence and to condemn it not because it poses a threat to this or that law but because it threatens the juridical order itself (*die Rechtsordnung,* "the legal system"). Whence the law's interest—for it does have an interest in laying itself down and conserving itself, or in representing the interest that, *justement,* it represents. Law's interest may seem "surprising," that is Benjamin's word, but at the same time it is in its nature as interest, and in this sense there is nothing surprising here at all, to pretend to exclude any individual violence threatening its order and thus to monopolize violence, in the sense of *Gewalt,* which is also to say authority. Law has an "interest in a monopoly of violence" (p. 281), (*Interesse des Rechts an der Monopolisierung der Gewalt*). This monopoly doesn't strive to protect any given just and legal ends (*Rechtszwecke*) but law itself. This seems like a tautological triviality. But isn't tautology the phenomenal structure of a certain violence in the law that lays itself down, by decreeing to be violent, this time in the sense of an outlaw, anyone who does not recognize it? Performative tautology or *a priori* synthesis, which structures any foundation of the law upon which one performatively produces the conventions that guarantee the validity of the performative, thanks to which one gives oneself the means to decide between legal and illegal violence. The expressions "tautology" and "*a priori* synthesis," and especially the word "performative" are not Benjaminian, but I'll venture to suggest that they do not betray his purposes.

The admiring fascination exerted on the people by "the figure of the "great' criminal," (p. 281) (*die Gestalt des "grossen" Verbrechers*), can be explained as follows: it is not someone who has committed this or that crime for which one feels a secret admiration; it is someone who, in defying the law, lays bare the violence of the legal system, the juridical order itself. One could explain in the same way the fascination exerted in France by a lawyer like Jacques Verges who defends the most difficult causes, the most indefensible in the eyes of the majority, by practicing what he calls the "strategy of rupture," that is, the radical contestation of the given order of the law, of judicial authority and ultimately of the legitimate authority of the state that summons his clients to appear before the law. Judicial authority before which, in short, the accused appears without appearing and claims the right to contest the order of right or law. But what order of law? The order of law in general or this order of law instituted and enforced by this state? Or order as inextricably mixed with the state in general?

The telling example would here be that of the right to strike. In class struggle, notes Benjamin, the right to strike is guaranteed to workers who are therefore, besides the state, the only legal subject (*Rechtssubjekt*) to find itself guaranteed a right to violence (*Recht auf Gewalt*) and so to share the monopoly of the state in this respect. Certain people may have thought that since the practice of the strike, this cessation of activity, this *Nicht-Handeln,* is not an action, we cannot here be speaking about violence. That is how the concession of this right by the power of the state (*Staatsgewalt*) is justified when that power cannot do otherwise. Violence would come from the employer and the strike would consist only in an abstention, a non-violent withdrawal by which the worker, suspending his relations with the management and its machines, would simply become alien to them. The man who will become Brecht's friend defines this withdrawal (*Abkehr*) as an "*Entfremdung*" ("estrangement"). He puts the word in quotation marks. But Benjamin clearly does not believe in the non-violence of the strike. The striking workers set the conditions for the resumption of work, they will not end their strike unless a list, an order of things has changed. And so there is violence against violence. In carrying the right to strike to its limit, the concept or watchword of *general strike* thus manifests its essence. The state can hardly stand this passage to the limit. It deems it abusive and claims that there was a misunderstanding, a misinterpretation of the original intention, and that *das Streikrecht "so" nicht gemeint gewesen sei,* "the right to strike was not 'so intended' " (p. 282). It can then condemn the general strike as illegal and, if the strike persists, we have a revolutionary situation. Such a situation is in fact the only one that allows us to conceive the homogeneity of law or right and violence, violence as the exercise of *droit* and *droit* as the exercise of violence. Violence is not exterior to the order of *droit*. It threatens it from within. Violence does not consist essentially in exerting its power or a brutal force to obtain this or that result but in threatening or destroying an order of given right and precisely, in this case, the order of state law that was to accord this right to violence, for example the right to strike. How can we interpret this contradiction? Is it only *de facto* and exterior to law? Or is it rather immanent in the law of law (*au droit du droit*)?

What the state fears (the state being law in its greatest force) is not so much crime or *brigandage,* even on the grand scale of the Mafia or heavy drug traffic, as long as they transgress the law with an eye toward particular benefits, however important they may be. The state is

afraid of fundamental, founding violence, that is, violence able to justify, to legitimate, (*begründen,* "to found," p. 283) or to transform the
relations of law (*Rechtsverhältnisse,* "legal conditions"), and so to
present itself as having a right to law. This violence thus belongs in
advance to the order of a *droit* that remains to be transformed or
founded, even if it may wound our sense of justice (*Gerechtigkeitsge-
fühl*). Only this violence calls for and makes possible a "critique of
violence" that determines it to be something other than the natural
exercise of force. For a critique of violence—that is to say, an interpretative and meaningful evaluation of it—to be possible, one must
first recognize meaning in a violence that is not an accident arriving
from outside law. That which threatens law already belongs to it, to
the right to law (*droit*), to the law of the law (*droit*), to the origin of
law (*droit*). The general strike thus furnishes a valuable guiding
thread, since it exercises the conceded right to contest the order of
existing law and to create a revolutionary situation in which the task
will be to found a new *droit,* if not always, as we shall see in a moment, a new state. All revolutionary situations, all revolutionary discourses, on the left or on the right (and from 1921, in Germany, there
were many of these that resembled each other in a troubling way,
Benjamin often finding himself between the two) justify the recourse
to violence by alleging the founding, in progress or to come, of a new
law. As this law to come will in return legitimate, retrospectively, the
violence that may offend the sense of justice, its future anterior already
justifies it. The foundation of all states occurs in a situation that we
can thus call revolutionary. It inaugurates a new law, it always does
so in violence. Always, which is to say even when there haven't been
those spectacular genocides, expulsions or deportations that so often
accompany the foundation of states, great or small, old or new, right
near us or far away.

In these situations said to found law (*droit*) or state, the grammati-
cal category of the future anterior all too well resembles a modification of the present to describe the violence in progress. It consists,
precisely, in feigning the presence or simple modalization of presence.
Those who say "our time," while thinking "our present" in light of a
future anterior present do not know very well, by definition, what they
are saying. It is precisely in this ignorance that the eventness of the
event consists, what we naively call its presence.[8]

These moments, supposing we can isolate them, are terrifying moments. Because of the sufferings, the crimes, the tortures that rarely
fail to accompany them, no doubt, but just as much because they are
in themselves, and in their very violence, uninterpretable or indecipherable. That is what I am calling "mystique." As Benjamin presents

it, this violence is certainly legible, indeed intelligible since it is not alien to law, no more than *polemos* or *eris* is alien to all the forms and significations of *dikè*. But it is, in *droit*, what suspends *droit*. It interrupts the established *droit* to found another. This moment of suspense, this *épokhè*, this founding or revolutionary moment of law is, in law, an instance of non-law. But it is also the whole history of law. *This moment always takes place and never takes place in a presence.* It is the moment in which the foundation of law remains suspended in the void or over the abyss, suspended by a pure performative act that would not have to answer to or before anyone. The supposed subject of this pure performative would no longer be before the law, or rather he would be before a law not yet determined, before the law as before a law not yet existing, a law yet to come, *encore devant et devant venir*. And the being "before the law" that Kafka talks about[9] resembles this situation, both ordinary and terrible, of the man who cannot manage to see or above all to touch, to catch up to the law: because it is transcendent in the very measure that it is he who must found it, as yet to come, in violence. Here we "touch" without touching this extraordinary paradox: the inaccessible transcendence of the law before which and prior to which "man" stands fast only appears infinitely transcendent and thus theological to the extent that, so near him, it depends only on him, on the performative act by which he institutes it: the law is transcendent, violent and non-violent, because it depends only on who is before it—and so prior to it, on who produces it, founds it, authorizes it in an absolute performative whose presence always escapes him. The law is transcendent and theological, and so always to come, always promised, because it is immanent, finite and so already past. Every "subject" is caught up in this aporetic structure in advance.

Only the yet-to-come (*avenir*) will produce intelligibility or interpretability of this law. Beyond the letter of Benjamin's text, which I stopped following in the style of commentary a moment ago but which I am interpreting from the point of its *avenir*, one can say that the order of intelligibility depends in its turn on the established order that it serves to interpret. This readability will then be as little neutral as it is non-violent. A "successful" revolution, the "successful foundation of a state" (in somewhat the same sense that one speaks of a "felicitous performative speech act") will produce *après coup* what it was destined in advance to produce, namely, proper interpretative models to read in return, to give sense, necessity and above all legitimacy to the violence that has produced, among others, the interpretative model in question, that is, the discourse of its self-legitimation. Examples of this circle, this other hermeneutic circle, are not lacking;

near us or far from us, right here or elsewhere, whether it's a question of what happens from one neighborhood to another, one street to another in a great metropolis or from one country or one camp to another around a world war in the course of which states and nations are founded, destroyed or redesigned. This must be taken into account in order to de-limit an international law constructed on the western concept of state sovereignty and non-intervention, but also in order to think its infinite perfectibility. There are cases in which it is not known for generations if the performative of the violent founding of a state is "felicitous" or not. Here we could cite more than one example. This unreadability of violence results from the very readability of a violence that belongs to what others would call the symbolic order of law, if you like, and not to pure physics. We might be tempted to reverse this "logic" like a glove ("logic" in quotation marks, for this "unreadable" is also very much "illogical" in the order of *logos,* and this is also why I hesitate to call it "symbolic" and precipitately send it into the order of Lacanian discourse), the "logic" of this readable unreadability. In sum, it signifies a juridico-symbolic violence, a performative violence at the very heart of interpretative reading. And the example or index could be carried by metonymy back toward the conceptual generality of the essence.

We might say then that there is a possibility of general strike, a right to general strike in any interpretative reading, the right to contest established law in its strongest authority, the law of the state. One has the right to suspend legitimating authority and all its norms of reading, and to do this in the most incisive, most effective, most pertinent readings, which of course will sometimes argue with the unreadable in order to found another order of reading, another state, sometimes not; for we shall see that Benjamin distinguishes between two sorts of general strikes, some destined to replace the order of one state with another (general political strike), the other to abolish the state (general proletarian strike). In short, the two temptations of deconstruction.

For there is something of the general strike, and thus of the revolutionary situation in every reading that founds something new and that remains unreadable in regard to established canons and norms of reading, that is to say the present state of reading or of what figures the State, with a capital S, in the state of possible reading. Faced with such a general strike, we can in various cases speak of anarchism, skepticism, nihilism, depoliticization, or on the contrary of subversive overpoliticization. Today, the general strike does not need to demobilize or mobilize a spectacular number of people: it is enough to cut the electricity in a few privileged places, for example the services, public and private, of postal service and telecommunications, of radio and television or to introduce a few efficient viruses into a well-chosen computer network or, by analogy, to introduce the equivalent of AIDS into the organs of transmission, into the hermeneutic *Gespräch.*[10]

Can what we are doing here resemble a general strike or a revolution, with regard to models, structures but also modes of readability of political action? Is that what deconstruction is? Is it a general strike or a strategy of rupture? Yes and no. Yes, to the extent that it assumes the right to contest, and not only theoretically, constitutional protocols, the very charter that governs reading in our culture and especially in the academy. No, at least to the extent that it is in the academy that it has been developed (and let's not forget, if we do not wish to sink into ridicule or indecency, that we are comfortably installed here on Fifth Avenue—only a few blocks away from the inferno of injustice). And besides, just as a strategy of rupture is never pure, since the lawyer or the accused has to "negotiate" it in some way before a tribunal or in the course of a hunger strike in the prison, so there is never a pure opposition between the general political strike looking to re-found another state and the general proletarian strike looking to destroy the state.

And so these Benjaminian oppositions seem to me to call more than ever for deconstruction; they deconstruct themselves, even as paradigms for deconstruction. What I am saying here is anything but conservative and anti-revolutionary. For beyond Benjamin's explicit purpose, I shall propose the interpretation according to which the very violence of the foundation or position of law (*Rechtsetzende Gewalt*) must envelop the violence of conservation (*Rechtserhaltende Gewalt*) and cannot break with it. It belongs to the structure of fundamental violence that it calls for the repetition of itself and founds what ought to be conserved, conservable, promised to heritage and tradition, to be shared. A foundation is a promise. Every position (*Setzung*) permits and promises (*permet et pro-met*), it positions *en mettant et en promettant*. And even if a promise is not kept in fact, iterability inscribes the promise as guard in the most irruptive instant of foundation. Thus it inscribes the possibility of repetition at the heart of the originary. With this, there is no more a pure foundation or pure position of law, and so a pure founding violence, than there is a purely conservative violence. Position is already iterability, a call for self-conserving repetition. Conservation in its turn refounds, so that it can conserve what it claims to found. Thus there can be no rigorous opposition between positioning and conservation, only what I will call (and Benjamin does not name it) a *différantielle contamination* between the two, with all the paradoxes that this may lead to. No rigorous distinction between a general strike and a partial strike (again, in an industrial society, we would also lack the technical criteria for such a distinction), nor, in Sorel's sense, between a general political strike and a general proletarian strike. Deconstruction is also the idea of—and the idea adopted by necessity of—this *différantielle* contamination. It is in thinking about this *différantielle* contamination, as the contamination at the very heart of law that I single out this sentence of Benjamin's, which I hope to come back to later: there is, he says "something rotten in law" (p. 286) (*etwas Morsches im Recht*). There is something decayed or rotten in law, which condemns it or ruins it in advance. Law is condemned, ruined, in ruins, ruinous, if we can risk a sentence of death on the subject of law, especially when it's a question of the death penalty. And it is in a passage on the death penalty that Benjamin speaks of what is "rotten" in law.

If there is something of strike and the right to strike in every interpretation, there is also war and *polemos*. War is another example of this contradiction internal to law (*Recht* or *droit*). There is a *droit de la guerre* (Schmitt will complain that it is no longer recognized as the very possibility of politics). This *droit* involves the same contradiction as the *droit de grève*. Apparently subjects of this *droit* declare war in order to sanction a violence whose object seems natural (the other wants to lay hold of territory, goods, women; he wants my death, I kill him). But this warlike violence that resembles "*brigandage*" outside the law (*raubende Gewalt*, "predatory violence," p. 283) is always deployed *within* the sphere of law. It is an anomaly *within* the legal system with which it seems to break. Here the rupture of the relation is the relation. The transgression is before the law. In so-called primitive societies, where these meanings would be more clearly brought out, the peace settlement shows very well that war was not a natural phenomenon. No peace is settled without the symbolic phenomenon of a ceremonial. It recalls the fact that there was already ceremony in war. War, then, did not simply amount to a clash of two interests or of two purely physical forces. Here an important parenthesis emphasizes that, to be sure, in the pair war/peace, the peace ceremonial recalls the fact that the war was also an unnatural phenomenon; but Benjamin apparently wants to withhold a certain meaning of the word "peace" from this correlation, in particular in the Kantian concept of "perpetual peace." Here it is a question of a whole other "unmetaphorical and political" (*unmetaphorische und politische*) signification, the importance of which we may weigh in a moment. At stake is international law, where the risks of diversion or perversion for the benefit of individual interests (whether those of a state or not) require an infinite vigilance, all the more so as these risks are inscribed in its very constitution.

After the ceremony of war, the ceremony of peace signifies that the victory establishes a new law. And war, which passes for originary and archetypal (*ursprüngliche und urbildliche*, "primordial and paradigmatic," p. 283) violence in pursuit of natural ends, is in fact a violence that serves to found law or right (*rechtsetzende*, "law making"). From the moment that this positive, positional (*setzende*) and founding character of another law is recognized, modern law (*droit*) refuses the individual subject all right to violence. The people's shudder of admiration before the "great criminal" is addressed to the individual who takes upon himself, as in primitive times, the stigma of the lawmaker or the prophet. But the distinction between the two types of violence (founding and conserving) will be very difficult to trace, to found or to conserve. We are going to witness an ambiguous and laborious movement on Benjamin's part to preserve at any cost a distinction or a correlation without which his whole project could collapse. For if violence is at the origin of law, we must take the critique of this double violence ("lawmaking and law-preserving violence," p. 386) to its logical conclusion.

To discuss the conservative violence of law, Benjamin sticks to relatively modern problems, as modern as the problem of the general strike was a moment ago. Now it is a question of compulsory military service, the modern police or the abolition of the death penalty. If, during and after World War I, an impassioned critique of violence was developed, it took aim this time at the law-conserving form of violence. Militarism, a modern concept that supposes the exploitation of compulsory military service, is the forced use of force, the compelling (*Zwang*) to use force or violence (*Gewalt*) in the service of the state and its legal ends. Here military violence is legal and *conserves* the law, and thus it is more difficult to criticize than the pacifists and activists believe; Benjamin does not hide his low esteem for these declaimers. The ineffectiveness and inconsistency of anti-military pacifists results from their failure to recognize the legal and unassailable character of this violence that conserves the law.

Here we are dealing with a *double bind* or a contradiction that can be schematized as follows. On the one hand, it appears *easier* to criticize the violence that founds since it cannot be justified by any preexisting legality and so appears savage. But on the other hand, and this reversal is the whole point of this reflection, it is *more difficult*, more illegitimate to criticize this same violence since one cannot summon it to appear before the institution of any preexisting law: it does not recognize existing law in the moment that it founds another. Between the two limits of this contradiction, there is the question of this ungraspable revolutionary instant that belongs to no historical, temporal continuum but in which the foundation of a new law nevertheless plays, if we may say so, on something from an anterior law that it extends, radicalizes, deforms, metaphorizes or metonymizes, this figure here taking the name of war or general strike. But this figure is also a contamination. It effaces or blurs the distinction, pure and simple, between foundation and conservation. It inscribes iterability in originarity, in unicity and singularity, and it is what I will call deconstruction at work, in full negotiation: in the "things themselves" and in Benjamin's text.

As long as they do not give themselves the theoretical or philosophical means to think this co-implication of violence and law, the usual critiques remain naive and ineffectual. Benjamin does not hide his disdain for the declamations of pacifist activism and for the proclamations of "quite childish anarchism" that would like to exempt the individual from all constraints. The reference to the categorical imperative ("Act in such a way that at all times you use humanity both in your person and in the person of all others as an end, and never merely as a means," p. 285), however uncontestable it may be, allows no critique of violence. Law (*droit*) in its very violence claims to recognize and defend said humanity as end, in the person of each individual. And so a purely moral critique of violence is as unjustified as it is impotent. For the same reason, we cannot provide a critique of violence in the name of liberty, of what Benjamin here calls "*gestaltlose Freiheit*," "formless freedom," that is, in short, purely formal, as empty form, following a Marxist-Hegelian vein that is far from absent throughout this meditation. These attacks against violence lack pertinence and effectiveness because they remain alien to the juridical essence of violence, to the *Rechtsordnung*, the order of law (*droit*). An effective critique must lay the blame on the body of *droit* itself, in its head and in its members, in the laws and the particular usages that law adopts under protection of its power (*Macht*). This order is such that there exists one *unique* fate or history (*nur ein einziges Schicksal*, "only one fate," p. 285). That is one of the key concepts of the text, but also one of the most obscure, whether it's a question of fate itself or of its absolute uniqueness. That which exists, which has consistency (*das Bestehende*) and that which at the same time threatens what exists (*das Drohende*) belong inviolably (*unverbrüchlich*) *to the same order* and this order is inviolable because it is unique. It can only be violated *in itself*. The notion of threat is important here but also difficult, for the threat doesn't come from outside. Law is both threatening and threatened by itself. This threat is neither intimidation nor dissuasion, as pacifists, anarchists or activists believe. The law turns out to be threatening in the way fate is threatening. To reach the "deepest meaning" of the indeterminacy (*Unbestimmtheit*, "uncertainty," p. 285) of the legal threat (*der Rechtsdrohung*), it will later be necessary to meditate upon the essence of fate at the origin of this threat.

In the course of a meditation on fate, which includes along the way an analysis of the police, the death penalty, the parliamentary institution, Benjamin thus comes to distinguish between divine justice and human justice, between the divine justice that destroys law and the mythic violence that founds it.

The violence that conserves ("law-preserving violence"), this threat which is not intimidation, is a threat *of droit*. Double genitive: it both comes from and threatens *droit*. A valuable index arises here from the domain of the right to punish and the death penalty. Benjamin seems to think that the arguments against the *droit de punir* and notably against the death penalty are superficial, and not by accident. For they do not admit an axiom essential to the definition of law. Which? Well, when one tackles the death penalty, one doesn't dispute one penalty among others but law itself in its origin, in its very order. If the origin of law is a violent positioning, the latter manifests itself in the purest fashion when violence is absolute, that is to say when it touches on the right to life and to death. Here Benjamin doesn't need to invoke the great philosophical arguments that before him have justified, in the same way, the death penalty (Kant, Hegel, for example, against early opponents like Beccaria).

If the legal system fully manifests itself in the possibility of the death penalty, to abolish the penalty is not to touch upon one *dispositif* among others, it is to disavow the very principle of law. And that is to confirm, says Benjamin, that there is something "rotten" at the heart of law. The death penalty bears witness, it must bear witness, to the fact that law is a violence contrary to nature. But what today bears witness in an even more "spectral" (*gespenstiche*) way in mixing the two forms of violence (conserving and founding) is the modern institution of the police. It is this mixture (*Vermischung*) that is spectral, as if one violence haunted the other (though Benjamin doesn't put it this way in commenting on the double meaning of the word *gespenstich*). This absence of a frontier between the two types of violence, this contamination between foundation and conservation is ignoble, it is, he says, the ignominy (*das Schmachvolle*) of the police. For today the police are no longer content to enforce the law, and thus to conserve it; they invent it, they publish ordinances, they intervene whenever the legal situation isn't clear to guarantee security. Which these days is to say nearly all the time. The police are ignoble because in their authority "the separation of the violence that founds and the violence that conserves is suspended" (*in ihr die Trennung von recht-setzender und rechtserhaltender Gewalt aufgehoben ist,* "in this authority the separation of lawmaking and lawpreserving is suspended," p. 286). In this *Aufhebung* that it itself is, the police invent law, they make themselves "*rechtsetzend,*" "lawmaking," legislative, each time law is indeterminate enough to give them the chance. The police behave like lawmakers in modern times, not to say lawmakers of modern times. Where there are police, which is to say everywhere and even here, we can no longer discern between two types of violence, conserving and founding, and that is the ignoble, ignominious, disgusting ambiguity. The possibility, which is also to say the ineluctable necessity of the modern police force ruins, in sum, one could say deconstructs, the distinction between the two kinds of violence that nevertheless structure the discourse that Benjamin calls a new critique of violence. He would like either to found it or conserve it but in all purity he can do neither. At most, he can sign it as a spectral event. Text and signature are specters. And Benjamin knows it, so well that the event of the text *Zur Kritik der Gewalt* consists of this strange exposition: before your eyes a demonstration ruins the distinctions it proposes. It exhibits and archivizes the very movement of its implosion, leaving instead what we call a text, the ghost of a text that, itself in ruins, at once foundation and conservation, accomplishes neither and remains there, up to a certain point, for a certain amount of time, readable and unreadable, like the exemplary ruin that singularly warns us of the fate of all texts and all signatures in their relation to law, that is, necessarily, in their relation to a certain police force. Such would be (let it be said in passing) the status without statute, the statute without status of a text considered deconstructive and what remains of it. The text does not escape the law that it states. It is ruined and contaminated, it becomes the specter of itself. But about this ruin of signature, there will be more to say.

What threatens the rigor of the distinction between the two types of violence is at bottom the paradox of iterability. Iterability requires the origin to repeat itself originarily, to alter itself so as to have the value of origin, that is, to conserve itself. Right away there are police and the police legislate, not content to enforce a law that would have had no force before the police. This iterability inscribes conservation in the essential structure of foundation. This law or this general necessity is not a modern phenomenon, it has an *a priori* worth, even if Benjamin is right to give examples that are irreducibly modern in their specificity. Rigorously speaking, iterability precludes the possibility of

pure and great founders, initiators, lawmakers ("great" poets, thinkers or men of state, in the sense Heidegger will mean in 1935, following an analogous schema concerning the fatal sacrifice of these
founders).

I do not see ruin as a negative thing.[11] First of all, it is clearly not a
thing. And then I would love to write, maybe with or following Benjamin, maybe against Benjamin, a short treatise on love of ruins. What
else is there to love, anyway? One cannot love a monument, a work
of architecture, an institution as such except in an experience itself
precarious in its fragility: it hasn't always been there, it will not always be there, it is finite. And for this very reason I love it as mortal,
through its birth and its death, through the ghost or the silhouette of
its ruin, of my own—which it already is or already prefigures. How
can we love except in this finitude? Where else would the right to love,
indeed the love of right, come from? (*D'où viendrait autrement le
droit d'aimer, voire l'amour du droit?*)

Let us return to the thing itself, to the ghost, for this text is a ghost
story. We can no more avoid ghost and ruin than we can elude the
question of the rhetorical status of this textual event. To what figures
does it turn for its exposition, for its internal explosion or its implosion? All the exemplary figures of the violence of law are singular
metonymies, namely, figures without limit, unfettered possibilities of
transposition and figures without figures. Let us take the example of
the police, this index of a phantom-like violence because it mixes
foundation with conservation and becomes all the more violent for
this. Well, the police that thus capitalize on violence aren't simply the
police. They do not simply consist of policemen in uniform, occasionally helmeted, armed and organized in a civil structure on a military
model to whom the right to strike is refused, and so forth. By definition, the police are present or represented everywhere that there is
force of law. They are present, sometimes invisible but always effective, wherever there is preservation of the social order. The police
aren't just the police (today more or less than ever), they are there, the
faceless figure (*figure sans figure*) of a *Dasein* coextensive with the
Dasein of the *polis*. Benjamin recognizes it in his way, but in a double
gesture that I don't think is deliberate and in any case isn't thematized.
He never gives up trying to contain in a pair of concepts and to bring
back down to distinctions the very thing that incessantly exceeds them
and surpasses them. In this way he admits that the problem with the
police is that they are a faceless figure, a violence without a form (*ges-
taltlos*). As such, they are ungraspable in every way (*nirgends fass-
bare*). In so-called civilized states the specter of its ghostly apparition
is all-pervasive (*allverbreitete gespenstische Erscheinung im Leben der*

zivilisierten Staaten, "all pervasive ghostly presence in the life of civilized states," p. 287). And still, this formless ungraspable figure of the police, even as it is metonymized, spectralized, and even as it installs its haunting presence everywhere, would if Benjamin had his way remain a determinable figure proper to the civilized states. He claims to know what he is speaking of when he speaks of the proper meaning of the police and tries to determine that phenomenon. It is hard to know whether he's speaking of the police of the modern state or of the state in general when he mentions the civilized state. I'm inclined toward the first hypothesis for *two reasons:*

1. He selects modern examples of violence, for example that of the general strike or the problem of the death penalty. Earlier on, he speaks not only of civilized states but of another "institution of the modern state," the police. It is the *modern* police, in politico-technical *modern* situations that have led to *produce* the law that they are only supposed to *enforce.*

2. While recognizing that the phantom body of the police, however invasive it may be, always remains equal to itself, he admits that its spirit (*Geist*), the spirit of the police, does less damage in absolute monarchy than it does in modern democracies where its violence degenerates. Let us stay with this point a moment. I am not sure that Benjamin worked out the *rapprochement* I'm attempting here between the words *gespenstische,* "spectral," and "*Geist,*" spirit also in the sense of the ghostly double.[12] But the profound logic of this analogy seems hardly contestable to me, even if Benjamin didn't recognize it. The police become hallucinatory and spectral because they haunt everything; they are everywhere, even there where they are not, in their *Fort-Dasein* to which we can always appeal. Their presence is not present, any more than any presence is present, as Heidegger reminds us, but the presence of their spectral double knows no boundaries. And it is in keeping with the logic of *Zur Kritik der Gewalt* to note that anything having to do with the violence of *droit*—here the police themselves—is not natural but spiritual. There is a spirit, both in the sense of specter and in the sense of the life that exalts itself, through death, precisely, by means of the possibility of the death penalty, above natural and biological life. The police bear witness to this. Here I shall invoke a passage from the *Ursprung der deutschen Trauerspiel* that speaks of *Geist* as the capacity to exercise dictatorship. I thank my friend Tim Bahti for bringing this passage to my attention (but one ought to read the whole chapter, which earlier on discusses the apparition of specters [*Geisterscheinungen,* p. 273]): "Spirit (*Geist*)—so the epoch would have it—manifests itself in power (*weist sich aus in Macht*); spirit is the capacity to exercise dictatorship (*Geist*

ist das Vermögen, Diktatur auszuüben). This capacity requires a rigorous internal discipline just as much as it requires the most unscrupulous external action (*skrupelloseste Aktion*)" (p. 276). And further on it is again a question of the evil genius (*böse Geist*) of despots.

Instead of being itself and being contained within democracy, this spirit of the police, this police violence *as spirit* degenerates there. It bears witness in modern democracy to the greatest degeneracy imaginable for violence (*die denkbar grösste Entartung der Gewalt bezeugt,* "bears witness to the greatest conceivable degeneration of violence," p. 287). Why? In absolute monarchy, legislative and executive powers are united. In it violence is therefore normal, in keeping with its essence, its idea, its spirit. In democracy, on the other hand, violence is no longer accorded to the spirit of the police. Because of the supposed separation of powers, it is exercised illegitimately, especially when instead of enforcing the law the police make the law. Here Benjamin indicates the principle of an analysis of police reality in industrial democracies and their military-industrial complexes with high computer technology. In absolute monarchy, police violence, terrible as it may be, proves to be what it is and what it ought to be in its spirit, while the police violence of democracies denies its proper principle, making laws surreptitiously, clandestinely. The consequences or implications are twofold: (1) democracy is a degeneracy of *droit* and of the violence of *droit;* (2) there is not yet any democracy worthy of this name. Democracy remains to come: to engender or to regenerate. And so Benjamin's argument, which then develops into a critique of the parliamentarism of liberal democracy, is *revolutionary,* even *marxisant,* but in the two senses of the word "revolutionary," which also includes the sense "reactionary," that is, the sense of a return to the past of a purer origin. This equivocation is typical enough to have fed many revolutionary discourses on the right and the left, particularly between the two wars. A critique of "degeneracy" (*Entartung*) as critique of a parliamentarism powerless to control the police violence that substitutes itself for it, is very much a critique of violence on the basis of a "philosophy of history": a putting into archeo-teleological, indeed archeo-eschatological perspective that deciphers the history of *droit* as a decay (*Verfall*) since its origin. The analogy with Schmittian or Heideggerian schemas does not need to be spelled out. This triangle could be illustrated by a correspondence, I mean the epistolary correspondence that linked these three thinkers (Schmitt/Benjamin, Heidegger/Schmitt). And it is still a question of spirit and revolution.

The basic question would be: what about liberal and parliamentary democracy today? As means, all violence founds or preserves *droit*. Otherwise it would lose all value. There is no problematic of *droit* without this violence of means. The result: every juridical contract, every *Rechtsvertrag* ("legal contract," p. 288) is founded on violence. There is no contract that does not have violence as both an origin (*Ursprung*) and an outcome (*Ausgang*). Here a furtive and elliptical allusion by Benjamin is decisive, as is often the case. The violence that founds or positions *droit* need not be immediately present in the contract (*nicht unmittelbar in ihm gegenwärtig zu sein:* "it need not be directly present in it as lawmaking violence," p. 288). But without being immediately present, it is replaced (*vertreten*, "represented") by the supplement of a substitute. And it is in this *différance*, in the movement that replaces presence (the immediate presence of violence identifiable as such in its *traits* and its spirit), it is in this *différantielle* representativity that originary violence is consigned to oblivion. This amnesic loss of consciousness does not happen by accident. It is the very passage from presence to representation. Such a passage forms the trajectory of decline, of institutional "degeneracy", their *Verfall* ("decay"). Benjamin had just spoken of a degeneracy (*Entartung*) of originary violence, for example, that of police violence in absolute monarchy, which is corrupted in modern democracies. Here is Benjamin deploring the *Verfall* of revolution in parliamentary spectacle: "When the consciousness of the latent presence of violence in a legal institution disappears, the institution falls into decay" (p. 288) (*schwindet das Bewußtsein von der latenten Anwesenheit der Gewalt in einem Rechtsinstitut, so verfällt es*). The first example chosen is that of the parliaments of the time. If they offer a deplorable spectacle, it is because these representative institutions forget the revolutionary violence from which they are born. In Germany in particular, they have forgotten the abortive revolution of 1919. They have lost the sense of the founding violence of *droit* that is represented in them ("*Ihnen fehlt der Sinn für die rechtsetzende Gewalt, die in ihnen repräsentiert ist*," "They lack the sense that a lawmaking violence is represented by themselves," p. 288). The parliaments live in forgetfulness of the violence from which they are born. This amnesic denegation is not a psychological weakness, it is their *statut* and their structure. From this point on, instead of coming to decisions commensurable or proportional to this violence and worthy (*würdig*) of it, they practice the hypocritical politics of *compromise*. The concept of compromise, the denegation of open violence, the recourse to dissimulated violence belong to the spirit of violence, to the "mentality of violence" (*Mentalität der Gewalt*) that goes so far as to accept coercion of the adversary to avoid the worst, at the same time saying to itself with the sigh of the parliamentarian that this certainly isn't ideal, that, no doubt, this would have been better otherwise but that, precisely, one couldn't do otherwise. Parliamentarism, then, is in violence and the renunciation of the ideal. It fails to resolve political conflicts by non-violent speech, discussion, deliberation, in short by putting liberal democracy to work. In face of the "decay of parliaments" (*der Verfall der Parlamente*), Benjamin finds the critique of the Bolshevists and the trade-unionists both pertinent (*treffende*) overall and radically destructive (*vernichtende*).

Now we must introduce a distinction that once again brings together Benjamin and one Carl Schmitt and in any case gives a more precise sense of what the historical configuration could have been in which all these different modes of thinking were inscribed (the exorbitant price Germany had to pay for defeat, the Weimar Republic, the crisis and impotence of the new parliamentarism, the failure of pacifism, the aftermath of the October revolution, conflict between the media and parliamentarism, new particulars of international law, and so forth). We just saw, in sum, that in its origin and its end, in its foundation and its conservation, *le droit* was inseparable from violence, immediate or mediate, present or represented. Does this exclude all non-violence in the elimination of conflicts, as we might placidly conclude? Not at all. Benjamin does not exclude the possibility of non-violence. But the thought of non-violence must exceed the order of public *droit*. Union without violence (*gewaltlose Einigung*, "non-violent agreement," p. 289) is possible everywhere that the culture of the heart (*die Kultur des Herzens*) gives men pure means with accord (*Ubereinkunft*) in view. Does this mean we must stop at this opposition between private and public to protect a domain of non-violence? Things are far from that simple. Other conceptual divisions will delimit, in the sphere of politics itself, the relation of violence to non-violence. This would be, for example, in the tradition of Sorel or Marx, the distinction between the general *political* strike, violent since it wants to replace the state with another state (for example the one that just flashed forth in Germany) and the general *proletarian* strike, that revolution that instead of strengthening the state aims at its suppression, as it aims at the elimination of "sociologists, says Sorel, men of the world so fond of social reforms, intellectuals who have embraced the profession of thinking for the proletariat" ("sociologists, elegant amateurs of social reforms or intellectuals who have made it their profession to think for the proletariat," p. 292).

Another distinction seems even more radical and closer to what concerns the critique of violence as a means. It opposes the order of means and representation, precisely, to the order of *manifestation*. Once again it is very much a question of the violence of language, but also of the advent of non-violence through a certain language. Does the essence of language consist in signs, considered as *means* of communication as re-presentation, or in a manifestation that no longer arises, or not yet, from communication through signs, from communication in general, that is, from the means/end structure?

Benjamin intends to prove that a non-violent elimination of conflicts is possible in the private world when it is ruled by the culture of the heart, cordial courtesy, sympathy, love of peace, trust. Dialogue (*Unterredung*, "conference"), as technique of civil agreement, would be the most profound example. But by what token can violence be considered excluded from the private or proper sphere (*eigentliche Sphäre*)? Benjamin's response may be surprising to some. The possibility of this non-violence is attested to by the fact that the lie (*die Lüge*, "lying," p. 289) is not punished, nor is deception (*Betrug*, "fraud"). Roman law and Old German law did not punish them. To consider a lie an offence is a sign of decadence (*Verfallsprozess*, "declining vitality"). Modern law loses faith in itself, it condemns deception not for moral reasons but because it fears the violence that it might lead to on the victims' part. They may in return threaten the order of *droit*. It is the same mechanism as the one at work in the concession of the right to strike. It is a matter of limiting the worst violence with another violence. What Benjamin seems to be dreaming of is an order of non-violence that withholds from the order of *droit*— and so from the right to punish the lie—not only private relations but even certain public relations as in the general proletarian strike that Sorel speaks about, which is a strike that would not attempt to refound a state and a new *droit;* or again certain diplomatic relations in which, in a manner analogous to private relations, certain ambassadors settle conflicts peacefully and without treaties. Arbitration is non-violent in this case because it is situated beyond all order of *droit* and so beyond violence ("beyond all legal systems, and therefore beyond violence," p. 293). We shall see in a moment how this non-violence is not without affinity to pure violence.

Here Benjamin proposes an analogy that we should linger over for a moment, particularly because it brings in this enigmatic concept of fate. What would happen if a violence linked to fate (*schicksalsmässige Gewalt*, "violence imposed by fate," p. 293) and using just means (*berechtigte*) found itself in an insoluble conflict with just (*gerechten*) ends? And in such a way that we had to envision another kind of violence that regarding these ends would be neither a justified nor an unjustified means? Neither a justified nor an unjustified means, undecidably, it would no longer even be a means but would enter into a whole other relation with the pair means/end. Then we would be dealing with a wholly other violence that would no longer allow itself to be determined in the space opened up by the opposition means/end. The question is all the more grave in that it exceeds or displaces the initial problematic that Benjamin had up to this point constructed on the subject of violence and *droit* and that was entirely governed by the concept of means. Here it will be noticed that there are cases in which, posed in terms of means/ends, the problem of *droit* remains undecidable. This ultimate undecidability which is that of all problems of *droit* (*Unentscheidbarkeit aller Rechtsprobleme,* "ultimate insolubility of all legal problems," p. 293) is the insight of a singular and discouraging experience. Where is one to go after recognizing this ineluctable undecidability?

Such a question opens, first, upon another dimension of language, on an *au-delà* beyond mediation and so beyond language as sign in the sense of mediation, as a means with an end in view. It seems at first that there is no way out and so no hope. But at the impasse, this despair (*Aussichtslosigkeit,* "insolubility," "hopelessness") summons up decisions of thought that concern nothing less than the origin of language in its relation to the truth, destinal violence (*schicksalhafte Gewalt,* "fate-imposed violence") that puts itself above reason, then, above this violence itself, God: another, a wholly other "mystical foundation of authority." It is not, to be sure, Montaigne's or Pascal's, but we shouldn't trust too much in this distance. That is what the *Aussichtslosigkeit* of *droit* in some way opens up on, that is where the impasse of *droit* leads.

There would be an analogy between "the undecidability (*Unentscheidbarkeit*) of all the problems of *droit*" and what happens in nascent language (*in werdenden Sprachen*) in which it is impossible to make a clear, convincing, determinant decision (*Entscheidung*) between true and false, correct and incorrect (*richtig/falsch,* "right/wrong"). This is only an analogy proposed in passing. But it could be developed on the basis of other Benjamin texts on language, notably "The Task of the Translator" (1923) and especially the famous essay of 1916, five years before, "On Language in General and Human Language." Both put into question the notion that the essence of language is originally communicative, that is to say semiological, informative, representative, conventional, hence *mediatory.* It is not a means with an end in view—a thing or signified content—to which it would have to adequate itself correctly. This critique of the sign was political then as well: the conception of language as means and as sign would be "bourgeois." The 1916 text defined original sin as that fall into a language of mediate communication where words, having become means, incite babbling (*Geschwätz*). The question of good and evil after the creation arises from this babbling. The tree of knowledge was not there to provide knowledge of good and evil but as the "*Wahrzeichen*," the sign betokening judgment (*Gericht*) borne by he who questions. "This extraordinary irony," Benjamin concludes, "is the sign by which the mythical origin of *droit* is recognized" (*das Kennzeichen des mythischen Ursprungs des Rechtes*, Bd 11, 1, p. 154).

Beyond this simple analogy, Benjamin here wants to conceive of a finality, a justice of ends that is no longer tied to the possibility of *droit*, in any case to what is always conceived of as universalizable. The universalization of *droit* is its very possibility, it is analytically inscribed in the concept of justice (*Gerechtigkeit*). But in this case what is not understood is that this universality is in contradiction with God himself, that is, with the one who decides the legitimacy of means and the justice of ends *over and above reason and even above destinal violence*. This sudden reference to God above reason and universality, beyond a sort of *Aufklärung* of law, is nothing other than a reference to the irreducible singularity of each situation. And the audacious thought, as necessary as it is perilous, of what I shall here call a sort of justice without *droit* (this is not one of Benjamin's expressions) is just as valid for the uniqueness of the individual as for the people and the language, in short, for history.

To explain this "nonmediate function of violence" (p. 294) (*Eine nicht mittelbare Funktion der Gewalt*), Benjamin again takes the example of everyday language as if it were only an analogy. In fact, it seems to me, we have here the true mechanism, and the very place of decision. Is it by chance and unrelated to such a figure of God that he speaks then of the experience of anger, an example of an immediate manifestation that has nothing to do with any means/end structure? The explosion of violence, in anger, is not a means that looks toward an end; it has no object other than to show and show itself. Let us leave the responsibility for this concept to Benjamin: the in some way disinterested, immediate and uncalculated manifestation of anger. What matters to him is a manifestation of violence that would not be a means looking toward an end. Such would be mythic violence as manifestation of the gods.

Here begins the last sequence, the most enigmatic, the most fascinating and the most profound in this text. For lack of time but not only time, I cannot claim to do it justice. I will have to content myself with stressing on the one hand the terrible ethico-political ambiguity of the text, on the other hand the exemplary instability of its status and its signature, what, finally, you will permit me to call this heart or courage (*ce coeur ou ce courage*) or a thinking that knows there is no *justesse,* no justice, no responsibility except in exposing oneself to all risks, beyond certitude and good conscience.

In the Greek world, the manifestation of divine violence in its mythic form founds a *droit* rather than enforcing an existing one by distributing compensations and punishments. It is not a distributive or retributive justice, and Benjamin evokes the legendary examples of Niobe, Apollo and Artemis, Prometheus. As it is a matter of founding a new *droit,* the violence that falls upon Niobe comes from fate; and this fate can only be uncertain and ambiguous (*zweideutig*), since it is not preceded or regulated by any anterior, superior or transcendant *droit.* This founding violence is not "properly destructive" (*eigentlich zerstörend,* "actually destructive"), since, for example, it respects the mother's life in the moment it brings a bloody death to Niobe's children. But this allusion to blood spilled, as we shall see, is here a discriminating index for identifying the mythical and violent foundation of *droit* in the Greek world and distinguishes it from the divine violence of Judaism. Benjamin offers multiple examples of this ambiguity (*Zweideutigkeit,* the word returns at least four times), and even of the "demonic" ambiguity of this mythical positioning of *droit*[13] which is in its fundamental principle a power (*Macht*), a force, a position of authority and so, as Sorel himself suggests, with Benjamin's apparent approval here, a privilege of kings, of the great or powerful: at the origin of all *droit* is a privilege (*in den Anfängen alles Recht "Vor"recht der Könige oder der Grossen, kurz der Mächtigen:* "in the beginning all right was the prerogative of the kings or the nobles—in short of the mighty," p. 296). At this originary and mythic moment, there is still no distributive justice, no chastisement or penalty, only expiation (*Sühne,* badly translated as "retribution").

To this violence of the Greek *mythos,* Benjamin opposes feature for feature the violence of God. From all points of view, he says, it is its opposite. Instead of founding *droit,* it destroys it; instead of setting limits and boundaries, it annihilates them; instead of leading to error and expiation, it causes to expiate; instead of threatening, it strikes; and above all, this is the essential point, instead of killing with blood, it kills and annihilates *without bloodshed.* Blood makes all the difference. The interpretation of this thought of blood is as troubling, despite certain dissonances, in Benjamin as it is in Rosenzweig (especially if we think of the "final solution"). Blood is the symbol of life, he says. In making blood flow, the mythological violence of *droit* is exercised in its own favor (*um ihrer selbst willen*) against life pure and simple which it causes to bleed, even as it remains precisely within the order of natural life (*das blosse Leben*). In contrast, purely divine (Judaic) violence is exercised on all life but to the profit or in favor of the living (*über alles Leben um des Lebendigen willen:* "Mythical violence is bloody power over mere life for its own sake, divine violence pure power over all life for the sake of the living," p. 297). In other words, the mythological violence of *droit* is satisfied in itself by sacrificing the living, while divine violence sacrifices life to save the living, in favor of the living. In both cases there is sacrifice, but in the case where blood is exacted, the living is not respected. Whence Benjamin's singular conclusion, and again I leave to him responsibility for this interpretation, particularly for this interpretation of Judaism: "The first (the mythological violence of *droit*) demands (*fordert*) sacrifice, the second (divine violence) accepts it, assumes it (*nimmt sie an*)." In any case, this divine violence, which will be attested to not only by religion but also in present life or in manifestations of the sacred, may annihilate goods, life, *droit,* the foundation of *droit,* and so on, but it never mounts an attack to destroy the soul of the living (*die Seele des Lebendigen*). Consequently, we have no right to conclude that divine violence leaves the field open for all human crimes. "Thou shalt not kill" remains an absolute imperative once the principle of the most destructive divine violence commands the respect of the living being, beyond *droit,* beyond judgment. It is not a "criterion of judgment" but a "guideline for the actions of persons or communities who have to wrestle with it in solitude and in exceptional cases, to take on themselves the responsibility of ignoring it. That for Benjamin is the essence of Judaism which forbids all murder, except in the singular cases of legitimate self-defense, and which sacralizes life to the point that certain thinkers extend this sacralization beyond man, to include animal and vegetable. But here we should sharpen the point of what Benjamin means by the sacrality of man, life or rather human *Dasein.* He stands up vigorously against all sacralization of life *for itself,* natural life, the simple fact of life. Commenting at length on the words of Kurt Hiller, according to which "higher even than the happiness and the justice of existence stands existence itself" (p. 298), Benjamin judges the proposition that simple *Dasein* should be higher than just *Dasein* (*als gerechtes Dasein*) to be false and ignoble, if simple *Dasein* is taken to mean the simple fact of living. And while noting that these terms "*Dasein*" and "life" remain very ambiguous, he judges the same proposition, however ambiguous it may remain, in the opposite way, as full of a powerful truth (*gewaltige Wahrheit*) if it means that man's non-being would be still more terrible than man's not-yet-being just, than the not yet attained condition of the just man, purely and simply. In other words, what makes for the worth of man, of his *Dasein* and his life, is that he contains the potential, the possibility of justice, the yet-to-come (*avenir*) of justice, the yet-to-come of his being-just, of his having-to-be just. What is sacred in his life is not his life but the justice of his life. Even if beasts and plants were sacred, they would not be so simply for their life, says Benjamin. This critique of vitalism or biologism, if it also resembles one by a certain Heidegger and if it recalls, as I have noted elsewhere, a certain Hegel, here proceeds like the awakening of a Judaic tradition. Because of this ambiguity in the concepts of life and *Dasein,* Benjamin is both drawn to and reticent before the dogma that affirms the sacred character of life, as natural life, pure and simple. The origin of this dogma deserves inquiry, notes Benjamin, who is ready to see in it the relatively modern and nostalgic response of the West to the loss of the sacred.

Which is the ultimate and most provocative paradox of this critique of violence? The one that offers the most to think about? It is that this critique presents itself as the only "philosophy" of history (the word "philosophy" remaining in unforgettable quotation marks) that makes possible an attitude that is not merely "critical" but, in the more critical and diacritical sense of the word "critique," *krinein,* an attitude that permits us to choose (*krinein*), and so to decide and to cut decisively in history and on the subject of history. It is the only one, Benjamin says, that permits us, in respect to present time, to take a decisive position (*scheidende und entscheidende Einstellung,* "discriminating and decisive approach," pp. 299–300). All undecidability (*Unentscheidbarkeit*) is situated, blocked in, accumulated on the side of *droit,* of mythological violence, that is to say the violence that founds and conserves *droit.* But on the other hand all decidability stands on the side of the divine violence that destroys *le droit,* we could even venture to say deconstructs it. To say that all decidability is found on the side of the divine violence that destroys or deconstructs *le droit* is to say at least two things:

1. That *history* is on the side of this divine violence, and history precisely in opposition to myth. It is indeed for this reason that it's a matter of a "philosophy" of *history* and that Benjamin appeals in fact to a "new historical era" (*ein neues geschichtliches Zeitalter,* "a new historical epoch," p. 300) that should follow the end of the mythic reign, the interruption of the magic circle of the mythic forms of *droit,* the abolition of the *Staatsgewalt,* of the violence or authority of the state. This new historical era would be a new political era on the condition that politics not be tied to state control, as Schmitt for example would have it.

2. If all decidability is concentrated on the side of divine violence in the Judaic tradition, this would come to confirm and give meaning to the spectacle offered by the history of *droit* which deconstructs itself and is paralyzed in undecidability, since what Benjamin calls the "dia-

lectic of up and down" (*ein dialektisches Auf und Ab,* "dialectical rising and falling") in the founding or conserving violence of *droit* constitutes an oscillation in which the violence that conserves must constantly give itself up to the repression of hostile counter-violences (*Unterdrückung der feindlichen Gegengewalten*). But this repression—and *droit,* the juridical institution, is essentially repressive from this point of view—never ceases to weaken the founding violence that it represents. And so it destroys itself in the course of this cycle. For here Benjamin to some extent recognizes this law of iterability that insures that the founding violence is constantly represented in a conservative violence that always repeats the tradition of its origin and that ultimately keeps nothing but a foundation destined from the start to be repeated, conserved, reinstituted. Benjamin says that founding violence is "represented" (*repräsentiert*) in conservative violence.

To think at this point that we have cast light and correctly interpreted the meaning, the *vouloir-dire* of Benjamin's text, by opposing in a decidable way the decidability of divine, revolutionary, historical, anti-state, anti-juridical violence on one side and on the other the undecidability of the mythic violence of state *droit,* would still be to decide too quickly and not to understand the power of this text. For in its last lines a new act of the drama is played, or a *coup de théâtre* that I couldn't swear was not premeditated from the moment the curtain went up. What does Benjamin in fact say? First he speaks in the conditional about revolutionary violence (*revolutionäre Gewalt*): "if," beyond *droit,* violence sees its status insured as pure and immediate violence, then this will prove that revolutionary violence is possible. Then we would know, but this is a conditional clause, that it is this revolutionary violence whose name is the purest manifestation of violence among men. But why is this statement in the conditional? Is it only provisional and contingent? Not at all. For the *decision (Entscheidung)* on this subject, the determinant decision, the one that permits us to know or to recognize such a pure and revolutionary violence *as such,* is a *decision not accessible to man.* Here we must deal with a whole other undecidability, and I prefer to cite Benjamin's sentence *in extenso:* "But it is neither equally possible nor equally urgent for man to decide when pure violence was effected in a determined case." (*Nicht gleich möglich, noch auch gleich dringend ist aber für Menschen die Entscheidung, wann reine Gewalt in einem bestimmten Falle wirklich war,* "Less possible and also less urgent for humankind, however, is to decide when unalloyed violence has been realized in particular cases," p. 300).

This results from the fact that divine violence, which is the most just, the most historic, the most revolutionary, the most decidable or the most deciding does not lend itself to any human determination, to any knowledge or decidable "certainty" on our part. It is never known in itself, "as such," but only in its "effects" and its effects are "incomparable," they do not lend themselves to any conceptual generalization. There is no certainty (*Gewißheit*) or determinant knowledge except in the realm of mythic violence, that is, of *droit,* that is, of the undecidable we have been talking about. "For only mythical violence, not divine, will be recognizable as such with certainty, unless it be in incomparable effects . . ." (p. 300). To be schematic, there are two violences, two competing *Gewalten:* on one side, decision (just, historical, political, and so on), justice beyond *droit* and the state, but without decidable knowledge; on the other, decidable knowledge and certainty in a realm that structurally remains that of the undecidable, of the mythic *droit* of the state. On one side the decision without decidable certainty, on the other the certainty of the undecidable but without decision. In any case, in one form or another, the undecidable is on each side, and is the violent condition of knowledge or action. But knowledge and action are always dissociated.

Questions: What one calls in the singular, if there is one and only one, deconstruction, is it the former or the latter? Something else entirely or something else again? If we trust the Benjaminian schema, is the deconstructive discourse on the undecidable more Jewish (or Judaeo-Christian-Islamic) or Greek? More religious, more mythic or more philosophical? If I do not answer questions that take this form, it is not only because I am not sure that such a thing as "Deconstruction," in the singular, exists or is possible. It is also because I think that deconstructive discourses as they present themselves in their irreducible plurality participate in an impure, contaminating, negotiated, bastard and violent way in all these filiations—let's call them Judaeo-Greek to save time—of decision and the undecidable. And then, the Jew and the Greek, that may not be exactly what Benjamin had in mind for us. And finally for what remains to come in deconstruction, I think that something else runs through its veins,perhaps without filiation, an entirely different blood or rather something entirely different from blood.[14]

And so in saying *adieu* or *au-revoir* to Benjamin, I nevertheless leave him the last word. I let him sign, at least if he can. It is always necessary that the other sign and it is always the other that signs last. In other words, first.

In his last lines, Benjamin, just before signing, even uses the word "bastard." That in short is the definition of the myth, and so of the founding violence of *droit.* Mythic *droit,* we could say juridical fiction, is a violence that will have "bastardized" (*bastardierte*) the "eternal forms of pure divine violence." Myth has bastardized divine violence with *droit* (*mit dem Recht*). Misalliance, impure genealogy: not a mixture of bloods but bastardy which at its root will have created a *droit* that makes blood flow and exacts blood as payment.

And then, as soon as he has taken responsibility for this interpretation of the Greek and the Jew, Benjamin signs. He speaks in an evaluative, prescriptive, non-constative manner, as we do each time we sign. Two energetic sentences proclaim what *must* be the watchwords, what one *must do*, what one *must reject*, the evil or perversity of what must be rejected (*Verwerflich*). "But one must reject (*Verwerflich aber*) all mythical violence, the violence that founds *droit*, which we may call governing (*schaltende*) violence. One must also reject (*Verwerflich auch*) the violence that conserves *droit*, the governed violence (*die verwaltete Gewalt*) in the service of the governing." (The English translation is, as it often is, insipid: "But all mythical, lawmaking violence, which we may call executive, is pernicious. Pernicious, too, is the law-preserving, administrative violence that serves it," p. 300).

Then there are the last words, the last sentence. Like the *shophar* at night or on the brink of a prayer one no longer hears or does not yet hear. Not only does it sign, this ultimate address, and very close to the first name of Benjamin, Walter. It also names the signature, the sign and the seal, it names the name and what calls itself "*die waltende.*" But who signs? It is God, the Wholly Other, as always, it is the divine violence that always will have preceded but also will have *given* all the first names: "*Die göttliche Gewalt, welche Insignium und Siegel, niemals Mittel heiliger Vollstreckung ist, mag die waltende heißen*": "Divine violence, which is the sign and seal but never the means of sacred execution, may be called sovereign violence (*die waltende heissen*)." [15]

Jacques Derrida

Post-scriptum

This strange text is dated. Every signature is dated, even and perhaps all the more so if it slips in among several names of God and only signs by pretending to let God himself sign. If this text is dated and signed (Walter, 1921), we have only a limited right to convoke it to bear witness either to Nazism in general (which had not yet developed as such), or to the new forms assumed there by the racism and the antisemitism that are inseparable from it, or even less to the final solution: not only because the project and the deployment of the final solution came later and even after the death of Benjamin, but because within the history itself of Nazism the final solution is something that some might consider an ineluctable outcome and inscribed in the very premises of Nazism, if such a thing has a proper identity that can sustain this sort of utterance, while others—whether or not they are Nazis or Germans—might think that the project of a final solution is an event, indeed something entirely new within the history of Nazism and that as such it deserves an absolutely specific analysis. For all of these reasons, we would not have the right or we would have only a limited right to ask ourselves what Walter Benjamin would have thought, in the logic of this text (if it has one and only one) of both Nazism and the final solution.

And yet in a certain way I will do just that, and I will do it by going beyond my interest for this text itself, for its event and its structure, for that which it allows us to read of a configuration of Jewish and German thinking right before the rise of Nazism, as one says, of all the shared portions and all the partitions that organize such a configuration, of the vertiginous proximities, the radical reversals of pro into con on the basis of sometimes common premises. Presuming, that is, that all these problems are really separable, which I doubt. In truth, I will not ask myself what Benjamin himself thought of Nazism and antisemitism, all the more so since we have other means of doing so, other texts by him. Nor will I ask what Walter Benjamin himself would have thought of the final solution and what judgments, what interpretations he would have proposed. I will seek something else, in a modest and preliminary way. However enigmatic and overdetermined the logical matrix of this text might be, however mobile and convertible, however reversible it is, it has its own coherence. This coherence also marks a number of other texts by Benjamin, both earlier and later ones. It is by taking account of certain insistent elements in this coherent continuity that I will try out several hypotheses in order to reconstitute not some possible utterances by Benjamin but the larger aspects of the problematic and interpretive space in which his discourse on the final solution might have been inscribed.

On the one hand, he would probably have taken the final solution to be the extreme consequence of a logic of Nazism that, to take up again the concepts from our text, would have corresponded to:

1. The radicalization of evil linked to the fall into the language of communication, representation, information (and from this point of view, Nazism has indeed been the most pervasive figure of media violence and of political exploitation of the modern techniques of communicative language, of industrial language and of the language of industry, of scientific objectification to which is linked the logic of the conventional sign and of formalizing registration);

2. The totalitarian radicalization of a logic of the state (and our text is indeed a condemnation of the state, even of the revolution that replaces a state by another state, which is also valid for other totalitarianisms—and already we see prefigured the question of the *Historikerstreit*);

3. The radical but also fatal corruption of parliamentary and representative democracy through a modern police that is inseparable from it, that becomes the true legislative power and whose phantom commands the totality of the political space. From this point of view, the final solution is both a historico-political decision by the state and a decision by the police, the civil and the military police, without anyone ever being able to discern the one from the other and to assign the true responsibilities to any one decision whatsoever.

4. A radicalization and total extension of the mythical, of mythical violence, both in its sacrificial founding moment and its most conservative moment. And this mythological dimension, that is at once Greek and aestheticizing (like fascism, Nazism is mythological, Grecoid, and if it corresponds to an aestheticization of the political, it is in an aesthetics of representation), this mythological dimension also responds to a certain violence of state law, of its police and its technics, of right totally dissociated from justice, as the conceptual generality propitious to the mass structure in opposition to the consideration of singularity and uniqueness. How can one otherwise explain the institutional, even bureaucratic form, the simulacra of legalization, of juridicism, the respect for expertise and for hierarchies, in short, the whole judicial and state organization that marked the techno-industrial and scientific deployment of the "final solution"? Here a certain mythology of right was unleashed against a justice which Benjamin believed ought to be kept radically distinct from right, from natural as well as historic right, from the violence of its foundation as well as from that of its conservation. And Nazism was a conservative revolution of right.

But, on the other hand and for these very reasons, because Nazism leads logically to the final solution as to its own limit and because the mythological violence of right is its veritable system, one can only think, that is, also remember the uniqueness of the final solution from a place other than this space of the mythological violence of right. To take the measure of this event and of what links it to destiny, one would have to leave the order of right, of myth, of representation (of juridico-political representation with its tribunals of historian-judges, but also of aesthetic representation). Because what Nazism, as the final achievement of the logic of mythological violence, would have attempted to do is to exclude the other witness, to destroy the witness of the other order, of a divine violence whose justice is irreducible to right, of a violence heterogeneous to the order both of right (be it that of human rights or of the order of representation) and of myth. In other words, one cannot think the uniqueness of an event like the final solution, as extreme point of mythic and representational violence, within its *own* system. One must try to think it beginning with its other, that is to say, starting from what it tried to exclude and to destroy, to exterminate radically, from that which haunted it at once from without and within. One must try to think it starting from the possibility of singularity, the singularity of the signature and of the name, because what the order of representation tried to exterminate was not only human lives by the millions, natural lives, but also a demand for justice; and also names: and first of all the possibility of giving, inscribing, calling and recalling the name. Not only because there was a destruction or project of destruction of the name and of the very memory of the name, of the name as memory, but also because the system of mythical violence (objectivist, representational, communicational, etc.) went all the way to its limit, in a demonic fashion, on the two sides of the limit: *at the same time,* it kept the archive of its destruction, produced simulacra of justificatory arguments, with a terrifying legal, bureaucratic, statist objectivity and paradoxically produced a system in which its logic, the logic of objectivity made possible the invalidation and therefore the effacement of testimony and of responsibilities, the neutralization of the singularity of the final solution; in short, it produced the possibility of the historiographic perversion that has been able to give rise both to the logic of revisionism (to be brief, let us say of the Faurisson type) as well as a positivist, comparatist, or relativist objectivism (like the one now linked to the *Historikerstreit*) according to which the existence of an analogous totalitarian model and of earlier exterminations (the Gulag) explains the final solution, even "normalizes" it as an act of war, a classic state response in time of war against the Jews of the world, who, speaking through the mouth of Weizman in September, 1939, would have, in sum, like a quasi-state, declared war on the Third Reich.

From this point of view, Benjamin would perhaps have judged vain and without pertinence—in any case without a pertinence commensurable to the event, any juridical trial of Nazism and of its responsibilities, any judgmental apparatus, any historiography still homogeneous with the space in which Nazism developed up to and including the final solution, any interpretation drawing on philosophical, moral, sociological, psychological or psychoanalytical concepts, and especially juridical concepts (in particular those of the philosophy of right, whether it be that of natural law, in the Aristotelian style or the style of the *Aufklärung*). Benjamin would perhaps have judged vain and without pertinence, in any case without pertinence commensurable to the event, any historical or aesthetic objectification of the final solution that, like all objectifications, would still belong to the order of the representable and even of the determinable, of the determinant and decidable judgment. Recall what we were saying a moment ago: in the order of the bad violence of right, that is the mythological order, evil arose from a certain undecidability, from the fact that one could not distinguish between founding violence and conserving violence, because corruption was dialectical and dialectically inevitable there, even as theoretical judgment and representation were determinable or determinant there. On the contrary, as soon as one leaves this order, history begins—and the violence of divine justice—but here we humans cannot measure judgments, which is to say also decidable interpretations. This also means that the interpretation of the final solution, as of everything that constitutes the set and the delimitation of the two orders (the mythological and the divine) is not in the measure of man. No anthropology, no humanism, no discourse of man on man, even on human rights, can be proportionate to either the rupture between the mythical and the divine, or to a limit experience such as the final solution. Such a project attempts quite simply to annihilate the other of mythic violence, the other of representation: destiny, divine justice and that which can bear witness to it, in other words man insofar as he is the only being who, not having received his name from God, has received from God the power and the mission to name, to give a name to his own kind and to give a name to things. To name is not to represent, it is not to communicate by signs, that is, by means of means in view of an end, etc. In other words, the line of this interpretation would belong to that terrible and crushing condemnation of the *Aufklärung* that Benjamin had already formulated in a text of 1918 published by Scholem in 1963 honoring Adorno on his 60th birthday.

This does not mean that one must simply renounce Enlightenment and the language of communication or of representation in favor of the language of expression. In his *Moscow Diary* in 1926–27, Benjamin specifies that the polarity between the two languages and all that they command cannot be maintained and deployed in a pure state, but that "compromise" is necessary or inevitable between them. Yet this remains a compromise between two incommensurable and radically heterogeneous dimensions. It is perhaps one of the lessons that we could draw here: the fatal nature of the compromise between heterogeneous orders, which is a compromise, moreover, in the name of the justice that would command one to obey at the same time the law of representations (*Aufklärung*, reason, objectification, comparison, explication, the taking into account of multiplicity and therefore the serialization of the unique) and the law that transcends representation and withholds the unique, all uniqueness, from its reinscription in an order of generality or of comparison.

What I find, in conclusion, the most redoubtable, indeed (perhaps, almost) intolerable in this text, even beyond the affinities it maintains with the worst (the critique of *Aufklärung*, the theory of the fall and of originary authenticity, the polarity between originary language and fallen language, the critique of representation and of parliamentary democracy, etc.), is a temptation that it would leave open, and leave open notably to the survivors or the victims of the final solution, to its past, present or potential victims. Which temptation? The temptation to think the holocaust as an uninterpretable manifestation of divine violence insofar as this divine violence would be at the same time nihilating, expiatory and bloodless, says Benjamin, a divine violence that would destroy current law through a bloodless process that strikes and causes to expiate. Here I will re-cite Benjamin: "The legend of Niobe may be confronted, as an example of this violence, with God's judgment on the company of Korah (Numbers 16: 1–35). It strikes privileged Levites, strikes them without warning, without threat, and does not stop short of annihilation. But in annihilating it also expiates, and a deep connection between the lack of bloodshed and the expiatory character of this violence is unmistakable" (p. 297). When one thinks of the gas chambers and the cremation ovens, this allusion to an extermination that would be expiatory because bloodless must cause one to shudder. One is terrified at the idea of an interpretation that would make of the holocaust an expiation and an indecipherable signature of the just and violent anger of God.

It is at that point that this text, despite all its polysemic mobility and all its resources for reversal, seems to me finally to resemble too closely, to the point of specular fascination and vertigo, the very thing against which one must act and think, do and speak, that with which one must break (perhaps, perhaps). This text, like many others by Benjamin, is still too Heideggerian, too messianico-marxist or archeo-eschatological for me. I do not know whether from this nameless thing called the final solution one can draw something which still deserves the name of a lesson. But if there were a lesson to be drawn, a unique lesson among the always singular lessons of murder, from even a single murder, from all the collective exterminations of history (because each individual murder and each collective murder is singular, thus infinite and incommensurable) the lesson that we can draw today—and if we can do so then we must—is that we must think, know, represent for ourselves, formalize, judge the possible complicity between all these discourses and the worst (here the final solution). In my view, this defines a task and a responsibility the theme of which (yes, the theme) I have not been able to read in either Benjaminian "destruction" or Heideggerian "*Destruktion.*" It is the thought of difference between these destructions on the one hand and a deconstructive affirmation on the other that has guided me tonight in this reading. It is this thought that the memory of the final solution seems to me to dictate.

NOTES

1. On the *oblique,* cf. my *Du droit à la philosophie* (Paris: Galilée, 1990), esp. pp. 71ff, and "Passions: An Oblique Offering," *Derrida: A Critical Reader,* David Wood, ed. (London: Blackwell, 1992).

2. On this notion of credit, see my *Given Time I: Counterfeit Money,* trans. Peggy Kamuf, forthcoming University of Chicago Press.

3. Minneapolis: University of Minnesota Press, 1987.

4. On animality, cf. my *Of Spirit: Heidegger and the Question,* trans. Geoffrey Bennington and Rachel Bowlby (Chicago: University of Chicago Press, 1989). Other references are collected in this volume. As for sacrifice, see the interview with Jean-Luc Nancy, trans. Peter T. Connor, in *Topoi,* vol. 7, no. 2.

5. And as for what consists, as St. Augustine would have said, in "making the truth," see my *Circonfession,* in Geoffrey Bennington and Jacques Derrida, *Jacques Derrida* (Paris: Le Seuil, 1991).

6. Editors' note: The following comprises the introduction to this second part of the essay when it served as a lecture delivered at the UCLA colloquium, "Nazism and the 'Final Solution'":

   Rightly or wrongly, I thought that it would perhaps not be entirely inappropriate to interrogate a text by Walter Benjamin, singularly an essay written in 1921 and entitled *Zur Kritik der Gewalt* (*Critique of Violence*), at the opening of such a meeting on Nazism, the final solution, and the limits of representation, especially since my lecture is also presented (and I am greatly honored by this double hospitality) under the auspices of a center for Critical Studies and the Human Sciences. If I have therefore chosen to present a somewhat risky reading of this text by Benjamin, it is for several reasons that seem to converge here.

   1. I believe this uneasy, enigmatic, terribly equivocal text is, as it were, haunted in advance (but can one say "in advance" here?) by the theme of radical destruction, extermination, total annihilation, beginning with the annihilation of the law and of right, if not of justice, and, among those rights, human rights, at least such as these are interpreted within a tradition of natural law of the Greek type or the "*Aufklärung*" type. I purposely say that this text is *haunted* by the themes of exterminating violence because first of all, as I will try to demonstrate, it is haunted by *haunting* itself, by a quasi-logic of the phantom which, because it is the more forceful one, should be substituted for an ontological logic of presence,

absence or representation. Now, I ask myself whether a community that assembles or gathers itself together in order to think what there is to be thought and gathered of this nameless thing that has been called the "final solution" does not have to show, first of all, its readiness to welcome the law of the phantom, the spectral experience and the memory of the phantom, of that which is neither dead nor living, more than dead and more than living, only surviving, the law of the most commanding memory, even though it is the most effaced and the most effaceable, but for that very reason the most demanding.

This text by Benjamin is not only signed by a thinker who is considered and considered himself to be, in a certain fashion, Jewish (and I most especially would like to talk about the enigma of this signature). *Zur Kritik der Gewalt* is also inscribed in a Judaic perspective that opposes just, divine (Jewish) violence that would destroy the law to mythical violence (of the Greek tradition) that would install and conserve the law.

2. The profound logic of this essay puts to work an interpretation of language—of the origin and the experience of language—according to which evil, that is to say lethal power, comes to language by way of, precisely, *representation*, in other words, by that dimension of language as means of communication that is re-presentative, mediating, thus technical, utilitarian, semiotic, informational—all of those powers that uproot language and cause it to decline, to fall far from or outside of its originary destination which was appellation, nomination, the giving or the appeal or presence in the name. We will ask ourselves how this thinking about the name is articulated with haunting and the logic of the specter. This essay by Benjamin, which treats thus of evil, of that evil that is coming and that comes to language through representation, is also an essay in which the concepts of responsibility and of culpability, of sacrifice, decision, solution, punishment or expiation play a major role, one which is most often associated with the value of what is demonic and "demonically ambiguous" (*dämonisch zweideutig*).

3. *Zur Kritik der Gewalt* is a critique of representation not only as perversion and fall of language, but as a political system of formal and parliamentary democracy. From that point of view, this revolutionary essay (revolutionary in a style that is at once Marxist and messianic) belongs, in 1921, to the great anti-parliamentary and anti-"*Aufklärung*" wave on which Nazism so to speak surfaced and even surfed in the 1920s and the beginning of the 1930s.

4. This very polyhedric and polysemic question of representation is posed as well from another point of view in this strange essay. Having begun by distinguishing between two sorts of violence, founding violence and conserving violence, Benjamin must concede at one moment that the one cannot be so radically heterogeneous to the other since the violence called founding violence is sometimes represented (*repräsentiert*) by the conserving violence.

For all of these reasons and according to all of these interlaced threads to which I am going to return, one can ask oneself a certain number of questions. They will be on the horizon of my reading even if I do not have the time here or the means to make them explicit. What would Benjamin have thought, or at least what thought of Benjamin is potentially formed or articulated in this essay—and can it be anticipated—on, the "final solution," its project, its *mise en oeuvre*, the experience of its victims, the judgments, trials, interpretations, narrative, explicating, literary, historical representations which have attempted to measure up to it? How would Benjamin have spoken, how would he have wished one to speak, to represent, or to forbid oneself from representing the "final solution"? How might he have attempted to identify it, to assign places in it, origins to it, responsibilities for it (as a philosopher, a historian, judge or jurist, as moralist, man of faith, poet, filmmaker). The very singular multiplicity of the codes that converge in this text, to say nothing of other texts; the graft of the language of marxist revolution on that of messianic revolution, both of them announcing not only a new historical epoch, but also the beginning of a true history that has been rid of myth; all of this makes it difficult to propose any hypotheses about a Benjaminian discourse on the "final solution" or about a Benjaminian discourse on the possibility or impossibility of a discourse on the "final solution." A "final solution" of which it would be reckless to say, relying on the objective dates of the Wannsee conference in 1942 and Benjamin's suicide on the Franco-Spanish border in 1940, that Benjamin knew nothing about it. One will always find ways to support the hypothesis according to which Benjamin, already in 1921, was thinking about nothing else than the possibility of this final solution that would be all the more challenging to the order of representation from having perhaps arisen, in his view, from radical evil, from the fall as fall of language into representation. And if one relies on a constant logic of his discourse, many signs allow one to think that for Benjamin, after this unrepresentable thing that will have been the "final solution," not only are discourse and literature and poetry not impossible but, more originarily and more eschatologically than ever, they must offer themselves to the dictation of the return or the still promised advent of a language of names, a language or a poetics of appellation, in opposition to a language of signs, of informative or communicative representation: beyond myth and representation but not beyond the language of names. Something I tried to show elsewhere about Celan on the subject of dates and acts. At the end, after the end of a reading in the course of which the horizon of Nazism and the final solution will appear only through signs or brief flashes of expectation and will be treated only in a virtual, oblique or elliptical fashion, I will propose a few hypotheses on the ways in which this text from 1921 can today be read, after the event of Nazism and the event of the final solution.

Before proposing a reading of this singular text, before articulating some questions that concern it more strictly, I must also say a few words, in this already too lengthy introduction, about the contexts in which I began to read the essay. That context was double and I will define it as schematically as possible, while limiting myself to the aspects that may interest us here, this evening, because they will have left some traces on my reading.

1. First of all, within a three-year seminar on "philosophical nationalities and nationalisms," there was a year-long sequence subtitled *Kant, the Jew, the German* in which, while studying the varied but insistent recurrence of the reference to Kant, indeed to a certain Judaism in Kant, on the part of all those who, from Wagner and Nietzsche to Adorno, sought to respond to the question *"Was ist Deutsch?"*, I became very interested in what I then called the *Judeo-German psyche*, that is, the logic of certain phenomena of a disturbing sort of specularity (*Psyché* also meaning in French a sort of mirror) that was itself reflected in some of the great German Jewish thinkers and writers of this century: Cohen, Buber, Rosenzweig, Scholem, Adorno, Arendt—and, precisely, Benjamin. I believe that a serious reflection on Nazism—and the "final solution"—cannot avoid a courageous, interminable and polyhedral analysis of the history and structure of this Judeo-German "psyche." Among other things that I cannot go into here, we studied certain analogies, which were sometimes of the most equivocal and disquieting sort, between the discourse of certain "great German" thinkers and certain "great

German Jewish" thinkers, a certain German patriotism, often a German nationalism, and sometimes even a German militarism (during and after the First World War) being not the only example, far from it, for instance in Cohen or Rosenzweig or, to some extent, in Husserl. It is in this context that certain limited but determinable affinities between Benjamin's text and some texts by Carl Schmitt, even by Heidegger, began to intrigue me. Not only because of the hostility to parliamentary democracy, even to democracy as such, or to the *Aufklärung*, not only because of a certain interpretation of the *polemos*, of war, violence and language, but also because of a thematic of "destruction" that was very widespread at the time. Although Heideggerian *Destruktion* cannot be confused with the concept of destruction that was also at the center of Benjaminian thought, one may well ask oneself what such an obsessive thematic might signify and what it is preparing or anticipating between the two wars, all the more so in that, in every case, this destruction also sought to be the condition of an authentic tradition and memory, and of the reference to an originary language.

2. Other context: On the occasion of a recent colloquium held at the Cardozo Law School of Yeshiva University of New York on the topic "Deconstruction and the Possibility of Justice," I began, after a long consideration of "Deconstruction and Justice," to examine this text by Benjamin from another point of view. I followed there precisely, and as cautiously as possible, a dismaying trajectory, one that is at the same time aporetic and productive of strange events in its very aporia, a kind of self-destruction, if not a suicide of the text, that lets no other legacy appear than the violence of its signature—but as divine signature. How to read this text with a "deconstructive" gesture that is neither, today any more than it has ever been, Heideggerian nor Benjaminian? In brief, that is the difficult and obscure question that this reading would like to risk putting forth.

7. "Psyche: Invention of the Other," trans. Catherine Porter, in *Reading de Man Reading* (Minneapolis: University of Minnesota Press, 1989), p. 36.

8. Cf. "Declarations of Independence," trans. Tom Keenan and Tom Pepper, *New Political Science*, no. 15, Summer, pp. 7–15.

9. Cf. "Before the Law," trans. Avital Ronell, in *Kafka and the Contemporary Critical Performance: Centenary Readings,* ed. Alan Udoff. (Bloomington, Ind.: Indiana University Press, 1987).

10. Cf. my "Rhétorique de la drogue," in *Autrement*, no. 106.

11. Cf. my *Mémoires d'aveugle. L'autoportrait et autres ruines* (Paris: Réunion des Musées Nationaux, 1990).

12. Cf. *Of Spirit*, op. cit., and "Philopolemogy: Heidegger's Ear (Geschlecht IV)," forthcoming, Indiana University Press.

13. This "mythic" dimension of *droit* in general could no doubt be extended, according to Benjamin, to any theory of the "rights of man," at least to the extent that the latter would not proceed from what in this text is called "divine violence" (göttliche Gewalt).

14. In putting this text of Benjamin to the test of a certain deconstructive necessity, at least such as it is here determined for me now, I am anticipating a more ample and coherent work: on the relations between this deconstruction, what Benjamin calls "destruction" (*Zerstörung*) and the Heideggerian "*Destruktion*" (which I have already touched upon and to which I will return elsewhere, notably in "Philopolemology: Heidegger's Ear (Geschlecht IV)."

15. This "play" between *walten* and *Walter* does not afford any demonstration or any certainty. That, furthermore, is the paradox of its "demonstrative" force: this force results from the dissociation between the cognitive and the performative of which I spoke a moment ago (and also elsewhere), precisely in regard to the signature. But, touching on the absolute secret, this "play" is in no way ludic and gratuitous. For we also know that Benjamin was very interested, notably in *Goethe's Elective Affinities,* in the aleatory and significant coincidences of which proper names are properly the site. I would be tempted to give this hypothesis an even better chance after reading the very fine essay by Jochen Hörisch "L'ange satanique et le bonheur—Les noms de Walter Benjamin" in *Weimar: Le tournant esthétique,* G. Raulet, ed. (Paris, 1988).

2

The Philosophy of the Limit: Systems Theory and Feminist Legal Reform

Drucilla Cornell

INTRODUCTION

Feminists, for all of the divergence among them, continue to join in a united call for justice for women. But in 1991, as we watch the stripping away of women's most basic civil rights, such as the right of abortion, we need to ask ourselves why feminist legal reforms have been so difficult to sustain and why the conditions of women's inequality are continually *restored*. Of course, this backlash does not effect all women equally. It is not a coincidence that the first decisions undermining the right of abortion were directed against poor and working class women's attempt to get funding for their abortions.[1]

For the purposes of this essay, I am only using abortion as an example. I could just as easily have used examples from sex discrimination law, the debate over pornography or the changing law regarding date rape, etc. I have argued elsewhere that what we need is a program of equivalent rights for women if we are to even begin to lay the legal foundation for the equality of women.[2] I use the word foundation, because I am not suggesting that equality between men and women is only, or even principally, a matter of rights. Even so, "rights" expresses a symbolic as well as social reality. Symbols, in turn, cannot be separated from the broader, many-faceted social constructs we call

This paper was written in loving memory of Mary Joe Frug. It is dedicated both to her and to Joan Scott, whose friendship has been a source of support and inspiration. I want to thank Niklas Luhmann for our intellectual exchanges at several recent conferences, which have pushed me to a new direction in my conception of the relationship between social theory and philosophy. As always, I wish to thank my dedicated research assistant, Deborah Garfield, who helped me in every stage of the production of this paper.

society. As I have argued, the right of abortion should only be understood as part of a broader program of equivalent rights. Furthermore, a comprehensive program of reproductive rights would obviously have to address the needs of heterosexual and lesbian women, as well as the needs of others who live in arrangements other than the nuclear family. But in 1991 we are equally obviously very far from having developed and implemented such a program of reproductive rights, let alone a program of equivalent rights such as the one I advocate.

My purpose in this essay is to suggest that we cannot understand the backlash against even the most meager civil rights of women through the traditional explanations of the distribution of political power. The very word restoration demands an analysis of the set of relations being restored and an explanation of how and why they are being restored. What we are seeing restored is the gender hierarchy, in which anything associated with the feminine is disparaged, devalued, feared and, ultimately, repudiated. To fully explain this process of restoration, we need a systems explanation of how the gender hierarchy is perpetuated and intersects with the law so as to effectively undermine the legitimacy of women's demands for justice.[3] I will argue that the systems theory of Niklas Luhmann can help us explain how the gender hierarchy can be understood as a system. In addition, Luhmann's systems theory can also give us the conceptual framework to explain the relationships between different subsystems within the social order, including the relationship between gender and law. Alone, such an explanation would seemingly lead only despair. To move beyond this dilemma we also need an account of how the gender hierarchy can be transformed and an idea of the ethical basis of a new alliance between the sexes which would overcome the current relations of domination.

This essay combines Jacques Derrida's deconstructive interventions into the writings of Jacques Lacan and Emmanuel Levinas with the systems theory of Niklas Luhmann to encompass the divergent aspects I have just described as necessary for a feminist narration of the gender hierarchy, including an analysis of how and in what direction it should be changed.[4] It is important to note at the outset that I disagree with Derrida's critics who argue that deconstruction can play no role whatsoever in providing us with a social analysis of the current conditions of society and the possibilities of social change. Although Derrida is not a sociologist, his insistence on the centrality of sexual difference to philosophical discourse has important implications for developing a social analysis that does not itself become an expression of the current gender hierarchy. It is precisely this reminder of the centrality of sexual difference that becomes important to the feminist addition to Luhmann's systems theory. As we will see, the rethinking of the relationship between deconstruction and systems theory is particularly important to feminists.

LACAN'S ANALYSIS OF THE GENDER HIERARCHY

To understand the significance of Derrida's deconstructive interventions and Luhmann's systems theory now translated into the field of gender we must first turn to Jacques Lacan's account of how the semantics of desire perpetuate the illusion of masculine physiology which is then expressed in gender hierarchy. By the semantics of desire, I mean to indicate Lacan's analysis of the relation, or lack thereof, between the "sexes." We can then focus on the relationship between the semantics of desire and the semantic code of law. Lacan's central insight was to provide a corrective to biologistic readings of Freud's account of gender differentiation. According to Lacan, children of both sexes enter into the world of culture and, more specifically, the signifying system we know as language only by enduring a severe wound to their own narcissism. This wound is the result of the recognition that the mother is not just there for the baby. With this recognition comes the inevitable question, "Who does Mommy want if she does not just want me?" The answer, in a society governed by patriarchal conventions, and in which, correspondingly, heterosexuality has been institutionalized as the norm, is "Daddy." Lacan's addition is to understand that it is not the real Daddy but the phallus that triggers the mother's desire. The implicit recognition that the desire of the mother is directed to what she does not have, the phallus, shatters the illusion that the mother is complete in herself, omnipresent and, therefore, always able to meet the child's needs. Lacan refers to this imaginary figure as the Phallic Mother. The choice of words is deliberate, because the illusion of omnipotence demands that the mother be able to satisfy herself so that no other can pull her away from the child. To read the mother's desire as lack is to know that there is something else, and to begin the quest to find it. This quest turns the child into a speaking "being" and turns him or her toward the Imaginary Father. The separation of the child from the mother becomes identified in the child's unconscious with the separation of the mother from the phallus. Her now apparent lack becomes a threat to the child's very security. Her incompleteness makes her desire the other who is not the child. It is the break-up of this idealized symbiotic unity that forces the child to speak in order to articulate his or her desires. But the most profound desire, the desire to be one with the mother again, cannot be spoken because of the intervention of the symbolic father, whose presence on the scene is associated with the very demand for articulation of what is now perceived as lack. Thus we speak out of a desire we cannot articulate because of the constraints of a conventional order based on the incest taboo. Given the incest taboo, the child cannot actually have the mother. As a result, the Phallic Mother is repressed into the unconscious as the idealized, if often feared, Woman. The incest taboo and the fear of the symbolic father prevent the child from articulating his desire. When Lacan says "the Woman does not exist," he means that the idealized Woman, the desired Other who lives on only in the imaginary, is just that: a figure of the imagination. In her place are actual women with their lack and the resulting failure "to live up to" the imaginary figure.

This schema obviously turns on a "reading" of the mother's desire and this "reading," in turn, can only be guaranteed to yield the same message if there is an already-established system in place. Lacan's analysis, which explains why the gender hierarchy is the very basis of culture, is inevitably circular, given the relationship between what he calls the realm of the symbolic—the established order of signification—and the differentiation between the genders. To quote Lacan, "[t]he symbolic order is, in its initial workings, androcentric. This is a fact."[5]

For Lacan, the Oedipal complex is the very basis for the child's entry into a cultural world which has significance. It is only once we grasp this central insight that we can understand how the gender hierarchy is perpetuated in and through the reality and the very idea of culture. Indeed, it is the implicit isomorphism that Lacan assumes, between what he defines as the symbolic and the social more generally, that accounts for his political pessimism. If the gender differentiation is the very basis for the difference between what "is" and what is given meaning through language itself, then the very entry of human beings into culture demands its perpetuation. And, if sacrifice, in the sense of being separated from the Phallic Mother, is demanded of both sexes as the price we all must pay to become speaking subjects, the toll extracted nevertheless diverges according to "sex." The assumption of castration—in Lacan's specific sense of the repression of the desire for the Phallic Mother—means one thing for masculine subjects and quite another for their feminine counterparts. Masculine identity is the illusion of wholeness that represses its differential relation to what "it" is not—feminine. To "be" a man is to not "be" a woman.

Both sexes read the mother's desire as for the phallus. Although Lacanians are always careful to distinguish the actual penis from the phallus (the phallus represents the supposed loss of symbiotic connection with the mother that triggers desire in both sexes), the cultural significance given to the penis within patriarchal society allows for the fantasy that to have the penis is to have the phallus. For the male child the entrance of the third, the symbolic father, and the culture he represents, symbolizes potency. The little boy's renunciation of the imagined symbiotic unity with the mother is rewarded by identification with the father who also, needless to say, has the penis. In Lacan, the relation of the little boy to the father is premised on the substitution allowed by metaphoric transference. The sacrifice demanded by the establishment of social order is thus compensated for by the fantasy that the little boy has what the father has. In fantasy, then, the little boy can make up for his primary narcissistic wound through the illusion that he at least has what it takes to bring the mother back. Once the identification with the father takes place, the mother's sex is viewed as lack. As a result, Woman is now "seen" as the castrated Other. Because the little girl cannot assume the little boy's position in the Oedipal complex she is denied the fantasy compensation given to the little boy. The little girl cannot, like the little boy, make up for her primary narcissistic wound.

The recognition of "sex" difference thus derives from a reading of the mother's desire. It has nothing to do with biology. Mother wants Daddy. She wants the phallus that she does not have. And, as the mother is devalorized, so that men can assume the identity of the not woman, so is the female child. Eleanor Galenson has provided empirical evidence that gives credence to the Lacanian schema.[6] In Galenson's studies, little girls show signs of hopelessness once they are confronted with their lack. One manifestation of this recognition is their fear of losing anything else that may lead to further disempowerment, such as hair, fingernails, etc. The devalorized mother is hardly a persona who can promote a desire to become like her. So the girl's normative identificatory trajectory is to become nor-mâle. Woman's sex, defined as lack, only has meaning as the castrated mother of man, as what he is not.

It is important to note that in Lacan's account it is not the penis itself that the little girl envies, but rather the illusion of potency that comes from the identification with the father. This envy leads to the repudiation of the feminine, even by women themselves. Furthermore, because there is nothing to be said about lack except that it is not, it is only as the limit of culture that the possibility for a cultural re-evaluation of woman's sex is foreclosed within patriarchal culture. The result is that women are left in a state of *dereliction*. This means that they are not allowed into the "boys' club" and that they are cut off from a system of language in and through which they could positively represent their sex so as to provide an affirmative basis for identification with one another.

THE LEGAL SIGNIFICANCE OF THE ASSUMPTION OF THE ISOMORPHISM BETWEEN THE SYMBOLIC AND THE SOCIAL CONTRACT

The idea that the very basis for culture is an unconscious social pact among men has influenced much feminist literature. Carole Pateman, for example has argued that the so-called social contract, which has continued to serve as a useful fiction in liberal jurisprudence, is itself yet another patriarchal construct.[7] Although I cannot adequately summarize Pateman's rich argument here, it is important to at least note that for Pateman the very basis of social order is an implicit *sexual contract* that gives men access to women. Once this sexual contract is noted, it is then possible to give a different meaning to the public/private distinction as it has been traditionally developed in social contract theory. For Pateman, access to women including violent access to women, is rendered beyond the scope of the terms of the male social pact. Contact only regulates relations between men, not between men and women. Implicit in this idea of the contract is that what men do with women is considered "private" and, thus, not to be regulated by the state. After all, what rational man would even hypothetically agree to have his "affairs" with women regulated? Women, by definition, cannot be equal to men under this arrangement. They can never be subjects of the social contract; they can only be subjected to it. Thus, Pateman argues that gender consolidation influences our conceptualization of civil society. The political significance of Pateman's analysis is that we cannot hope to change our social order if we do not take sexual difference into account. As Pateman explains, "To argue that patriarchy is best confronted by endeavouring to render sexual difference politically irrelevant is to accept the view that the civil (public) realm and the 'individual' are uncontaminated by patriarchal subordination."[8] Obviously, the actual law of most Western democracies has changed, allowing women to enter into contracts in their own name. Pateman, however, is suggesting that this change alone does not alter the patriarchal "foundation" of the myths which justify civil society. If Pateman's analysis is correct, it is not surprising that Mary Joe Frug could so graphically show the masculine bias that continues to underpin much of our current doctrine in contract law.[9]

Pateman's ultimate argument is that we should understand the social pact through Freud's account in *Moses and Monotheism* which, even if it only gives us another fiction, can much more effectively illuminate the patriarchal roots of social order. One cannot help but be reminded here of Lacan's own analysis of the relationship between the Oedipal complex, the incest taboo and language itself. Indeed, Lacan's analysis justifies one of the crucial moves in Pateman's argument. Pateman must show that there is an inevitable entanglement of relations relegated to the "private" realm of individual and familial development and the "public" realm of political and legal relations. Of course, Pateman understands that her argument demands that she challenge the traditional categories of public and private. But, like other social theorists, she is ultimately unable to explain why a psychoanalytic account of the gender hierarchy can be successfully transposed into the arena of public relations, without collapsing psychic structures into the social, a move that most psychoanalytic theorists are careful to avoid.[10] A related error is the attempt to directly apply to groups the findings of psychoanalytic studies, such as Galenson's, which are based on individual experiences. An account of how the gender hierarchy is constituted as a social system can provide a corrective for these errors. Gender must be grasped as a set of imperatives which, then, defines what is meant by a man and what is meant by a woman in an actual culture. The very introduction of the word meaning presupposes the Lacanian account just given, which radically separates the construction of gender from biological determinism. Lacan not only shows us the relationship between the Oedipal complex and language, he also shows us that gender is a system of meaning indeed, the very basis of the possibility of meaning. But, of course, feminists want more than a mere account of how gender identity is constructed as the system of signification. We also need an analysis of how the individual observer can critically assess the system and why change is possible. The collapse of psychic operations into social structures would negate the possibility of a critical observer, because the individual psyche would be completely determined by his or her social order.[11]

The first problem of how one can justify applying the insights of psychoanalysis to the social can be answered by the assumption that there is a relation of causality between the realm of the symbolic and the social order more generally. I have suggested that this assumption is implicit in much feminist literature and particularly in the work of Lacanian feminists.[12] We will see shortly just how Niklas Luhmann has displaced the problematic concept of causality with a different understanding of the relationship between subsystems. For now I want to note a political problem. The problem with the assumption of a relation of causality or worse yet, of identity between the system of gender and the social order, is that it would foreclose the possibility of change in another subsystem because that subsystem would itself be determined by the gender hierarchy. In much feminist literature it is assumed that the gender hierarchy is the leading system. In other words, there is not even the hope implicit in the idea of mutual causality as one subsystem influences another. In other words one of our problems is solved at the expense of the other.

Pateman, for example, brilliantly argues that the social contract is itself contaminated by patriarchy. Thus, she can help us explain why "neutral" language in law will itself not be "neutral" at all, but an expression of the gender hierarchy. By so doing, she has helped us solve the problem of why it is so difficult to sustain and justify legal reform under the traditional concepts of the legal system. But if we take Pateman's argument to its logical conclusion, we would have difficulty explaining the possibility of legal reform at all. If there is truly an isomorphic relationship between the symbolic and the social contract, then the social contract could only reinforce the gender hierarchy. I seek to maintain a feminist analysis of the structures of gender identity which I do not think can be developed without an appeal to psychoanalysis generally and, more specifically, the theories of Jacques Lacan. Thus, I agree with Pateman that we should criticize legal myths and legal institutions for being contaminated by patriarchy. But I think her argument about how this contamination takes place must be developed through Niklas Luhmann's systems theory. The question becomes how are we to understand that contamination if we are not to assume with Lacanians that the symbolic contract *is* the social contract which serves as the basis of culture and social order.

WHY GENDER HIERARCHY IS A SYSTEM

I have already suggested that an alternative explanation can be found if feminists incorporate certain crucial concepts of Niklas Luhmann's systems theory into their own critical account of patriarchy. To do so, we must understand gender as a system in Luhmann's sense. Luhmann himself does not argue that gender is a system. Similarly, Lacan does not understand the need for systems theory to effectively explain the intersection of the semantics of desire and the gender hierarchy with the social order. Thus, I am arguing that it is only by combining the work of Lacan and Luhmann that we can develop an adequate understanding of the hold of the gender hierarchy in modern society. A review of Luhmann's systems theory that would portray his work in all its richness and complexity is beyond the scope of this essay. Therefore, I will focus only on the terms essential for the feminist analysis of the relationship between the legal system and the gender hierarchy that I am advocating.

Simply put, a system for Luhmann is an entity that delimits itself from its environment by continually stabilizing the distinction between "inside" and "outside." Systems consists of communications which construct reality as a field of meaning as that reality is relevant to the definitional structures of the system. The goal of social science, given the circular "nature" of systems, is not to test hypotheses by reference to an outside world of "facts," because what would be designated as "facts" would already be established by the system, but rather to understand the functioning of the system itself. The definition of a system as meaningful communications about the environment, rather than with it, distinguishes Luhmann's systems theory from the input/output model of competing sociological approaches to society. We grasp the reality given to us by the system by understanding the operations of the system as these operations in turn promote the achievement of the system's self-referentiality. Self-referentiality is what allows the system to achieve codification and, thus, closure of its own semantic structures.

Luhmann is very specific in the definition of what he means by closure. To quote Luhmann, "In theoretical terms the ultimate problem always consists in combining external and internal references, and the real operations which produce and reproduce such combinations are always internal operations. *Nothing else is meant by closure.*" [13] It is Luhmann's unique concept of closure that necessitates his rejection of the traditional input/output model and leads to his understanding of the relations between systems as one based not causality. As Luhmann explains:

> The emergence of closed systems requires a specific form of relations between systems and environments; it presupposes such forms and is a condition of their possibility as well. The theory of "open systems" describes these forms with the categories of *input and out-*

put. This model postulates a causal chain in which the system serves as the connecting part linking inputs and outputs. The theory of autopoietic systems replaces the input/output-model with the concept of *structural coupling*. It renounces the idea of an overarching causality (admitting it, of course, as a construct of an observer interested in causal attributions), but retains the idea of highly selective connections between systems and environments . . .

Structural couplings are forms of simultaneous (and therefore, not causal) relations. They are analogical, not digital, coordinations.[14]

I return later to how Luhmann's concept of structural coupling can help us understand the relationship between the semantics of desire and the semantics of law. For now, we can take the preliminary step of translating Lacan's understanding of gender into Luhmann's systems theory. Using Luhmann's terminology, we can define the gender hierarchy as a closed self-referential system that codifies its semantic code through the meaning given to the Oedipal complex. And, in turn, the meaning given to the Oedipal complex within the system differentiates the human species into two sexes, male and female, even though the masculine is only defined against the feminine, and therefore is itself illusionary, not really a "sex." Luhmann recognizes the importance of binary codes within systems: "The most important function systems structure their communication through a binary or dual-valued code that, from the viewpoint of its specific function, claims universal validity and excludes further possibilities."[15] I am further arguing that gender differentiation takes place through the consolidation of the binary code which defines each one of us as a man or a woman. Gender, then, is a classic example of how a functional system structures itself through a binary opposition. Furthermore, Lacan's analysis shows why the binary code of male and female claims universal validity in all cultures with the incest taboo and why it excludes, through its own operations, further possibilities for sexual differentiation or what Derrida has called "a new choreography of sexual difference." Using Luhmann's language, Lacan, then, shows us why the structure of this binary opposition, as a set of duplication rules, perpetuates itself through the repudiation of the feminine. All human beings may suffer from gender consolidation, which in turn reinforces heterosexuality as the norm.[16] But men and women do not suffer in the same way and, of course, all women are not equally victimized. Lacan's analysis of gender differentiation is structured not only as a binary opposition but as a hierarchy in which the feminine is pushed under, since the very definition of masculinity is against the feminine. Thus, it can only be a system in Luhmann's sense precisely because sex is only given to us by the system and not by a pre-given biological reality. Yes, men have a penis and women don't, but it is the meaning given to that fact within the system of the gender hierarchy that continually re-inscribes the de-valuation of women as the castrated other.

THE FEMINIST ADDITION TO SYSTEMS THEORY

I want to make two observations which may help us understand why Luhmann has never written of gender as a system when it can be so successfully translated into his own theory. I am suggesting that gender differentiation can serve as a powerful example of why we need systems theory to adequately understand our reality. Yet Luhmann glosses over the full significance of the gender hierarchy in modernity. Luhmann himself always turns us to the observer to assess a particular social analysis. In this case the observer is a man. But I would argue that there is a second, perhaps more important, reason for Luhmann's lack of attention to the gender hierarchy. As Luhmann himself notes, his social theory encompasses the following two fundamental hypotheses:

> 1. That the transition from traditional societies to modern society can be conceived of as the transition from a primarily stratified form of differentiation of the social system to one which is primarily functional
> 2. That this transformation occurs primarily by means of the differentiation of various symbolically generalized media of communication.[17]

Both hypotheses are important for a feminist analysis of modern society, but it is the first that helps us to understand why Luhmann has not focused on the hold of the gender hierarchy in modern society. If the transition to modernity implies the dismantling of a system of social differentiation based on stratification, then it should follow that gender, as one of the traditional hierarchies, would also be dismantled. In other words, Luhmann's optimism about the situation of women follows from his theory.

It is not surprising to find that in 1991, as women watch the civil rights gains of the last twenty years quickly being undermined, if not taken away altogether, feminist social historians have turned to the study of how the dynamics of restoration work against functional differentiation. In her pathbreaking work, Joan Scott has begun to elaborate the process of restoration of the gender hierarchy in the succession of French revolutions.[18] Not surprisingly, Scott's work has been influenced by Lacan. It is not surprising, because Lacan provides us with one of the most powerful analyses of how and why the gender hierarchy will be restored in spite of the efforts of women and men to undermine it. If, however, Scott is right that there is a non-random character to this process of restoration in the great upheavals against stratified differentiation, and I believe that she is, then we need a systems explanation for this phenomenon. If we are to have a full analysis of the complex social order we associate with modernity, we need to both analyze the shift to functional differentiation, as well as examine the barriers against it. In this sense, a feminist analysis makes an important addition to Luhmann's systems theory, even as it relies on its categories.

Turning to Luhmann's second hypothesis, we see that for Luhmann, as society moves from stratified to functional differentiation, there is an ever-increasing differentiation of subsystems. This ever-increasing differentiation of subsystems is important to feminists, because it can help us explain the possibility of the feminist observer. If there were a true relationship of isomorphism between the symbolic and the social contract, then gender would be a kind of leading system, which would determine the development of other systems, such as the legal system and the system we know as the individual. The assumption of isomorphism means that one system can be reduced to another. If it was truly the case that the system of the individual could be reduced to the system of gender, then there could be no explanation of the critical feminist observer, because she would be encompassed by the system of gender, in which woman's allotted place does not include the voice of the critic, because she is silenced before her own oppression.[19] For Luhmann, on the other hand, functional differentiation enhances the possibilities of divergent individual positionings, of which feminism could clearly be considered one. To quote Luhmann:

> [T]he transition from stratified to functional differentiation within society leads to greater differentiation of personal and social systems (or, to be exact, of system/environment distinctions within personal or social systems). This is the case because with the adoption of functional differentiation individual persons can no longer be firmly located in one single subsystem of society, but rather must be regarded a priori as socially displaced. As a consequence, not only do individuals now consider themselves unique owing to the

supposed greater diversity of individual attributes (which may not all be true), but also a greater differentiation occurs of system/environment relations, necessary for personal systems to refer to specific systems. . . .

This trend towards differentiation, easily comprehensible from the point of view of systems theory, means that individuals are all the more provoked into interpreting the difference between themselves and the environment (and in the temporal dimension, the history and future of this difference) in terms of their own person, whereby the ego becomes the focal point of all their inner experiences and the environment loses most of its contours.[20]

This ever increasing differentiation of systems is easily comprehensible by Luhmann's theory because his theory emphasizes functional differentiation. Because each system is related to a function, it is irreplaceable by other systems which take care of another function. By autonomy, Luhmann means to indicate the way in which functional irreplaceableness in turn yields a unique set of operations which define the system as a system. Luhmann is very careful in his explanation of the linkage between systems, particularly as each system constructs reality:

As far as reality references are concerned, this peculiar, devious systems structure, oriented towards almost simultaneous dissolution and recreation, has a particular advantage. It can allow events to act simultaneously on several systems, as long as only their selectivity and their self-referential interweaving with other events always belong to different systems. Thus, communications are always also events in the consciousness of the participants. Nevertheless, the systems remain separate, because the events (which can be identified by an observer as *one* event of conscious communication) select in each case from different systems in relation to different other possibilities; this constitutes the meaning of the event in each case. That the elementary operations have the character of events can guarantee a high degree of interpenetration of the various systems, preventing, through the disappearance of the events, the systems from becoming stuck to one another. Thus, albeit in extremely precarious form, especially close relationships between system and environment can be produced. The transience of the "material" is exploited in two ways; for the reproduction of the system and for the interpenetration of system and environment.[21]

This explanation of linkage helps us to understand why different "realities" can appear, as they are constructed by different systems. It also allows us to understand the close relationship between systems without reducing them or the reality they construct to a shared identity.

THE LEGAL SIGNIFICANCE OF STRUCTURAL COUPLING

With the foregoing explanation of the gender hierarchy as a system in Luhmann's sense, I can now show why feminists need a conception of the structural coupling of systems to understand the restoration of the gender hierarchy within the legal system. I have already argued that feminists clearly do not want to deny that the system of the gender hierarchy intersects with other systems. Such an argument only reinforces the illusion that gender has been successfully cleansed from systems such as the legal system, because at least on the formal level, these systems have seemingly come to express what Luhmann has called functional differentiation. As I have already noted, feminists such as Pateman have insisted that the categories of the legal system express the "reality" of the gender hierarchy. My own argument bolsters that suggestion by elaborating on how Lacan can help us understand gender as a system that does, indeed, intersect with other systems. What I want to stress, and this is clearly an argument that has been at the forefront of much feminist literature, is that the category of functional differentiation may itself disguise the way in which this differentiation can only seemingly be functional, as opposed to stratified, if one implicitly takes for granted the already-in-place gender hierarchy.

An obvious example of the way this assumption operates is the hour requirements for the ascension to partnership in a law firm. Firms can argue that putting in long hours is a functional requirement for making partner. Women, so the story goes, are unable to meet this so-called functional requirement, because the demands of personal life make it impossible to do so. To remedy this problem, the firms have introduced solutions like the "mommy track," that purportedly allow women to function in both systems, law and the family.[22] Mothering can, for our purposes here, be considered a classic example of an "event" that takes place in a number of systems. But how does one system intersect with another so as to express stratification or, on the other hand, functional differentiation? Does the legal system not define mothering according to the pre-given gender hierarchy? By pregiven I mean only the recognition of the "past" in which gender hierarchy was clearly a fundamental stratification. Has this hierarchy been effectively dismantled? If so, why is it assumed that the burdens of parenting will be differentially distributed according to sex? Does just having a penis mean that you can't take care of children? Does it mean that you can't cook? If one can't make a philosophical argument that one can have the direct access to nature necessary in order to make such an argument feasible—and most modern as well as "post-modern" philosophers would agree that direct access to nature is impossible—then we are inevitably returned to the system in which the meanings given to gender are perpetuated.

Luhmann, of course, would be the first to insist that we should look to the system for an understanding of social reality. But, as we have also seen, Luhmann does not study gender as a system and, as a result, he cannot adequately explore the hold of stratified differentiation in a modern society. The situation the "mommy track" leaves us in exemplifies what this hold means for women. Our access to the labor market is curtailed by the operations of the gender hierarchy, which define what mothering supposedly means for women.

From examples such as the "mommy track," which demonstrate the severe limitations the gender hierarchy imposes on women's lives, we can understand why a feminist analysis of social "reality" demands more than just a conception of how systems are linked with another. Such an analysis also requires an explanation of how we can account for change. If the legal system were not autonomous in Luhmann's sense, then there could be no explanation for how we ever achieved the reforms of the late 1960s and 1970s. Even the fact that the operations of the legal system cannot be justified by an explicit appeal to gender opens up what I would call the rhetorical space for change. We can use Luhmann's rhetoric of functional differentiation against the gender hierarchy. Although it is important for me to note here that since I think the dawn of a new age in which the gender hierarchy is truly dismantled awaits us only in the distant future, I do not think that the call for functional differentiation is enough. As I have argued elsewhere, we must affirm feminine sexual difference now.[23] The need to affirm the feminine within sexual difference now is why my own understanding of how one should interact with the rhetorical space opened by the autonomy of the legal system would undoubtedly differ from Luhmann's systems theory. Feminists need both an analysis of the repetition compulsion that in the political and legal arena I have called restoration as well as the assurance that legal and political reform will nevertheless not be completely foreclosed.

Having argued that gender hierarchy shows the continuing hold of stratified differentiation, I would also suggest that race and national differences can be understood in a similar, although certainly not identical manner. Patricia Williams has given us a brilliant analysis of how race intersects with the legal system.[24] In addition to such an analysis, however, feminists also need to account for how the system of gender intersects with the system of racism. If we assume that there is an intersection between two systems then we can better understand that what it means to be a woman can never be the same for an African-American woman and a "white" woman. Moreover, we need not deny that gender operates as a system to be able to make this statement and the assumption it is premised upon. We can also refute the *hubris* too often associated with feminism that gender is a leading system that can give us an understanding of the oppression of women across race and class lines. This insight is perfectly consistent with the "postmodern"[25] insight that to be a woman is always to be a woman differently depending on race, class, sexuality and age and yet there is meaning to the statement that one is a woman, even if that meaning constantly shifts.

THE PHILOSOPHY OF THE LIMIT AND SYSTEMS THEORY

I can now turn to a discussion of the relationship between the feminist revision of systems theory I have just advocated and what has come to be called deconstruction or, as I have renamed it, the philosophy of the limit.[26] Luhmann has frequently used the word "irritation" to describe how a system that does not deal consciously with its structural couplings must still accommodate "outside" systems. For my purposes here, I would like to replace the irritant with the symptom. The word "symptom" more exactly expresses the structural coupling of the semantics of desire and the legal system I have described, because it reflects the psychoanalytic approach I have adopted to explain the gender hierarchy. I also use the word "symptom" to indicate that from the standpoint of the gender hierarchy the repressed feminine "is" only as symptom and, indeed, from within the meaning given to it in that hierarchy it can only be read as symptom, which may explain why so much feminine writing is read as hysterical.

I am also using the word "symptom" here in the way Derrida uses the term, to indicate the outside observer. For Derrida, "The symptom is always a foreign body, and must be deciphered as such; and of course a foreign body is always a symptom, and behaves as a symptom in the body of the ego—it is a body foreign to the body of the ego."[27] What Derrida says about the symptom in the body of the ego can and should be said of the feminine within the gender hierarchy.

But the concept of the symptom also reminds us that from the vantage point of the "symptom," the system is de-limited by its other and is not just self-limiting. For the foreigner, there is an "outside," because she is the banished, the marginalized. But is this just her definition by the system and, thus, an internal definition of the system?

Luhmann would seem to say "yes" to this question. He describes his difference with Derrida as follows:

> Information is, according to Gregory Bateson's oft-cited dictum "a difference that makes a difference." Regardless of what one thinks of their ontological and metaphysical status, or their incarnation as "script" (Derrida), or similar approaches, differences direct the sensibilities which make one receptive to information. Information processing can only take place if, beyond its pure facticity, something has been experienced "as this way and only this way," which means that it has been localized in a framework of differences. The difference functions as a unity to the extend that it generates information, but it does not determine which pieces of information are called for and which patterns of selection they trigger off. Differences, in other words, do not de-limit a system; they specify and extend its capacity for self-delimitation.[28]

But is Luhmann completely correct in his understanding of the difference between his theory and Derrida's? I would argue that we need to redefine the terms of the disagreement between the two.

Luhmann always turns us toward the observer. From the vantage point of the foreigner, the system is "seen" as de-limited by her "outside" position. In other words, as soon as a theory emphasizes the observer, the difference between whether or not a particular difference will appear as a self-delimitation or a de-limitation by the system's other will turn on just that, the standpoint of the observer. Derrida himself reminds us that the question of whose observation is in any fundamental sense "accurate" would have to remain undecidable. Moreover, both Derrida and Luhmann accept what Luhmann calls "epistemological constructivism," meaning that there can be no direct access to the "real" or to definitive conceptualizations of the real. The difference that makes a difference, upon which Luhmann himself remarks, is precisely that the status given to difference does matter for Derrida, which is why he continually stresses the quasi-transcendental analysis which shows why, if a system is self-limited, it is *necessarily* de-limited by its other. For my purposes here, it does not matter if that other is identified as a system. This quasi-transcendental analysis is what Derrida calls "the logic of parergonality."[29] The insight is based on the realization that the only system that could truly be self-limiting and only self-limiting would, by definition, have to encompass all other systems. This insight can be translated back into Luhmann's own language. Regardless of how one describes the other, as symptom or as irritation, the very idea of structural coupling implies an other, that remains other to the system, so that at the very least she can irritate and, in that sense, demand a response. Derrida incorporates that demand for a response into Levinas' ethical philosophy of alterity. I will return to Levinas' ethical philosophy of alterity as it is relevant for our purposes here shortly. For now I want to turn to another important exchange between Derrida's categories and Luhmann's, this time around the difference between what Luhmann calls self-referentiality and what Derrida calls iterability. I will do so from within Derrida's specific deconstructive intervention into Lacan's analysis of the gender hierarchy.

Derrida tells us that Lacan's insight into the relationship between *signifiance* and *jouissance*[30] undermines his own pessimistic political conclusions. Derrida argues that the very slippage of language, which breaks up the coherence of gender identity, makes it possible for us to undermine the rigid gender divide that has made dialogue between men and women impossible and the acceptance of violence toward women not only inevitable, but also not "serious." This slippage in language that always allows for the possibility of reinterpretation is what Derrida means by iterability. He uses the term to indicate that the very repeatability of language implies both sameness and difference. What allows language to be repeatable is that it can be repeated in different contexts. But if there is no context of context, then what is repeated does not yield an identical meaning. In this sense if we assume that all systems are constructed in language there could never be any *pure* self-referentiality, because as the system seeks to perpetuate itself it would always be doing so by responding to its irritations or symptoms and, thus, repeating itself in a slightly different context. This, in turn, means that as it repeats itself the system also transforms itself.

Within the context of the gender hierarchy iterability means the repetition compulsion of imposed gender identity can never completely foreclose transformative possibility. It is Lacan's very insight into the linguistic structures that construct gender identity that allows Derrida to turn Lacan's analysis against himself by showing how his insight into the semantics of desire could give way to another reading. It is important to note here that I refer to this possibility as transformative to distinguish it from the position that would allow for shifts within the binary code itself. In other words, it is not just that we can shift the meanings of male and female within the binary code that produces the distinction male and female. Such shifts would clearly be comprehensible within Luhmann's understanding of how binary codes are perpetuated by systems. Since the code cannot be separated from its meanings, this process can never be protected from the effective undermining of the code itself. It is precisely the undermining of the rigid code of binary oppositions that the philosophy of the limit seeks to effectuate. Within the code of the gender hierarchy this process itself has an ethical aspiration. That aspiration is Derrida's dream of a new choreography of sexual difference, in which our singularity, not our gender, would be loved by our Other. This dream of a new choreography might be reconciled with Luhmann's own dream of love.

I realize that to associate the word "dream" with Luhmann's systems theory may seem to go against the grain of his theory itself. I am suggesting that it does not, in light of the poem Luhmann offers us at the end of *Love as Passion*, which indicates that he does, indeed, have such a dream:

> Transparency only exists in the *relationship* of system and system, and by virtue, so to speak, of the difference of system and environment, which constitutes the system in the first place. Love and love alone can be such a transparency:

> A face in front of
> one
> neither now any more subject
> only reference
> intangible
> and fixed.[31]

But Luhmann does not offer us an explanation of why that dream is only too often lived as a nightmare within our current gender hierarchy. As I have already argued, he does not do so because he does not understand gender hierarchy as a system. If we are to translate gender hierarchy into the terms of his system, does that mean that we are left with the bleak, even if socially constructed reality that would seemingly block love? The answer, I think, is "no," but only once we understand the structural relationship between self-referentiality, with its illusion of consolidated identity, the "logic of parergonality," and the concept of iterability. Once we understand that no system can guarantee itself against the constant shift of its boundaries because of structural coupling and, I would add, iterability, then we can only understand self-referentiality as a future-oriented aspiration that can never be a completed. Although this is not Luhmann's own conception of self-referentiality, I believe it is the necessary outcome of under-standing just how structural coupling itself is what continually opens every system to its deconstruction.

Therefore, there is a very specific sense in which the philosophy of the limit can itself be understood as an operation within Luhmann's system theory, as it can also be understood as the quasi-transcendental condition of the system and thus as its other, its limit. How does one decide? Again, we are returned to the undecidable because we can only decide by a further reference to the observer. Is the philosophy of the limit the "discourse" of the outside observer? Maybe so; but, as a woman, I am thankful for such a "discourse."

THE RELEVANCE OF LEVINAS

Let me now try to connect Derrida, Lacan, and Levinas. A discus-sion of the intricacies of either Emmanuel Levinas' philosophy of al-terity or Jacques Derrida's engagement with it is beyond the scope of this essay.[32] For my purposes here, I want to focus on the significance of Derrida's deconstruction of Levinas' own conceptualization of *both* the ethical and phenomenological asymmetry of the Other for femi-nism. To do so, I will focus on the relationship of Derrida's engage-ment with Levinas to his deconstructive encounter with Lacan. Why is Levinas relevant to Derrida's intervention into Lacan? Levinas chal-lenges the idea that justice can ever be identified with any descriptive set of conditions or rights. Justice cannot be reduced to convention, no matter how conceived, and certainly not to the current definitions of any system. Levinas' messianic conception of justice demands the recognition of the call of the Other, which always remains as a call and can never be fully answered. Put somewhat differently, and this is exactly the notion of justice as aporia that Derrida emphasizes,[33] jus-tice is the limit to what is, not its endorsement. Once we introduce Levinas' messianic concept of justice, we can think more profoundly about Derrida's intervention into Lacan. Levinas argues for the asym-metry of the *ethical* relationship. For Levinas, the Other precedes the ethical subject. She cannot be grasped only in a relationship to the subject or in a conceptualization of her as like the subject who exam-ines her, because such knowledge would ultimately only be derivative of the subject's own self-conception. There can be no pre-given uni-versality that would allow for phenomenological symmetry in which the I understands the Other through a set of common properties that are supposedly shared. For Levinas, to try to know the Other is itself unethical, because to do so would be to deny her difference and her otherness. Instead, our responsibility is to hear her call, which demands that we address her and seek redress from the wrongs done to her. The Other, then, is "there" in the ethical relationship, only as the subject's responsibility to her.

Derrida demonstrates that ethical asymmetry must be based on a *phenomenological* symmetry if it is not to be reduced to another excuse for domination and, thus, for violation of the Other. My addition is that phenomenological symmetry demands the specific recognition of the symmetry of woman as ego, and that this is precisely what the psychical fantasy of woman described by Lacan makes impossible.[34] Without phenomenological symmetry, the asymmetry of the ethical relationship is nothing but violation of woman once again, which is why, on one interpretation, there is an indelible universality upon which Derrida insists, even if it cannot be positively described as a set of properties that define the subject. Such a positive definition, if one accepts that the masculine is defined as the subject, would perpetuate, not undermine, the gender hierarchy. But let me return to the relationship between phenomenological symmetry and ethical asymmetry. I am arguing that Derrida's intervention demands phenomenological symmetry as possible and necessary to the aspiration to the ethical relationship as ethical. Very simply put, to think the ethical relationship, one has to think the question of sexual difference as it has been constituted through the gender hierarchy. Derrida has shown us that the relationship between phenomenological symmetry and the ethical asymmetry values the Other as different, indeed as difference.

CONCLUSION

I am now taking this intervention into what, at first glance, seems to be a very foreign context, the context of equality. The recognition of phenomenological symmetry can be understood as the very basis for any theory of equality. Thus, for me, equal citizenship turns on the phenomenological symmetry that demands the end of violation of women. Derrida's contribution to legal and political philosophy and, more specifically, his interventions into Lacan and Levinas show us that unless we challenge the reduction of Woman to an imaginary fantasy, to the *phenomenologically* asymmetrical Other, there will be nothing but the perpetuation of violence and violation of women. On this analysis, the sweeping away of our civil rights is not a political coincidence. Rather, it reflects the denial of the phenomenological symmetry of women. The feminist alliance with deconstruction, the philosophy of the limit, is precisely Derrida's specific intervention into the work of Lacan and Levinas.

The feminist alliance with Luhmann, on the other hand, is in his explanation of how systems are perpetuated. As we have seen, we need Luhmann to adequately understand how the gender hierarchy functions as a system so as to be structurally coupled with other systems. In light of the current situation, we need to understand why hope is still possible. If systems theory and the philosophy of the limit are in alliance with feminism, then it can only be as an alliance, because theory does not change the world, although it can help us see how and why it can be changed. It is still up to feminists to elaborate the dream of a different world for women beyond the gender hierarchy and to try to make it a reality. All of us know the beginnings of such a world. It would be a world in which we would not lose such an important feminist thinker as Mary Joe Frug to a brutal, tragic and, as yet, unaccounted for murder. Yet her death is also a call, an obligation to continue to critique the subordination of women and to dream. In her death she remains as the limit of the system in which she was killed. In the death that demands redress we will always hear the call of the Other.

NOTES

1. Webster v. Reproductive Health Svcs., 492 U.S. 490 (1989).

2. See Gender, Sex and Equivalent Rights, in Feminists Theorize the Political (J. Butler & J. Scott eds. 1992).

3. Developing such a system explanation of the perpetuation of the gender hierarchy and its intersection with the legal system is the project of my forthcoming book, Sexual Difference, Politics and the Law (New York: Routledge, Chapman & Hall, forthcoming 1993).

4. I am relying primarily on the following texts by Niklas Luhmann: Ecological Communication (J. Bednarz trans. 1986) (originally published as Ökologische Kommunikation: Kann die moderne Gesellschaft sich auf ökologische Gefährdungen einstellen? West Germany: Westdeutsches Verlag, 1986); Love as Passion: The Codification of Intimacy (J. Gaines & D. Jones trans. 1986); Closure and Openness: On Reality in the World of Law (EUI Working Paper No. 86/234, Badia Fiesolana: European University Institute, 1986); Operational Closure and Structural Coupling: The Differentiation of the Legal System, 13 Cardozo L. Rev. 1419(1992)

5. J. Lacan, Le Séminaire, livre II: Le moi dans la théorie de Freud et dans la technique de la psychanalyse 303 (1978).

6. See Galenson & Roiphe, The Impact of Early Sexual Discovery on Mood, Defensive Organization, and Symbolization, in 26 Psychoanalytic Study of the Child, no. 195 (1972).

7. See C. Pateman, The Sexual Contract (1988).

8. Pateman, supra note 7, at 17.

9. Frug, Re-reading Contracts: A Feminist Analysis of a Contracts Casebook, 34 Am. U. L. Rev. 1065 (1985).

10. For my critique of the way the American object relations theorists make this exact mistake, see Cornell, The Limits of Object Relations Theory—The Maternal and the Feminine: Social Reality, Fantasy and Ethical Relation, in Beyond Accommodation: Ethical Feminism, Deconstruction, and the Law (1991).

11. For a complete discussion of the distinction between Stanley Fish and Niklas Luhmann, see Cornell, The Relevance of Time to the Relationship Between The Philosophy of the Limit and Systems Theory: The Call to Judicial Responsibility, in The Philosophy of the Limit: Justice and Legal Interpretation, (New York: Routledge, Chapman & Hall 1992).

12. See generally Brennan, History After Lacan, in 19 Economy & Society no. 3 (1990); J. MacCannell, Figuring Lacan: Criticism and the Cultural Unconscious (1986); J. Rose, Sexuality in the Field of Vision (1986); M. Whitford, Luce Irigaray: Philosophy in the Feminine (1991).

13. Luhmann, Operational Closure and Structural Coupling, supra note 4, at 1431.

14. Id. at 1431–32 (emphasis in original and footnote omitted).

15. Luhmann, Ecological Communication, supra note 4, at 36.

16. For an illuminating discussion of the problems associated with gender consolidation, see J. Butler, Gender Trouble: Feminism and the Subversion of Identity (1990).

17. Luhmann, Love as Passion, supra note 4, at 5.

18. See J. Scott, Historical Perspectives on Equality and Difference: French Feminists in 1848 (unpublished lecture delivered at the New School for Social Research, May 13, 1991).

19. It should be noted that this is a position adopted by many feminists critics, including Catharine MacKinnon.

20. Luhmann, Love as Passion, supra note 4, at 15 (footnotes omitted).

21. Luhmann, Closure and Openness, supra note 4, at 14.

22. The term "mommy track" refers to an arrangement whereby women who need flexible work schedules to be able to meet the needs of their families are given the "opportunity" to work part-time. Unfortunately, in terms of career goals, this accommodation serves only to relegate these women to positions where they have no hope of reaching senior management positions or achieving partnership.
    Some women have taken the position that corporations ought to recognize two different groups of women managers: those who put career first and those who need a flexible schedule for personal reasons. See, e.g., F. Schwartz, Management Women and the New Facts About Life, Harv. Bus. Rev., January–February 1989,

at 65. Others take a stronger stance, demanding equal pay and an equal sense of entitlement for women. See, e.g., Mann, The Demeaning "Mommy Track": Separate and Unequal, in The Washington Post, at C3 (March 15, 1989).

23. One of the main purposes of my book, *Beyond Accommodation: Ethical Feminism, Deconstruction and the Law,* is to argue that the affirmation of the feminine and, specifically, feminine sexual difference, is crucial to any feminist theory.

24. P. Williams, The Alchemy of Race and Rights (1991).

25. As I have explained in the context of other discussions, I use the word "postmodern" reluctantly. First, I do not think that periods of history can be so rigidly separated. Moreover, I believe that in using this terminology we run the risk of losing what is unique in the messages offered by the various philosophical positionings that get defined under the catch-all description "postmodern."

26. For a comprehensive exploration of the reasons I have chosen to rename deconstruction as "the philosophy of the limit," see Cornell, What is Postmodernity Anyway? in The Philosophy of the Limit: Justice and Legal Interpretation (1991).

27. Derrida, Geopsychoanalysis: ". . . and the rest of the world," in 48 American Imago: Studies in Psychoanalysis and Culture 203 (1991).

28. Luhmann, Love as Passion, supra note 4, at 84.

29. Derrida uses this phrase to indicate his notion that the very "frame" by which we denote our context, our "reality," also implies more, precisely because our reality is enframed. See J. Derrida, The Truth in Painting (G. Bennington & I. McLeod trans. 1987).

30. Throughout his work, Lacan uses the term *signifiance* to refer to that "movement in language against, or away from, the positions of coherence which language simultaneously constructs." J. Rose, Sexuality in the Field of Vision 75 (1986). As Jacqueline Rose goes on to explain, "[t]he concept of jouissance (what escapes in sexuality) and the concept of significance (what shifts within language) are inseparable." Id. at p. 76.

31. Luhmann, Love as Passion, supra note 4, at 177–78 (quoting Friedrich Rudolf Hohl) (emphasis in original).

32. For a fuller discussion of the complex relationship between Derrida and Levinas, see Cornell, The Philosophy of the Limit: Justice and Legal Interpretation (1991).

33. See Derrida Force of Law: The "Mystical Foundation of Authority," 11 Cardozo Law Rev. 919, 959–73 (1990).

34. When I say the "psychical fantasy of woman" I am referring to what Lacan means when he says that what man "relates to is the objet a, and that the whole of his realisation in the sexual relation comes down to fantasy." Lacan, A Love Letter, in Feminine Sexuality: Jacques Lacan and the école freudienne 157 (J. Mitchell & J. Rose eds. 1982).

Part Two

Deconstruction and Legal Interpretation

3

The Idolatry of Rules: Writing Law According to Moses, With Reference to Other Jurisprudences

Arthur J. Jacobson

Moses, unlike Socrates, writes. He writes about writing. He writes about writing law. He writes about reading it, erasing it, learning and teaching it.

The first mention of writing in the *Five Books* occurs in the second, which English speakers call by the Greek name *Exodus*, but which Hebrew speakers call *Names*.[1] The scene is the first battle of the people of Israel after their flight from Egypt. The battle is against Amalek, in Refidim. It is the occasion in Moses' text for the introduction of Joshua, Moses' aide-de-camp.[2] It is also the moment in which the people of Israel, who have been slaves in Egypt for 430 years,[3] first collaborate as partners with God in fighting the enemies of Israel.[4]

Moses makes seven more references to writing in *Names*, all during the sojourn of the Israelites at Mr. Sinai.[5] He also includes a reference to reading,[6] directly after the first Sinaitic reference to writing, and one to erasure,[7] between the fourth and fifth Sinaitic references to writing. Moses thus refers to writing eight times and the activities surrounding it twice immediately before, during, and immediately after the revelations at Mt. Sinai.[8]

The point of view of the narrator in Moses' text is virtually unavailable to modern writers. Modern narrators speak in one of two voices. Either the author narrates, or a character narrates.[9] The first voice presents a narrator who knows everything about the world in the novel, because the voice of the narrator has created it.[10] The narrator is a god. "He" rules the novel directly, if not frankly. The second voice, by contrast, speaks only as a particular consciousness in the world created by the author. The narrator knows only certain things, because he has not created the world. The author remains all-knowing and powerful. He is a hidden god, alternately embracing and rejecting the limited point of view of the narrator. He rules the novel indirectly, behind the back of the narrator.

The narrator in Moses' "novel" does not take the perspective of the all-knowing, powerful creator. He does not play God. He resists the temptation to be Pharaoh. Moses knows only what he sees and what God tells him, nothing more. He writes, and acknowledges that he writes. He writes about his own writing, and God's. Nor does the narrator take the perspective of the ordinary, limited consciousness. Moses is not God, but he has spoken with God. He is the "friend" of God.[11] The claim of the narrator, that he has spoken with God, is a lesser claim than the claim of modern authors, one less familiar to moderns.

Moses was not unfamiliar with those who assume the godlike perspective of modern authors. He calls them *"elohim"*—"rulers," "judges," or "gods." He also calls God "Elohim"—"Rulers"—when he wishes to refer to God as an author—the all-knowing, powerful creator of the narrative's world. (To call God "Elohim" is to criticize the opinion that rulers are the source of their own rule. "Rulers" rules, not rulers.) He calls God "Yahweh," when he wishes to refer to Him as a character interacting with other characters in the world created, and therefore ruled by Elohim. The name "Yahweh" in Hebrew makes no sense in ordinary terms. It is said to be made up of particles from the tenses—past, present, and future—of the verb "to be." "Yahweh" is "That Which Is What Has Been And Will Be." [12] Yahweh is character defining itself through past interactions and committed to change through further interactions. Yahweh is "Friend." Where Elohim rules, Yahweh interacts. Man approaches Elohim as a child approaches a parent, a creation approaches a creator, a subject approaches a ruler. He approaches Yahweh as a collaborator, a friend.[13]

Moses, who is both narrator of the *Five Books* and a character in them, has relations with both Elohim and Yahweh. As narrator, Moses "takes dictation" from Elohim, the all-knowing, powerful God of the narrative. As a character, Moses is friend of Yahweh. The story of Elohim's narrative is the drama of Moses and Yahweh. It is the conflict between Moses as narrator and Moses as character.

The drama of Moses and Yahweh, the conflict between Moses as narrator and Moses as character, may be seen as a struggle over the names of God, "Elohim" and "Yahweh." Elohim rules over types and classes. Single characters cannot be the friend of Elohim. To be a character is to challenge the rule of types and classes. Yahweh is the name of God who befriends characters, who tolerates challenges to Elohim. Yahweh challenges his own rule, the rule of Elohim. The drama of the text is the question: Does Elohim rule or does Yahweh collaborate with characters?

The text gives the question a legal formulation: Do legal rules rule or do characters? Legal rules rule by commanding or prohibiting classes of specific acts, and by punishing disobedience with sanctions. Characters rule by ruling themselves according to ten propositions (ten *d'varim, dekalogoi*). Propositions rule by assent, by the aspirations of characters, not by commanding or prohibiting classes of specific acts using sanctions. To rule by propositions is to engage in ceaseless conversation with Yahweh.[14] The text at once poses rules to substitute for the collaboration of characters with Yahweh, and challenges rules when characters reconstruct themselves through action according to propositions.

The text also formulates the drama as a relentless concern with graven images.[15] An idol is a completed creation. Creation is complete, when Elohim rules. When Yahweh collaborates with characters, creation is ongoing. To approach God only as Elohim is to treat creation as finished. It is to consider things as products, not as constituents of further creation. It is to treat things as idols. Everything that will be has been given. It is, because it has been. Yahweh asserts that what will be, is not, because it has not been. Nothing is given. Creation is incomplete. Things are constituents of further creation, not idols. To bow to idols is to assert that what will be has been given. It is to treat God only as Elohim. It is to approach Him as a subject, rather than as a collaborator. If Elohim must rule and not characters, then rules too must be graven: Moses must reduce the rules to writing. Yet Moses warns repeatedly against graven images at crucial moments in the drama. The crisis of Mt. Sinai is a crisis of graven images. It is a crisis of writing.

The text thus poses the drama as a struggle over writing: Does Elohim write or does Moses? If only Elohim writes, then characters have no role in creation. Moses must write in order to befriend Yahweh. He must destroy and replace Elohim's writing. But if Moses writes, then people will bow to the text as a graven image. They will want Moses to be Pharaoh. They will be without character. Yahweh/Moses must write a second time what Elohim first wrote and Moses destroyed. Moses must write as a collaborator of Yahweh, not as *elohim/ Pharaoh*.

WRITING AND THE EPISODES AT MT. SINAI

The sojourn at Mr. Sinai covers the climactic weeks in Moses' entire narrative of the *Five Books*, from the beginning of time[16] to Moses' death just before the arrival of the Israelites in Canaan. The text presents an elaborate and puzzling sequence of events during these weeks. One must know the sequence in order to appreciate the role of writing in the Sinaitic revelation. In outlining the sequence, I want to avoid two tendencies, each of which is, nevertheless, quite instructive.

The first is the effort to order and rationalize the sequence in a prosaic chronology. Rashi, the authoritative French commentator, proceeds in this manner.[17] He does so, I believe, for two reasons. He wants the text not to offend strict dramatic logic. He also wants the multiple references to writing in the text—Moses' writing, God's writing, and Moses' account of his own and God's writing—to work together without conflict. Rashi thus seeks to make sense of the text in ordinary terms, a sense not directly available from the text without interpretation.

Take, as an example Rashi does not discuss for this point, Jethro's criticism of Moses, just prior to the revelation at Mt. Sinai.[18] In the two-or-so months from the departure from Egypt to the arrival in Refidim, Moses sat to judge the people without the aid of other leaders. Jethro, who was Moses' father-in-law, arrived in Refidim with Tsipporah, Moses' wife, and their two sons, directly after the battle with Amalek. When Jethro observed Moses judging, he sternly criticized him for undertaking too heavy a burden. Moses, he said, must appoint subordinate judges for ordinary matters. Otherwise he will wear himself out.[19] Moses closes the scene by stating that "Moses sent away his father-in-law; and he went his way into his own land [*Midyan*]."[20] The very next statement in the text records the arrival of the Israelites at Mt. Sinai. Thus it would appear that Jethro left the Israelite encampment prior to the arrival at Mt. Sinai. Yet we know from later scenes that Jethro was present in the encampment after the revelation at Mt. Sinai.[21] The text does not record his return from Midian. Was Jethro present in the camp during the sojourn at Mt. Sinai? We do not know. The mystery of the passage deepens when we consider that Jethro's departure precedes the bulk of the revelations recorded in *Names* and the following books. We know that God revealed "a decree [*h.ok*] and a rule [*mishpat*]" at Marah, just after the departure from Egypt.[22] But Moses did not have much revelatory law to use in Refidim.[23] Did he use the customary law the Hebrews undoubtedly possessed prior to Sinai?[24] Moses tells Jethro that he is using revelatory, not customary law. Why does Moses choose to discuss the burdens of judging at this moment, in Refidim? Or was the discussion after Mt. Sinai, as the Jethro story suggests? Again, we do not know.

The second tendency I want to avoid is the critical dissolution of the text into distinct traditions, separated by purpose and origin, only to be united by a hypothetical single or group compiler in later ages.[25] Apart from the "interpretive" grounding of this approach, lacking as it is in documentation outside the text, we must be permitted to assume that the compiler, at least, was an artful arranger. Why would the compiler leave oddities and inconsistencies in the text, such as the Jethro episode? Surely, one purpose of the compiler would be to eliminate oddities and inconsistencies. If he or they did not, we must ask what purpose the compiler had in leaving them in. All we can do, reading as we must behind the veil of ignorance, is puzzle out for ourselves the purposes, whether those of an historical Moses, or some later compiler or compilers of diverse traditions, whom we might as well give the name, Moses.

An overview of the events at Mt. Sinai encompasses eight (or possibly six) ascents Moses made to confer with God, together with two (or possibly four) episodes in which Moses conferred with God without going to the top of the mountain. In the first of the two episodes, Moses met with God on the slopes of the mountain; in the second, in the Tent of Meeting.[26]

First meeting (first ascent): Yahweh's first message to the people.[27]

[Moses tells the people Yahweh's propositions and the people answer.][28]

Second meeting (second ascent): Moses tells Yahweh the people's propositions; Yahweh gives preparatory instructions.[29]

[Moses prepares the people and brings them to meet Elohim; Yahweh comes down upon Mt. Sinai.][30]

Third meeting (third ascent): Yahweh repeats the preparatory instructions, adding special instructions for the priests.[31]

[Elohim speaks the ten propositions (ten *d'varim, dekalogoi*) to Moses and the people; the people ask Moses to mediate.][32]

Fourth meeting (and the first without an ascent): "Moses drew near to the fog where Elohim was"; Yahweh introduces His teaching of the legal rules (*mishpatim*) to Moses with three prohibitions against idolatrous cults (precious metals, hewn stone altars, uncovered genitals), and teaches Moses the legal rules.[33]

[Yahweh orders Moses to bring Aaron, Aaron's sons, and seventy of the elders to "come up to Yahweh," warning that only Moses shall come near; Moses speaks all the propositions and all the rules to the people; *he writes "all the propositions" of Yahweh (W2); he reads the "book of the covenant in the ears of the people" (R);* he performs a covenant ceremony (dashing blood against an altar and throwing it on the people); Moses, Aaron, Aaron's sons and seventy of the elders go up, see Elohim, and celebrate a meal; *Yahweh orders Moses to ascend, saying, "I will give you the tablets of stone, the doctrine and the commandment which I have written that you may teach them." (W3)*][34]

Fifth meeting (fourth ascent): Moses spends forty days and nights on Mt. Sinai; Yahweh instructs Moses to make the implements of the cult, to install Aaron and his sons in the priest's office, to use Betsalel ("and I have filled him with the spirit of Elohim")[35] and Oholiav to help him, and to instruct the Israelites to keep the Sabbath (not doing work);[36] *Yahweh gives Moses the "two tablets of testimony, tablets of stone, written with the finger of Elohim." (W4)*[37]

[Moses delayed: crisis of the golden calf, Aaron fashions the calf "with an engraving tool."][38]

Yahweh orders Moses to return to the pople; Moses pleads with Yahweh, who relents; Moses returns with the two tablets; *"the writing was the writing of Elohim, graven on the tablets." (W5)*[39]

[Moses smashes the tablets; Aaron pleads with Moses; division of the camp and slaying of recalcitrant idolaters.][40]

Sixth meeting (fifth ascent): *"Yet now, if You will forgive their sins, and if not, erase me, please, from Your book" (E);* Yahweh tells Moses He will erase from his book anyone who has sinned against Him; Yahweh smites the people, "because they made the calf, which Aaron made."[41]

Seventh meeting (possibly the sixth ascent): Yahweh tells Moses to order the people to depart for Canaan, and says He will send an angel before them; "The people heard this evil tiding [that Yahweh would not be 'present' on the journey to Canaan] and they mourned."[42]

Eighth meeting (possibly the seventh ascent): Yahweh tells Moses to order the people to remove their ornaments (Moses records that prior to this meeting no one put on ornaments, since they were mourning over the loss of Yahweh's presence); "They stripped themselves of ornaments." [43]

Ninth meeting (in the Tent of Meeting): Moses negotiates a second covenant ("Yahweh spoke to Moses face to face, as a man speaks to his friend"); *Yahweh orders Moses to hew two tablets of stone like the first, and says He will write on the tablets the propositions that were on the first tablets. (W6)*[44]

Tenth meeting (either the sixth or eighth ascent, depending on the place of the sixth and seventh meetings): Moses hews the two tablets and goes up to Mt. Sinai; the second covenant, warnings against making covenants with others and against idolatry; *Yahweh orders Moses to write "these propositions," on the basis of which Yahweh had made a covenant with Moses and Israel; "He [referring to either Yahweh or Moses wrote [in Moses' presence] the propositions of the covenant, the ten propositions" (W7)*; after forty days and nights, Moses descends with the two tablets, his face glowing.[45]

> [Moses carries out the instructions of the fifth meeting;[46] *Betsalel, and Oholiav "made the plate of the holy cross of pure gold, and wrote on it a writing, like the engraved pattern of a seal: Holy to Yahweh." (W8)*[47] (Yahweh had instructed Moses to order Betsalel and Oholiav "to engrave," not "to write.")][48]

We may abstract the eight references to writing (W), the one to reading (R) and the one to erasing (E);

W1 Refidim, the battle with Amalek: Yahweh commands Moses to "write this to remember it in the book." [49]

W2 Moses writes "all Yahweh's propositions" (just prior to Moses' fourth ascent of Mt. Sinai).[50]

R Moses reads his book of the covenant in the ears of the people.[51]

W3 Yahweh offers tablets of stone, on which He has already written "the doctrine and the commandment." [52]

W4 Yahweh delivers the tablets, "written with the finger of Elohim." [53]

> [Moses delayed; interruption of the conversation with Yahweh by the episode of the golden calf; Aaron fashions the calf "with an engraving tool."][54]

W5 Conversation resumes; Moses descends with the tablets; "the writing was the writing of Elohim, graven on the tablets."[55]

E   Moses requests that Yahweh either forgive the Israelites for the golden calf or "erase me from Your book which You have written."[56]

W6 Yahweh offers two more tablets; "I will write on the tablets the propositions which were on the first tablets, which you broke."[57]

W7 Yahweh commands Moses to write down "these propositions," according to which Yahweh has made a covenant with Moses and Israel; "He [referring to either Yahweh or Moses] wrote [in Moses' presence] on the tablets the propositions of the covenant, the ten propositions."[58]

W8 Betsalel and Oholiav write, "Holy to Yahweh" on Aaron's crown.[59] (Yahweh had instructed Moses to order Betsalel and Oholiav "to engrave," not "to write.")[60]

The ten references, broken as they are by the crisis of the golden calf into two sets of five, form the following array:

Before	During	After
W1 W2	Golden	W5 W8
R	Calf	E
W3	Crisis	W6
W4		W7

W1 occurs in Refidim, just prior to the Mt. Sinai episodes. W8 occurs just after Moses descends the mountain for the last time. W2 through W4 (including R) occur during the meetings prior to the crisis. W5 through W7 (including E) occur during the meetings after the crisis.

READING THE REFERENCES TO WRITING

The content of the references suggests a pattern of appositions. Read the sequence in pairs from outside in, as one would remember them, looking backwards, having finished reading the text:

1. W8 – W1
2. W7 – W2

3. W6 – R
4. E – W3
5. W5 – W4

A reading from memory[61] suggests that people can come to regard what Elohim "engraves," either on the tablets or in creating the world, as writing, if they actively collaborate with Yahweh. They collaborate with Yahweh by writing—by listening to an inner voice, by reading the writing of their actions to an inner ear. They also collaborate with Yahweh by reading and rewriting. All three collaborations—writing, reading, and rewriting—are made possible by "erasure." Erasure rescues writing from the idolatrous threat of engraving.

Engraving Becomes Writing (W8–W1)

The apposition of W8 with W1 suggests that the drama at Mt. Sinai taught the people to regard engraved patterns of words as writings rather than as graven images, or idols. Written words do not complete creation. They are constituents of further creations. The "subjects" or rules should not regard them as commands backed by sanctions. They are further propositions in ceaseless conversation.

W1 records Yahweh's command to Moses to write a record of the battle with Amalek. It does not record Moses obeying the instruction. It does, instead, record Moses constructing an altar to memorialize the battle, which he names: "Yahweh is my banner."[62] W8 records Betsalel and Oholiav obeying Yahweh's instruction "to engrave" "Holy to Yahweh" on a plate to be worn by Aaron.[63] But they do not engrave, they "write." Hence, W1 records Moses' delay in obeying Yahweh's instruction to write, and W8 records Betsalel and Oholiav obeying Yahweh's instruction "to engrave" by writing instead of engraving. Moses' "delay" for forty days in delivering Elohim's writing of the ten propositions had fomented the crisis of the golden calf, in which the people reverted to making graven images. Moses' second "delay" for forty days, during which Yahweh and he write, allows Betsalel and Oholiav to regard engraving as writing rather than a graven image, or idol. Moses has rescued writing from engraving.

Writing as Collaboration: Inspiration (W7–W2)

The aposition of W7 with W2 begins a contrast of collaborative writing with writing on one's own, without textually explicit authority. The W7–W2 apposition captures the first of three collaborations: inspiration. (The W6–R apposition will capture the others: reading and rewriting.) Writing requires collaboration with Yahweh. It requires a voice, an ear, even prior to reading. This collaboration is the inner voice, the inner ear, of writing. Writing requires inspiration.

W2 records Moses writing "all Yahweh's propositions" during the meeting on the slopes of Mt. Sinai in a "book of the covenant." It does not record Yahweh instructing Moses to write this book. Moses' book was all the people had, when Moses disappeared on the mountain for forty days. The authority of the book, which Moses wrote on his own, was not enough to keep them from making the golden calf. W7 records Yahweh commanding Moses to write down "these propositions," according to which Yahweh has made a covenant with Moses and Israel. W7 also records "he," referring either to Moses or Yahweh, writing down "the propositions of the covenant, the ten propositions." Hence W2 records Moses writing, without recording Yahweh's command to write. W7 records Yahweh's command to write, leaving an ambiguity whether Yahweh or Moses is writing. Moses writes on his own in W2. The writing in W7 is a collaboration. It is not an explicit collaboration. (Moses does not say that Yahweh and he wrote together.) It is a collaboration signified by the ambiguity in the text. It is textual collaboration.

Writing as Collaboration: Read and Rewriting (W6–R)

The apposition of W6 with R captures the second and third collaborations. The writer's audience collaborates with the writer by reading. Readers always rewrite texts. Writing too is a reading, a rewriting of texts already written. Writing collaborates in a tradition.

R records Moses reading the book he has written on his own, aloud to the people. W6 records Yahweh offering to "rewrite" the ten propositions that were on the first set of tablets, "which you broke." Moses' reading, like Yahweh's offer, is a rewriting of matters already written. The writing Moses reads—containing the legal rules—supplements and substitutes for the ten propositions. Moses' writing is itself a "reading" of the spoken propositions. It is a rewriting of them as rules. Yahweh's rewriting of Elohim's broken tablets constitutes a reading—a rewriting—of the rules, to restore the propositions. The rewritten propositions are Yahweh's, not Elohim's. The R–W6 apposition folds into the W2–W7 apposition: rewriting, hence reading, is a species of collaboration.

Collaborative Writing Flows From Erasure (E–W3)

The apposition of E with W3 suggests that reading and rewriting, the second and third collaborations involved in writing, flow from erasure.

W3 records Yahweh offering the first tablets of stone, upon which He has already written "the doctrine and the commandment." The writing, W4 and W5 will reveal, is the writing of Yahweh as Elohim. E records Moses asking Yahweh to erase him from the book Yahweh has written, if Yahweh will not forgive the people for the sin of the golden calf.[64] The writing in W3 has already been written, prior to Yahweh's delivery of the writing to Moses. Moses' request for erasure in E suggests the possibility that the writing Elohim has already written can be erased, rewritten by Yahweh. Moses shows that Elohim's writing can even be destroyed altogether.

Engraving: Writing That Is Not Erasure (W5–W4)

The apposition of W5 with W4 suggests that collaboration between Moses and Yahweh, the first collaboration involved in writing, rescues writing from the threat that people will regard it as engraving. Moses demonstrates the possibility of collaboration with Yahweh by smashing—by erasing—Elohim's writing.

W4, immediately before the crisis of the golden calf, records Yahweh's delivery of the writing, "written with the finger of Elohim." W5, immediately after the crisis, states that "the writing was the writing of Elohim, graven on the tablets." The crisis of the golden calf causes Moses to regard Elohim's writing as a sort of engraving. The writing is not a graven image, but the people could confuse it with one. Moses thereupon fails to deliver it to the people. He breaks it, just as he breaks the golden calf.

The innermost apposition returns to the outermost: Betsalel's and Oholiav's reworking of Yahweh's command "to engrave" into "to write" is proof that the people need not regard writing as engraving.

Now read the series of appositions the other way, from inside out, as one discovers them during the drama of reading:[65]

1. (W5–W4) The people will regard writing that is not a product of erasure as an engraving, a graven image, an idol.

2. (E–W3) Reading and rewriting are two sorts of erasure.

3. (W6–R) Reading and rewriting are collaborative in two senses. To read is to collaborate as audience. To write is to rewrite, hence to collaborate with tradition.

4. (W7–W2) The act of writing requires collaboration with Yahweh, or inspiration.

5. (W8–W1) If writing collaborates in all three senses, then the people will not regard it as an engraving, a graven image, an idol.

The struggle over writing in *Names*—between Elohim and Yahweh, between Yahweh and Moses—rescues it from idolatry. The struggle supplies the necessary collaborations. To write is to rewrite. To rewrite is to erase. To erase is to rescue writing from idolatry.

The theme has a legal formulation. When Elohim speaks the ten propositions, the people are too frightened to understand them. When Elohim writes the propositions, Moses must smash the writing so that the people do not bow to it as an idol. Moses will not let the people read Elohim's writing, because they will bow to it as an idol. They will not rewrite its contents in deeds. Elohim's writing is superfluous, since Elohim has already written—spoken and by speaking created—the propositions in creation. But the propositions cannot serve as propositions, unless Yahweh, not Elohim, rewrites them in collaboration with Moses. Short of a collaborative rewriting of the propositions— by Yahweh/Moses on the top of Mt. Sinai and by the people in deeds—Yahweh specifies the propositions as rules backed by sanctions. The people fear sanctions. They cannot collaborate with Yahweh.

Moses considers that he must record the rules in writing. He writes without authority clearly indicated in the text—with inspiration, but without the collaboration of the people. He will let the people read the propositions only once they are written for a second time, ambiguously by Yahweh/Moses. The people will not regard the second writing, the rewriting of a writing they saw Moses smash, as an idol. They will read the propositions, rewrite them in deeds, use them as further propositions in conversations with Yahweh.

MOSES' LAW: THREE WRITINGS

The revelation of law in *Names* requires not one, but three writings. The first is Elohim's writing—the world, along with the laws of the world, as a finished, created product. The second is Yahweh's collaborative writing—human deeds continuing creation. The third is Moses' writing, which records the struggle over the first two. It is the writing Moses delayed—the record Yahweh commanded Moses to write at Refidim. It is the writing Moses does not explicitly say he wrote with clear authority—the writing of rules backed by sanctions. It is dangerous writing.

To require fewer than three writings to make law is not to have Moses' law. Other legal systems do require fewer than three writings. Naturalism requires only one (or perhaps two, a writing and a reading). Positivism requires two, a procedure for marking rules as law and the actual marking of rules according to the procedure. Moses' is not the only legal system to require three writings. The common law system in force today in the United States does so, as does the rights jurisprudence of theorists such as Hobbes.

Moses' two forty-day sojourns at the top of Mt. Sinai recall Noah's forty days in the ark. During Noah's sojourn, Elohim "erased all existing things," [66] because Elohim saw that flesh was degenerate and filled the earth with violence. [67] After Noah built an altar to Yahweh, "Yahweh said in His heart: I will not curse the ground any more for the sake of man." [68] He reconstructed physical and moral order. He gave Noah a code resembling "law." [69] Noah's "code" binds, hence defines, all humanity. This most primitive law—so primitive that it does not merit any of the terms Moses ordinarily uses for law[70]— expresses Yahweh's regret for erasing all existing things. It prohibits murder and eating live animals—nothing more. Yahweh did not call Noah back for a second forty days. Noah thus learned only one of the propositions by which Elohim rules creation—the one against murder—and none of the rules. Moses, by contrast, learns all the propositions. He learns rules.

Yahweh uses the same word, "degenerate" (*sheeh.et*), to describe the idolaters of the golden calf. [71] The word means "that which is reversing creation," "destroying," "de-constructing." The English "destroy" derives from the Latin "*struere*," to "pile up" or "construct." [72] So "destruction" is "deconstruction." Elohim thus tells Noah that he will "*mashh.eetam* [destroy, deconstruct] all flesh [*basar*]." [73] Instead, Yahweh "erased [*vayeemah.*] all existing things." [74] To "erase" is to leave without record. Yahweh did not "destroy" the degenerate flesh, as He proposed, but rather "erased all existing things"—left them without record.

Yahweh threatens—not to destroy, not to erase—but to "*akhalem*"—"annihilate"—the idolaters. [75] To "annihilate" is to turn into nothing, to deprive of material substance. To "destroy" is to reverse creation to its primordial state, which was "the breath of Elohim" and "water." [76]

Moses' request for Yahweh to "erase" him from the book if Yahweh does not forgive the idolaters (E) powerfully recalls the Noahide erasure. [77] It also recalls Moses' first reference to writing in *Names,* in which Yahweh tells Moses to write the battle with Amalek in a book, "for I will utterly erase the memory of Amalek from under the heavens." [78]

To erase is to kill by depriving of a record. "Moses," Moses tells us, means "pulled out from water."[79] So Moses, like all Elohim's creation, is "pulled out" from the water. Moses, pulled out from the water, is rewriting creation, drawing all existing things from the erasing waters of the flood. Moses does not regenerate, reconstruct creation. By writing—by creating alphabetic writing—he rescues the memory of creation from erasure. He does not draw pictures or symbolize creation. He makes a record of it.

Who pulled Moses from the water? Not "the breath of Elohim," as in creation, but Pharaoh's daughter. In fact, Moses was a product of a union that his own rules could come to call "incestuous."[80] Amram, Aaron's and Moses' father, married Yokheved, Amram's aunt and Aaron's and Moses' mother.[81] Moses' mother was his great-aunt. (By writing a record, Moses reconstructs moral order, forbidding incestuous unions.) Moses was the product of a quasi-pharaonic union, since Pharaoh's mother was always supposed to be his aunt. But Moses was adopted by Pharaoh's daughter. So Moses' adoptive great-aunt was his adoptive grandmother. Was his adoptive great-aunt his real mother? Was Moses a future Pharaoh?

Freud argues that Moses was a future Pharaoh, and that the Israelites killed him in the desert.[82] He has it backwards. The text is not hiding the secret that Moses was an Egyptian prince. Moses is telling us that he risked setting up as Pharaoh. Just before Moses asks Yahweh either to forgive the sin of the golden calf or erase him from Yahweh's book, Yahweh made a tempting offer to Moses:

> Now leave Me alone. I will be furious with them. I will annihilate them, and make you a great nation.[83]

Moses did not let Yahweh alone. Instead, he persuaded Yahweh not to annihilate the Israelites. He resisted the pharaonic temptation. After all, the Egyptian political model was the only one the Israelites knew after 430 years. The highest political drama of the text is whether Moses will become a new Pharaoh. He did not. He created a new political model based on law—based on rules drawn from conversations with Yahweh. He rejected the pharaonic model, based on slavery.

Moses' text describes the extraordinary power of the pharaonic temptation quite frankly. Shortly after Moses records Yahweh's fury and His offer, Moses records Moses' reaction: Instead of threatening to annihilate the Israelites, he broke Elohim's tablets:

> And then, when he came close to the camp, and saw the calf and the dancing, Moses became furious, and he cast the tablets out of

his hands, and he broke them beneath the mountain. And he took the calf which they had made, and he burned it with fire, and he ground it thin, and he sowed it on the face of water, and made the children of Israel drink it.[84]

Moses records himself having the same reaction as Yahweh. He was furious. Instead of threatening to annihilate the Israelites, he broke Elohim's tablets. He then turned to the calf, burned it, ground it thin, sowed it on the face of water, and made the people of Israel drink it.

This strange "turn," from destruction of the tablets to destruction of the calf, tactfully accomplishes three poetic goals. First, by burning, grinding and sowing the calf in water, Moses does to the calf exactly what Yahweh threatened: he "destroys" the calf—through fire, grinding and sowing (a word of rebirth!)—to water, and "annihilates" it by making the people drink the water.[85] Moses does to the calf what Elohim did not do to "all flesh" in the time of Noah, and what Yahweh did do to Sdom and Amorrah through fire. Second, the burning, grinding, sowing and drinking are exactly what Ugaratic (pre-Hebraic) god-kings did to sacred objects when the people failed to receive them with proper enthusiasm.[86] Moses here records himself unconsciously performing the actions of an Ugaratic god-king. Third, Moses stops himself from completing these actions on Elohim's tablets. He turns his rage—appropriately, realistically—to the calf. The entire scene powerfully establishes Moses' unreflective, furious imitation of a known local god, even after he has rejected Yahweh's tempting offer.

Until Sinai, collaboration with Yahweh remained limited after the flood. Elohim still ruled creation, "unconsciously." Yahweh brings Elohim's propositions to consciousness: He propounds them to Moses as rules. The propositions cannot work strictly in Elohim's manner, as rules of nature, of human nature. They can work only if consciousness possesses them, only if people use them in conversations with Yahweh.

Humans do not administer propositions. The sanctions attached to them are sanctions in the order of nature. Tribunals enforce only certain propositions. Humans do administer rules. Yahweh asks humans to supplement the natural sanctions of the propositions with legal sanctions according to rules. People must talk about rules. They must use them, work with them, appreciate their link to the propositions. The rules are Elohim's propositions carried on, specified, and transformed in conversations with Yahweh. Rules supplement propositions. They are further propositions. They are dangerous propositions.

After Yahweh regrets wanting to annihilate the Israelites, Moses goes back to the top of the mountain for a second forty days. He enlarges Yahweh's realm. The first sojourn had not rescued Elohim's propositions from the unconscious. The people who made the golden calf because Moses delayed his return from the top of the mountain were prepared only to make idols, to make rules as idols. They were not prepared to use rules as further propositions, to recognize the "delayed" authority of rules as every judge (*el*) makes and uses them—always after the behavior the rule seeks to rule. Moses persuades Yahweh to regret His offer to annihilate the Israelites and start over, pharaonically, with Moses' descendants. By rejecting the temptation to be Pharaoh, Moses collaborates with Yahweh in completing creation.

Moses' rejection of the pharaonic temptation demonstrates tolerance for the delay of the people in accepting Yahweh's covenant, even before Yahweh tolerates the delay. Moses teaches Yahweh and the people to tolerate delay—the people's delay, Moses' delay and the delayed authority of rules. Moses thus creates a consciousness—a delayed authority—of Elohim's propositions. Consciousness of propositions is conversation with Yahweh about rules. Men and women, now conscious that Elohim's propositions are rules they themselves must administer, are more perfect "images" of Elohim, as Elohim created them to become "in the beginning of" creation. Elohim too has changed, according to Moses' image. He is more Yahweh, tolerating delay.[87]

The rules humans administer as further propositions cannot successfully be written in fewer than three writings: Elohim's, Moses', and Yahweh's.

To write law only once is to get only Elohim's propositions. These are unconscious, hence incomplete. The people on their own cannot specify them or take responsibility for administering them as rules. Natural law is law written without delay, only once, by Elohim. (Natural law is written twice, if we count reading nature as a writing. But if natural law admits that the reading is a writing, it probably remits to positivism, the jurisprudence of two writings. The matter is quite complicated.) But natural law is not Moses' law.

To write law twice is to get the rules Moses wrote. It is to tolerate some delay. The people will administer rules as idols, and obey them out of fear of sanctions. Ordinary people will not use the rules as premises for action. Ordinary rulers will not administer them as further propositions. Positive law is law written only twice, by humans such as Moses. It is not Moses' law either.

Moses' law needs three writings: Elohim's propositions defining perfection in action; Moses' further propositions assisting humans to achieve the perfection of Elohim's propositions; and Yahweh's rewriting of Elohim's propositions providing standards propelling the further propositions even further towards perfection.

Moses' law poses rules as instruments to assist humans to realize Elohim's propositions. It also puts rules in play, opens them to change through consciousness, through ceaseless collaboration of the people with Yahweh. Law requires both movements: posing rules and putting them in play. To deny one or the other is not to know Moses' law. It is not to know law altogether.[88]

Legal traditions (and the traditions interpreting Moses' rules are no exception) take a host of positions on these two necessary movements, posing rules and putting them in play. Some try to suppress the need to pose rules, favoring instead assessments of character and moral education. Others try to suppress putting rules in play by various well-known devices. One such device distinguishes between the rules and its applications: conditions have changed, they say, not the rule. Another device points to the ambiguities, imprecisions, and dynamism of language: we are interpreting the rule, they say, not changing it. There are others.

No legal tradition, however, has successfully eliminated either movement, posing rules or putting them in play. Though pragmatic considerations seem to favor retaining both, the heart of the matter is not pragmatic. Every legal tradition supports a struggle over rules, because the struggle over rules defines the moral situation of the legal person. To be a person is to engage in struggle over rules. Persons are not creatures, herded by rules into neat, eternal categories. Persons do not obey rules out of fear of sanctions. They engage rules—put them in play in action.

Positivism and naturalism suppress the character of persons engaging the struggle over rules. Positivism asserts that the struggle is irrelevant, beside the point, a private matter. Naturalism asserts there is no struggle. Moses, I believe, does not at all reject the struggle over rules. He is neither a naturalist nor a positivist.

Each of the writings in *Names* erases the other two. Each is written as an erasure. Elohim's writing rules all of creation. It leaves no room for writing as collaboration—Yahweh's writing and Moses'. It deprives Moses' writing of authority. Yahweh's writing replaces Elohim's engraving. Yahweh erased the "existing things" in Noah's time, will erase Moses himself, and will erase Moses' rules in collaboration with future generations. Moses' writing, not Elohim's or Yahweh's, is the only record of the drama at Mt. Sinai.

Yahweh depends on Moses to write the record. Moses earns the right to write the record by his godlike anger at Aaron's engraving of the golden calf. He earns the right by destroying Elohim's engraving. He earns it by tolerating delay, by teaching Yahweh and the people to tolerate delay, and by rejecting the temptation to be Pharaoh. Moses earns the right to write by collaborating with Yahweh in erasure.

THE BATTLE WITH AMALEK: MAKING A RECORD

Moses, like Yahweh, erases. What does he erase? How does he erase it?

Moses erases the immediate experience of events. He erases the rule of immediate experience, the rule of presence. He erases the rule of rulers, such as Joshua, in collaboration with Yahweh. He erases the rule of Elohim—the realm of immediate experience, the realm of presence. He makes a record.

The themes we learn from the pattern of Moses' references to writing turn us to the first reference, Yahweh's command to record the first battle of the slave army after their departure from Egypt. Moses writes (**W1**):

> And Yahweh said to Moses: Write this to remember it in the book, and put it in the ears of Joshua, for I will utterly erase the memory of Amalek from under the skies. And Moses built an altar, and he called the name of it "Yahweh is my banner." And he said: The hand upon the thro[ne] of Yah[weh], Yahweh will have war with Amalek from generation to generation.[89]

The text records Yahweh's command to Moses to record the battle with Amalek in a book. We cannot be sure from Moses' description whether Yahweh is commanding him to record the battle in a book Moses has already begun on his own, or whether Yahweh is now directing Moses to begin the book upon the occasion of the battle. Either way, we may infer that the book Moses refers to here is just the *Five Books*. (Moses will continue writing this book all through the rest of the narrative, finishing it only just before his death in the last book.)[90] If the inference is correct, then Yahweh's command to "write ... in the book" is Moses' first reference to writing the book in the book that he is writing.

We know that Moses did obey Yahweh's command (we are reading the book), but we do not know when. Moses does not record, as he might, that he wrote in the book the very moment Yahweh commanded. The next mention of writing (after Moses' fourth meeting with Yahweh, on the slopes of Mt. Sinai, when Yahweh presents the rules) does record Moses writing, but does not say Yahweh commanded it. Has Moses finally obeyed Yahweh's command, at Mt. Sinai rather than Refidim? If so, he has delayed. He may also have differed with Yahweh, since Moses does not record Yahweh commanding him to write the events—most importantly the rules—between Refidim and the fourth meeting at Mt. Sinai. If Moses has indeed deferred obeying Yahweh's command or differed with it, this would be only one amongst a series of deferrals and differences during the sojourn at Mt. Sinai.

Yahweh accompanies the command to write with a command to put the record in the ears of Joshua. This is strange for two reasons. Joshua was the leader of the Israelite forces. Why would Yahweh command Moses to put the record of the battle in Joshua's ears when Joshua was present at that very battle? Also, Yahweh commands Moses to write in order to remember, and then tells Moses, "I will utterly erase the memory of Amalek." If Yahweh wished to erase the memory of Amalek, why preserve the record in a book "to remember"? The first mention of writing in the *Five Books* thus sets two paradoxes. The first is a paradox of presence: Yahweh asks Moses to put the record of the battle in Joshua's ears, even though Joshua was present at the battle. The second is a paradox of erasure: Yahweh asks Moses to record the battle with Amalek to remember it, while planning to erase the memory of Amalek.

Moses' paradox of presence marks all writing, not just the writing Yahweh commanded Moses in Refidim. Writing changes *what* we remember, and the *way* we remember it. We write in order to remember what we wish or fear to forget. Writing to remember is writing to forget—to forget in order to be reminded by the writing. To remember through the written record of an event is to forget the immediate experience of it. Writing erases immediate experience. Yahweh commands Moses to put the record in Joshua's ears in order to replace Joshua's immediate experience with Moses' record. Joshua's experience, after all, is Joshua's, not Moses'. Putting the record in Joshua's ears is the education of Joshua to Moses' perspective. The record commands a perspective. Moses writes in order to forget or to cause others to forget—to command a perspective.

What is the difference between Joshua's perspective and Moses'? Joshua is a commander, after all, like Pharaoh or any other ruler. Moses is a prophet, as well as a ruler. He speaks with Yahweh. Joshua's immediate experience of the battle was undoubtedly that *he* won the battle, because his skills and personality were commanding. If Joshua believes this, he has the wrong perspective. Only Elohim rules. Joshua's command is Elohim's. That is the correct perspective, the one Moses puts in Joshua's ears.

"Elohim rules and not rulers" is not a completely correct perspective. Elohim rules through immediate experience. Joshua was a talented commander, and he was absolutely correct to believe that his deeds were crucial to victory. (Moses does not advocate oriental fatalism.) Rulers do rule, after all. "Elohim," "Rulers," is plural. Yahweh does not tell Moses to "erase" Joshua's experience, only to supplement it. Joshua has the experience of ruling—he commands the army and leads it to victory—supplemented by the experience of Moses' record. Moses makes removing Joshua from the immediate experience of ruling into one of Joshua's experiences. The record does not destroy Joshua's experience. The record only memorializes it.

Memory too forms part of experience. We experience remembering. Unlike Plato, however, Moses held that remembering does not form all of experience. Change need not be only disintegration. Moses, unlike Plato, is interested in the godlike virtue of freedom. Elohim's creation is incomplete, because human freedom is part of creation. Collaboration with Yahweh—conversations with Yahweh, self-consciousness—completes creation. Moses might agree that remembering forms all of experience, so long as remembering includes reference to the possibility of creation. Creative memory—the memory Moses wishes to pursue—is remembering the present as if one were already living in the future. Ordinary memory is memory of the past from the point of view of the present. Ordinary memory rules the present, weighs it down with the past. Ordinary memory treats creation as complete. It is "*elohim*" memory. Moses wishes to convert Joshua from ordinary memory to Yahweh's creative memory—living in the present as if one is remembering it from the future.[91]

Moses puts a record in Joshua's ear, the record Yahweh orders Moses to put there. Joshua's education draws him away from the "*elohim*" perspective—the perspective of rulers—to the collaborative perspective of Yahweh. It teaches Joshua the experience of memory. It accustoms Joshua to experiencing events as if they were memory. The correct perspective, Yahweh's perspective, is that by participating in events Joshua is creating a record. His own, casual recollections of events will not form the basis of that record. Joshua must act knowing that he is collaborating with Yahweh in making a record.

Moses' solution to the paradox of presence is the erasure of casual recollections in favor of memory. A record replaces casual recollection with a single, recorded memory. The correct perspective is a record drawing participants in an event away from immediate experience and casual recollection. The truth—that Elohim rules, not Joshua—appears only in a record. Removal from events supplements experience. Records create memory. They do not erase experience. They make memory into experience. Those present at events then live them from the perspective of memory. They write events. The writing supplements (is) the experience. It is experience as the erasure of experience.

The very next scene in the text—Moses building and naming an altar to memorialize the battle—directly takes up Moses' second paradox, the paradox of erasure.

The name Moses gives the altar—"Yahweh is my banner"—is an instance of erasure: the overt erasure of a name, rather than the covert erasure of experience in a record. To say, "Yahweh is my banner," is to say that Moses does not have a banner—a sign, a rallying point for his troops—in the ordinary sense. Yahweh, not an object, is his banner. Moses' sign in battle is not a sign as we understand it.[92] Moses rallies and leads his troops with an invisible banner. Also, his name for the altar is not a name in the ordinary sense. It is a phrase, not a name. It is a phrase that denies its own content. To say, "Yahweh is my banner" is to say, "I have no banner in the ordinary sense." Moses gives a name to the altar that is not a name, and the name itself denies that it is a name.

The theme of the "anti-name" for the altar continues: "And he said: The hand upon the thro[ne] of Yah[weh], Yahweh will have war with Amalek from generation to generation." Moses' text fails to complete two words, "throne" and "Yahweh." The text, if not the speech it records, is incomplete. Rashi interprets Moses' omissions as a statement that Yahweh's name and throne will not be whole until the name "Amalek" is completely erased.[93] (Joshua "weakened" Amalek, he did not destroy him.)[94] Moses preserves the name "Amalek" in a text, so that future generations can finish destroying Amalek. The text commands the Israelites to repeat the recorded event: future generations will fight Amalek, because they read Moses' record. But the text itself, which is necessary for the destruction of Amalek, preserves the memory of Amalek by virtue of the very command to erase it.

Records allow or command future generations to repeat events recorded in the record. Without a record, the events will be forgotten, or not remembered according to the correct perspective. The events that will be repeated are not the events individual participants personally remember: they are events recorded according to the perspective established by the record. Amalek's memory has disappeared into the record. Moses' solution to the paradox of erasure is that the record erases the memory of Amalek by preserving it in a record hostile to Amalek. The record preserves the erasure of Amalek's perspective.

Moses' record of the battle with Amalek transforms the individual recollections of participants in the battle into a collective recollection, into a memory. The collective recollection will completely take over only once the actual participants, with their own stories, have died out or lost practical interest in recounting them. The collective recollection springs to life in future generations. Collective recollection depends on writing and upon the death or inactivity of participants in the events recorded in the writing.

The incomplete name "Yah" invites us to recall the only other instance Moses uses it in his writing. Moses and the Israelites sang, "Yah is my strength and song," after Yahweh, collaborating with Moses, drowned Pharaoh's troops in the Red Sea.[95] The song is a song of joy to the victory of Yahweh over Pharaoh. The victory required little collaboration from the Israelites. Moses' record of the song makes no mention of writing. Moses' last reference to writing, in *Propositions*, records Yahweh's command to Moses to write the words of a darker song, recording the difficult victory of Yahweh's collaboration with the people:

> Now therefore write for yourself this song, and teach it to the children of Israel. Put it in their mouths, that this song may be for Me a witness of the children of Israel.[96]

(Moses has just referred to reading.)[97] Moses records that "Moses wrote this song at that day."[98] He records that Moses charged Joshua to be strong, and to bring the Israelites into the land He swore to them.[99] He records that "Moses had finished writing the propositions of this doctrine in a book."[100] He records that "Moses spoke the propositions of this song in the ears of all the assembly of Israel until they were done."[101] He records Moses speaking the propositions of the song.[102]

The last reference to writing in the *Five Books* thus shows Moses obeying Yahweh's command to write, which the first reference to writing in the *Five Books* omitted. The last reference shows Yahweh commanding Moses to write a song, where the first shows Yahweh commanding Moses to write a record of strength. The first reference ties the song of Yahweh's strength only indirectly to writing by the incomplete name, "Yah." The last reference links the song of collaborative strength directly to Moses' writing. The first reference is Yahweh's command to put the song in Joshua's ears. Joshua's role in the writing is passive. The last reference is Yahweh's command to put the song in the people's mouths. The people's role in the writing is active.

The last reference is flanked by Joshua's strength and the beauty of a song. Because the song is beautiful, it will testify to the people as a witness.[103] These will be the defenders of Moses' doctrine, Joshua's strength and the people's song. Deeds complete the incomplete record of Yahweh's name through strength. The record bears witness to the incomplete deeds of Israel through beauty.

THE DEED OF WRITING

Moses' first mention of writing establishes the significance of a record. His second mention establishes the significance of writing as an act or deed.

The second mention directly follows Moses' fourth meeting with Yahweh, the first meeting off the top of the mountain, in which Yahweh presented him with the rules (W2):

> And Moses came and told the people all Yahweh's propositions and all the rules. And all the people answered with one voice and said: All the propositions Yahweh has spoken we will do. And Moses wrote all Yahweh's propositions, and rose up early in the morning and built an altar beneath the mountain and twelve monuments according to the twelve tribes of Israel.[104]

The passage records Moses' only clear reference to his own act of writing. Moses reflects here on writing as an act or deed. The author of a text writes about writing the text—witnesses writing the text in the text—in order to establish its authority. Self-witnessing writings in law—acts, wills, deeds—seek to establish the legal authority of the writing. Moses' writing is an act or deed, since it too seeks to establish its authority by witnessing its own writing.[105]

The only other possible reference to Moses actually writing occurs in the next-to-last mention of writing in *Names*, at the end of Moses' final meeting with Yahweh on the top of Mt. Sinai (W7):

> And Yahweh said to Moses: Write these propositions, because on the basis of these propositions I have made a covenant with you and with Israel. And he was there with Yahweh forty days and forty nights. He did not eat bread and he did not drink water. And he

wrote on the tablets the propositions of the covenant, the ten propositions.[106]

This last passsage too is ambiguous—intentionally, we must assume—both as to the content of the writing on the tablets and as to who did the writing. When Yahweh says "write these propositions," He is undoubtedly referring to the commands of a covenant Yahweh has just finished offering Moses and Israel.[107] These are the "propositions" Yahweh ostensibly orders Moses to write down. But then the text records someone, Moses or Yahweh, actually writing down "the propositions of the covenant" on the tablets. If we take the text literally and stop before the apposition, we would suppose that Moses, having just been instructed to "write these propositions," wrote "the propositions of the covenant" on the tablets. But we know from other texts that the second set of tablets have on them only the "ten propositions," and that Yahweh wrote them.[108] The text places "the ten propositions" in apposition to "the propositions of the covenant." It thus appears to be intentionally mixing Yahweh's instruction to Moses to write with Yahweh actually writing, and the content of what Yahweh instructed Moses to write with the content of what we know from other texts Yahweh wrote.

The significance of the ambiguity sharpens when we note that "the propositions of the covenant" that Yahweh ordered Moses to write in the last meeting on the mountain recalls the first reference to actual writing, the writing Moses records himself doing after the fourth meeting with Yahweh. In the very next reference after the one to Moses actually writing, a reference to reading, Moses calls the writing he records himself having written, "the book of the covenant" (R):

> And he took the book of the covenant, and read in the ears of the people, and they said: All that Yahweh has said, we will do and we will hear.[109]

Moses makes it clear that Moses wrote the book of the covenant. But he does not record Yahweh commanding him to write it. He does record Yahweh commanding him to write the propositions of the second covenant, during the last meeting on top of the mountain, but leaves us confused as to whether he wrote the propositions directly after the command, and whether he wrote them on the tablets.

Moses' writing of the book of the covenant is similarly laced with ambiguity. Moses does not make it clear that Yahweh commanded Moses to write it. More importantly, Moses does not tell us exactly what Moses wrote. Rashi comments that "And Moses wrote" means to say Moses wrote *In the Beginning Of* and the portions of *Names* up to "the giving of doctrine." [110] He also maintains that the prior reference to "all Yahweh's propositions," put side-by-side with "all the rules," refers to the propositions Yahweh asked Moses to speak to the people during the first three meetings on top of the mountain. [111] These included preparatory instructions for speaking the ten propositions before Moses and the people. The people's fear upon hearing Elohim's speech led to Moses' fourth meeting, on the slopes, where Moses received the rules. Rashi does not include the ten propositions in the book of the covenant, though Elohim did speak them to Moses and the people prior to the reference to Moses actually writing. [112] Nor does Rashi include the rules, though they too, at least according to the order in the text, have already been spoken to Moses prior to his writing the book of the covenant. "And Moses wrote all Yahweh's propositions," may or may not mean to exclude the rules from the writing.

Moses could be describing Yahweh ordering him to write down the rules (or Moses actually writing them) at only one other place in the text, the very place Yahweh orders Moses to "write these propositions," during the last meeting on the top of the mountain. After having implicitly rejected the writing of the rules in the book of the covenant, Rashi does not clearly tell us that Yahweh commanded Moses to write the rules during the last meeting. Rashi's only comment on "write these propositions" is revealing: "But you are not permitted to write down the oral doctrine." [113] The oral doctrine (*mesirah*, handing over) is an oral tradition, tracing its authority to transmission from Moses, through Joshua, to generations of authoritative interpreters. [114] Rashi locates the textual source of the oral doctrine here, where Yahweh commands Moses to "write these propositions": *these* and not others, which also have been spoken during the eighty days at the top of Mt. Sinai. Rabbinic tradition uses the oral doctrine as a system of exegesis of Moses' rules. It also uses oral doctrine as a source of unwritten rules, of the same order as Moses' written rules, and as a source of canons of interpretation, both of written and unwritten rules.

Though the necessities of Rome's occupation forced the Rabbis to abrogate the command not to write down the oral doctrine, the spirit of the command remains an essential norm of the system of law in the *Five Books*. Without oral doctrine the written rules could not be put in play, could not be "changed." Rules such as "an eye for an eye," [115] which the oral doctrine construes to mean "money compensation for an eye," [116] could not be read: they could only be slavishly obeyed. The oral doctrine gives authority to future generations to put the written rules in play, to "change" them. The oral doctrine rescues the written rules from positivism.

The mystery of Moses' legal system is not that Moses did not write down certain of the rules (together with principles of exegesis and interpretation), which Yahweh had spoken to him either on the slopes or on top of Mt. Sinai, but that he did write down some of the rules spoken to him "near the fog," [117] on the slopes of the mountain. The writing itself puts the writing in question. First, the rules Moses came to write were spoken to him on the slopes of the mountain. The oral doctrine is superior to these rules, since Yahweh spoke it to Moses on top of the mountain. Second, Yahweh spoke the rules Moses came to write in reaction to the fright of the people when they heard Elohim (as the text says) speaking the ten propositions:

> And all the people see the loud noises and torches, and the voice of the horn, and the mountain smoking. And when the people feared, they moved, and stood in the distance. And they said to Moses: You speak with us, and we will hear, for if Elohim will speak with us, we will die. [118]

The rules—backed by frightful sanctions—are a reaction to fright. The people "see . . . the voice"; they do not hear it. The rules are rules for people whose reactions to the ten propositions are frightened reactions, who "see" the ten propositions as "loud noises and torches" rather than "hear" their intellectual content. Though rules are "further propositions" whose preferable sanctions is reason, the people will treat them only as triggers for sanctions. One rules frightened people by sanctions, not by reason. The oral doctrine rules by reason. It subjects sanctions, such as "an eye for an eye," to reason.

Moses reduces the "frightening" rules to writing, because frightened people must see. They cannot hear. But he is very careful to show us, his readers, that his reduction of the frightening rules to writing does not have clear textual authority—Yahweh's authority, if you will. How could it? How could the name of God as collaboration sanction the fright of the people? How could the writing of rules calculated to frighten them further be collaborative writing in any sense?

Though Moses' dangerous writing may be necessary, it does not serve to complete creation. The written rules, like all engraved objects, treat creation as already completed by Elohim. They can be rescued from engraving only by rewriting, only by correction and supplementation through oral doctrine. The oral doctrine is a doctrine of speech and hearing, not a doctrine of seeing, as are written rules. Without the oral doctrine, the people would bow to the written rules as they bowed to the golden calf, out of fright. The oral doctrine rescues the people from fright. It reads the written rules, and rewrites them. It erases the written rules. It stops people from regarding them as idols.

Rashi's anchor for the oral doctrine is not the only possible anchor.

First, Moses invites us to compare the structure of his references to writing with the structure of his meetings with Yahweh at Mt. Sinai. ("T" stands for a meeting at the top of the mountain; "S," for the meeting on the slopes; and "M," for the meeting in the Tent of Meeting):[119]

	Golden	
T1	Golden	T5
T2	Calf	T6
T3	Crisis	T7
S		M
T4		T8

The center of both structures is the crisis of idolatry, the golden calf.[120] Moses has eight (possibly six) meetings with Yahweh at the top of Mt. Sinai, just as *Names* has eight references to writing.[121] The meeting on the slopes, "near the fog" (S), in which Moses hears the rules he will write down and read to the people, mirrors the reference to reading (R). The meeting in the Tent of Meeting (M), in which Moses persuades Yahweh not to be absent (to be "present") on the journey to Canaan, mirrors the reference to erasure (E). Altogether Moses makes ten references to writing and its allied activities (reading and erasure), just as he recounts ten meetings (and hears ten propositions).

The structure of meetings draws attention to a symmetry between S–T4 and M–T8.[122] Thus, in S Yahweh tells Moses the rules. Between S and T4 Moses writes down the rules (without "authority"), reads them to the people, and performs a covenant ceremony "of his own devising"[123] sprinkling the people with the blood of a sacrifice. In T4 Moses receives Elohim's tablets. Also, in M Moses persuades Yahweh to be "present"—to accompany the Israelites to Canaan, not to send an angel (a physical manifestation, according to the tradition) instead. Yahweh also orders Moses to carve a second set of tablets, on which He promises to write the propositions on the first set, which Moses broke. Between M and T8 Moses hews the second set of tablets. In T8 Yahweh makes a covenant with Israel, and writes the ten propositions ("because on the basis of these propositions I have made a covenant with you and with Israel") on the second set of tablets, apparently with Moses' collaboration.

The difference between S–T4 and M–T8 focuses on the two covenants and their link to writing. Moses' blood covenant and his writing and reading of the rules (S–T4) take place on the ground. Yahweh's covenant (M–T8) takes place on top of the mountain, and is "sealed" by Moses' and Yahweh's collaborative writing of the ten propositions on the tablets. Looking backward after the crisis of the golden calf, Moses' blood covenant, his writing and reading of rules with bloody sanctions, smacks of idolatry. It is an "inauthentic" version of the true covenant—collaborative writing and conversations with Yahweh. Not covenants of blood and written rules, but ten propositions and conversations with Yahweh about them escapes the snares of idolatry.

Moses writes the rules without indicating clear authority in the text where he records his writing. He tells us that writing them risked idolatry. It might have been better had he not written the rules, had they stayed oral. Then the people would not be tempted to bow to them as they are tempted to bow to idols.

Second, Moses suggests that he himself interpreted Yahweh's commands when he related them to the people, and that Yahweh Himself interpreted His own commands. Moses' interpretive suggestion requires expository patience. But Moses rewards patience.

In Moses' first ascent of Mt. Sinai,[124] Yahweh tells Moses to tell the people:

> You have seen what I did to Egypt, and how I bore you on eagles' wings, and brought you to Me. And now, if you will diligently hear what I tell you, and keep My covenant, then you will be My own treasure of all the peoples, for all the earth is Mine. And you will be to Me a kingdom of priests, and a holy nation. These are the propositions which you shall speak to the children of Israel.[125]

Moses set "all these propositions" before the elders of the people, and the people answered: "All that Yahweh has spoken we will do."[126]

In the second ascent,[127] Moses reported the people's response to Yahweh, and Yahweh told Moses:

> Go to the people and sanctify them today and tomorrow, and let them wash their clothes. And they will be ready on the third day, for on the third day Yahweh will come down before the eyes of the people on Mt. Sinai. And you shall set bounds to the people round about, saying: Beware of going onto the mountain or touching its edge. Whoever touches the mountain shall surely be put to death. No hand shall touch him, but his hand shall surely be stoned, or shot through. Whether beast or man, it will not live. When the ram's horn sounds long, they shall come up to the mountain.[128]

In executing Yahweh's command to get the people ready, Moses added one preparation to those Yahweh listed, which according to Moses' *own* account he could only have inferred by interpreting Yahweh's propositions:

> And Moses went down from the mountain to the people. And he sanctified the people. And they washed their clothes. And he said to the people: Be ready against the third day. Do not come near a woman.[129]

The sanctification ritual Yahweh ordered Moses to perform and Moses reports himself performing is presumably the set of decrees (h.ookah)[130] of the red heifer, which he reports in the fourth book, *In the Wilderness:*

> And Yahweh spoke to Moses and Aaron, saying: This is the set of decrees of the doctrine which Yahweh has commanded, saying: Speak to the children of Israel, that they take to you a faultless red heifer,[131] in which there is no blemish and on which there came no yoke. And you shall give her to Eleazar [Elohim helped] the priest, and she shall be brought outside the camp, and he shall slaughter her before his face. And Eleazar the priest shall take blood from her with his finger and sprinkle her blood seven times in the face of the Tent of Meeting. And one shall burn the heifer in front of his eyes. Her skin, her flesh and her blood with her dung shall be burnt. And the priest shall take cedar-wood and hyssop and scarlet, and cast them into the burning of the heifer. Then the priest shall launder his clothes and wash his flesh in water, and afterward he will come into the camp, and the priest shall be unclean until the evening. And he that burns her shall wash his clothes in water, and wash his flesh in water, and shall be impure until the evening. And a man that is pure shall gather up the ashes of the heifer and place them outside the camp in a pure place. And it shall be for the congregation of the children of Israel for a keeping for a water of separation. It is a purification from sin. And there he that gathers the ashes of the heifer shall wash his clothes, and be unclean until the evening. And it shall be a decree forever to the children of Israel and to the proselyte that lives among them.[132]

Rashi comments that the set of decrees of the red heifer is the decree that Yahweh gave at the first revelation, prior to Mt. Sinai, in Marah.[133] Rashi's reasoning is undoubtedly that Yahweh gave the set of decrees of the red heifer in order to enable the Israelites to sanctify themselves at Mt. Sinai, as Yahweh ordered. The set of decrees of the red heifer requires laundering clothes, as Yahweh had ordered at Mt. Sinai, but nowhere does it mention staying clear of women. (The sacrifice, however, is female, and anyone who touches its product becomes unclean.) The evidence is persuasive that Moses added: "Do not come near a woman." [134]

Moses records Moses supplementing the commands Yahweh gave Moses in the second ascent. Moses' own text gives evidence that Moses was prepared to interpret the words Yahweh spoke to him, that he was not content, at least as far as reporting Yahweh's messages to the people, to be a "stenographer." Since Moses gives evidence in his own text that he interpreted Yahweh's commands, he puts us on warning that he may have engaged in other interpretations. Unlike the people, however, we who are reading Moses' text know the "inside story" of his conversations with Yahweh. Are we then privileged to know *all* the instances of Moses' interpretation, carefully comparing the words of Yahweh with Moses' transmissions? But Moses does not make it clear that he writes for us all his conversations, and does not assure us that he is not engaging in written interpretation in the text, as well as oral interpretation before the people. The text thus puts in question here any superiority we might have thought our privileged reading of the text had given us over the Israelites receiving Moses' oral reports. Our relationship to Moses, as readers to author of a text, is not less dependent or uncertain than the relationship of the Israelites to Moses at Mt. Sinai. And we know from the rebellions against Moses' authority and God's authority to come in the fourth book, *In the Wilderness*,[135] that the relationship of the Israelites to Moses, and through Moses to Yahweh, is dependent, rebellious, and uncertain.

The last rebellion in *In the Wilderness* concerns the sexual relations of a Midianite woman with an Israelite man during the punishment of the Israelites for Israelite men having consorted with Moabite women. Yahweh commanded Moses to "harass the Midianites and smite them" [136] and to "avenge the vengeance of the children of Israel on the Midianites." [137] Moses' troops, acting in the usual manner, did not at first kill the Midianite women and male children. But Moses commanded them to kill every male child and every woman who had had sexual relations with any man, and to purify themselves in a manner reminiscent of the set of decrees of the red heifer.[138] Again, Yahweh had not instructed Moses to kill the women and male children, an act of interpretation echoing what I claim to be his first interpretation of Yahweh's command during the second ascent of Mt. Sinai. The last rebellion in *In the Wilderness*—the sexual relations of an Israelite man with a Midianite woman—recalls the first rebellion in

In the Wilderness, of Miriam and Aaron against Moses for having taken a Cushite woman as his second wife. Moses' first wife was a Midianite, Tsipporah. Also, the last rebellion recalls Moses' "interpretation" of Yahweh's command during his second ascent of Mt. Sinai: "Do not come near a woman."

"Interpretation" is necessary. It is also tempting. It is dangerous enough when it is necessary. When interpretation is done because it is tempting, it masks rebellion.[139] Moses ties the act of interpretation to the purification ritual of the red heifer—the sacrifice of a female animal that has never born offspring, touching whose product creates impurity. He ties the content of his interpretations to temptation and impurity—the necessity and danger, as he regards it, of women.

Interpretation, Moses tells us, is a woman.

Other moments in the text alert us that Moses' Midianite marriage was dangerous. Moses records that Yahweh tried to kill Moses directly after their first meeting in Midian, as Moses was on his way back to Egypt with Tsipporah and their uncircumcised son, Gershon:

> And on the way, at the inn, Yahweh met him and sought to kill him. Then Tsipporah took a flint, and cut off the foreskin of her son, and flung it at his feet, and said: For you are a bridegroom of blood to me. So He let him alone. Then she said: You are a bridegroom of blood in regard of the circumcision.[140]

Gershon had not been circumcised, presumably because Moses was married to a Midianite. Yahweh was prepared to kill Moses, even after Yahweh had chosen him in the meeting at the burning bush. Moses began his collaboration with Yahweh. But he had been unable to collaborate with Tsipporah. She saves him, angrily. She saves him from the anger of his future collaborator.

The danger posed by Midianite women looms over the text. Moses' interpretations loom over it as well.

As we have come to expect in Moses' collaboration with Yahweh, Yahweh echoes Moses' supplement with a supplement of His own during their third meeting and conversation:

> And Yahweh said to Moses: Go down, charge the people, so that they will not destroy their position to gaze at Yahweh, and many of them perish. And the priests that come near to Yahweh will sanctify themselves, lest Yahweh break through upon them. And Moses said to Yahweh: The people cannot come up to Mt. Sinai, for you have charged us, saying: Set bounds to the mountain, and sanctify it. And Yahweh said to him: Go, get down, and you shall come up,

you and Aaron with you, and the priests. And the people shall not destroy through to come up to Yahweh, lest He break through upon them. So Moses went down to the people, and told them.[141]

Moses complains that Yahweh is repeating the command to charge the people. In fact, Moses' complaint is not well founded, for two reasons. The original charge concerned "touching" rather than "gazing." One might say that Yahweh Himself is anticipating a possible "misinterpretation" of His first charge, that people will "destroy through to gaze," believing they are not physically "touching" the mountain. Yahweh is "interpreting" His own charge. Also, in the course of repeating His charge Yahweh adds to it an "implied" license for the priests to come closer than the people. Yahweh may be "adding" the license, but He may again be "interpreting" a possible "misinterpretation" of His original charge, that priests must obey the same restrictions as the people. Either way, Yahweh is changing the words of His original charge in a manner similar to Moses. Both are interpreting.

Yahweh shows irritation with Moses for not permitting Him the same interpretive "license" that Moses permitted himself. Moses must learn the rules of their collaboration. If man is made in Elohim's image, and man must interpret Elohim's commands in order to collaborate with Yahweh, then Yahweh too must interpret His own—Elohim's—commands. The text ratifies the act of interpretation, by showing Yahweh reflect the act of interpretation. Yahweh is Elohim by reflection—the image of an image.[142]

Moses places the text of Yahweh's interpretation of His own command in apposition with the text of Moses' interpretation. The position of the priests, we expect, will mirror the position of women. They too are necessary and dangerous.

What is a priest? Moses tells us:

> And all the people see the loud noises and torches, and the voice of the horn, and the mountain smoking. And when the people feared, they moved, and stood in the distance. And they said to Moses: You speak with us, and we will hear. For if Elohim will speak with us, we will die. And Moses said to the people: Do not fear, for in order to try you Elohim has come, and in order that His fear will be on your faces, so that you will not sin. And the people stood in the distance, but Moses drew near to the fog where the Elohim was.[143]

"Seeing" the voice of Elohim frightens the people. They want Elohim to speak to Moses, and Moses to speak to the people. They want

Moses to mediate between them and Elohim. They do not want to collaborate with Yahweh, without mediators. A priest is one who mediates between the people and Elohim.

Yahweh's response is instructive:

> And Yahweh said to Moses: Thus you shall say to the children of Israel: You have seen that I have talked with you from the skies. You shall not make with Me gods of silver, and gods of gold you shall not make for yourselves. You shall make to Me an altar of earth and sacrifice on it your burnt offerings and your peace offerings, your sheep and your cattle. In every place where I will mention My name I will come to you and bless you. And if you shall make Me an altar of stones, you shall not build it of hewn stones. For if you lift your sword on it, you have profaned it. Neither shall you go up by steps to My altar, that your genitals not be uncovered on it.[144]

Yahweh's first response to the people's request that Moses mediate is to repeat the warning, already stated in the ten propositions, against making idols. Yahweh then lists two likely substitutes for idols: beautifully (violently) carved altars, and uncovered genitals. He then tells Moses the rules.[145]

The rules close with a further warning against making and bowing to idols.[146] Yahweh follows the rules immediately with a call:

> And He said to Moses: Come up to Yahweh, you and Aaron, Nadav and Avihu, and seventy of the elders of Israel, and bow in the distance. And Moses alone came near to Yahweh. And they did not come near. And the people did not come up with him.[147]

Yahweh establishes the priority of the priests—Aaron, Nadav and Avihu—over the people.

The very next passage records Moses engaging in his writing without clear textual authority. The full passage is also instructive (*W2* and *R*):

> And Moses wrote all Yahweh's propositions, and got up early in the morning, and built an altar beneath the mountain, and twelve monuments for the twelve tribes of Israel. And he sent the young lads of the children of Israel, who offered burnt offerings, and they sacrificed peace offerings of oxen to Yahweh. And Moses took half the blood, and put it in basins. And he threw half the blood against the altar. And he took the book of the covenant, and read it in the ears of the people. And they said: All that Yahweh has said we will do and hear. And Moses took the blood, and threw it on the people.

> And he said: Here is the blood of the covenant, which Yahweh has made with you concerning all these propositions. Then Moses and Aaron, Nadav and Avihu and seventy of the elders of Israel went up. And they saw the Elohim of Israel. And under His feet there was the like of a brickwork of sapphire, the like of heaven for purity. And He did not lay His hand on the nobles of the children of Israel. And they saw the Elohim, and ate and drank.[148]

Then Moses, together with young Joshua (not the priests or elders), rose up and Moses went alone to the top of the mountain for his first forty-day sojourn, where he reports learning instructions about the cult.[149]

The passage records Moses carrying out Yahweh's instructions regarding altars and sacrifices, with three characteristic and fateful additions. Moses retains the blood of the sacrifices and sprinkles it on the people in a convenant ceremony of his own devising. He also adds writing "all Yahweh's propositions" and reading them to the people. He calculates that the sprinkling of blood will remind us of one element of the set of decreases of the red heifer—an inappropriate, partial repetition of the purification ceremony Yahweh had reserved for the preparation of the people.[150]

This covenant ceremony—Moses' effort to collaborate with Yahweh—will not stick. The people, aided and abetted by Aaron, will turn from Moses' ceremony to making the golden calf. The reason they cite for turning the idols is Moses' delay. He is "delayed" for forty days on top of the mountain receiving instructions about the priestly cult and Elohim's tablets. He will smash the tablets, unerring (I am arguing) in his instinct that the people will bow to them as idols. Will they also bow to the mediators—Moses and Aaron? If they turn to Moses and Aaron because they are frightened, will they collaborate with Yahweh? Will those to whom they turn as mediators—Moses, Aaron, and Aaron's sons—betray the trust the people place in them?[151]

The balance of the text of the *Five Books* circles about these questions with an extraordinary variety of hints and further questions. I can touch only one or two.

Moses leaves no doubt about the uniqueness of his own abilities. When Miriam and Aaron rebel against Moses for marrying a Cushite woman, Moses writes:

> And Yahweh spoke suddenly to Moses and Aaron and Miriam: Come out the three of you to the Tent of Meeting. And the three came out. And Yahweh came down in a pillar of cloud, and stood

at the door of the tent, and called Aaron and Miriam, and they both came forth. And He said: Please listen to My propositions: If there will be a prophet among you, in a vision I will make Myself known to him. In a dream I speak to him. My servant Moses is not so. He is trusted in all My house. I speak with him mouth to mouth, even with sight, and not in riddles. And he can look at the image of Yahweh. And why were you not afraid to speak against My servant, against Moses?[152]

Moses retains his super-prophetic ability to speak directly with Yahweh throughout the *Five Books*. No other person has it:

And Yahweh came down in a cloud, and He talked to him and shaded the spirit [wind, breath] on him and on the seventy men, the elders. And then, when the spirit rested on them and they prophesied and did so no more. And two men stayed in the camp. The name of one was Eldad [Elohim's breast] and the name of the other is Maidad [breast's water]. And the spirit rested on them and they were in the scriptures [*ktubim*, writings]. And they did not go out to the tent, and they prophesied in the camp. And the lad ran and told Moses. And he said, Eldad and Maidad are prophesying in the camp. And there responded Joshua-bin-Nun, the servant of Moses and one of his lads. And he said: My sire Moses, jail them. And Moses said to him: Are you jealous for me? If it was only possible that all of Yahweh's people were prophets, for whom Yahweh would give his spirit on them.[153]

Others can be prophets, but they will not be able to speak face to face with Yahweh, as Moses can. Moses' super-prophetic abilities have an important consequence. If the people have questions about the rules, Moses can ask Yahweh to answer the questions.[154] Others cannot. After Moses dies, the people must answer their legal questions on their own, without Moses' super-prophetic mediation.

When Moses renegotiates the covenant, after the failure of the covenant ceremony "of his own devising," Yahweh says that the condition of his remaining "inside" the people is that no human will ever see His face after Moses.[155] Yahweh will remain "inside" people. They talk with Him by talking to themselves. They will not talk with Yahweh face to face, as did Moses.[156] They will collaborate with Yahweh by collaborating with themselves, and with each other.

The second covenant, unlike the first, is not a covenant initiated by Moses with the people. Yahweh simply calls His "proper" name, twice, and promises works, deeds, in exchange for deeds of the people.[157] The first covenant was a covenant of blood. The second, a covenant of deeds, self-witnessing acts, not words or blood. Moses simply reports the words of the second covenant to the people. He does not ask them to say anything in response, just do and hear.[158]

OTHER JURISPRUDENCES

Moses' is not the only jurisprudence to require three writings. Common law and the jurisprudence of right do as well. Moses' is a jurisprudence of duty. These three—Moses' law, common law and the jurisprudence of right—make up a family of jurisprudences that are dynamic.[159] The universe of norms in a dynamic jurisprudence is never static. Legal persons must change the universe of norms in a dynamic jurisprudence in order to follow a single one of them. A dynamic jurisprudence requires persons to make law in order to fulfill the fundamental obligations of legality.

The dynamic jurisprudences treat law as an expression of the personality rather than an instrument of order. They are dynamic because the personality is dynamic. The amount of personality in the three dynamic jurisprudences differs. In Moses' law, the jurisprudence of duty, the personality strives towards a communally shared image of perfection. In the jurisprudence of right the personality strives towards liberation, defined as recognition by other, similarly striving personalities. In common law, the personality attempts to suppress uncertainty of norms through concerted reciprocal action. The two non-dynamic jurisprudences—positivism and naturalism—treat law as an instrument of order. The static jurisprudences suppress personality, in any form, in the interests of order. They treat personality as anarchic. They acknowledge fewer than three writings.

Positivism insists that law achieves order only by force, and only by confining the exercise of force to a central bureaucratic apparatus. The "author" of law in a positivist system makes law in two steps. First, the author makes a procedure for making law. The procedure "marks" or "franks" certain norms as law. The procedure marks—makes—law, such as enacting a statute according to the procedures of statutory enactment or rendering a judicial decision according to the norms of rendering decisions. Persons do not make law directly, only by working the procedures. Unmarked norms are "customs."[160] The first "writing" is the authoritative enactment of the procedure. The author of the first writing is either a single person backed by charismatic force, or a group of persons agreeing to a procedure and backing it by collective physical force or by tradition or a divine author donating a procedure and backing it by force in the way of the world. The second writing is the marking or franking of certain norms as law according to the procedure. Positivism treats the application of norms to cases as uninteresting, unproblematic—a private matter. True law in positivism is the product of two writings and two writings only.[161]

Naturalism asserts that law achieves order naturally, according to norms "written" or "engraved" in nature. Some forms of naturalism suppress the fact that persons "read" the "writing," both when they act and when they apply law to cases. Once again, persons do not make law, and true law is the product of one or two writings.

The static jurisprudences assert that a person cannot have a legal right unless another person simultaneously has a mirror-image legal duty, and vice versa. Rights must always be correlated with duties, and duties with rights. The dynamic jurisprudences agree that rights can never be correlated with duties. They break the correlation of rights with duties. They are dynamic because they break the correlation.

The jurisprudence of duty—of which Moses' law is the supreme example—breaks the correlation of rights with duties by abolishing right as an operative category in the jurisprudence. Persons have duties, not rights. A complainant goes to court, not because she is enforcing a right to compel another person to fulfill her mirror-image duty, but because she has a duty to report the other person's failure to the court. The duty to report is the duty of every person in the community. Persons in this jurisprudence are propelled to legal action by a drive to transform their personality in the direction of an image of perfection. In Moses' jurisprudence Yahweh/Elohim offers the image. Other jurisprudences of duty have other images.

The jurisprudence of right—of which Hobbes' *Leviathan*[162] and Hegel's *Philosophy of Right*[163] are examples—breaks the correlation by suppressing or de-emphasizing the role of duty. Persons want rights, but they do not want other persons to reflect the rights as duties. They want other persons to recognize the rights, not to obey duties. They are willing to engage in contractual exchanges of recognition in order to get what they want, which is recognition. Persons have duties only when they fail to provide recognition.[164]

Common law is the dynamic jurisprudence that asserts that law is just the application of law—the doctrine of precedent. Making or knowing a legal norm requires three applications. The first is the application of the norm in a prior case, a precedent. The second is the application of the norm in the case at hand, using the precedent. The third is application of the norm in the case at hand to a future case.

Persons in common law learn law first by reading prior applications. But they cannot know law just by reading prior cases. The norms generated by the prior cases must be applied in their case before they can know the norm, since the norm is just its application. Persons learn more about the norm as they plan action and act in light of their reading of the prior cases. The norm itself changes as persons act. It is general when they start. It becomes specific and calculable as they continue. Only once they "finish" the actions constituting their case does the norm "exist" as a full judgment on the propriety of their actions. One knows the norm by making it, in action. All action in common law (for that matter, in all dynamic jurisprudence) is legal action. All persons are constantly applying law. No moment in their lives is legally indifferent. Law drenches life and fills the universe. (In static jurisprudence large parts of the universe are legally indifferent, and what persons do in the gaps is their own business. Nothing in dynamic jurisprudence is the person's "own" business.) But completing action in a case does not finish making or knowing the common law norm. In order to know the norm thoroughly, persons must await a further application. The present case yields a complete norm only once it serves as a precedent for further action, a future application.

Common law breaks the correlation of rights with duties, but eliminates or suppresses neither right nor duty. It recognizes that rights and duties are correlated, but that the correlations themselves are dynamic, constantly changing as persons act, and as further applications revise norms generated in prior application.[165]

The dynamic jurisprudences agree that persons make law, and that they cannot make it in one or two writings. Persons make law in three writings. The third writing makes the jurisprudence dynamic.

The dynamic jurisprudences always allocate one writing each to a past, a present, and a future. The static jurisprudences allocate writings only to a past and a present. There is no future, hence no dynamic driving the jurisprudence.

Moses' law allocates Elohim's writing to a past, Moses' writing to the narrative present, and Yahweh's writing to a collaborative future. Common law allocates precedent to the past, application to the present, and further application to the future. The jurisprudence of right allocates the state of nature to the past, the contract leading out of the state of nature to the present, and law application to the future.

The dynamic jurisprudences differ only with respect to the writing—the past, present, or future—that drives persons in the jurisprudence, making it dynamic.

Collaboration with Yahweh—the writing of the future—drives persons in the jurisprudence of duty. Persons act in order to collaborate with Yahweh. They rewrite a model of perfection in an incessant struggle toward future perfection. The present is a flight towards the past. The past supplies the judgment of perfection. The future is a prospect that the present will attain past perfection.

The legal state of nature—the writing of the past—drives persons in the jurisprudence of right. They act—they struggle to get mutual recognition of rights—in order to flee the state of nature. The present is flight from a threatening past, from the state of non-recognition. The future guarantees that the present will successfully distinguish itself from the terrors of non-recognition.

Acting according to precedent with an awareness that actions create further precedents—the writing of the present—drives persons in common law. Persons act in order to achieve reciprocal certainty according to the doctrine of precedent. They seek certainty of norms, in the present. Past applications and future applications fold into action. Action makes norms by remaking past applications, and by offering further applications for remaking in the future.[166]

The writing driving each dynamic jurisprudence is the source of law in the jurisprudence. The originating state of each dynamic jurisprudence supplies energy propelling persons into action (necessarily always legal action, no action being legally indifferent). In the jurisprudence of duty the originating state is the future—collaboration with Yahweh. In the jurisprudence of right the originating state is the past—the state of nature. In common law the originating state is the present—action according to precedent with an awareness that action creates precedents.

The static jurisprudences, by contrast, recognize only a past and a present. They propose no originating state. The writing of the past serves only to establish a foundation for the writing of the present. The writing of the present neither flees from nor seeks the writing of the past. Neither present nor past propels the person into action.

The static jurisprudences claim that persons can know law thoroughly at every moment. Law is always fully present. It never changes its relation to an originating state, in either past or future. Unlike common law, the static jurisprudences do not treat the present as an originating state, perpetually unfolding law as persons apply and create precedents in action. Law is fixed. It is fixed forever, even in positivism, which fixes law forever until it marks another norm as law. The marks of positivism, the maxims of the legal state of nature, refer only to the present. Persons know them completely in the present. Every legal person is conscious at all times of every legal norm. There is no "legal unconscious."

The common experience of persons is to the contrary. Even if positivism and naturalism could fulfill the promise that legal norms be fully present—fully presented by marks and maxims—the bulk of norms must be thin enough to guarantee that legal persons could know all of them at a single moment. That is why positivists, at least, often regard the physical inscription of law as crucial: inscription of law expands the effective memory of persons. When lawmakers reduce law to writing, the bulk of norms with which persons can be charged enlarges, since persons have "access" to the writing, a legal "preconscious." [167] Naturalism, by contrast, simply asserts the "preconscious" accessibility of all norms.

Dynamic jurisprudence asserts that legal norms may be unconscious. Unlike static jurisprudence, it does not require that norms be present to consciousness or accessible to consciousness (preconscious). Dynamic jurisprudence allows for normative material that is not present and not accessible in the present. The normative material is irredeemably past or future. Yet like the unconscious, the normative material affects the normative structure of the legal present. The legal present is a breaching or broaching through action of normative material which is not otherwise present. The dynamic jurisprudences tolerate, indeed require, a legal unconscious.

Positivism makes the clearest statement of any jurisprudence that law to be law must be "marked" or written—once, according to a given procedure. The danger for every non-positivist jurisprudence is a collapse into positivism, a sacrifice of legal material to the apparent needs of unitary order, self-denial or self-rejection by persons, loss of interest in all but the vulgar, narrow version of writing.

Moses' law is not the only jurisprudence to face the positivist threat. Common law too has constantly been challenged by positivist distortion. When common law judges began writing opinions in the first third of the nineteenth century, the content and flavor of their judgments altered. Before they wrote opinions, students or reporters recorded the colloquies of judges, prior to voting. The written record of early common law decisions does not contain "opinions," but debates amongst judges. The written record presents a debate, followed by a vote and a verdict. It does not present an "opinion," a justification of a vote after the vote has been taken. [168]

The style of the modern record is a style of justification, not debate. Old records contain "hypotheticals" on every page—invented facts used by law-debaters to attack the statement of a rule. Hypotheticals are sparse in modern opinions. If we find them at all, we find a very different hypothetical. Modern judicial hypotheticals tend to show that a rule works and how it works, not that it fails to work. We find the attacking hypothetical mostly in the law school classroom. The main institution supporting the common law today is legal education, not the judiciary.[169]

Positivism and naturalism share a specific claim that the dynamic jurisprudences always reject, each in its own way. The claim is that the rule is complete, fully formed, prior to any case applying it. Common law and Moses' law never treat rules as complete, fully formed, prior to applying them.

To consider rules complete, from Moses' perspective, is to treat them as engravings. To apply rules to cases as if they are already formed bows to rules as idols. Creation is not complete, even if we want to treat it so. Rules rule only when persons struggle at every moment with them, use them in deeds to create a record. Common law holds a similar doctrine. Rules rule only when persons make them in applications. To make prior applications the last word is to deny that law is application.

Positivism and naturalism regard the incessant creation or re-creation of rules out of the very action the rules are supposed to govern as a destabilizing invitation to anarchy. The dynamic jurisprudences regard the incessant creation or re-creation of rules as at once the striving of persons (toward salvation, liberation, or reciprocity, as the case may be) and a spur to action.

Moses' account of the jurisprudence he discovered is our most passionate, thorough, profound and illuminating discourse on the rewards and perils of writing law. His warnings against positivism speak directly to common lawyers, as well as to practitioners of his own legal system. The warnings are as difficult to do and hear today, as they were for those first legal persons in the wilderness, struggling to free themselves, body and soul, from slavery. Positivism and naturalism are our own pharaonic temptations.

NOTES

1. Names, XVII, 14–16. From now on I will refer to citations from *Names* by a roman numeral chapter and an arabic numeral verse only.

   I prefer to use English translations of the Hebrew names of the *Five Books*, rather than the (mostly) Greek translations, which are more familiar. The tradition names each book by the first significant word in the text of the book. Hence:

Genesis	In the Beginning of (*Bereshit*)
Exodus	Names (*Sh'mot*)
Leviticus	He Called (*Vayikra*)
Numbers	In the Wilderness (*Bamidbar*)
Deuteronomy	Propositions (*D'varim*)

English calls the last book *Deuteronomy,* but *d'varim* means words, propositions, discourses, matters, or things. *Propositions* contains the last propositions or discourses of the dying lawgiver. The best Greek translation is *Logoi,* not *Deuteronomos* ("second law").

Moses also uses the word "*d'varim*" to describe the "ten *d'varim,*" usually translated as "ten commandments." Moses does not call them "commandments"—"*mitsvot*"—a word he reserves for other matters. In order to reveal the Hebrew text as well as possible in English, I translate "*d'varim*" as "propositions" wherever it occurs, regardless of better English choices in context.

These names resonate more powerfully than the anglicized Greek with various themes woven elaborately and carefully into the fabric of the *Five Books.*

2. XVII, 9. Joshua will figure prominently at two further points in the *Five Books:* the second and third of three covenants between God and Israel, at Names, XXXIII, 11 ("but his servant Joshua-bin-Nun, a young lad, did not depart out of the tent"), and at Propositions, XXXI, 14, 23 and XXXII, 44.

3. XII, 40.

4. The Israelites played a passive role in prior collaborations. During the departure, when Pharaoh decided to pursue the Israelites, Moses comforted the people, saying: "Yahweh will fight for you." XIV, 14. Moses writes, "Thus Yahweh saved Israel that day." XIV, 30. And: "And Israel saw the great hand which Yahweh did upon the Egyptians, and the people feared Yahweh and believed in Yahweh and in Moses His servant." XIV, 31. The Israelites did not fight for themselves, up to Refidim.

5. XXIV, 4; XXIV, 12; XXXI, 18; XXXII, 15–16; XXXIV, 1; XXXIV, 27–28; XXXIX, 30.

   Though Refidim is the first mention of writing, the first mention of "book" (*sefer*) is in the first verse of the fifth chapter of *In the Beginning Of.* Moses describes *In the Beginning Of* as the "book of the generations of man [*adam*]."

6. XXIV, 7.

7. XXXII, 32.

8. Moses thus refers to writing and the activities surrounding it altogether ten times—the number of propositions that are the subject of God's writing on the two tables and the number of meetings between Moses and God at Mt. Sinai.

9. In the epistolary novel, more than one character narrates. The narrative voice of the epistle, at least in the Western tradition, is a late Judaic or early Christian invention. Given the ceaseless search of moderns for markets, I'm sure there are exceptions to my categories.

   Maurice Blanchot has written about the narrative voice along these lines in "La Voix narrative," first published in *L'Entretien infini* (1969). See Blanchot, The Narrative Voice (the "he," the neuter), in The Gaze of Orpheus and other literary essays 133–43 (L. Davis trans. 1981).

10. Sometimes authors who speak in this voice nonetheless suggest a distance between the narrator and the author. To that extent, the narrator shifts to the second voice,

becoming a character. Often, narrators of the first sort assume the voice of a reporter, without assuming the responsibilities of a creator. The "fate" of the characters excuses the author from responsibility. Here too, the narrator shifts partly to the second voice, assuming the role of a character subject to the same fate as his creations.

11. XXXIII, 11. Jose Faur has discussed the special status of the narrator in the *Five Books*. See Faur, God as a Writer: Omnipresence and the Art of Dissimulation, 6 Religion & Intell. Life 31 (1989). Erich Auerbach's comparison between the Homeric and Mosaic narratives in Mimesis is less useful. See E. Auerbach, Mimesis (1946).

12. A suitable English translation of "Yahweh" might be a word formed from the first letters of "That Which Is What Has Been and Will Be": "Twiwhbawb." Yahweh is simply four letters in Hebrew: *Yud-Hay-Vov-Hay* (the Tetragrammaton). One writes it, in Hebrew, but does not say it. One says, instead, "*Adonai*," "Our Sire," "*Notre Seigneur.*" So one would write, "Twiwhbawb," and say, "Our Sire." See infra note 17.

    Unlike the Greek "*ousia*," which asserts changeless "being," "Yahweh" asserts "becoming," ceaseless moving from past to future through present. Maimonides equates "Yahweh" with "*ousia*":

    > Accordingly it has become clear to you that all names are derived or are used equivocally, as *Rock* and others similar to it. He, may He be exalted, has no *name* that is not derivative except the *name having four letters*, which is *the articulated name*. This name is not indicative of an attribute but of simple existence [*ousia*] and nothing else. Now absolute existence implies that He shall always be, I mean He who is necessarily existent. Understand the point at which this discourse has finally arrived.

    M. Maimonides, The Guide of the Perplexed, pt. I, ch. 63, at 156 (S. Pines trans. 1963) (footnote omitted). I do not feel the same need to conform to Aristotelian philosophy. I start with Hegel's critique of Aristotle. See G. Hegel, Science of Logic 94–118 (W. Johnston & L. Struthers trans. 1929).

    Maimonides does not disagree, however, that "Yahweh" signifies God in relation to persons. That is the significance of his striking claim that the Tetragrammaton is the "articulated name" of God. See infra note 123.

    The etymology of the English word "God" is disputed. According to the Oxford English Dictionary, a probable Aryan root is "*ghuto-m*," the neuter of the passive pluperfect of "*gheu*," whose root is either "to invoke" (Sanskrit, "*hu*") or "to pour, to offer sacrifice" (Sanskrit, "*hu*"). Hence, "*ghuto-m*" has been interpreted as "what is invoked" and "what is worshipped by sacrifice." 4 The Oxford English Dictionary, "god," at 267 (1970). Translators of the *Five Books* correctly use "God" for "Elohim," since "*elohim*," just like "god," names any object of worship as well as the one, true object. They also translate "Yahweh" by the spoken Hebrew substitute: "Our Lord." This translation is, of course, wrong, since the written English should translate the written Hebrew.

13. Rashi accounts for the different names of God:

    > This name (Elohim) denotes the attribute of justice (*din*), but it was changed into the attribute of mercy (*rah.amim*) through the prayers of the righteous. But the evil behavior of wicked people changes the attribute of mercy into the attribute of justice, as it is said, "and Y saw that the wickedness of man

was great," etc., "and Y said, I will erase," although it is the name denoting the attribute of mercy.

The Pentateuch and Rashi's Commentary: A Linear Translation into English (A. Ben Isaiah & B. Sharfman trans. 1950) ("Rashi's Commentary"), In the Beginning Of, VIII, 1 ("And Elohim remembered Noah"). (I use the system of transliteration which sounds "h." as "ch." I have altered the translation when I have thought necessary for consistency or precision.)

"Mercy" is the standard translation of the Hebrew "*rah.amim.*" The idea, more exactly, is "pardon," refraining from imposing a just sanction. Rashi thus views Yahweh as "anti-Elohim," inasmuch as Yahweh refrains from imposing Elohim's sanctions. I believe that the text gives evidence that Yahweh is something other than "anti-Elohim," though "anti-Elohim" overlaps with the attribute I claim for Yahweh. I call this attribute "collaboration," "friendship," the sympathy generated by working together on a joint project. (The notion of "collaboration" is also distinct from "*h.esed,*" which means "benevolence," the gratuitous conferral of a benefit, apart from duty.)

Thus collaborators can and should be merciful towards one another—release each other from duties, refrain from imposing sanctions suggested by justice. But collaborators will not approach pardon from the emotional posture of "mercy," which I believe to be the posture of a superior towards a fractious inferior. Collaborators approach pardon as the sympathy generated by working together on a joint project, as friends. To join Yahweh with mercy is to retain the "*elohim*" perspective, the perspective of a subject to a ruler. Yahweh's perspective, I suggest, is the perspective of coworkers on a joint project. Moses, we shall see, influences Yahweh, makes an impression on Yahweh, causes Him to change. He could not do this did Yahweh advocate only release from justice. See infra text accompanying notes 86–87, 140.

14. Today, following Hegel, we would characterize this ceaseless conversation as "self-consciousness." Though the parallels are by no means exact, perhaps the best translation of "Yahweh" is "Self-consciousness" (*Selbstbewusstsein*), and "Elohim," "Consciousness" (*Bewusstein*).

15. The Hebrew "*pesel,*" which is usually translated as "idol" or "graven image," has the root meaning of "statue."

16. Unlike Laurence Sterne, Elohim knows how to begin a novel. See L. Sterne, The Life and Opinions of Tristram Shandy, passim (1759).

17. See, e.g., Rashi's Commentary, Names, XXXI, 18 ("And he gave unto Moses, etc."):

> There is no "earlier" or "later" (i.e., there is no chronological order necessary) in Scripture. The incident of the (golden) calf preceded the commandment of the construction of the tabernacle by many days, for on the seventeenth of Tammuz were the Tables broken and on the Day of Atonement was the Holy One Blessed Be He reconciled to Israel, and on its morrow they began the contributions for the tabernacle, and it was set up on the first of Nisan (tanh.uma).

For an example of Rashi's deconstructive technique, look at his commentary on the missing letter "*vov*" in the word "*le-olam*" ("forever") in the sentence, "This is My name forever." Rashi says that concealment of the letter means that

God's name, Yahweh, ought to be concealed, that is, written but not spoken. See Rashi's Commentary, Names, III, 15 ("This is My name forever").

The refusal to say "Yahweh" may be seen as a sign of respect, flowing from the expected mutuality of the relationship with Yahweh, which in turn flows from the individuality of both Yahweh and the person addressing Him.

18. These events are described in Names, XVIII.

19. XVIII, 17–23.

20. XVIII, 27.

21. In the Wilderness, X, 29–32.

22. XV, 25.

23. Apart from Marah, the following are the references to decree (*h.ok*), rule (*mishpat*), and doctrine (*torah*—"teaching" or "learning," in non-latinate English):

    1. In the Beginning Of, XXVI, 5 (Yahweh promising Isaac to establish the oath He swore to Abraham and to multiply Isaac's seed, etc.): "because that Abraham harkened to My voice, and kept My charge, My commandments, My decrees and My doctrines."
    2. Names, XII, 14: "And you shall celebrate it [the Passover day] as a feast to the Yahweh throughout your generations, as a decree forever shall you celebrate it."
    3. XII, 17: "[T]herefore shall you keep this day [Passover] throughout your generations a decree forever."
    4. XII, 24: "And you shall observe this thing [smearing blood on the lintels], for a decree to you and to your children forever."
    5. XII, 43: "And Yahweh said to Moses and to Aaron: This is the decree of the passover".
    6. XII, 49: "One doctrine shall be to the native and to the stranger that sojourns in the midst of you [referring to the passover feast]."
    7. XIII, 9–10: "And it [the passover feast] shall be to you for a sign upon your hand, and for a memorial between your eyes; in order that the doctrine of Yahweh may be in your mouth; for with a strong hand Yahweh has taken you out from Egypt. And you shall keep this decree in its season from year to year."
    8. XV, 25–26: "There [Marah] He made for them a decree and a rule, and there He tried them. And He said: If you will diligently hearken to the voice of Yahweh your Elohim, and what is right in His eyes will you do, and you will listen to His commandments, and you will keep all His decrees, all the diseases which I have put on the Egyptians I will not put on you; for I am the Yahweh your doctor."

    There is one other reference to a "decree" prior to the Sinaitic revelation: Joseph's decree levying a tax of the fifth of each harvest for Pharaoh. In the Beginning Of, XLVII, 26.

24. Moses does not refer to the "Noachide Commandments" as any form of decree, rule, doctrine, or commandment. In the Beginning Of, IX, 1–7.

25. An excellent (and typical) text in the critical tradition is M. Noth, Exodus: A Commentary (J. Bowden trans. 1962) (first published as Das Zweite Buch Mose, Exodus in 1959).

26. XXXII, 30–XXXIII, 3, and XXXIII, 12–XXXIV, 3.

   I use brackets in the following summary to indicate that Moses is off the top of the mountain and not in solo conference with God. The numbered passages indicate that Moses is in solo conference, either on the top or slopes of the mountain, or in the Tent of Meeting.

   I also use boldface to indicate references to writing, reading and erasure. "**W1**" etc. indicate the references to writing; "**R**" indicates reading; and "**E**" indicates erasure.

   Moses met with God ten times at Mt. Sinai—eight (or possibly six) ascents, one meeting on the slopes of the mountain and one in the Tent of Meeting. The meeting on the slopes follows upon the scene in which God speaks the ten propositions. Moses hears God's rules (*mishpatim*), or specifications of the ten propositions (*dekalogoi*), during this meeting on the slopes, and writes them down. In the meeting in the Tent of Meeting Moses renegotiates the covenant. The eight meetings at the top of the mountain echo the eight references to writing, excluding reading and erasure. The meeting on the slopes echoes the reference to reading (reading is a sort of writing), and the meeting in the Tent of Meeting, where Moses renegotiates the covenant, echoes the reference to erasure (a sort of renegotiation).

   The text is silent in the venue of the seventh and eithth meetings (XXXIII, 1–3 and XXXIII, 5), unlike the venues of the other eight meetings, with respect to which the text is quite explicit. Though I choose to regard the venue of the two meetings about which the text is silent as the top of the mountain, the silences may be calculated to reinforce what the text will reveal as ambiguities about writing: W7 expresses an ambiguity as to whether Moses or Yahweh is writing the second set of tablets, and W8, an ambiguity as to whether the activities of Betsalel and Oholiav constitute writing or engraving. See infra text accompanying notes 45–48. The first reference to writing (*W1*) was in Refidim.

27. XIX, 3–6.

28. XIX, 7–8.

29. XIX, 8–13.

30. XIX, 14–20.

31. XIX, 20–24

32. XX, 1–17.

33. XX, 18–XXIII, 33.

34. XXIV, 1–14.

35. XXXI, 3.

36. Unlike the legal rules (*mishpatim*), Moses does not classify the instructions of the cult systematically as one sort or another of legal material. He does not call them either "*mishpatim*" (rules) or "*torah*" (doctrine). He refers to three of the instructions as "*h.ukim*" (decrees): XXVIII, 43 (a perpetual decree to Aaron and his sons to wear the priest's clothes); XXIX, 9 (the priesthood is a perpetual decree to Aaron and his sons); XXX, 21 (a perpetual decree to Aaron and his sons to wash their hands and feet when they minister at the altar).

   Rashi comments that decrees are "propositions" (*d'varim*) which are only the decree of the king, without any reason given for them. He cites the prohibition against wearing a mixture of wool and linen, against the eating of the flesh of swine, and the law of the red heifer, as examples. Rashi's Commentary, Names, XV, 26 ("All His decrees").

He opposes decree (*h.ok*) to rule (*mishpat*): rules have reasons:

> The Holy One Blessed Be He said to Moses: "It should not enter your mind to say, "I shall teach them the chapter or the law [*halakhah*] two or three times, until it will be fluent in their mouths as it is worded, but I shall not trouble myself to make them understand the reasons of the thing and its explanation." Therefore it is stated, "which thou shalt set before them"— like a table which is set and prepared for eating before a person.

Rashi's Commentary, Names, XXI, 1 ("Now these are the rules which you shall set before them").

I translate "*mishpatim*" as "legal rules", rather than the usual translation, "ordinances." "*Mishpat*" in other contexts means "sentence," either the sentence on a page or the sentence a judge imposes on a criminal, just as in English. The word "rule" in English has come to mean law accompanied by reason. It might have been better to translate "*mishpat*" as "ruling", since the Hebrew preserves an identity between "rule," which is general, and "sentence," which judges tailor to the individual. ("*Lish-pot*" means "to adjudicate.") The English does not. The closest one comes in English to preserving the identity between rule and sentence is the word "ruling": "The judge made a ruling." The English word "ordinance" has come, by contrast, to mean a minor municipal regulation. It is quite irrelevant here.

The use in Hebrew of the same word for rule and sentence may be asserting that rules are not "general" in the sense American law treats them as general. A "*mishpat*" speaks directly to the souls of individuals, as if it were a sentence.

37. XXIV, 15–XXXI, 18.
38. XXXII, 1–6.
39. XXXII, 7–16.
40. XXXII, 17–30.
41. XXXII, 31–34.
42. XXXIII, 1–3.
43. XXXIII, 5.
44. XXXIII, 12–XXXIV, 3.
45. XXXIV, 6–29.
46. XXXV, 1–XL, 38.
47. XXXIX, 30.
48. XXVIII, 36 and XXXI, 1–6.
49. XVII, 14–16.
50. XXIV, 4.
51. XXIV, 7.
52. XXIV, 12
53. XXXI, 18.
54. XXXII, 1–6.

55. XXXII, 15–16.

56. XXXII, 32.

57. XXXIV, 1.

58. XXXIV, 27–28. The last book (remembering the event in the form of writing, as opposed to writing a memory of the event, as in the second book) resolves the ambiguity in favor of Yahweh. Propositions, X, 4.

59. XXXIX, 30.

60. XXVIII, 36.

61. We will learn, or have already learned by reading the first reference to writing preceding the revelations at Mt. Sinai, that to read from memory is to read a record. See infra text accompanying notes 89–103.

62. XVII, 15.

63. XXVIII, 36.

64. XXXII, 32. See infra text accompanying Notes 66–79.

65. We will learn, or, as we shall see, have already learned by reading the Amalek, episode, to regard "forward reading" as "creative memory," acting as if one is in the process of creating a record. See infra text accompanying notes 89–103.

66. In the Beginning Of, VI, 7; VII, 4; VII, 23.

67. In the Beginning Of, VI, 11–13.

68. In the Beginning Of, VIII, 20–21.

69. In the Beginning Of, IX, 1–17.

70. See supra note 23.

71. XXXII, 7.

72. See 3 The Oxford English Dictionary, "destroy," at 260 (1970).

73. In the Beginning Of, VI, 13.

74. In the Beginning Of, VI, 7; VII, 4; VII, 23.

75. XXXII, 10 and 12.

76. In the Beginning Of, I, 2. Or, to "destroy" is to return creation to thought and extension.

    The text also offers the other logical formulation of "destruction." Yahweh "destroyed," In the Beginning Of, XVIII, 21, etc., Sdom and Amorrah with "sulphur and fire," In the Beginning Of, XIX, 24. Fire deconstructs creation to the other elemental substance, the "breath of Elohim."

77. See supra text accompanying note 64.

78. XVII, 14. See infra text accompanying notes 89–103.

79. II, 10. From the root *mashah* (to pull out from water).

80. He Called, XVIII, 13.

81. VI, 20.

82. S. Freud, Moses and Monotheism (1939). On the links between Freud's thesis and his discovery of psychoanalytic interpretation, see Susan Handelman's extraordinary work. S. Handelman, The Slayers of Moses: The Emergence of Rabbinic Interpretation in Modern Literary Theory 129–53 (1982).

83. XXXII, 10.

84. XXXII, 19–20. Blanchot has recognized the significance of Moses' destruction of the first set of tablets and the two writings of his "L'Absence du Livre," first published in *L'Entetrien infini* (1969). See M. Blanchot, The Absence of the Book, in The Gaze of Orpheus and other literary essays, supra note 9, at 145–60.

85. Though apparently false etymology, the Hebrew word for "eat" (*akhal*) is similar to the word for "annihilate" (*khalah*).

86. Compare the Baal Epic:

> With a sword split them asunder, with [another weapon] winnowed them, hacked them to pieces, scattered them, by fire burnt them, ground them, sowed the flesh in the field, portions to be eaten by birds.

Translated by Rabbi Marvin Petruck from the Ugaritic text in C. Gordon, Ugaritic Textbook, Texts in Transliteration: Cuneiform Selections, IABII, at 168, col. A (1965). For a poetic translation, see Ancient Near Eastern Texts Relating to the Old Testament, IABII, lines 31–35, at 140 (J. Pritchard ed. 3rd ed. 1969):

> With sword she [Anat] doth cleave him [Baal].
> With fan she doth winnow him—
> With fire she doth burn him.
> With hand-mill she grinds him—
> In the field she doth sow him.

> Birds eat his *remnants,*
> Consuming his *portions,*
> *Flitting from remnant to remnant.*

Baal, of course, was the god of the golden calf.

87. See supra note 13.

88. I am specifically not taking a positivist perspective here, which always tempts any observer of a legal system or other facts. A positivist perspective would regard putting rules in play as amending or ousting them. A positivist legal system would be "frank" (positivists are always "frank") about putting rules in play. That is one perspective. Nor do I reject the positivist perspective. It just does not supply the appropriate language to "play" non-positivistic legal systems, such as Moses'. One cannot be a persuasive positivist lawyer in Moses' system. One could in a positivist system.

89. XVII, 14–16. The brackets in "throne" and "Yahweh" are an attempt in English to mimic the omitted portions of the words in the Hebrew text. The word "*nissi*" refers ambiguously to both "banner" and "miracle."

90. Propositions, XXXI, 24.

91. When Moses first met Elohim, at the burning bush in Midian, he said:

> When I come to the children of Israel, and I say to them: The Elohim of your ancestors has sent me to you; and they say to me: What is His name? what shall I say to them? And Elohim said to Moses: I Will Be What I Will Be; and He said: Thus shall you say to the children of Israel: I Will Be has sent me to you. (III, 13–14)

Elohim leaves out the past and the present from the report Moses is to give of His name. Elohim thus tells Moses to draw the people away from their present and past as slaves. They should regard Elohim as future only.

92. Nor as Moses understood it at the burning bush, when he asked God for material, miraculous signs. IV, 1–9.

93. Rashi's Commentary, Names, XVII, 16.

94. XVII, 13.

95. XV, 2.

96. Propositions, XXXI, 19.

97. Propositions, XXXI, 11 ("you shall read this doctrine before all Israel in their ears").

98. Propositions, XXXI, 22.

99. Propositions, XXXI, 23.

100. Propositions, XXXI, 24.

101. Propositions, XXXI, 30.

102. Propositions, XXXI, 30–XXXII, 43.

103. Propositions, XXXI, 21.

104. XXIV, 3–4.

105. Rashi's first commentary is that the *Five Books* are a deed of Israel to the land of Canaan. Rashi's Commentary, In the Beginning Of, I, 1 ("In the beginning of").

106. XXXIV, 27–28.

107. XXXIV, 10–26.

108. And Yahweh said to Moses: Make two tablets of stone like the first, and I will write on the tablets the propositions that were on the first tablets, which you broke. (XXXIV, 1 [W6])

109. XXIV, 7.

110. From *In The Beginning Of* until the giving of the doctrine, and he wrote the commandments which were commanded at Marah.

Rashi's Commentary, Names, XXIV, 4 ("And Moses wrote").

111. Rashi's Commentary, Names, XXIV, 3 ("All Yahweh's propositions").

112. I mean "prior" in the text. Rashi's chronology is undoubtedly consistent with his omission of the ten propositions.

113 Rashi's Commentary, Names, XXXIV, 27 ("Write these propositions").

114 The Principles of Jewish Law 53 (M. Elon ed. 1975). For an extraordinary discussion of the relationship between writing and the oral tradition, see J. Faur, Golden Doves with Silver Dots: Semiotics and Textuality in Rabbinic Tradition (1986). See also G. Vermes, Scripture and Tradition in Judaism: Written and Oral Torah, in The Written Word: Literacy in Transition 79–95 (G. Baumann ed. 1986).

115. XXI, 24.

116. See Babylonian Talmud, Baba Kamma 83b.

117. XX, 18.

118. XX, 15–16.

119. See supra text accompanying notes 26–48.

120. See supra text accompanying notes 60–61.

121. Moses does not tell us the venue of two meetings, T6 and T7. Even so, my argument does not depend on assuming that T6 and T7 take place on top of the mountain. Moses' silence on the venue of T6 and T7 is significant for other reasons. In particular, Moses raises the issue of Yahweh's "presence" in two "placeless" meetings. Yahweh also tells Moses to tell the people to remove ornaments which they never put on and Yahweh knows they never put on.

122. Amongst others, which I do not explore.

123. When I say, "of his own devising," I mean nothing more than "without clear authority indicated in the text." Since one of Moses' doctrines is that Elohim absolutely rules all of creation, nothing can truly or strictly be "our own." But another of Moses' doctrines is that Elohim—the God of categorical, ruled and ruling attributes—is also Yahweh—the God of textual authority, the God of texts, the God of articulated (proper) names. See supra note 12. To look in Moses' text for clear authority, I would argue, is to regard God only as Elohim—God dictating the narrative to Moses as God dictates all of creation in the narrative. To say that Moses' text does not show clear authority for the covenant ceremony is to say that Moses, an articulated name, is endeavoring to collaborate with Yahweh, God as an articulated name. Moses' text must show an absence of clear textual authority—"*elohim*" authority—in order to establish collaboration with Yahweh. The absence of clear textual authority does not imply the absence of actual authority—the authority of deeds done collaboratively with Yahweh. On these matters, see M. Maimonides, supra note 12, pt. III, ch. 17, at 464–74.

Maimonides takes a contrary position in his Mishnah with Commentary, Sannhedrin Tenth Chapter, at 143–44 (Mossad Ha-Rav Kuk 1984–85):

> And the eighth principle [of Maimonides' thirteen basic principles of Judaism] is the Torah from the skies. And that we believe that this entire Torah found in our hands today is the Torah that was given to Moses. And that it stems in its entirety from the Mouth of Might. That is to say that there reached [arrived to, touched] him, entirely from Yahweh, a reaching which we call speech [*dibbur*], by a borrowing [metaphor]. [In note 29, at 151, Kapach prefers a Hebrew translation of Maimonides' Arabic as "transfer" rather than "borrowing".] And none knows the quality of this reaching but he, peace be upon him, to whom the reaching came. And that he is in the status of a scribe before whom we read, and he writes down everything— her [the Torah's] dates, stories and commands—and is thus called a decree- maker [*m'h.okek* also means engraver, or legislator]. And there is no differ- ence between "And the children of Ham and Kush and Egypt and Phut and Canaan," "And the name of his wife—Mehitabel, daughter of Matred," or, "I am Yahweh," and "Hear Israel, Yahweh is our Elohim, Yahweh is One." All is from the Mouth of Might, and all is Yahweh's Torah, perfectly whole, pure, sanctified, and true. And to them [the Rabbis] Menashe was not made a denier more than any other denier because he thought that within the Torah exist an inner core and an outer shell, and that these dates and ac- counts have no utility in them, and that Moses said them from his own knowledge, and this is the notion, "There is no Torah from the skies." They [the Rabbis] said that it comes with one who declares that the entire Torah is from the mouth of The Holy One Blessed Be He but for one verse that

The Holy One Blessed Be He did not say, but that Moses said from his own mouth. And this is, "Because he has scorned the word of Yahweh." May Yahweh rise above what the deniers say. But each letter in her [the Torah] has in her wisdom and wonders to whoever understands Him, Yahweh. And the end of her [the Torah's] wisdom will not be reached, "Longer in measure than land and broader than the sea." And a human has nothing to do but pray, following in the footsteps of David, the messiah [the annointed] of the Elohim of Jacob, who prayed, "Open my eyes that I may see wonders from Your Torah." And so, the Torah's interpretive tradition also comes from the Mouth of Might. And that which we make today, the form of the Sukkah, and the Lulav, and the Shofar, and fringes and Phylacteries and the rest, that is the form itself that Yahweh said to Moses, and that Moses said to us. And he merely acted as a conduit of Yahweh's agency, a faithful agent of Yahweh in what he brought. And the speech [*dibbur*] in which the eighth principle is indicated is said in: "With this shall you know that Yahweh sent me; for I have not done them of my own mind.

What I claim to be Moses' description of the authority of writing is, I believe, an accurate description of writing any of us does that we believe to be true. The writing is "our own," but we do not "properly" write it. The words flow as they must according to the logic of the text. We write, and we do not write. The text is written "through" our name. We must, as Derrida says in his paper for this colloquim, sign our name to take responsibility for the text. This is also Moses' theme.

124. XIX, 3–6.

125. XIX, 4–6.

126. XIX, 8.

127. XIX, 8–13.

128. XIX, 10–13.

129. XIX, 14–15.

130. In modern Hebrew "*h.ookah*" means "constitution." I translate it as "set of decrees," since I do not believe constitutions were a known art-form in Moses' time, and "*h.ookah*" is clearly closely related to "*h.ok*"/ "*h.ookim*".

131. "Heifer:" "A young cow, that has not had a calf." 5 The Oxford English Dictionary, "heifer," at 195 (1970).

132. In the Wilderness, XIX, 1–10.

133. Rashi comments:

> At Marah He gave them a few sections of a doctrine that they will be engaged with them: Sabbath, red heifer and legal procedures (*dinim*).

Rashi's Commentary, Names, XV, 25 ("There He put for them"). The rule was the rule of the Sabbath. The decree was the set of decrees (*h.ookah*) of the red heifer.

134. Rashi is silent on the question whether "Do not come near a woman" constitutes Moses' interpretation. He does, however, comment that the immediately preceeding words in Moses' text—"Be ready against the third day"—may be what we may interpret to be either error or interpretation:

> At the end of three days, which is the fourth day, for Moses added one day on his own accord, according to Rabbi Jose. However, according to he who says that on the sixth day of the month the ten propositions were given, Moses did not add anything. . . .

Rashi's Commentary, Names, XIX, 15 ("Be ready against the third day"). Rashi finds textual support for "Do not come near a woman" in Moses' second meeting with Yahweh, when Yahweh says, "And be ready." Rashi Commentary, Names, XIX, 11 ("And be ready"). It is interesting to note that Rashi's textual support for the proposition that Moses added a day is in the words immediately following "And be ready," when Yahweh says, "against the third day." In his comment, Rashi refers to XXIV, 4, which is the place where Moses engaged in writing without indicating in his text clear textual authority. May we read a tactful concession into Rashi's reference?

Professor Bleich agrees that the textual evidence for Moses' interpretation is clear, but tells me that the tradition does not regard "Do not come near a woman" as the correct example. He follows Rashi. Professor Bleich argues that Moses would have understood "sanctify them" as including the prohibition against touching a woman, since the portions of *He Called* devoted to ritual purity, XI–XVII, make this prohibition clear.

Apart from doubts I have about Moses' knowledge of the revelations in *He Called* at this moment in the narrative, my claim that Moses is interpreting when he adds "Do not come near a woman" does not depend on Moses being ignorant of all the revelations in *He Called*. Even under Professor Bleich's interpretation, it is undeniable that Moses "put together" Yahweh's command to sanctify with certain revelations in *He Called*. Moses' "putting together" constitutes interpretive activity, albeit less extensive than the activity I attribute to Moses at this point.

In any case, I do not see what in the tradition depends on choosing Moses adding a day over "Do not come near a woman" as the evidence that Moses is interpreting. Perhaps what is at stake is the nature of interpretation.

135. In the Wilderness, XI (rebellion of lusts); In the Wilderness, XII, 1–15 (Miriam and Aaron rebel against Moses for marrying a Cushite woman); In the Wilderness, XIII, 1–XIV, 39 (the people refuse to go immediately to Canaan); In the Wilderness, XVI, 1–35 (Korach's rebellion against Moses); In the Wilderness, XX, 1–13 (Moses struck the rock twice to produce water at Merivah [quarrel]); In the Wilderness, XXI, 4–9 (the people spoke against Elohim and Moses); In the Wilderness, XXV, XXXI (sexual relations with Moabite women; Baal and Pinchas' intervention; sexual relations of an Israelite man with a Midianite woman; war against the Midianites).
    In the Wilderness contains seven rebellions. An interesting number.

136. In the Wilderness, XXV, 17.

137. In the Wilderness, XXXI, 2.

138. In the Wilderness, XXXI, 17–20.

139. Korach rebels against Moses' and Aaron's claim to superior interpretive authority: "You take too much upon you, seeing the whole congregation are every one of them holy and Yahweh is in them." In the Wilderness, XVI, 3. Korach's is the fate of a "groundless" interpreter:

> And Moses said: Hereby you shall know that Yahweh has sent me to do all these works, for I have not done them of my own heart. If these men [Ko-

rach's party] die the common death of all men, and the visitation of all men be visited over them, Yahweh has not sent me. But if Yahweh create a creation, and the ground open her mouth, and swallow them up with all unto them, and they go down alive into the pit, then you shall know that these men have despised Yahweh. And when he finished talking all these propositions, the ground did cleave asunder that was under them. And the earth opened her mouth, and swallowed them up, and their households and all the men unto Korach and all their goods.

In the Wilderness, XVI, 28–32. Not all battles over interpretive authority have been resolved so definitively.

140. IV, 24–26.

141. XIX, 21–25.

142. Like Eve (*Khavah*). The text places Yahweh/Elohim in the same position as Eve—the image of an image. In *In the Beginning Of,* Adam gave Eve two names—*Khavah* (mother of life) (III, 20) and *Eeshah* (woman) (II, 24). God also has two names, Yahweh and Elohim.

The text links the Elohim name of God with the equal creation of man and woman, and the Yahweh name of God with the creation of *Khavah* from *Adam* (human) as the image of an image. In the first chapter of *In the Beginning Of,* Elohim creates both man and woman as equals. In the second chapter, Yahweh enters the text, and Yahweh/Elohim (a double) creates *Khavah/Eeshah* (a double) from the side of *Adam* (human), the image of an image. Yahweh/Elohim and *Khavah/Eeshah* are the equivalent relationships with *Adam* (human). They both have two names. They both collaborate with *Adam. Adam* (meaning "human") has no name.

Unlike the Christian tradition, in which God manifests "Himself" definitively as a male human, the Jewish tradition does not take a position on the gender of the Deity. Though it would be utterly perverse in traditional terms to press the point, Moses' text, inasmuch as it calls our attention to any notion of gender in speaking of the Deity, associates the articulated, proper name of God—God as collaborator, Yahweh—with *Khavah,* a woman.

143. XX, 15–18.

144. XX, 19–23.

145. XXIII.

146. XXIII, 32–33.

147. XXIV, 1–2.

148. XXIV, 4–11.

149. XXIV, 13.

150. In the Wilderness, XIX, 4.

151. Nadav and Avihu, Aaron's sons, clearly do betray the trust. In the only narrative "event" in *He Called,* Nadav and Avihu, "offered a foreign fire in the face of Yahweh, which He had not commanded them. And there came forth fire before Yahweh and annihilated them, and they died before Yahweh" (He Called, X, 1–2). Note the connection with Yahweh's threatened "annihilation" of the Israelites who made the golden calf, XXXII, 10. See supra notes 71–83 and accompanying text.

Meshekh Khokhmah, Meir, Simkhah ha-Kohen, Yerushalaim, Even Yisra'el (1980), an anthology of interpretations of the *Five Books,* contains the following comment: "And Yahweh was angry with me for what you have spoken . . . since I will die in this land and I shall not pass the Jordan" (Propositions, IV, 21–22). What is the purpose of this verse here, at this point in a chapter which deals with a warning against idolatry, both in the first and latter verses?

However, it is possible to say that the rationale for Moses' death in the desert is to prevent the Israelites from making him a god later on. As long as the generation which knew Moses from his childhood is still alive and sometimes may have had claims and grudges against him, there was no place for such fear. But the new generation which will enter Israel and will hear of all the signs and exemplars which Moses our Rabbi did, for it is possible that they may think of placing the shade of divinity upon him. For that purpose, Moses our Rabbi died in the desert together with that generation.

Therefore, when Moses our Rabbi warns Israel from idolatry, he is saying: "And Yahweh was angry with me for what you have spoken." It is your eyes that see that the Name-Blessed decreed death in the desert only because of you, so that you will not mistake me and make me too holy. From this it is easy for you to understand how much the Name-Blessed is fearful of your idolatry. And so, "watch yourself not to forget . . . and you have made yourself a statue [idol].

" Watch yourself . . . and you have made yourself a statue, a picture of all that Yahweh commanded you." (Propositions, XXIII, 23)

And so the writing should have said: "that Yahweh has not commanded you?" However, "statue and picture" means to say: that which makes an image or a copy of a living object, so that the statue in itself is by no means original, but it is an imitation and a mirror of something else.

That should have been the interpretation of the writing: You shall not make "a statue and a picture" from the commands that Yahweh commanded you, but you shall follow the original command as it is, and not an imitation of that command . . . (Ad-Mo-Re HH'K from Kutzahk Z-tz'l).

152. In the Wilderness, XII, 4–8.

153. In the Wilderness, XI, 25–29.

154. In the Wilderness, IX, 6–13.

155. XXXIII, 3, 20.

156. XXXIII, 11.

157. XXXIV, 6, 10–26.

158. XXXIV, 32. "Do" first, and "hear" after. A nice description of monitoring action according to conscience.

159. For a more detailed exposition of dynamic jurisprudence, in the context of a jurisprudence of right, see Jacobson, Hegel's Legal Plenum, 10 Cardozo L. Rev. 877 (1989). For the connection between dynamic jurisprudence and the revelatory tradition, see Jacobson, Autopoietic Law: The New Science of Niklas Luhmann, 87 Mich. L. Rev. 1647, 1685–87 (1989).

160. Some positivists, led by Hobbes, reject the legal status of customs. See T. Hobbes, Leviathan, ch. 26, at 204–06 (reprinted from the edition of 1651, 1909). To give legal status to customs, to unmarked norms, is to reject positivism: customary law

has no authoritative mechanism for marking. See, e.g., Montesquieu, The Spirit of the Laws 104 (T. Nugent trans. 1949) (loss of written codes, which imitated the Roman codes, led to the re-establishment of customary law during the Dark Ages).

Hobbes calls unwritten law "natural law," not custom. See T. Hobbes, supra, at 205–06. Natural law describes the legal state of nature—the way of the world in the absence of civil law (norms marked as law by a sovereign). The way of the world includes the laws of force, together with the drives and talents of persons. The talents include the capacity to discover laws of natural reason. Customary law, by contrast, includes attitudes and patterns of action that cannot be justified or explained by universal reason. Custom becomes law only when it is marked as such by a sovereign.

One could—and Montisquieu does—have a very different account of custom, in which the attitudes and patterns of action can be justified or explained by reasoning creatures in the exact situation of creatures with the attitudes or patterns constituting the custom. The reason justifying or explaining such attitudes and patterns is not universal, Spinozist reason, as it is for Hobbes, but the empathetic reason employed by Montesquieu in the doctrine of spirit (*esprit*). Custom becomes spoken law that need not be written; natural law, the unspoken law that need not be written.

161. H. L. A. Hart addresses the relevance of writing to law in H. Hart, The Concept of Law 92 (1961):

> The simplest form of remedy for the *uncertainty* of the regime of primary rules is the introduction of what we shall call a "rule of recognition." This will specify some feature or features possession of which by a suggested rule is taken as a conclusive affirmative indication that it is a rule of the group to be supported by the social pressure it exerts. The existence of such a rule of recognition may take any of the huge variety of forms, simple or complex. It may, as in the early law of many societies, be no more than that an authoritative list or text of the rules is to be found in a written document or carved on some public monument. No doubt as a matter of history this step from the pre-legal to the legal may be accomplished in distinguishable stages, of which the first is the mere reduction to writing of hitherto unwritten rules. This is not itself the crucial step, though it is a very important one: what is crucial is the acknowledgement of reference to the writing or inscription as *authoritative*, i.e., as the *proper* way of disposing of doubts as to the existence of the rule. Where there is such an acknowledgement there is a very simple form of secondary rule: a rule for conclusive identification of the primary rules of obligation.

Hart's insight, limited by his narrow, pre-Derridean understanding of "writing," can have pernicious intellectual effects in the wrong hands. For example, see M. Gagarin, Early Greek Law 2–17, 51–97, 121–41 (1986), one of the few texts to discuss the significance of reducing law to writing. Gagarin is most misled in his brief comments, heavily influenced by Hart, on the legal quality of Moses' code:

> The various Hebrew codes of law preserved in the Old Testament are different [than the early Greek codes]. They cover many different areas of human behavior, and some of the rules can scarcely be considered legal. (Id. at 133 n.37)

162. See T. Hobbes, supra note 160.

163. G. Hegel, Hegel's Philosophy of Right (T. Knox trans. 1967).

164. See Rosenfeld, Hegel and the Dialectics of Contract, 10 Cardozo L. Rev. 1199 (1989).

165. I shall leave unexplored the connections between common law and constitutionalism, in both its English and American versions. Suffice it to say that common law probably requires a background political doctrine of constitutionalism. On the connections between common law and English culture, see Goodrich, Rhetoric, Grammatology and the Hidden Injuries of Law, 18 Economy & Society 167 (No. 2, 1989), reprinted in P. Goodrich, Languages of Law: From Logics of Memory to Nomadic Masks 111–48 (1990).

166. Our founding text on writing in American jurisprudence is John Marshall's opinion in *Marbury v. Madison,* 5 U.S. (1 Cranch) 137 (1803). Marshall's insistence that written constitutions require judicial review of legislation for conformity to the constitution is a corollary of the common law position on writing. See also *Goldberg v. Kelly,* 397 U.S. 254, 272–74 (1969) (Black, J., dissenting). For commentary on Marshall's position, see Ferguson, We Do Ordain and Establish: The Constitution as Literary Text, 29 Wm. & Mary L. Rev. 1 (1987); Grey, A Constitutional Morphology: Text, Context, and Pretext in Constitutional Interpretation, 19 Ariz. St. L.J. 587 (1987); Grey, The Constitution as Scripture, 37 Stan. L. Rev. 1 (1984). See also Levinson, Writing and its Discontents, 3 Tikkun 36 (1988). Cf. supra note 165.

167. Inasmuch as positivist law is inscribed law, positivism assumes complete, cost-free access by ordinary legal persons to the written legal corpus. Positivism suggests two ways to assure access: (1) a simple, spartan code "put up in the market-place" in plain view of all citizens, or (2) a complex body of laws mastered by a coterie of legal specialists whom ordinary citizens hire upon need. The first either requires repression of variety and eccentric activity, or leaves most activities legally unregulated. The second makes two assumptions: (1) that citizens will know when they need to employ the services of a legal specialist prior to undertaking an activity, and (2) that they will have enough money to engage the services of the specialist once they know the need for one. If either assumption fails, then citizens will not have the adequate access to the services of legal specialists that written law requires. Failure of the first assumption is a failure of public legal education. Failure of the second is an economic failure respecting the distribution of legal services.

168. For an account of the growth and decline of case law in England see J. Dawson, The Oracles of the Law 1–99 (1968). For an account of the effects of literacy on English legal culture, see M. Clanchy, From Memory to Written Record: England 1066–1307 passim (1979). See also B. Danet & B. Bogoch, From "Say is Doing" to "Writing is Doing": The Institutionalization of the Written Word in Medieval English Legal Documents (1988) (unpublished manuscript on file with the author).

169. Philip Shuchman has collected and assessed data about the longevity and utility of published opinions in modern American law. See Shuchman, The Writing and Reporting of Judicial Opinions, in The Role of Courts in Society 319 (S. Shetreet ed. 1988).

4

Deconstruction and Legal Interpretation: Conflict, Indeterminacy and the Temptations of the New Legal Formalism
Michel Rosenfeld

DECONSTRUCTION AND THE CRISIS IN LEGAL INTERPRETATION

The practice of legal interpretation is mired in a deep and persistent crisis. This crisis extends both to the realm of private law[1] and to that of public law.[2] Even justices on the United States Supreme Court have increasingly become pitted against one another in fierce and often vituperative debate over questions of legal interpretation.[3]

In the broadest terms, the crisis reflects a loss of faith concerning the availability of objective criteria permitting the ascription of distinct and transparent meanings to legal texts. Moreover, this loss of faith manifests itself in the intensification of the conflict among the community of legal actors, the dissolution of any genuine consensus over important values, the seemingly inescapable indeterminacy of legal rules, and the belief that all the dispositions of legal issues are ultimately political and subjective. The roots of the crisis affecting legal interpretation can be traced back to the Legal Realists' critique of legal formalism,[4] and a comprehensive exposition of the multifaceted dimensions of this crisis can be found in writings of scholars associated with the Critical Legal Studies Movement ("CLS").[5]

Deconstruction appears to buttress the proposition that application of legal rules and legal doctrine is ultimately bound to lead to conflict, contradiction and indeterminacy. Any attempt at defining deconstruction is hazardous at best as there is disagreement over whether deconstruction is a method, a technique or a process based on a particular ontological and ethical vision.[6] Nevertheless, leaving these difficulties aside for now, it seems fair to assert that deconstruction postulates that writing precedes speech instead of operating as a mere supplement to speech,[7] stresses that every text refers to other texts,[8] and emphasizes that discontinuities between the logic and rhetoric of texts create inevitable disparities between what the author of a text "*means to say*" and what that text is "nonetheless *constrained to mean.*"[9] In other words, in the context of deconstruction, all texts (whether oral or written) are writings that refer to other writings. A text is not a pure presence that immediately and transparently reveals a distinct meaning intended by its author. Instead, from the standpoint of deconstruction, every writing embodies a failed attempt at reconciling identity and difference, unity and diversity and self and other. A writing may give the impression of having achieved the desired reconciliation, but such impression can only be the product of ideological distortion, suppression of difference or subordination of the other. Consistent with these observations, legal discourse—and particularly modern legal discourse with its universalist aspirations—cannot achieve coherence and reconciliation so long as it produces writings that cannot eliminate from their margins ideological distortions, unaccounted differences or the lack of full recognition of any subordinated other.

For those who take the challenge posed by deconstruction seriously, there can be no easy solution to the crisis affecting legal interpretation. Thus, for example, there cannot be a return to the narrowly circumscribed and simpler jurisprudence of original intent where the meaning of legal texts can be precisely framed by reference to some transparent, self-present intent of the framer of a constitution, a legislator or a party to a private contract. As Arthur Jacobson has persuasively argued in the course of his contribution to this symposium, even divinely prescribed law involves multiple writings, erasure and intersubjective collaboration.[10] Accordingly, in light of deconstruction, resort to the jurisprudence of original intent can only lead to a paralyzing idolatry[11] that forecloses any genuine intertextual elucidation of legal relationships. In other words, by isolating a particular writing and by elevating it above all other writings in such a way as to sever the intertextual links that constitute an indispensable precondition to the generation of meaning, the jurisprudence of original intent both promotes blind worship of the arbitrary and the unintelligible and blocks discovery of the intertextual connections necessary to endow legal acts with meaning.

Other attempts at overcoming the crisis affecting legal interpretation do not fare significantly better in the face of the challenge posed by deconstruction. For example, the claim that an adequate standard of legal interpretation can be fashioned by reference to the intersubjective perspective of an "interpretive community," [12] can only prevail through the suppression of difference and the subordination of the dissenting other. Indeed, as evinced by the very crisis sought to be overcome, legal interpretation becomes manifestly problematic *because* of conflict and fragmentation *within* the interpretive community. Therefore, unless appeal to the interpretive community comes on the heels of a genuine resolution of the aforementioned conflict and fragmentation, such an appeal would only make sense if it were accompanied by suppression of some of the clashing voices found in the interpretive community.

Attempts at solving the crisis affecting legal interpretation through submission of legal issues to an interpretive framework informed by extra-legal values also prove ultimately unsatisfactory. Take, for example, the law and economics approach according to which, in the most general terms, legal rules and legal doctrine should be interpreted in such a way as to promote wealth maximization.[13] Even assuming that law and economics were capable of yielding determinate outcomes, it would still fail to meet the challenge posed by deconstruction. This is because there is no consensus that the sole purpose of law is to advance the interests of *homo economicus*. And, to the extent that such consensus is lacking, the canons of legal interpretation derived from the law and economics approach would operate in disregard of the extra-legal values of a substantial portion of the community of legal actors. More generally, unless there is a society-wide consensus on extra-legal values, no canons of legal interpretation based on extra-legal values can possibly meet the objections raised from the standpoint of deconstruction.

There is a different kind of approach to the crisis of legal interpretation which may initially seem particularly attractive because it does not apparently rely on a concrete definition of the object of legal interpretation or on contested extra-legal values. This kind of approach stresses the *process* of interpretation above the object of interpretation or the substantive values espoused by the interpreter. It is a procedural approach in so far as it suggests that so long as legitimate interpretive procedures are followed, the interpretive outcome will be justified regardless of actual substantive disagreements concerning the object of interpretation or extra-legal values held by members of the community of legal actors.

A prime example of the approach under consideration is provided by Ronald Dworkin's theory of law as integrity developed in his *Law's Empire*. In its broadest outlines, the theory of law as integrity maintains that legal interpretation does not take place in a vacuum, but that it is an historically situated practice. An interpreter confronted with the task of determining what the law requires in a particular case must refer to relevant past instances of legal interpretation in order to be in a position to provide the best possible interpretation of the law in the case at hand. Dworkin analogizes the task of legal interpretation with that of writing a chain novel.[14] A chain novel, in Dworkin's conception, is a work of collective authorship, with each chapter being written by a different individual author. Each one of these authors is constrained by the previously written chapters and must insure that the chapter that he or she is about to write "fits" with the preceding chapters and contributes to the preservation of the integrity of the novel. Moreover, each author must endeavor to write the best possible novel consistent with the aesthetic constraints imposed by the need to incorporate already completed chapters. Similarly, in Dworkin's view, a judge confronting a hard case, must decide it on the basis of the best possible legal interpretation compatible with establishing a fit between the case at hand and the line of relevant historical judicial precedents in a way that preserves the integrity of law as a practice that evolves over time.

Dworkin's approach is intertextual, and while formal and procedural, it is not purely abstract. The substantive values of the community of legal actors do not directly figure in legal decisions but they are not simply severed from the process of legal interpretation. Traces of these substantive values are embedded in the legal precedents that confront the legal interpreter and must therefore be implicitly taken into account by the latter in his or her formulation of an interpretation that is compatible with precedent while preserving the integrity of the legal process.

Under closer scrutiny, Dworkin's theory of law as integrity fails to provide an acceptable solution to the crisis affecting legal interpretation. The principal reason for this failure is, as Alan Brudner has perceptively indicated, that the criterion of fit is too indeterminate to endow Dworkin's principle of integrity with a sufficiently concrete meaning.[15] Indeed, Dworkin's requirement of fit and integrity is reducible to an appeal to coherence made in an interpretive universe that has been stripped of intelligible criteria of coherence.[16] Either the measure of fit and integrity is based on some set of substantive values such as those embedded in certain relevant judicial precedents, or it is reducible to a purely formal and abstract notion that cannot be given any non-arbitrary concrete instantiation. If fit and integrity depend on particular substantive values—even if these values have been filtered through the interpretive process involved in the attempted reconciliation of judicial precedents—then Dworkin's theory is ultimately subject to the same criticisms as those theories which select one set of contested substantive extra-legal values over others or which posit some such values as dominant and the remainder as subordinate. On the other hand, if fit and integrity are to be understood in purely formal and abstract terms, cut off from all extra-legal substantive values, then the coherence which they seek is a mere transcendent ideal devoid of any particular concrete purchase.[17]

Although Dworkin's principle of integrity fails to deliver the means to overcome the challenge posed by deconstruction, the notion of integrity should not be discarded altogether. Indeed, integrity may play a useful, if more modest, role than that reserved for it by Dworkin, in the quest for a satisfactory solution to the crisis affecting legal interpretation. That role is a critical one, and it consists in serving as a constant reminder against the acceptability of a conception of law that tolerates the reduction of law to mere politics—that is, politics in the pejorative sense of the unprincipled, shrewd and often manipulative quest for advantage in the political arena. Even if no concrete embodiment of law as integrity is presently attainable, drawing attention to the absence of integrity may foster resistance against abandoning law to politics. In short, while legal interpreters may lack a positive conception of integrity, integrity can nevertheless still play the important negative role of standing in for the coherence and the principles that law that is reducible to politics lacks.[18]

DECONSTRUCTION AND THE RELATIONSHIP BETWEEN LAW AND POLITICS

What has been established thus far is that deconstruction confirms the genuine nature of the crisis affecting legal interpretation, and that from the standpoint of deconstruction none of the above mentioned approaches designed to overcome this crisis is capable of achieving success. An important question, however, has not been addressed yet, namely whether deconstruction lends support to the proposition that law is ultimately reducible to politics. In this section I address this question and conclude that deconstruction, as I understand it, requires rejecting that proposition. This conclusion, moreover, leads to a further question concerning what there is about law—or more precisely about legal interpretation—which makes legal practice irreducible to the practice of politics (in the sense specified above). This last question will be explored in the next section, principally by means of an assessment of the hypothesis that law can overcome the interpretive crisis that besets it and escape the strangehold of politics through a return to legal formalism. As we shall see, the legal formalism to be considered in the next section is not the same as that attacked by the Legal Realists and by members of CLS. It is a new, more sophisticated kind of legal formalism, and I shall concentrate on two significantly different conceptions of it put forth respectively by Stanley Fish and Ernest Weinrib. Finally, although I will argue that neither of these two conceptions of legal formalism is ultimately consistent with the insights derived from deconstruction, both of them will nevertheless prove useful in pointing towards ways in which law may be understood to remain distinct from politics.

The Meaning of Destruction and the Deconstruction of Meaning

To determine properly whether deconstruction supports the proposition that law is reducible to politics, it is necessary first both to further specify what is understood by deconstruction in the context of the present discussion and to articulate the rudimentary outlines of a workable conception of law. So far, I have stressed the following features of deconstruction: the priority of writing over speech, the intertextual nature of all writings, the dichotomy between what a writing is intended to mean and what it is constrained to mean, and the failure of every writing fully to account for difference or for the other. Moreover, the combination of the priority of writing and of its intertextual nature causes all meaning to be *deferred*. The meaning of a writing is neither immediately given nor self-present, but depends on some future reading (or re-collecting) of that writing's past. And since all reading involves a rewriting,[19] all meaning depends on a future rewriting of past writings as rewritten in the present writing which confronts the interpreter. A present writing is a rewritten past writing and a not yet rewritten future writing. Or put somewhat differently, a present writing is both a completion and an erasure[20] of a past (or no longer present) writing, and a text which must face erasure and completion by some future (or not yet present) writing in order to acquire meaning. In a word, from the standpoint of deconstruction, meaning depends on the transformation of what is no longer present by what is not yet present.

To the extent that meaning requires both a constant reinterpretation of the past and a perpetual openness to future reinterpretation, it would appear to dissolve in an infinite regress that travels in both temporal directions. Every past was once a future and then a present, and every future shall become a present and then a past, and accordingly meaning can seemingly never become ascertained. Or more precisely, inasmuch as present writings are opaque, paradoxically, the meaning of a text could possibly be anything except that which it presently appears to be. Consistent with this analysis, moreover, the crisis affecting legal interpretation could never be overcome so long as one shared the perspective of deconstruction. Indeed, if the search for meaning leads to an infinite regress, those with the greatest power or cunning will impose their (arbitrary) meaning, and law will dissolve into politics.[21]

In the conception referred to above, deconstruction is viewed exclusively as an interpretive method or technique. And, taken as a mere interpretive technique disconnected from any larger framework, deconstruction seems only fit to destabilize all meanings by systematically unveiling the contradictions embedded in every writing and by constantly but fruitlessly inverting the binary oppositions (e.g., mind/nature, subject/object, masculine/feminine) that circumscribe every text. In contrast to this latter conception of deconstruction, however, there is another which, while preserving a necessary link between past, present and future writings, does not inescapably lead to the conclusion that all ascriptions of meaning turn out to be arbitrary.[22] This alternative conception does not cut off the process of deconstruction from the realm of ontology or from that of ethics.[23] Indeed, in this alternative conception, the deconstructive process implies an ontology of the unbridgeable separation of the self from the other (or put in a way that seems less likely to provoke a return to the sterile interplay of binary oppositions, an ontology of infinite postponement of the complete reconciliation of self and other). Moreover, this ontology is supplemented by an ethic of inclusion of, and care for, the other—an ethic which must always be attempted and renewed but which can never be satisfied because the meaning of "inclusion" and of "care" can never be sufficiently determined to the extent that the self always remains (somewhat) estranged from the other. In short, in this alternative conception of deconstruction, on the ontological plane, difference can never be fully reintegrated within a totality that encompasses self and other, whereas on the ethical plane, difference both incessantly requires and perpetually frustrates the gesture of inclusion and caring extended towards the other.[24]

Within the alternative conception of deconstruction just outlined, meaning although never permanently fixed does not thereby become purely arbitrary. Because the requirements of ontology and those of ethics are inscribed in history—that is, because they leave their mark on the succession of concrete historical social formations—at every moment, they constrain the range of possible legitimate meanings without ever imposing a single, fully determinate meaning. Hence, ontology and ethics, which are always projected both towards the past and towards the future, constantly open and close possible paths of interpretation without ever settling on any single, distinct, clearly articulated and exhaustively circumscribed meaning.

Given that the alternative conception of deconstruction advanced here is thoroughly committed to the intertextual nature of all writings, the escape from the pure arbitrariness of meaning can only be effectuated by engaging texts at a proper level of abstraction. Indeed, at too high a level of abstraction, all meanings appear to be fully interchangeable, as every writing is grasped in its infinite regress along the opposite directions of its endless past and its perpetually incompleted future. At too low a level of abstraction, on the other hand, meanings would remain completely opaque as myopic concentration on the features of individual texts would tend to conceal or obscure the relationships between such texts and other texts.

A proper level of abstraction can be reached, however, by grasping texts in their unfolding as part of the process of historical formation that gives shape to the ontology of postponement of the reconciliation of self and other and to the ethical call to the other renewed by each such postponement. In each historical epoch, there are writings which are *meant* to reflect a concrete vision of the desired reconciliation between self and other, but which are *constrained* by the very vision they embrace to produce yet another picture of the further postponement of such reconciliation. Moreover, the latter picture serves to expose the limits of the particular vision or reconciliation which it reflects. And, as they become manifest, these limits suggest particular forms which the renewed ethical call to the other might have to take under the circumstances. In other words, the very limits of a vision of reconciliation indicate how that vision has failed, and suggest to the about to be renewed ethical call to the other which particular failures should be avoided, and which obstacles need to be overcome. Similarly, each emerging vision of reconciliation is informed by the particular failures and contradictions of its historical predecessors as well as by the shortcomings of recent ethical calls to the other.

Conducted at the proper level of abstraction and applied to the historical succession of diverse forms of attempted reconciliation between self and other, intertextual interpretive practice does not culminate in aimless conflict and hopeless indeterminacy. Whereas it cannot avoid conflict, such interpretive practice can reveal particular conflicts which invite a finite range of possible solutions. Similarly, such interpretive practice unavoidably leads to indeterminacy, but not to the kind of indeterminacy which justifies virtually every conceivable meaning. Rather, it is the kind of constrained indeterminacy that results from the interplay between semantic path openings and closings guided by the actual historical succession of intertextual forms of attempted reconciliation between self and other.

It may seem implausible, given the unlimited intertextuality of all writings, that any particular meaning should be able to muster sufficient strength—albeit only for a short fleeting moment—to resist being swept away in the ceaseless exchange of semantic markers. Or put somewhat differently, it may seem inconceivable, in light of the past and future infinite regresses to which the intertextual ascription of meaning is subject, that the temporary emergence of any particular meaning would be the product of anything but an arbitrary purely subjective choice. And if this proved to be the case, then we would all wind up permanently trapped between the poles of an insurmountable binary opposition pitting the subjective against the objective.

Meaning, however, is neither subjective nor objective, but intersubjective. Also, acknowledgment of a ceaseless exchange of semantic markers does not compel the conclusion that on a given historical occasion any meaning could be legitimately substituted for any other meaning. These two propositions may not be self-evident, but are consistent nonetheless with the alternative conception of deconstruction being advanced here.

Analogies Between Semantic Value in Intertextual Exchanges and Economic Value in Market Exchanges

To shed further light on the plausibility of these two propositions, it might be useful to refer to certain parallels between the production of semantic value through intertextual exchange and the production of economic value through the exchange of commodities in the marketplace.[25] Assuming a fully developed rational market with participants who are utility-maximizers, the exchange of commodities depends on such commodities having value.[26] More specifically, exchange depends on commodities having two different kinds of value: use value and exchange value.[27] Unless a commodity had some use value for some ultimate consumer, no one would desire to acquire it, and there would be no point in exchanging it. On the other hand, unless commodities had exchange value, that is unless they were commensurable, they could not become objects of rational exchange.

In the most rudimentary market imaginable, counting with two individual participants who possess equality in bargaining power, exchange value and use value appear to be closely linked to one another, and all market values appear to be subjective. In such a market, for example, it would seem as rational for the market participants to exchange two apples for three oranges as it would for them to exchange three apples for two oranges. That is because the choice between these two transactions is heavily dependent on the participants' respective relative subjective preference as between apples and oranges, and because the exchange value of apples relative to oranges appears to be a direct function of the relative use value of apples to oranges for each of the two participants.

In a fully developed market economy with huge numbers of market participants, on the other hand, market values seem to be objective, while use value and exchange value appear devoid of any palpable connection. Indeed, in a fully developed perfect market, the well-established and well-publicized price of a widely traded commodity does not seem susceptible to change as the result of the efforts of any individual competitor.[28] Moreover, no matter how intense the desire of an individual consumer may be for a particular commodity, such consumer would appear to have no measurable effect on the exchange value of the commodity in question. In a fully developed market, therefore, it would be irrational for anyone to buy a commodity (significantly) above, or to sell it (significantly) below, its market price.

Upon closer scrutiny, the values of commodities on the rudimentary market are no more purely subjective than they are strictly speaking objective on the fully developed market. In both cases, such values are intersubjective as they are the product of a combination of, or a compromise between, the diverse subjective desires which seek fulfillment through market transactions.[29] Even in a rudimentary market with two participants, the terms of the contract for the exchange of commodities are not the product of the subjective will of either of the two participants, but rather the product of their common will which is intersubjective.[30] On the other hand, in a fully developed market, if the value of a widely traded commodity appears to be objective, it is not because it is determined in relation to some objective criterion that is independent from the subjective desires of the market participants. Indeed, in a fully developed market just as in a rudimentary one, value is the product of an intersubjective compromise involving the subjective input of each market participant. The only difference between these two markets is that in the fully developed market the subjective input of each individual participant becomes so infinitesimal relative to the sum of subjective inputs as to become virtually imperceptible.

As we move from the rudimentary to the fully developed market the precise relationship between use and exchange value becomes more difficult to grasp. In a fully developed market, most exchanges may be made among traders who are several steps removed from a commodity's ultimate consumer. To the extent that such traders concentrate on trading the commodities in which they deal they are likely, for the most part, to ignore the use value of those commodities. On the other hand, in a sophisticated, fully developed market, the use value of a commodity may be more the product of an intersubjective compromise between the exchange objectives of traders and the subjective desires of ultimate consumers than merely the product of only the latter.[31] Be that as it may, however, even in the most sophisticated of modern markets, where money makes all commodities fungible from the standpoint of exchange, the exchange of commodities only makes sense so long as there is some dynamic relationship between use value and exchange value.

Useful parallels can be drawn between the production of semantic value through intertextual exchange and the production of economic value through the exchange of commodities in two principal areas. First, the intersubjectivity of all meaning is produced in a way that is analogous to the generation of intersubjective values in the economic marketplace. Second, the manner in which the interchange of semantic markers is prevented from resulting in a senseless and arbitrary ritual structurally resembles the process by which use values become engrafted upon exchange values in order to prevent market transactions from becoming irrational and pointless.

All meaning—or at least all meaning relating to events and transactions in the social and political sphere where the community of legal actors is located—is intersubjective in that it requires some collective consensus or compromise concerning the setting of certain particular intertextual relationships. In other words, all meaning-endowing interpretations in the context of the social and political sphere require a collaborative collective rewriting of historically situated textual material that confronts a group of actors. Moreover, such collaborative rewriting may be the product of a pre-existing agreement concerning relevant values among the group of actors involved, or the product of a dialogical compromise bearing a marked resemblance to the process of contract formation in the economic marketplace.[32]

The size of the group of actors that engages in collaborative rewriting can range from a minimum of two to a maximum of all actors confronted with the task of interpreting the same text. Moreover, any actual community of actors is confronted with the task of interpreting a multitude of different texts. Agreement concerning the interpretation of some of these texts may be widespread, while at the same time the interpretation of other texts may be highly contested. Also, the nature and scope of particular widespread agreements is bound to affect the kind of interpretive disagreements likely to be produced in a given community of actors.[33] In general, consensus, compromises and conflicts are fluid rather than fixed because the relationship between them is dynamic as any change in one of the three is bound to produce corresponding changes in the other two. Finally, even when an attempt at a particular collaborative rewriting fails completely because not even two actors can agree to take a common standpoint, such failure need not undermine intersubjective values and may in fact serve to reinforce them. Indeed, the search that culminates in the failure to reach agreement with respect to some values may itself have been prompted by agreements concerning other values, and that search may serve to reinforce commitment to those other values. Thus, for example, two would-be contractors, whose efforts fail because they cannot agree on mutually acceptable terms of exchange, may nevertheless by their very efforts reaffirm their joint commitment to the values of market competition and freedom of contract.

Any semantic value generated through a collaborative rewriting is intersubjective regardless of whether it seems subjective (as the product of only a handful of actors) or objective (as the product of virtually an entire community of actors). So far, therefore, the analogy between the intersubjective production of semantic value and the intersubjective production of economic value appears to hold nicely. It may be objected, however, that there is a crucial disanalogy between these two modes of producing values. According to this objection, the very nature of economic exchange makes it impossible for less than two actors to generate economic value in a free market economy. But there is nothing inherent in the nature of interpretive practice which compels the conclusion that a single individual acting alone cannot rewrite texts in a way that generates new semantic values.

If this objection were valid and rewriting were not necessarily collaborative, then meaning could be purely subjective and interpretation an essentially solipsistic activity. At least from the perspective of the alternative conception of deconstruction advanced here, however, this objection misses the mark. Indeed, even if interpretation were not collaborative in the sense of involving a group of actors jointly engaged in the present rewriting of a past writing, it would still have to be collaborative and intersubjective to be meaningful. At the very least, interpretation requires a collaboration over time between a past actor, a present actor and a future actor. A reading of a past writing can only be conceivable as a rewriting if there is some intersubjective basis upon which semantic connections between the past writing and the rewriting can be established. Furthermore, to the extent that the meaning of a rewriting depends on future readings of that rewriting, interpretation also depends on future readings of that rewriting, interpretation also depends on the existence of an intersubjective basis for the establishment of semantic connections between present and future writings. On the other hand, if such intersubjective basis were lacking, the interpretation of a past writing would not involve a rewriting (a reading being impossible unless writer and reader share a common language) but an original writing devoid of any *meaningful* connection to any past or future writing. Hence, a writing is meaningless unless it is the product of an intersubjective collaboration (or co-laboration) over time that involves a minimum of three actors.

That interpretation is intersubjective and collaborative may be a guarantee against meaninglessness, but it is no guarantee against the unrestricted interchangeability of all meaning. A rewriting must both bear some semantic connection to, and some semantic difference from, that of which it is a rewriting.[34] Accordingly, the question becomes whether the degree of such connection and difference is in any way constrained, or whether any degree of connection no matter how tenuous, and any degree of difference no matter how extreme, are acceptable provided that they are the product of a collaboration among a minimum of three persons. If the answer is the latter, then virtually every semantic marker would seem to be exchangeable for any other such marker, and rewriting would be encumbered by practically no constraints. If the answer is the former, on the other hand, then the question becomes one of knowing which constraints to impose and how those constraints would make it possible to distinguish between acceptable and unacceptable rewritings.

Consistent with the alternative conception of deconstruction advanced here, constraints regarding the process of rewriting are both necessary and provided by the ontology and ethics that underlie deconstruction. As already mentioned,[35] the operative ontological constraint narrows the range of acceptable rewritings to those which recast the concrete historical writing upon which they elaborate as a vision of a failed reconciliation between self and other and expose the specific aporias, contradictions and blind spots that require the further postponement of the desired reconciliation. Moreover, the operative ethical constraint requires that rewritings as writings (a rewriting being a writing for a future rewriter) specify a renewed ethical call to the other from the standpoint of exceeding the specific historically grounded limits of the vision of reconciliation which has just been interpreted as inadequate.

As also already pointed out,[36] the ontological and ethical constraints imposed by deconstruction do not usually dictate a single determinate meaning. Rather they operate through interconnected path opening and path closing mechanisms which legitimate certain meanings and bar others. Moreover, these mechanisms appear to be constraining without necessarily directly imposing or barring any isolated individual meaning in a way that is reminiscent of how use value indirectly constrains the definition of exchange value in a fully developed market. In both cases, an otherwise seemingly unconstrained, unstoppable and open ended exchange process is kept within certain bounds through the indirect application of normative markers that endow exchange with meaning through punctuation of its flow.

Ontological and Ethical Constraints of Deconstruction and Rejection of Mere Politics

The interconnected path opening and path closing mechanisms associated with the ontological and ethical constraints imposed by deconstruction frequently leave a fair amount of leeway to interpreters who are about to rewrite particular historical writings with which they are confronted. If two interpretive avenues are equally open, only in the future could it become possible to determine whether either of the two would have been better than the other.[37] Because of this, the indeterminacy that inevitably accompanies the interpretive process makes room for potential abuses. By weaving in and out of different open paths of argumentation, an interpreter may skirt his or her ethical obligation and subvert the interpretive process to personal advantage. Indeed, since the complete and definitive reconciliation of self and other is subject to perpetual postponement, every attempted reconciliation pursued along an open path produces a certain configuration of benefits and burdens to be divided between self and other. To the extent that these configurations vary from one form of attempted reconciliation to another, an unscrupulous interpreter may exploit the availability of several genuine avenues of attempted reconciliation, by shifting back and forth from one to the next so as to maximize personal benefits and to minimize personal burdens.

To prevent abuses, interpreters should be held to a standard of integrity according to which shifts from one available interpretive avenue to another would only be justifiable if accompanied by a full and

sincere assumption of all the burdens associated with the latter interpretive avenue. Consistent with this requirement of integrity, an
interpreter may not resort to an available interpretive avenue to press
for an advantage on one occasion, and then on the next occasion,
abandon that interpretive avenue in favor of another in order to avoid
a burden. On the other hand, an interpreter may switch from one
available interpretive perspective to another if that interpreter sin-
cerely believes that the latter perspective is better suited to promote
the attempted reconciliation sought and if he or she is fully prepared
to assume all the burdens that might flow from adoption of the new
perspective.[38]

Any interpretive practice that operates within the ontological and
ethical constraints of deconstruction, including the requirement of integrity, cannot be reducible to politics in the pejorative sense identified
above.[39] These constraints, indeed, are clearly incompatible with any
unprincipled, shrewd or manipulative quest for advantage in the arena
of intersubjective relationships. Accordingly, deconstruction may provide a satisfactory solution to the crisis affecting legal interpretation.
Whether deconstruction actually furnishes such a solution, however,
depends on whether its ontological and ethical presuppositions are
compatible with law and legal interpretation.

Before exploring whether deconstruction (in the alternative version
advanced here) may be legitimately applied to law, it is necessary
briefly to further consider the universe that lurks beneath the surface
of deconstruction. Deconstruction's presupposition of the perpetual
postponement of the reconciliation of self and other implies the existence of an intersubjective universe which is inevitably split into self
and other. Moreover, deconstruction's postulation of the ethical necessity of the constant renewal of the call to the other makes it imperative to engage in a search for vehicles of social interaction which
promise (although they will be eventually proven not to be able to
deliver on their promises) the possibility of a form of reconciliation
between self and other that allows for the concurrent full flourishing
of self and other. Finally, the concepts of self and other should not be
understood as referring to fixed entities, but instead as designating
relationships respectively of identity and of difference or alterity.
Thus, depending on the particular context, both "self" and "other"
may refer to an individual or a group, to an economic class or an
ethnic minority, to tribes or nations, and to temporary as well as to
permanent groups. Also two (individual or collective) actors may con-
currently be part of the same self for some purpose, while standing
vis-a-vis one another in a relation of self to other for some other pur-

pose. For example, white men and women may constitute a single self in the context of racism against blacks—that is, such men and women identify with one another as being white and relate to blacks as "the other"—and self and other in the context of the relationship between the sexes, where difference is defined along gender lines.

Modern Law's Possible Embrace of Deconstruction to Overcome Mere Politics

Consistent with the preceding observations, law can embrace deconstruction if it constitutes itself as a practice oriented towards a universe of social actors split into self and other, and if it conceives its mission as seeking to bridge the gap between self and other without sacrificing or compromising either of the two.[40] To be sure, not all conceptions of law satisfy these two conditions. Nevertheless, a strong case can be made that the complex legal systems of modern Western democracies in general, and the American legal system rooted in the common law and a written constitution, in particular, do in fact satisfy these two conditions.

In their broadest outlines, modern legal systems prevalent in Western democracies are characterized by, among other things, group pluralism;[41] general rules of law that are universally applicable to all regardless of status or group affiliation,[42] and that prescribe duties and entitlements to individuals;[43] and the separation of legislation from adjudication, which is designed to buttress the autonomy of law by sharply separating the function of applying legal norms to particular cases from the political function.

Group pluralism obviously entails social divisions into self and other. General rules of law universally applicable to all actors regardless of their group affiliations, on the other hand, can be viewed as evincing attempts at reconciliation of self and other within an order of duties and entitlements that transcends the divisions arising from the clash of divergent group interests. These attempts at reconciliation, however, are ultimately doomed to fail. This is because whereas they may reconcile antagonistic interests from a formal (and/or procedural) standpoint, even universal laws cannot avoid, from a substantive standpoint, privileging certain antagonistic interests over others.[44] So long as a legal system operates in the context of group pluralism, and through the application of general laws that are universally applicable, therefore, law meets the two conditions that entitle it legitimately to embrace deconstruction.

Because of its constitution and common law tradition, the American legal system encompasses a conception of law that seems particularly well suited to incorporate deconstruction. The American constitution is designed for a pluralistic society with antagonistic interests, and it seeks to reconcile self and other through prescriptions for accommodation designed to allow both of them to flourish. For example, the Constitution embraces federalism to reconcile local interests and national interests through a complex interplay between identity and difference.[45] Another proof of the Constitution's commitment to a pluralistic society and to the attempted reconciliation of self and other is provided by the adoption and judicial elaboration of the Bill of Rights. The Bill of Rights recognizes the split between the individual and the community, and seeks to prevent communal suppression of individual difference through the grant of entitlements that impose antimajoritarian limits on the democratic process. The long history of litigation under the Bill of Rights indicates, however, that no stable or lasting reconciliation between self and other, identity and difference, or individual and community seems likely under the auspices of the Constitution or as a consequence of the interplay between democratic majoritarianism and constitutional restraints.[46]

The very nature of the common law makes it a prime candidate for the incorporation of deconstruction. The common law involves the fashioning of legal rules and the allocation of duties and entitlements by judges who seek to reconcile precedents. As Arthur Jacobson notes, the common law requires three writings: a past writing, a present writing and a future writing.[47] The common law judge is confronted with antagonistic litigants and must extract a rule of law designed to settle the dispute before him or her from a reading (rewriting) of judicial precedents. The judge's decision is a present writing that rewrites the past writings that count as precedents. The present writing that embodies the judicial decision allocates entitlements and duties among the litigants and partakes in the formulation of a rule of law designed to provide a framework for the reconciliation of antagonistic interests such as those possessed by the litigants. The rule of law implicit in the present writing of a deciding judge, however, may well be insufficiently articulated to be grasped before it is "rewritten" in the writing of some future judicial decision.[48] Accordingly, the final formulation of the rules of law that account for the attempted judicial reconciliation of self and other in the hands of common law judges must always be postponed until the dusk will have settled on the last of the future adjudications.

As Jacobson has pointed out, common law is a "dynamic jurisprudence" rather than a "static" one.[49] For present purposes, the key distinction between these two kinds of jurisprudence is that dynamic jurisprudences fill the universe of social interaction with legal relationships whereas static jurisprudences draw sharp lines between legal relationships and other intersubjective relationships which remain beyond the reach of law. Dynamic jurisprudence is concerned primarily with legal personality while static jurisprudence is above all preoccupied with order.[50] Accordingly, as a dynamic jurisprudence common law appears to be more indeterminate and open-ended than static jurisprudences.[51] But because its dynamism is potentially all-encompassing, and because it is concerned with personality rather than mere order, common law is suited to undertake a comprehensive reconciliation of self and other within the sphere of legal relationships. Static jurisprudences, on the other hand, cannot even hope to seriously attempt such a reconciliation as they are structurally impeded from reaching the other whose intersubjective dealings extend beyond the realm of law.

In sum, some conceptions of law—and, in particular, the American legal system with its constitution and its common law tradition—are well suited to embrace deconstruction as an internal process designed to map a realm of legitimate legal relationships. Accordingly, deconstruction is in principle capable of solving the crisis affecting legal interpretation. It remains to be determined, though, *how* deconstruction might inform the practice of legal interpretation so as to successfully repel the threat of absorption into the universe of mere politics. One tempting hypothesis, which will be critically examined in the next section, is that law can escape from mere politics by embracing some recently conceived revamped versions of legal formalism.

THE NEW LEGAL FORMALISM

Two significantly different conceptions of legal formalism have emerged, which may be referred to respectively as the "old formalism" and the "new formalism." The old formalism holds that application of a legal rule leads to determinate results due to the constraints imposed by the language of the rule.[52] The new legal formalism envisions law as an internally unfolding dynamic practice that carves for itself a domain of social interaction that remains distinct from the sphere of politics.[53] The new legal formalism depends neither on the belief in the transparency of language nor on the requirement that legal doctrine or legal rules lead to determinate outcomes.[54] Nevertheless, the new legal formalism is properly considered to be a type of formalism to the extent that it maintains that something internal to law rather than some extra-legal norms or processes determines juridical relationships and serves to separate the latter from non-juridical social relationships, including political ones.

As will become obvious soon, the two different versions of the new legal formalism—respectively formulated by Stanley Fish[55] and by Ernest Weinrib[56]—which will be discussed here differ vastly from each other in several key respects. They do share certain important features in common, however, which make them both attractive candidates to carry out the interpretive tasks confronting law conceived as having internalized deconstruction.[57] Fish's central point is that legal formalism is not something given, but something which must be constantly made and remade.[58] In the dynamic process of making itself formal, moreover, law internalizes values from the ethical and political world and transforms them into legal values.[59] For Weinrib, on the other hand, what endows juridical relationships with a separate identity are the forms of justice, namely corrective and distributive justice. But to establish the meaning and separate identity of juridical relationships, it is not sufficient to contemplate the forms of justice like Platonic forms or the forms of geometry.[60] The relationship between the forms of justice and particular juridical relationships is immanent, and it can only be made explicit by unearthing the links that connect particular socially and historically situated juridical relationships to the more abstract forms of justice which endow such juridical relationships with meaning.[61]

The principal similarity between these two approaches to legal formalism lies in their reliance on a dynamic process that leads to the immanent unfolding of the connections pointing towards the unity of law's content and its form. With this in mind, let us now look more closely at these two versions of the new legal formalism to determine whether, and how, they might be used to solve the crisis affecting legal interpretation in the context of law conceived as having internalized deconstruction.

The New Formalism of Stanley Fish

The making of law's formal existence, according to Fish, involves a double gesture. Law must absorb and internalize that which threatens it from the outside, and in particular ethical and political values.[62] But, at the same time, law must deny that it is appropriating extra-legal values.[63] In other words, the law cannot simply carve for itself a path that remains beyond ethics and politics. Yet the law cannot admit dependence on the ethical and the political, for that would threaten to deprive law of any distinct identity. To resolve this dilemma, the law simultaneously incorporates ethical and political values and denies that it is doing so. This incorporation, however, is not all-encompassing. In the process of making itself formal, the law only incorporates certain ethical and political values while repelling others.

Law's efforts to achieve a formal existence must be ceaseless and energetic, according to Fish, because the law must constantly overcome formidable obstacles to carve out and sustain an identity of its own.[64] Economical, ethical and political pressures have been poised throughout history to overwhelm law, but legal doctrine, argues Fish, against all odds, has managed to survive. And it is this sheer survival that sustains law's identity.[65]

Fish believes that, through numerous stratagems, legal doctrine can not only defuse ethical and political controversy but also conflicts regarding interpretation.[66] Because he is thoroughly committed to the proposition that all meaning is contextual, Fish cannot endorse the old legal formalists' belief that the plain meaning of legal language enables the application of legal doctrine to produce determinate results. Fish's new legal formalism postulates instead that plain meaning is "made"—that is, that it is fashioned or contrived—through the force of rhetoric.[67]

The "making" of (plain) meaning also involves a dynamic process of incorporation and rejection which remains largely concealed through the force of rhetoric. But to preserve itself from a complete surrender of law to rhetoric, legal interpretation must be able to give the impression that something internal to law operates to constrain the unlimited exchange of semantic markers. According to Fish, it is legal doctrine which provides (or gives the impression of providing, depending on how one rewrites Fish's text) the means to constrain the free flow of legal meaning, and which thus sustains the autonomy of law as a practice.[68] Moreover, legal doctrine, according to Fish, fulfills its constraining function by requiring that legal arguments travel along those paths which make possible the avoidance of a head-on collision with legal doctrine.[69]

In the last analysis, the constraints which legal doctrine imposes in the context of Fish's theory of legal interpretation are purely formal. Legal doctrine, for example, does not bar the importation of ethically based arguments into legal discourse. But because it has incorporated selected ethical values which it privileges while concealing that it has done so, legal doctrine both skews the ethical landscape which it traverses and forces the submersion of the ethical values that inform legal arguments. Moreover, legal doctrine does not foreclose any legal interpretation, even one that directly contradicts that doctrine's traditionally accepted meaning, provided only that the interpretation in question follow a path that permits the avoidance of the appearance of contradiction. Thus, Fish believes that legal interpretation can succeed in totally contradicting the (accepted) meaning of a legal doctrine, provided that it present the new meaning as expanding and supplementing what is encompassed by the legal doctrine rather than as promoting a contrary legal doctrine.

In order to be in a better position to assess Fish's new legal formalism, it would be useful to examine one of the specific examples which he discusses—namely, that relating to the legal doctrine of consideration in contract law. "Consideration," a term of art, refers to the requirement of a *quid pro quo* which makes an agreement enforceable.[70] According to modern contract law, only agreements that satisfy the requirement of consideration—that is, agreements that embody a mutuality of bargained-for exchange—are legally binding.[71] Consideration, thus serves to distinguish between promises or agreements that are *legally* binding and those that are only *morally* binding.

Consistent with Fish's view of it, the requirement of consideration is purely formal in at least two senses. First, consideration operates to distinguish enforceable exchanges from all other events in the flow of history.[72] In other words, the doctrine of consideration is used to impose a given abstract form on certain transactions in order to lift the latter out of their concrete spatiotemporal context. Second, consideration is purely formal in the sense of requiring compliance with certain formalities—that is, each party to an agreement must exchange something for something else at the time of making the agreement[73]— without permitting any inquiry into the substantive terms of the exchange—that is, the relative values of the things exchanged.

On this view, consideration not only exemplifies the dichotomy between legal and moral obligation, but it also appears to play an active role in establishing it and maintaining (re-establishing) it. Indeed, consideration iterates (and reiterates) the difference between legal and moral obligation each time that it requires enforcing a contractual obligation that appears to be unfair (or not enforcing a morally compelling promise). Furthermore, consideration serves to abstract legal relationships from the general historical flow of intersubjective relationships. Under modern contract law, consideration brackets the moment of agreement and disconnects it from both its past and its future.[74] Thus, the operation of the doctrine of consideration seems to demonstrate how law strives to carve out an independent existence for itself, by ascending to a level of abstract formalism from which it can negate (or differentiate itself from) both history and morality.

Fish emphasizes, however, that for all that the doctrine of consideration marks a clear boundary between law and morality, it fails to keep morality from permeating contractual exchanges. The binary distinction of law/morality actively promoted by the doctrine of consideration masks another binary opposition that *actually* shapes the realm of modern contractual transactions. That latter binary opposition involves two different moralities: the morality of the marketplace, which is the morality of abstract and ahistorical agents engaged in arms-length dealings,[75] and a morality concerned with fairness, justice, sympathy and compassion. As envisaged by Fish, therefore, the doctrine of consideration proclaims a dichotomy between law and morals, but operates according to the canons of market morality.

It may appear, based on the preceding remarks, that the purpose of the doctrine of consideration is to imbue contract relationships with the morals of the market and to foreclose further moral debate concerning contracts by presenting law as being beyond morals. Fish, however, accords the doctrine of consideration a much more modest role. Indeed, as he sees it, consideration privileges the morality of the market, but does not exclude other moralities from silently penetrating into the realm of contractual transactions.[76] All that the requirement of consideration demands is that the other moralities be filtered through paths of argumentation that do not lead to head-on collisions with the official narrative designed to keep consideration in place. Accordingly, these other moralities can inform contract doctrines that are inconsistent with the doctrine of consideration, provided that the former doctrines do not appear to contradict the requirement of consideration.

As an example of a modern contract doctrine that is supposed to supplement the doctrine of consideration but that is clearly inconsistent with it, Fish cites the doctrine of contract implied in law.[77] Unlike a contract implied in fact, which is based on the parties' intent,[78] a contract implied in law allows a judge to disregard the intention of the parties and to impose terms based on justice and equity.[79] Thus, we seem to have come full circle. What the requirement of consideration bars makes a full fledged re-entry into the precincts of modern contract law through the deployment of the doctrine of contract implied in law.

Fish's treatment of the example of consideration clearly indicates that the constraints derived from law making, itself formal, are purely procedural and not substantive. The path closing mechanisms associated with legal doctrine amount to no more than the imposition of a rhetorical etiquette on the practice of legal argumentation. For all practical purposes, under Fish's theory, the meanings generated through legal interpretation are the exclusive product of rhetorical force.

Fish's equating of law with the rhetoric of the empowered appears to place him squarely in the camp of those members of CLS who claim that law is ultimately reducible to politics. Fish insists, however, that his position differs significantly from that of CLS. While he acknowledges that his conception of the development of legal doctrine as being *ad hoc* and contradictory is the same as theirs, Fish maintains that the conclusions he draws from this differ significantly from CLS conclusions.[80] Whereas CLS laments the use of the inherent indeterminacy of legal doctrine as a means to advance the political agenda of the powerful under the guise of a politically neutral rationality, Fish unabashedly celebrates such use.[81] Moreover, Fish contends that it is a mistake to insist that judicial precedents be reconciled.[82] Indeed, Fish goes on to argue, it is only in the particular circumstances of an individual controversy that given legal arguments actually succeed or fail. That cases are *decided* is law's triumph. Doctrinal inconsistencies spreading over numerous cases may be troubling from the standpoint of philosophy, but not from the internal perspective of legal practice.

In the last analysis, far from providing a solution to the crisis affecting legal interpretation, Fish's new legal formalism compels the conclusion that the only way to punctuate the ceaseless flow of exchange of semantic values produced by law as an interpretive practice is through *ad hoc* exercises in power. Thus, legal practice may feign to transcend, but is in fact animated by, politics. Also, the dynamism of Fish's legal formalism is ultimately deceiving, because it is the dynamism of someone who runs in place rather than the dynamism of those on the move towards a new destination.

Because it locates justification in the purely present act of the decisionmaker,[83] Fish's new legal formalism leads to a perpetual celebration of the *status quo* (of each decision regardless of its content). Accordingly, Fish's formalism lacks the means to launch any real attempted reconciliation of self and other. Due to the constraints imposed by its abstracting and atomizing features, Fish's formalism can only offer a temporary palliative to ease the pain of the fissure of the body politic into self and other. Yet for all the shortcomings of his theory, Fish's analysis does yield some salient insights into the crisis affecting legal interpretation. Chief among these insights are: the need for law constantly to carve out an identity for itself; the need for law to incorporate and rework extra-legal value-laden materials from the realms of ethics and politics; and the need for law as a practice not to be ultimately reducible to any other practice, such as politics or philosophy.

All three of these insights relate to the dialectic between law and the universe of extra-legal norms, practices and values. Fish is correct in insisting that law must simultaneously plunge into, and differentiate itself from, the realm of the extra-legal, and that in order to accomplish this law must remain constantly on the move. As we shall see, Fish's analysis becomes problematic, however, when it comes to assessing the law's incorporation and reworking of extra-legal materials, and the relationship between law as a practice and other practices.

What is most important about law's constant dynamic striving to carve out an identity for itself is the process of differentiation itself. *What* law is different from and *how* law is different from it may be subject to change (within certain limits beyond which juridical relationships would be altogether impossible). Thus, it seems futile to search for a universal form of mediation between legal and non-legal relationships. Instead, the task for law is, as Fish aptly indicates, to "make" a formal existence for itself, that is, to emerge and distinguish itself from the particular sociohistorical context in which it is located. In other words, although there is no universal form by which law becomes law, at each moment of its existence law must find *a* form (or several forms) through which it can express its difference from the particular extra-legal materials on which it presently depends.

Fish's analysis becomes unpersuasive, however, in its reduction of law into arbitrary rhetorical gamesmanship. While law and legal doctrine mediate the ethical material with which they deal, they do not necessarily dissimulate it. Moreover, while the meaning of a legal doctrine may not be simply or directly inferable form the moral vision which it incorporates, such moral vision places *substantive,* not merely formal or procedural, constraints on the legitimate use of that legal doctrine. In general, the extra-legal values that inform legal doctrine do not make its meaning transparent. Nevertheless, those values serve to open and close certain possible (substantive) semantic paths for legal interpretation.

These points can be profitably illustrated by a return to the modern contract doctrine of consideration. Fish is correct in stressing that this doctrine incorporates the morals of the market to the exclusion of other moral visions. The remainder of his account of consideration, however, is much more questionable. This becomes apparent, moreover, if one takes a closer look at the morals of the market.

One of Adam Smith's well known insights is that a market economy better serves the common good if every individual who trades in the market pursues his or her self-interest rather than that of society.[84] It does not follow, however, that because market participants ought to pursue self-interest rather than altruism, morals are altogether expelled from the economic sphere. If it made no difference whether market actors pursued their self-interest or acted out of altruistic motives, then arguably market relations would by and large escape the fetters of morality. But it does make a difference because altruism would not promote society's good as well as self-interest, and therefore it seems quite proper—if counterintuitive—to claim that individuals who participate in the market have a moral obligation to pursue self-interest.[85] Accordingly, consistent with Smith's theory, the individual is always subject to moral constraints, but these constraints differ depending on whether the individual is acting in the economic sphere or any other sphere of intersubjective interaction.[86]

Bearing in mind that "[a] regime of contract is just another legal name for a market," [87] let us now subject consideration to a Smithian conception of the morals of the market. The modern doctrine of consideration wholly incorporates, and is justifiable in terms of, the morals of the market.[88] Indeed, consideration requires the kind of *quid pro quo* which should be expected of agents who bargain to advance their self-interests.[89] Furthermore, consideration does not have to be interpreted as dissimulating its incorporation of the morals of the market by stressing the distinction between legal and moral obligation. Strictly speaking, the distinction that consideration highlights is that between the morals of the market and the morals of other spheres. Thus, it seems fair to interpret consideration both as not attempting to hide that it incorporates moral values, and as incorporating moral values derived from a single moral vision.

This leaves the more difficult question of how to reconcile the coexistence of consideration and contracts implied in law. The difficulty here is not the one raised by Fish, but rather one stemming from the fact that different hypotheses may provide equally persuasive accounts for the juxtaposition of consideration and contract implied in law. For example, such juxtaposition may be equally legitimate under the morals of the market[90] or under a clash of conflicting moral visions concerning the market and the law of contract.[91] Moreover, in both these cases legal doctrine and legal interpretation would be substantively constrained by the moral vision or moral visions which they incorporated. The nature and scope of the doctrine of consideration would vary depending on the particular moral vision which is deemed to be operative. But regardless of which plausible moral vision is adopted, *some* substantive constraints are bound to be imposed on what should count as legitimate interpretations of the doctrine of consideration.[92]

The last of Fish's insights which requires brief consideration is that law as a practice is not ultimately reducible to any other practice, such as politics or philosophy. The principal lesson taught by this insight is that law carves out an independent existence for itself, not because of the material which it incorporates, but because of the way in which it deals with such material. Philosophy and law, for example, may be concerned with the same ethical values, but whereas philosophy may consider how these values might fit within certain theoretical frameworks, law is likely to rework them and to give them expression (or to reinscribe them) in legal doctrine. Because of this, moreover, it would be just as inappropriate to engage in abstract philosophical debate concerning a moral value which happens to be embedded in legal doctrine before a court of law, as to cite judicial opinions as dispositive on controversies concerning moral values to an assembly of professional philosophers.

Not only does Fish assert that law is not reducible to any other practice, but that law as a practice is self-contained, so that there is no overlap between law and other practices. Fish acknowledges that law may be assessed from the standpoint of other practices, such as philosophy. But a philosophical assessment of law, he would insist, cannot form part of the practice of law. More generally, for Fish, any theory of law would involve the practice of theory but could not belong to the practice of law.[93]

There is a sense in which Fish's conception of law as a self-contained practice is unexceptionable. Indeed, to the extent that law is given structure by, and functions in accordance with, a particular combination of certain rules, norms, standards and conventions, it seems clear that it is a unique and self-contained practice. In this sense, law is a self-contained practice just as is a game like chess or checkers. Thus, although the same board can be used for both chess and checkers, it would be obviously inappropriate to claim that there is an "overlap" between the practice of chess and that of checkers. Moreover, on any given occasion, one would determine whether the board in question was a chess board or a checkers board, not by reference to the nature of the board, but to the dynamic relation between the board and the rules and conventions of the game being played on it. When two people are moving chess pieces according to the rules of chess on the board, then the board is a chessboard, and the practice involved—which incorporates the board as an element within it—is the practice of chess. Similarly, in the sense in which law is properly viewed as a self-contained practice, the same argument—for example, that equality requires equal treatment of those who are in the same essential category[94]—would belong to the practice of law, when made by a litigating attorney to a judge in court, and to the practice of philosophy, when made by a university professor conducting a philosophy class.

Because law as a practice is not simply a game like chess or checkers, however, there is an important sense—which Fish altogether fails to capture—in which law is a practice that is open to, and that overlaps in part, with other practices. Unlike a game such as chess or checkers, which is a self-contained practice, law is a highly complex and dynamic practice which can incorporate not only decontextualized materials from another practice, but also—albeit to a limited extent—the very processes by which the latter practice generates its materials. Thus, there are cases in which lawyers not only refer to ethical values, but also make philosophical or ethical arguments which are subject to the same processes of generation, validation and refutation as if they had been made in the course of a serious philosophical discussion. For example, there are cases in constitutional law, where neither the constitutional text, nor the intent of the framers, nor precedent can offer sufficient guidance to settle an actual controversy.[95] In such cases, ethical or philosophical arguments concerning such values as freedom, equality or privacy may be legitimately invoked and may well determine the judicial outcome.

As a specific illustration, consider the equal protection clause which constitutionalizes the conception of equality.[96] In several equal protection cases, the crucial question for the court to resolve is whether constitutional equality requires equal treatment or equality of result.[97] Frequently, this question cannot be answered by reference to the kinds of arguments that might be preferred by those who regularly engage in the practice of constitutional interpretation—namely, arguments from the text of the Constitution, or the framers' intent, or judicial precedent. Accordingly, the requisite decision must ultimately rely on the kinds of arguments and evaluations that are customary within the practice of moral and political philosophy.[98] In short, in those cases where only philosophical arguments can suggest whether one of two possible legal outcomes is preferable to the other, the practice of constitutional interpretation overlaps with that of philosophy. In other cases, philosophical arguments may be relevant but subordinate to other arguments, or may be altogether trumped by other arguments. Thus, there are overlaps between the practices of law and philosophy, albeit that these are limited in nature.[99]

It should not be surprising that law as a practice should be open to, and overlap with, other practices. Indeed, games such as chess, checkers or for that matter baseball or basketball can be seen as self-contained ends in themselves in a way that law cannot. These games bear no connection to one another as practices, and suggesting that the rules or conventions of one of them should be made applicable to another would be ludicrous. Law, however, is not an isolated practice, but rather one of a cluster of interrelated practices which need not be viewed exclusively as ends in themselves. These interrelated practices, which include ethics and politics as well as law, are linked at some level, by a common pursuit of the reconciliation of self and other within the sphere of social interaction. To be sure, each of these practices undertakes this common pursuit in its own way, and sometimes they may each diverge significantly from the other. But at other times they converge and overlap thus belying Fish's unduly reductionist thesis.

In the last analysis, Fish's atomistic tendencies and his underestimation of the richness and complexity of law as a practice lead him to the unwarranted conclusion that law is *in all relevant senses* a self-contained practice. Fish is right that law is a distinct practice which is capable of incorporating and transforming materials from other practices. To the extent that ethical, political and philosophical arguments have a genuine place *within* the practice of law, however, that practice is not self-contained. But if law as a practice is distinct but not self-contained, the question arises anew as to whether there is something internal to law (other than Fish's purely procedural and purely tautological conception of law as a self-contained practice) which makes it in essence different from the interrelated practices with which it overlaps. Weinrib's new legal formalism suggests an affirmative answer to this question. Accordingly, I shall briefly turn to Weinrib's theory to determine how it might contribute to the solution of the crisis affecting legal interpretation.

The New Formalism of Ernest Weinrib

Reduced to its bare essentials, Weinrib's new legal formalism postulates that law remains distinct from politics to the extent that law's structure is intelligible as an internally coherent practice.[100] Moreover, the internal coherence of law can be grasped, according to Weinrib, through interpretation.[101] As Weinrib specifies, "from a perspective internal to the law's content, formalism draws out the implications of a sophisticated legal system's tendency to coherence by making explicit the justificatory patterns to which the content of such a system must conform." [102] In other words, in a mature legal system, interpretation—and Weinrib has in mind principally judicial interpretation[103]—reveals law's tendency towards internal coherence through the articulation of immanent links between the form and the content of particular juridical relationships. At the most abstract level, the forms of juridical relationship envisaged by Weinrib are universal and ahistorical,[104] but the process of judicial interpretation nevertheless remains dynamic. This is because the concrete judicial relationships to which such forms must be immanently linked are embedded in particular social and historical contexts, and because judicial decisions must employ the public meanings developed in, and applicable to, such contexts.[105]

As already mentioned, the abstract forms that endow juridical relationships with meaning, according to Weinrib, are the forms of justice, namely corrective and distributive justice.[106] Weinrib further indicates that these two forms of justice are irreducible, and that accordingly particular juridical relationships come either within the sweep of corrective justice or within that of distributive justice, but never within that of both.[107] Moreover, drawing upon Aristotle's insight, Weinrib emphasizes that, paradigmatically, the juridical relationships that embody the forms of justice are those "that obtain between parties regarded as external to each other, each with separate interests of mine and thine." [108] In other words, juridical relationships involve agents who are connected through external links as opposed to such internal interpersonal links as those forged through love or virtue.[109]

Thus far, Weinrib's brand of new legal formalism seems to mesh well with law conceived as having internalized deconstruction. Indeed, the universe in which Weinrib locates juridical relationships is one in which there is a clear split between self and other. Juridical relationships understood in terms of the forms of justice, on the other hand, appear to provide a path towards the reconciliation of self and other, all the while permitting self and other to remain external to one another. But before any further assessment of the apparent virtues of Weinrib's new legal formalism is possible, it is necessary to take a somewhat closer look at the forms of justice which he invokes, and at the way in which they are supposed to endow juridical relationships with distinct meaning consistent with his conception of law as being irreducible to politics.

As understood by Weinrib, corrective justice involves the award of damages which simultaneously quantifies the wrongdoing of one party and the suffering of the other party in a bipolar (voluntary or involuntary) private transaction.[110] Moreover, under this view, all bilateral relationships characteristic of the private law of torts and contracts are ultimately intelligible in terms of the structure of corrective justice.[111] In other words, the legal universe carved out by juridical relationships intelligible in terms of corrective justice is one in which formally equal individual legal actors are initially placed side-by-side owing each other nothing but reciprocal negative duties (of noninterference).[112] The initial equilibrium maintained by a network of reciprocal negative duties which makes for purely external relationships among legal actors, however, is bound to become upset as individuals either seek the cooperation of others in the pursuit of self-interest (contract) or voluntarily or involuntarily interfere with others in the course of such pursuit (tort). Corrective justice, through the award of damages, undoes (erases) the positive entanglements of (unfulfilled) contracts and the interferences of torts, and thus purports to reestablish (reinscribe) the initial equilibrium between purely externally linked equals.

Corrective justice, argues Weinrib, deals with the immediate relationship of person to person,[113] and is completely removed from politics,[114] as it merely seeks to restore the initial equilibrium between a doer and a sufferer regardless of the actual wealth, merit or virtue of the interacting legal actors.[115] Thus, it apparently makes no difference whether one is politically inclined to advance the interests of the wealthy or the poor, as there is only one legitimate way to resolve legal disputes arising under private law: that is, by commanding payment of the quantity of damages which corrective justice requires in order to restore the initial equality between doer and sufferer. Accordingly, as Weinrib sees it, the judicial task in the context of dispensing the quantitative equality mandated by corrective justice is limited to the specification of the actual damages required in the particular case to be adjudicated.[116]

In contrast to the quantitative equality of corrective justice, distributive justice requires the implementation of proportional equality. Whereas corrective justice is concerned with the recovery of a status quo ante, distributive justice requires the allocation of the benefits and burdens of social cooperation in the proportions set by an applicable criterion of distribution.[117] Also, consistent with Weinrib's analysis, unlike corrective justice, distributive justice cannot be completely severed from politics. Indeed, settling on any given criterion of distribution for purposes of achieving proportional equality involves a political decision.[118] Thus, for example, whether certain benefits ought to be distributed equally in proportion to need or in proportion to merit depends not on anything inherent to law or to juridical relationships, but instead on some collective decision that remains extrinsic to law and that must draw, at least in part, on political considerations.

Although distributive justice cannot avoid politics, Weinrib maintains that the former is not thereby reducible to the latter.[119] Once a particular criterion of distribution has been selected, distributive justice requires that juridical relationships conform to the proportional equality mandated by that criterion.[120] Moreover, Weinrib also believes that inherent in the very notion of distributive justice there is a conception of personhood and of equality which constrains all legitimate juridical relationships falling within the scope of that form of justice.[121] The concept of personhood thus requires judges to make sure that people engaged in the relevant juridical relationships are not treated as things; the concept of equality, that each person be treated as an equal consistent with the dictates of the prevailing criterion of distribution.[122]

Distributive justice, particularly through its conception of personhood and equality, is supposed to preside, in Weinrib's formalist vision, over the domain of public law. On the one hand, Weinrib maintains that the notions of personhood and equality impose nonpolitical constraints on the legislative and administrative processes.[123] On the other hand, Weinrib argues,

> The positive law may give effect to the fundamental values of personhood and equality in a variety of ways: by incorporating them into the techniques for construing statutes, by elaborating notions of natural justice or fairness for administrative procedures or by enshrining specifications of personhood and equality into constitutional documents.[124]

Corrective and distributive justice, as conceived by Weinrib, may be viewed as offering two distinct (and irreducible to politics) paths towards the reconciliation of self and other as persons capable of engaging in mutually external relationships. Corrective justice promotes the minimal harmony of mutual non-interference through the spread of a quantitative equality that ritualistically effaces the encroachment of a wrongdoing self upon a suffering other. Moreover, since the self's devotion to its own interests is bound to cause interference with the negative rights of others, the completion of the mission of corrective justice must be deferred until such time as the self becomes completely self-sufficient—an impossibility in terms of deconstructionist ontology.

Distributive justice, on the other hand, also aspires to promote mutual non-interference by defusing the conflict between self and other over the allocation of collectively generated benefits and burdens. By instituting proportional equality, distributive justice circumscribes an order within which each person can see him or herself as a moral equal who is treated as an end rather than merely as means by being given his or her due. Because each individual self is ascribed a dignified place within the order carved out by the proportional equality of distributive justice, moreover, the self can presumably renounce confrontation with the other as a means to secure the socially generated goods which self-respect and dignity require. Thus, distributive justice, much like corrective justice, tends towards a harmony of purely external relationships of non-interference between a self and an other who have competing claims on the products of social cooperation.

Finally, the task of distributive justice, like that of corrective justice, can never be completed, both because presumably there will always be new goods to be distributed according to proportional equality, and because the particular criterion of distributive justice to be applied in given social and historical circumstances is likely to be a subject of political controversy so long as society remains divided into self and other.

Not only do corrective and distributive justice as the forms of justice seem highly compatible with law conceived as having internalized deconstruction, but they also allow for indeterminacy in the course of discharging their meaning-endowing function. Indeed, in Weinrib's assessment, indeterminacy is inevitable in the course of applying abstract forms to particular juridical relationships that necessarily comprise an element of contingency.[125] Indeterminacy, however, is only objectionable if it allows juridical relationships to be ultimately swept into the whirlwind of politics. The indeterminacy created due to the application of Weinrib's forms of justice does not. As Weinrib states,

> The forms of justice determine juridical relationships by representing the justificatory structures through which those relationships can be understood as the sorts of thing that they are and to which they must conform if they are to be intelligible. The forms of justice are thus determinative as the distinctive—not the exhaustive—modes for the understanding of law.[126]

In other words, although the forms of justice may not determine the outcome of every case, only those outcomes which are consistent with the forms of justice (and hence not merely reducible to politics) may

be legitimately defended. Thus, even when not completely determinative, the forms of justice operating in the context of Weinrib's formalism are supposed to perform a path closing function capable of preventing the slippage of the legal into the political.

If Weinrib's conception of the two forms of justice and of their potential for making juridical relationships immanently intelligible were
acceptable, then his new legal formalism would provide a genuine solution to the crisis affecting legal interpretation. Unfortunately, as con-
vincingly demonstrated by Alan Brudner, Weinrib's new legal formalism is ultimately unacceptable to the extent that it rests on certain
arbitrary and unwarranted premises.[127] In the remainder of this section, I briefly focus on these premises with a view to determining
whether, and to what extent, Weinrib's insights might still be incorporated in a satisfactory resolution of the crisis affecting legal interpretation.

From the standpoint of our own concerns, there are two basic flaws
with the premises underlying Weinrib's formalist thesis: the first relates to his conception of the forms of justice, the second, to his ap-
praisal of the relationship between corrective and distributive justice.
More specifically, the first flaw, as noted by Brudner, derives from
Weinrib's elevation of one (among many possible) historically
grounded and ideologically determined version of what is entailed by
corrective and distributive justice as the universal and ahistorical essence of those forms of justice.[128] Moreover, the reason why this flaw
is particularly troublesome is because it reveals that Weinrib's apparent depoliticization of the forms of justice is achieved through the
privileging and enshrining of a particular ideological vision which is
certainly subject to political debate. The second flaw stems from Weinrib's insistence on the existence of an unbridgeable gap between corrective and distributive justice, and from his assertion that corrective
justice is concerned with immediate relationships among persons. At
least under some conceptions of the forms of justice, there need be no
insurmountable gap between corrective and distributive justice. Also,
when all the relevant considerations are taken into proper account, it
becomes clear that the relationships that come within the sweep of
corrective justice must be mediated ones. Furthermore, to the extent
that there is no gap between the two forms of justice, and that all
relationships encompassed by either of two must be mediated ones,
these cannot be, contrary to Weinrib's claim, a total separation between politics and corrective justice.

Two of the principal unwarranted assumptions made by Weinrib
are that the domain of corrective justice must preside over a regime of

purely negative rights and that distributive justice necessarily involves respect for Kantian notions of equality and personhood. Corrective justice can operate in the context of purely negative rights under certain particular historical and ideological circumstances, namely those associated with a free market economy.[129] Thus, private law shaped so as to afford the greatest possible legal protection to free market transactions would undoubtedly be primarily oriented towards the protection of the negative rights and freedoms best suited to promote the orderly proliferation of market exchanges. And, under those circumstances, corrective justice would be quite properly confined to "undoing" the entanglements having resulted in infringements upon negative rights and freedoms. Nothing in corrective justice as a form of justice taken at the highest level of abstraction, however, precludes extending corrective justice to cover a regime of positive rights, or, in other words, a legal system in which private legal actors are charged with positive duties towards one another.

Corrective justice is necessarily backward looking, in that it must pick some point in the past and set it as a baseline. After selecting its baseline, corrective justice must compare the set of intersubjective relationships existing at the baseline and that which is in force at the subsequent time at which a claim for compensation arises. Corrective justice must also introduce a concept of "disruption" pursuant to which it can distinguish between compensable and non-compensable deviations from the baseline. Weinrib seems to assume that if we seek to establish the baseline logically, by carrying corrective justice to its highest level of abstraction, we will all be lead by reason to the same point: a static universe of purely abstract egos who remain entirely independent from each other and who scrupulously refrain from interfering with one another as a consequence of their strict adherence to a regime of purely negative rights and duties. Moreover, for those who accept this point as providing a purely logically compelled—and hence completely apolitical—baseline, the definition of what should count as a compensable disruption becomes self-evident: any deviation from the status quo of the baseline that involves a violation of a negative right.

Logic alone, however, does not compel acceptance of the atomistic universe that Weinrib projects at the highest level of abstraction. Indeed, it hardly seems contradictory to contend that at the highest level of abstraction, persons are cleansed of their selfish individualistic concerns, and that they are mutually dedicated to the maintenance of social harmony and welfare within their community through the deployment of care, concern and an elaborate network of positive rights and duties. Within this communitarian vision, moreover, the baseline would be one of solidarity and mutual assistance, and any deviation involving a violation of a positive duty would quite naturally qualify as a compensable disruption.

Neither Weinrib's atomistic vision nor its communitarian counterpart are in any sense logically compelled. Each of them figures as an originary myth suited to buttress a particular ethical and political ideology. More generally, setting a baseline for corrective justice involves an irreducibly arbitrary—i.e., political and ideological—element. And because of this, corrective justice no more requires the imposition of purely negative rights than a regime heavily composed of positive rights. Thus, for example, it seems entirely legitimate for tort law to impose, at least under certain conditions, on individual actors a positive duty to rescue fellow human beings who are in danger. Corrective justice in the latter case would have to extend to nonfeasance and not merely to misfeasance, as Weinrib would have it, but that would simply reflect one possible legitimate choice among several plausible alternative ethical and political visions.[130] In short, it is only by suppressing alternative political visions of the proper role of corrective justice, that Weinrib succeeds in conveying the impression that corrective justice is apolitical.

As we have seen, Weinrib does concede, on the other hand, that distributive justice has a political component, but he insists that it nevertheless transcends politics to the extent that it imposes a duty to abide by Kantian notions of personhood and equality. Unless one incorporates these Kantian notions tautologically in the very definition of distributive justice, however, there is no reason to assume that all plausible conceptions of distributive justice need include such Kantian notions. For example, there seems to be nothing contradictory about a feudalist conception of distributive justice, according to which persons are inherently unequal depending on the social class to which they are born, according to which much greater dignity attaches to those born into aristocratic families than to commoners, and according to which distributions should be made unequally, with a disproportionate share of society's goods going to the members of the aristocracy.[131] Once again Weinrib has taken one possible conception—or in this case more precisely a class of possible conceptions—of a form of justice and presented it as universally valid. But to the extent that distributive justice at the highest level of abstraction does not imply Kantian notions of personhood and equality, judicial protection of the latter is not likely to be apolitical in the sense that Weinrib intends.

Turning to the second principal flaw underlying Weinrib's premises, the unbridgeable gap which he perceives between corrective and distributive justice does not extend to all plausible conceptions of the relation between the two forms of justice. To be sure, there is one sense in which there is an irreducible difference between corrective and distributive justice: the former is backward-looking whereas the latter is essentially forward-looking.[132] In another sense—which is more important in terms of the relationship between law and politics—however, corrective and distributive justice may be harmonized (at least under certain conceptions) under a unified all-encompassing system of justice. Such a unified system may comprise several components such as distributive, corrective and procedural justice, but is above all characterized by its possession of an internal congruence and harmony that binds all its component parts together in a single whole which is greater than the sum of its parts. Such a unified system of justice may rely, for example, on an overriding criterion of justice to be applied to all distributions. Distributions, however, may be tampered with, either through interference with the process of distribution or with the products of such distribution. And, at least in the latter case, corrective justice, subsumed under the relevant overriding criterion of justice, may be called for as a means to preserve the integrity of the then operative all-encompassing system of justice.[133]

To the extent that the *measure* of compensation under corrective justice depends on a criterion of justice that is applicable across the board to all intersubjective dealings coming within the sweep of an all-encompassing system of justice, corrective justice cannot be completely apolitical. Indeed, selection of one among several available criteria of justice inevitably involves the making of a political choice, and that choice bears some imprint on the articulation of the dictates of corrective justice. Also, because of this, the intersubjective transactions that come within the purview of corrective justice necessarily involve mediated relationships between legal actors.[134]

Notwithstanding the failure of Weinrib's legal formalism persuasively to detach law from politics, some of his insights might be profitably incorporated in a proposed solution to the crisis affecting legal interpretation in the context of law understood as having internalized deconstruction. Specifically, whereas corrective justice cannot rid law of politics, it structures the relationships between self and other to which it applies in a distinctive manner that makes them distinguishable from political and ethical relationships. In other words, while not excluding the ethical or the political, corrective justice rearranges them in a way that gives a distinctive legal contour to the relationships that come within its scope. Furthermore, whereas Weinrib's conception of distributive justice is both timebound and ideologically conditioned, the Kantian constraints which it imposes nevertheless arguably provide a legitimate way to distinguish legal from purely political relationships in the context of those legal systems that share its ideological assumptions. Significantly, the contemporary American legal system with its constitutional rights to due process and to equality and with its numerous private law doctrines grounded on premises of individual autonomy and equality clearly seems to conform to the ideological assumptions embodied in Weinrib's conception of distributive justice. Finally, Weinrib's insight that law is concerned with external relationships between persons furnishes apparently cogent means of demarcation between legal relationships and purely ethical ones.

It remains to be determined *how* corrective justice conceived as inextricably linked to politics, and distributive justice imposing Kantian constraints interpreted as being ideological, as well as law construed as ordering external interpersonal relationships, may contribute to maintenance of the distinction between law and politics in the context of law understood in terms of having internalized deconstruction. These issues are addressed in the next section, as part of an attempt to shed some preliminary light on the question concerning deconstruction's potential for resolving the crisis affecting legal interpretation in spite of the above mentioned shortcomings of the new legal formalism.

LAW, ETHICS, POLITICS AND A PROPOSED SOLUTION TO THE CRISIS IN LEGAL INTERPRETATION: SOME PRELIMINARY OBSERVATIONS

While it is beyond the scope of this article to attempt a comprehensive examination of deconstruction's potential for resolving the crisis affecting legal interpretation, a few preliminary conclusions may be drawn from the preceding analysis. First, there is no single formula or form which underlies all juridical relationships or which could be relied upon to draw any clear cut boundaries between law and politics. Second, law as a practice is distinct from other practices but not self-contained, as it borrows and incorporates elements from other social practices, and as it partially overlaps with such other practices. These overlaps, moreover, are intelligible in relation to the common ultimate objective that animates all the practices involved, namely the reconciliation of self and other within the realm of social relationships. Third, the law's distinct existence is not given, but must be constantly fought for, through a dynamic process of differentiation operating in a specific social and historical context and constrained by the requirement of integrity. It is not sufficient, however, for law rhetorically to proclaim that it is different from other practices. To keep earning its distinct identity, law must (through interpretive work) constantly carve out a sufficiently determinate and differentiated meaning (identity) for itself as a practice, by processing and reworking the actual social and historical materials with which it happens to be confronted. But because law's meaning-endowing work cannot be carried out successfully if conducted at too high or too low a level of abstraction, one can make no general prescriptions concerning how law in general ought to operate as a distinct practice.

By concentrating on modern law, and in particular on the contemporary American legal system, however, one can gain useful insights into the means by which law in a given set of social and historical circumstances strives to carve out a distinct existence for itself. As a dynamic jurisprudence resting on a strong common law tradition and on a broadly encompassing constitutional vision, American law generally favors the proliferation of juridical relationships to suit the multiple needs of the legal personality—that is, the human personality to the extent that it is prone to being shaped, developed, perfected and fulfilled through *external* relationships that are distinguishable from the constantly waged struggles and *ad hoc* compromises typical of politics. Moreover, in the context of contemporary American law, juridical relationships can be distinguished from other external intersubjective relationships inasmuch as the former are much more prone to embrace corrective justice and a broadly interpreted version of the Kantian constraints attached to Weinrib's conception of distributive justice. On the other hand, although contemporary American law embraces corrective justice and a particular vision of distributive justice as part of its quest for a meaningful existence, the juridical relationships that it encompasses tend to remain distinct from internal intersubjective (moral) relationships based on the same forms of justice.

Before turning to a closer examination of each of the above points—and particularly since these points must be addressed one after another in a linear fashion—it bears emphasizing that none of these points *standing alone* allows law to fashion for itself a distinct identity in the context of the contemporary sociohistorical scene. Rather, if contemporary law can find such an identity it would have to be due to the convergence of these various points. Also, since there are bound to be significant changes of circumstances over time, yesterday's successes cannot be necessarily counted on today, and today's may not last past tomorrow.

Dynamic Jurisprudence and Multiplication of External Relationships

To understand how a dynamic jurisprudence may constantly produce new juridical relationships to meet the changing needs and aspirations of the legal personality, it is necessary to focus briefly on the difference between static and dynamic jurisprudences. A static jurisprudence bent on establishing its order[135] settles on certain kinds of potential external relationships and draws them into the realm of law, but it excludes others. For example, a static legal order may require subjecting all market transactions to law, but not the vast majority of relationships between family members. A dynamic legal order, on the other hand, would not be thus limited. To the extent that needs for external relationships arise within the family—as in the case of wife or child abuse—a dynamic legal order, like that framed by the common law, would be able to cope with them, through internal growth and evolution.[136] Accordingly, when no other road to reconciliation appears open, dynamic jurisprudence offers the hope of reconciliation through external relationships.

As previously mentioned,[137] external relationships, as described by Weinrib, involve persons engaged in the pursuit of self-interest, and are contrasted with internal relationships, such as those fostered by love or virtue. To the extent that external relationships mediate the pursuit of self-interest, they are not necessarily legal relationships. They may also be political relationships. Therefore, the characterization of legal relationships as external ones may suffice to distinguish them from purely ethical relationships, but does not contribute to the separation of laws from politics. Moreover, the very classification of intersubjective relationships into internal and external ones appears vulnerable to the deconstructionist charge that it sets another arbitrary invertible binary opposition.

The validity of the above deconstructionist charge must be conceded in part, insofar as it seems impossible to draw any clear cut lines between internal and external in relation to interacting subjects. But whereas the dichotomy between internal and external may lack ontological validity, it is not thereby deprived of phenomenological validity. Indeed, relative to the particular circumstances in which they find themselves, interacting actors may tend to perceive certain relationships as internal and others as external. These perceptions, moreover, provided that they are widespread among the members of an interacting community, can serve as *a* basis for distinguishing legal from nonlegal relationships. Thus, in contemporary society, moral relationships may be construed as involving an internal self-generated and self-policing curbing of self-interest whereas legal relationships may be perceived as only involving external constraints on the pursuit of self-interest, buttressed by external sanctions.

The separation of law from politics depends not on the phenomenological distinction between internal and external, but rather on law's embrace of forms not usually present in purely political relationships. In our contemporary setting, these forms may well be those of corrective justice and of the particular version of distributive justice invoked by Weinrib. Again, it bears repeating that law does not strictly depend on the presence of either of these forms of justice, and that, as we shall more fully elaborate below, mere presence does not necessarily transform the external relationships to which they apply into legal ones.

Corrective Justice: Legal and Political

As already mentioned,[138] corrective justice is backward-looking. It seeks to re-establish (reinscribe) a disrupted past by ritualistically erasing the wrongdoing and suffering that has opened a wedge between self and other. Corrective justice seeks to inscribe the return to a baseline projected into a particular point in time lifted from the flow of past events. This baseline, as we have seen, always involves an arbitrary—in the sense of political and ideological—element and is always established *ex post facto* (as is the particular point in time selected as its temporal anchor).[139] Moreover, the arbitrary element involved in selecting the baseline also extends to the definition of the "disruption" sought to be overcome through the application of corrective justice. Thus, what constitutes a compensable "disruption" as opposed to, for example, "the cost of doing business" or the "risk assumed" by motorists or consumers, under any particular conception of corrective justice depends on the political and ideological assumptions behind that conception of justice. In short, dispensing corrective justice involves an interpretive task which is not merely limited to the rewriting of past texts, but which also requires rewriting these as if they had already been rewritten in the past. In other words, corrective justice not only draws the past into the present, but also seeks to transform every present (here and now) into a past.[140]

The past writings defining disruptions and prescribing measures of compensation may be fairly straightforward legal statutes or judicial precedents giving rise to broad interpretive consensuses among particular groups of legal actors. On the other hand, the writings in question may appear to offer much less guidance—such as when no judicial precedent seems directly applicable—and may accordingly lead to much greater interpretive controversy. In either case, however, the past writing must be read—that is, rewritten—before it can be made to reveal what corrective justice requires in a particular instance. Accordingly, the projection of the present into the past that is supposed to accompany law's embrace of corrective justice may appear to be largely illusory. And if that proved to be the case, then there would be ostensibly no palpable difference between legal and political corrective justice.

The projection of the present into the past does not have to be viewed as a mere collapse of a present into a past. It may plausibly involve a dynamic effort to embed a present in its past, through the establishment of a network of interpretive links travelling between the two. As I have already pointed out[141] the rewriting involved in reading a past writing is not arbitrary, if it is constrained by the openings and closings of semantic paths that result from punctuation of the free flow of meaning attributable to genuine historically grounded efforts to reconcile self and other. Accordingly, whether the projection of the present into the past in the context of corrective justice involves a slight or very extensive rewriting of past writings is not crucial, so long as the travels between past writings and present rewritings take place over open semantic paths which are used with integrity.

Interpreting the here and now as a past in the context of external relationships, however, is not the exclusive preserve of the law. Indeed, politics can make use of the form of corrective justice in ways that do not seem to involve any legitimate legal relationships. For example, in a case involving political justice against a deposed tyrant where such tyrant is called upon to account for wrongdoings clearly not encompassed within any plausible interpretation of positive law, corrective justice—in the sense of the erasure of the tyrant's (wrong)doing—may well be carried out without recourse to anything genuinely interpreted by legal actors as law.

This last example is arguably illustrative of the ability of politics to mimic law. More generally, one may object that political justice often involves genuine appeals to law (as when a deposed tyrant is prosecuted in part for violations of the criminal code), and that even what seem to be purely legal matters are often imbued with politics (as when a rarely enforced criminal statute is invoked against a political enemy), thus negating the possibility of drawing any genuine boundary between politics and law.

To this one may reply that, whereas law and politics are often close bedfellows, and whereas it may be sometimes impossible as a practical matter to disentangle one from the other, in theory law as an embodiment of corrective justice remains distinguishable from politics. Indeed, not only does law's embrace of corrective justice, like that of politics, depend on collapsing presents into pasts but also on reinscribing such presents in a special kind of past—namely one in which the nature of future disruptions and the measure of compensation needed to erase such disruptions has already been identified in writings. These writings, moreover, cannot just be any writings, but only those which can be fairly read as revealing generally applicable norms, rules and standards that circumscribe an order within which external relationships can be intelligibly reconciled.

Consistent with this, legal corrective justice can be distinguished from its political counterpart. Indeed, in its legal embodiment, corrective justice involves a projection of a present into a past that preserves (or creates) a continuity in meaning over the temporal intervals which must be traversed. In its purely political embodiment, on the other hand, corrective justice faces an inevitable rupture which stems from its inability to find a sufficient continuity in meaning between the present texts and past texts which it must confront in the course of its efforts to reattach its present to its past. Finally, because of this difference, legal corrective justice gives the impression of operating according to pre-existing norms, rules and standards, whereas purely political corrective justice seems to operate on an essentially *ad hoc* basis.[142] In other words, whereas in legal corrective justice the return to a baseline through the dispensation of damages according to an intelligible measure is inscribed into a single and continuous order elaborated for the external reconciliation of self and other, in purely political justice there are two irreconcilable orders which make any such inscription impossible. In the case of purely political corrective justice, therefore, the selection of a baseline projected into the past is always bound to remain arbitrary from the standpoint of at least one of the two orders—that is, the order of the old regime or that of the new regime—with which that selection would have to be reconciled in order to avoid an unbridgeable rupture making any genuine reconciliation between past and present selves impossible.

That legal corrective justice is distinguishable from its purely political counterpart does not mean that the former is altogether detached from politics. Corrective justice, as I have argued[143] necessarily involves politics in the selection of a baseline and of a measure of damages, and its legal incarnation is no exception. Legal corrective justice, however, apparently successfully separates its legal function from its political one along temporal lines. The political process of selecting baselines, defining disruptions and settling on measures of compensation appears relegated to the past. The seemingly purely legal process of determining whether a particular plaintiff and defendant have become entangled in the kind of wrongdoing and suffering which requires legal compensation, on the other hand, appears to be always situated in the present—or more precisely in a point in time that is always a future from the standpoint of the past moment of political determination of the substantive components of legal corrective justice. Upon closer scrutiny, however, this temporal division between the law and politics of corrective justice does not hold up. Indeed, to the extent that all readings of past writings involve rewritings, no temporal division between law and politics could ever be consistently sustained.

In the last analysis, maintenance of the distinction between law and politics in the context of corrective justice is an interpretive matter. The political cannot be dislodged from legal interpretations of corrective justice. But such legal interpretations can transcend mere politics in their dynamic strivings to produce meaning by circulating with integrity through open semantic paths (and by opening new such paths) capable of binding past, present and future texts together in a single order oriented towards the external reconciliation of self and other—that is, the reconciliation of self and other through external relationships mediated through universally applicable norms, rules, and standards. Moreover, these norms, rules and standards may be interpretively found, inferred or created in the course of applying corrective justice, provided that they can be legitimately squared with the relevant set of past, present and future texts with which they must combine to sustain a single order of external reconciliation between self and other. Stated more generally, legal relationships, including those based on corrective justice, differ interpretively from purely political ones, principally because of the following. Law is supposed to reconcile (without suppressing or transcending) antagonistic self-interests within an external order dynamically sustained through the constant generation (and regeneration) of norms, rules and standards that can plausibly be interpreted as being universally applicable. Mere politics, on the other hand, only seems suited to produce *ad hoc* accommodations between clashing self-interests, which are intelligible solely in terms of the balance of power among the political actors with competing interests or of purely contingent convergences among such disparate interests. And this difference in the respective capacities of law and politics for dealing with the external relationships which they encounter is perhaps most vividly illustrated by the contrast between the legal and the political embodiment of corrective justice.

Distributive Justice: Legal and Ethical

Because it is forward-looking, distributive justice shapes legal relationships quite differently than does corrective justice. Whereas corrective justice projects juridical presents into the past, distributive justice projects such presents into the future. For example, in a school desegregation case where a black plaintiff seeks enforcement of his or her distributive constitutional right to a racially integrated education, the fashioning of an appropriate judicial remedy does not involve the restoration of a (now disrupted) past status quo. It requires, instead, the deployment of a scheme—such as mandatory busing—designed to produce future departures (towards school integration) from the present (racially segregated) status quo.[144]

Although distributive justice is essentially forward-looking, its judicial dispensation involves a past as well as a future. Indeed, whereas a judge must project a present into the future in order to fashion an appropriate distributive remedy, the particular criterion of distribution which the judge must use in order to arrive at an appropriate remedy always appears embedded in a past from the standpoint of the here and now of judging. Thus, consistent with Weinrib's conception, in judicial applications of distributive justice the political act of selecting a criterion of distribution seems separable from the legal act of applying such a criterion in a particular case: the political act is located in the past of judging; the legal act is projected towards its future.

Just as in the case of corrective justice, however, a closer examination of the legal embodiment of distributive justice reveals that no neat distinctions along temporal lines can be drawn between law and politics. Even if the criterion of distributive justice were always to be found in past writings, its application would require reading these past writings, and hence rewriting them. Because of this, the political cannot be expurgated from the legal application of distributive justice, as Weinrib would have it. Nevertheless, legal applications of distributive justice may still be legitimately distinguished from the purely political elements associated with distributive justice, along the same lines as the legal can be differentiated from the political in the case of corrective justice.

There is also another way in which the legal may be distinguished from the political in the case of those conceptions of distributive justice which impose the Kantian constraints stressed by Weinrib.[145] It seems that when these Kantian constraints are applicable, the law appropriates the ethical categories of personhood and equality and employs them to limit the reach of the purely political will engendered through the deployment of democratic majoritarian processes. Thus, judges are supposed to examine the legislative enactments expressive of the political will of the majority and validate them only to the extent that they are consistent with applicable Kantian constraints made legally enforceable by some generally accepted writing such as a (written or an orally transmitted) constitution. For example, under the American Constitution, the due process and equal protection clauses can be read as imposing broadly interpreted Kantian constraints on democratically generated legislation. Moreover, these constraints appear to impose extra-political limitations on the products of the democratic political process, regardless of whether they are very narrowly construed by "strict constructionists" or market libertarians or very broadly understood by "liberal" judges or welfare egalitarians—or, in other words, regardless of whether due process is narrowly conceived as only protecting certain procedural rights or broadly conceived as also encompassing an extensive domain of substantive rights, and of whether equal protection is narrowly restricted to sustaining formal political equality or broadly expanded to cover equal opportunity and basic social welfare rights.

Although the judicial implementation of Kantian constraints is a task that runs counter to the ordinary processes of majoritarian politics, it is not thereby altogether immune from politics. Indeed, interpretation of the relevant constraints—including such open-ended constitutional provisions as the due process and the equal protection clauses under the American Constitution—cannot help but involve politics to the extent that it requires the judicial (reading) rewriting of past texts.

In the last analysis, both legal distributive justice in general and the implementation of Kantian constraints in particular necessarily encompass political elements. Nevertheless, in the case of Kantian constraints, legal interpretation conducted with integrity leads to the transcendence of ordinary majoritarian politics. Moreover, in the cases of both legal distributive justice and Kantian constraints, execution of the requirement to bind pasts, presents and futures together so as to insert external relationships among legal actors in an order structured by universally applicable norms, rules and standards, if performed with integrity along the proper interpretive paths, succeeds in producing a difference between legally mandated distributions and purely political ones. Finally, even though the same criterion of distributive justice may inform ethical as well as legal relationships, and even though legal distributive justice may necessarily encompass ethical elements, legal implementations of distributive justice nevertheless are generally distinguishable from ethical ones. And the reason for this difference is that not all prescriptions and sanctions suitable for internal relationships are likewise applicable to external relationships, or in other words, that there can be no complete overlap between ethics as a practice based exclusively on self-constraint and law as practice that requires the imposition of external constraints.[146]

Assessing the Distinct Identity of Modern Law

If the preceding broadly based observations are warranted, then modern law viewed through the prism of deconstruction's ontology of postponement and ethics of reconciliation can interpretively carve for itself a distinct identity. Within this deconstructionist perspective, law like ethics and politics presupposes a social universe split into self and other and a call to attempt overcoming that split.[147] Law is, however, unlike ethics (as a practice) insofar as ethics operates by means of self-restraint and internal sanctions. On the other hand, law is also unlike politics, to the extent that politics can aspire to no more than *ad hoc* compromises among competing self-interested parties. By charting an intermediate course which uses external constraints and sanctions in order to channel disparate self-interests to a common ground of (possible) reconciliation buttressed by generally applicable norms, rules and standards, law can through its interpretive deeds sustain an identity of its own, and thus overcome the crisis affecting legal interpretation. Furthermore, whereas (at least Kantian) ethics seeks to overcome the dichotomy between self and other by completely subordinating the self to the universal other that is the categorical imperative; and whereas politics cannot prevent the self in pursuit of its interests from constantly threatening to destroy the tenuous *ad hoc* compromises on which the other depends for protection; law's promise of external reconciliation seems to strike a much better balance between the interests of the self and those of the other.

From the standpoint of the broader ontological and ethical concerns of deconstruction, the external impersonal reconciliation promised by law appears to fall far short of the mark. Indeed, the pluralism of interests assumed by modern law seems but a pale and partial image of the profound split between self and other which informs deconstruction's ethic of reconciliation. Perhaps the limitations of law could be overcome by supplementing its external relationships with internal relationships capable of fostering greater intimacy and solidarity between self and other. Perhaps, however, the ontological and ethical demands of deconstruction require the erasure of the distinction between external and internal relationships which may require superseding the very order established by law. These alternative possibilities raise important and vexing issues that cannot be pursued here. Therefore, it must suffice for now that whereas the status of law may be ontologically and ethically in doubt in the context of deconstruction, epistemologically, law's distinctness as a practice remains on firm ground.

NOTES

1. See, e.g., Dalton, An Essay in the Deconstruction of Contract Doctrine, 94 Yale L.J. 1007 (1985); Feinman, Critical Approaches to Contract Law, 30 UCLA L. Rev. 829 (1983); Abel, Torts in The Politics of Law 185–200 (D. Kairys ed. 1982).

2. See, e.g., Freeman, Legitimizing Racial Discrimination Through Antidiscrimination Law: A Critical Review of Supreme Court Doctrine, 62 Minn. L. Rev. 1049 (1978).

3. For examples of recent bitterly divided and acrimonious decisions, see Garcia v. San Antonio Metro. Transit Auth., 469 U.S. 528 (1985); Webster v. Reproductive Health Servs., 109 S. Ct. 3040 (1989); Texas v. Johnson 109 U.S. 2533 (1989); City of Richmond v. J. A. Croson Co., 109 S. Ct. 706 (1989). In *Croson*, for instance, Justice Marshall's dissent characterized the Court's majority as taking a "disingenuous approach." Id. at 746; see also Rosenfeld, Decoding Richmond: Affirmative Action and the Elusive Meaning of Constitutional Equality, 87 Mich. L. Rev. 1729 (1989) [hereafter Decoding Richmond].

4. See, e.g., Pound, Mechanical Jurisprudence, 8 Colum. L. Rev. 605 (1908); Cohen, Transcendental Nonsense and The Functional Approach, 35 Colum. L. Rev. 809 (1935); see also Yablon, Review: Law and Metaphysics, 96 Yale L.J. 613, 615–24 (1987).

5. See, e.g., Unger, The Critical Legal Studies Movement, 96 Harv. L. Rev. 561 (1983); Kennedy, The Structure of Blackstone's Commentaries, 28 Buffalo L. Rev. 205 (1979); Kelman, Interpretive Construction in the Substantive Criminal Law, 33 Stan. L. Rev. 591 (1981).

6. See C. Norris, Derrida 18–27 (1987).

7. See id. at 23–24, 127.

8. See id. at 25.

9. Id. at 19.

10. See Jacobson, The Idolatry of Rules: Writing Law According to Moses, With Reference to Other Jurisprudences, 11 Cardozo L. Rev. 1079 (1990) [hereafter Idolatry of Rules].

11. See id. at 1118–20, 1125–32.

12. Fiss, Objectivity and Interpretation, 34 Stan. L. Rev. 739, 744 (1982).

13. See generally R. Posner, Economic Analysis of Law (2d ed. 1977).

14. R. Dworkin, Law's Empire 228–32 (1986).

15. See Brudner, The Ideality of Difference: Toward Objectivity in Legal Interpretation, 11 Cardozo L. Rev. at 1133, 1156–57 (1990).

16. See id. at 1158.

17. Id.

18. A similar argument can be made concerning the interpretive value of Habermas' process based dialogical method designed to yield a rational consensus and the "ideal speech situation" which he employs as a means to that end. Habermas' aim to achieve a genuine rational consensus through an unconstrained dialogue (see T. McCarthy, The Critical Theory of Jürgen Habermas 306 [1978] certainly seems vulnerable to the Derridean charge of "logocentrism" as it belongs to the Western philosophical tradition that presupposes the possibility of achieving universal rationality. From the standpoint of deconstruction, the consensus generated through unconstrained dialogue is either purely formal and abstract and thus deprived of any particular content, or such consensus depends on the pre-dialogical acceptance of certain particular substantive values, in which case the dialogue that is supposed to lead to universal agreement is not genuinely unconstrained.

    Within the Habermasian project, the ideal speech situation is a counterfactual device designed to lead to the removal of the distortion which domination, deception and self-deception would bring to the dialogical process designed to produce a rational consensus. See id. at 306–07. Although from the perspective of deconstruction, Habermas' entire dialogical project lacks any genuine positive interpretive value, this does not foreclose the notions of consensus and of an ideal speech situation from playing a useful negative role analogous to that performed by Dworkin's concept of integrity. Thus, the absence of any form of consensus and the failure to devise legitimate means to combat domination, deception and self-deception from legal relationships may well constitute important obstacles standing in the way of a successful resolution of the crisis affecting legal interpretation.

19. See Jacobson, Idolatry of Rules, supra note 10.

20. All rewriting presumably seeks both to preserve and to supersede—i.e., to improve, to clarify—the writing which it seeks to restate. Hence, rewriting involves both completion and erasure of the text with respect to which it constitutes itself as a rewriting.

21. Derrida rejects the equation of knowledge and power. C. Norris, supra note 6, at 217.

22. No conception of deconstruction can be advanced with confidence, as every such conception is subject to further deconstruction. This, however, is not particularly distressing in the context of the present analysis, as the object is not to find the best conception of deconstruction. Rather, the object is to fasten onto *a* plausible conception of deconstruction that seems particularly well suited to shed light on the important questions raised by the crisis affecting legal interpretation.

23. While any conception of deconstruction presented in the course of this article involves, at best, one among many possible readings or rewritings of Derrida's conception of deconstruction, it is noteworthy that Derrida apparently conceives

of deconstruction as possessing a definite ethical dimension. See C. Norris, supra
note 6, at ch. 8. Moreover, according to Norris, "For Derrida, the realm of ethical
discourse is that which exceeds all given conceptual structures, but exceeds them
through a patient interrogation of their limits, and not by some leap into an unknown 'beyond' which would give no purchase to critical thought" (Id. at 224).

24. In this connection, it is worth mentioning Derrida's predominant preoccupation
with the writings of Hegel. See J. Derrida, Positions 77 (1981): "We will never be
finished with the reading or rereading of Hegel, and, in a certain way, I do nothing
other than attempt to explain myself on this point." For other among Derrida's
writings dealing with Hegel, see of Grammatology (1976); Margins of Philosophy
(1982); and Glas (1986). Turning the tables on Derrida, one could characterize
his deconstructive enterprise in Hegelian terms, as an ontological privileging of
difference which makes it irreducibly transcendent thus preventing its sublation
(*Aufhebung*) within a totality encompassing both self and other. Because of this
ontological privileging of difference, moreover, deconstruction requires the perpetual deferral of the reconciliation between individual morality—that is, Hegelian *Moralität*—and the ethical life of the community—that is, Hegelian *Sittlichkeit*.

For a particularly illuminating analysis of the relationship between the thought
of Derrida and that of Hegel, see Brudner, supra note 15, at 1191–98. For a
discussion of the conception of meaning within a Hegelian framework, see Rosenfeld, Hegel and the Dialectics of Contract, 10 Cardozo L. Rev. 1199 (1989).

25. Cf. Herrnstein Smith, Judgment After the Fall, 11 Cardozo L. Rev. 1291, 1304
(1990): "Value judgments may themselves be considered commodities—useful,
appropriable, and thus valuable, in numerous ways. Moreover, some of them are
evidently *worth more* than others *in the relevant markets*" (emphasis in original).

26. Indeed, since the exchange of commodities requires some effort and, when such
exchange is not simultaneous, some risk, utility-maximizing market participants
endowed with rationality of means would not engage in such exchange unless the
commodities involved had some value for them.

27. For a more comprehensive discussion of the relation between use value and exchange value and of the relation between subjective and objective values in the
context of a developed market economy, see Rosenfeld, Contract and Justice: The
Relation Between Classical Contract Law and Social Contract Theory, 70 Iowa L.
Rev. 769, 814–17, 832–39 (1985) [hereafter Contract and Justice].

28. Cf. P. Samuelson, Economics 455 (10th ed. 1976) ("A perfect-competitor is too
small and unimportant to affect market price.").

29. For an argument that is similar in many key respects and that concerns value in
general, see Herrnstein Smith, supra note 25.

30. See G. Hegel, Philosophy of Right g 40 (T. Knox trans. 1952) (contract is the
transfer of property from one to another in accordance with a common will).

31. Cf. id. at g 191A ("the need for greater comfort does not exactly arise within you
directly; it is suggested to you by those who hope to make a profit from its creation"); J. Galbraith, The Affluent Society 127 (1976) (consumer wants are to a
large extent created by producers).

32. Paradigmatically, contract formation involves a bargained-for intersubjective mediation between initially conflicting subjective desires. Both parties to a prospec-

tive contract seek to obtain as much as possible in exchange for as little as possible. A contract is struck when a compromise is reached. Such compromise is likely to provide each party with less than originally hoped for but with enough to make it more advantageous for each of them to enter into a contract than to walk away from it. Similarly, two actors with initially incompatible subjective value-laden approaches to an historically situated text by which they are jointly confronted cannot collaboratively rewrite it unless they first negotiate a mutually acceptable intersubjective standpoint from which they can produce a common interpretation.

33. In other words, a broad consensus concerning certain intersubjective values closes certain paths of legitimate disagreement while opening (or leaving open) other such paths. For example, if an entire community agrees that all human beings are created equal, then feminist claims for greater equality between the sexes cannot be contested legitimately by arguing that God created women to serve men. Such feminist claims could be legitimately contested, however, by an argument to the effect that while men and women are entitled to equal rights, they are not entitled to equal pay to the extent that physical differences between the sexes make women less desirable than men on the marketplace for jobs. But if a widespread consensus developed concerning the proposition that physical differences between the sexes do not justify different treatment on the job marketplace, then neither of the two above mentioned arguments could legitimately be advanced in opposition to the feminist claims.

34. It is conceivable in a purely formal sense that a rewriting would do no more than restate in different words the very meaning of that of which it is a rewriting. From the standpoint of deconstruction, however, rewriting involves erasure and projection into the past as well as into the future, and can therefore never be merely a plain restatement of that of which it is a rewriting.

35. See supra text accompanying note 24.

36. See supra text accompanying note 24.

37. This follows from the fact that whereas the ethical call to the other requires overcoming the particular shortcomings of the failed vision of reconciliation which gives such call its renewed impetus, since no definitive form of the reconciliation between self and other is possible, no blueprint for the ethical call to the other is ever available.

38. The requirement of integrity in the context of deconstruction is hence much more circumscribed than Dworkin's principle of integrity. See supra note 14 and accompanying text. Moreover, deconstruction's requirement of integrity is not an additional constraint to be added to existing ontological and ethical constraints. The requirement of integrity is implicitly contained in those constraints, but needs to be made explicit to better indicate the actual sweep of the constraints of which it forms part.

39. See supra text accompanying notes 17–18.

40. A distinction must be drawn between law embracing deconstruction—that is, availing itself of the interpretive process of deconstruction—and law as an object for deconstruction—that is, law as a subject matter submissible to the interpretive practices of deconstruction. In the former case, deconstruction becomes internalized within law, whereas in the latter, deconstruction remains external to law. In

the former case, moreover, law is irreducible to politics, whereas in the latter law might well be reducible to politics. Indeed, in the latter case, deconstruction might well reveal the aporias, blind spots and contradictions of a legal discourse that envisions itself as being severed from politics, and based on these revelations, deconstruction might quite conceivably lead to the conclusion that law is ultimately reducible to politics.

41. See R. Unger, Law in Modern Society 66 (1976).

42. See id. at 69.

43. See id. at 83, 86.

44. Cf. id. at 129 ("The conditions of liberal society require that the legal order be seen as somehow neutral or capable of accommodating antagonistic interests. . . . Yet every choice among different interpretations of the rules, different laws, or different procedures for lawmaking necessarily sacrifices some interests to others").

45. To the extent that it is accepted as the fundamental social charter by all the citizens of the United States, the Constitution plays a principal role in the formation of a national identity that promotes a nationwide notion of collective selfhood. On the other hand, the Constitution recognizes the split between the states and the nation, and proposes a reconciliation designed to preserve the respective identities of the states and of the nation. Because of the open-ended nature of the constitutional text, and because the practice of judicial review subjects it to endless rewriting, however, the work of reconciliation seems bound to remain forever incomplete. For a recent example of the difficulties involved in applying constitutional notions of federalism in an attempt to reconcile state and federal concerns, compare National League of Cities v. Usery, 426 U.S. 833 (1976) (Federalism bars imposing certain federal labor standards on employees of a state) with Garcia v. San Antonio Metro. Transit Auth., 469 U.S. 528 (1985) (Federalism permits imposing the same labor standards on employees of a state).

46. One notorious example of a recent failure to reconcile self and other or individual and community or identity and difference in the context of the constitutional jurisprudence of the Bill of Rights is furnished by the Supreme Court's series of decisions on the constitutional right to privacy since its landmark decision in Griswold v. Connecticut, 381 U.S. 479 (1965). See, e.g., Webster v. Reproductive Health Servs., 109 S. Ct. 3040 (1989); Bowers v. Hardwick, 478 U.S. 186 (1986); Roe v. Wade, 410 U.S. 113 (1973).

47. See Jacobson, Idolatry of Rules, supra note 10, at 1106.

48. Consider the following example involving a legal rule that cannot be grasped until it becomes further elaborated in a future judicial opinion. A landowner brings a lawsuit against his neighbor because the latter's cat has entered upon plaintiff's property where it has caused damage for which the plaintiff seeks to be reimbursed. Moreover, the only relevant precedent involves a case holding that the owner of a cow is liable to his neighbor for the damage caused to the latter's property by the cow following its unauthorized entry upon the plaintiff's property. Under those circumstances, the judge sitting in the case concerning the cat can infer at least two different rules from the precedent involving the cow. The first rule is that the owner of a large animal is liable for any damage caused by the latter following unauthorized entry upon the owner's neighbor property. The second rule, on the other hand, is that an owner is thus liable for any such damage

caused by any of his or her domestic animals. Since a cat is a small domestic animal, the plaintiff will lose his case if the judge infers the first rule from the precedent, but he will win if the judge infers instead the second rule.

Now, suppose further that the judge in the case of the cat rules in favor of the plaintiff after concluding that the situation involving the cat is in all relevant respects analogous to that regarding the cow. But the judge leaves unclear the basis for the analogy she draws between the case of the cow and that of the cat. Under those circumstances, it will be left to another judge before whom the next case in the series will be brought at some future date, to infer which legal rule might cover all three cases consistent with the results in the respective cases of the cow and the cat. Thus, the judge before whom the third case will be brought may decide, for example, that the rule to be inferred concerns all of an owner's domestic animals, or that it instead covers all animals, whether domestic or not, which usually live on the owner's property. The important point, however, is that no matter which of these two alternative legal rules is eventually chosen, the legal rule that accounts for the result in the case of the cat cannot become explicit until its articulation in the course of the judicial resolution of some subsequent case.

49. See Jacobson, Idolatry of Rules, supra note 10, at 1135; Jacobson, Hegel's Legal Plenum, 10 Cardozo L. Rev. 877, 889–90 (1989) [hereafter Legal Plenum].

50. Jacobson, Idolatry of Rules, supra note 10, at 1135.

51. Cf. Jacobson, Legal Plenum, supra note 49, at 890 (in the common law system persons cannot interact without generating rights and duties, but cannot know what those rights and duties are until after having interacted).

52. See Schauer, Formalism, 97 Yale L. J. 509, 510 (1988); see also Unger, supra note 5, at 564 (Legal formalism is usually understood to describe the "belief in the availability of a deductive or quasi-deductive method capable of giving determinate solutions to particular problems of legal choice.").

53. If "origins" for this new legal formalism need be sought, one place where they may be found is in the vigorously antiformalist writings of Roberto Unger. See Unger, supra note 5, at 564 (legal formalism evinces "a commitment to, and therefore also a belief in the possibility of, a method of legal justification that can be clearly contrasted to open-ended disputes about the basic terms of social life, disputes that people call ideological, philosophical or visionary"). For evidence of reliance by a proponent of the new legal formalism on Unger's formulations, see Weinrib, Legal Formalism: On the Immanent Rationality of Law, 97 Yale L.J. 949, 953 (1988).

54. See, e.g., Weinrib, supra note 53, at 1008 ("Nothing about formalism precludes indeterminacy. . . . For formalism the possibility of indeterminacy neither can, nor need be, avoided.").

55. Remarks by S. Fish, Symposium on Deconstruction and the Possibility of Justice (Benjamin N. Cardozo School of Law, Oct. 2–3, 1989).

56. See Weinrib, supra note 53.

57. It should be pointed out from the outset that neither Fish's nor Weinrib's version of legal formalism taken as a whole is likely to satisfy the requirements of the alternative conception of deconstruction advanced in this article. Indeed, Fish's legal formalism is based heavily on an identification of law with rhetoric which is more in tune with the conception of deconstruction as an interpretive technique

or method than with the alternative conception embraced here. Weinrib's legal formalism, on the other hand, places substantial reliance on the rationality of law, and is thus vulnerable to a Derridean charge of undue "logocentrism." Accordingly, in assessing the suitability of Fish's and Weinrib's theories for purposes of elaborating an interpretive practice consistent with a conception of law as embracing deconstruction, emphasis will be placed on those features of the respective theories which seem most compatible with the alternative conception of deconstruction adopted in this article.

58. Fish, supra note 55.

59. Id.

60. Weinrib, supra note 53, at 1002–03.

61. See id. at 1003.

62. Fish, supra note 55.

63. Id.

64. Id.

65. Id.

66. Id.

67. Id.

68. Id.

69. Id.

70. Restatement (Second) of Contracts §71 comment a (1979). Consideration has also been described as the "element of exchange required for a contract to be enforceable as a bargain." Id.

71. Fish, supra note 55.

72. Id.

73. Typically, the parties exchange promises of future performance, or such a promise in exchange for a present performance.

74. Under modern contract law, the mutuality of bargained-for exchange must occur in the present tense of the entering into the agreement. Under pre-modern contract law, in contrast, a past benefit conferred upon a promisor was deemed adequate consideration for his or her subsequent promise to become legally binding. See Rosenfeld, Contract and Justice, supra note 27, at 829. As a matter of fact, "[t]he old doctrine of consideration was presumably an attempt to confine legitimate contractual transactions within some broad parameters of fairness." Id.

75. Fish, supra note 55.

76. Id.

77. Id.

78. For example, when a person enters a restaurant and orders food, it can be reasonably inferred that the intention of both the patron and the restaurant owner is to exchange the ordered meal for the price of that meal calculated by reference to the menu that the patron consulted before ordering.

79. See, e.g., Continental Forest Prods., Inc. v. Chandler Supply Co., 95 Idaho 739, 743, 518 P.2d 1201, 1205 (1974).

80. Fish, supra note 55.

81. Id.

82. Id.

83. This act is "purely present" in that it is lifted out of the flow of historical events and has no past or future. Indeed, the decisionmaker's decision is legitimated because of the decisionmaker's present authority rather than because of any links to past or future writings.

84. See A. Smith, An Inquiry into the Nature and Causes of the Wealth of Nations 477–78 (E. Cannan ed. 1976). For a more extended discussion of Adam Smith's views and of the morals of the market, see Rosenfeld, Contract and Justice, supra note 27, at 873–77.

85. To the extent that individuals are naturally inclined to pursue their self-interest, it may sound odd to speak of an "obligation" to act out of self-interest. Nevertheless, if one is willing to admit that it is possible for individuals to chose to act out of motivations other than self-interest, then it is not inconsistent to claim that the individual has a moral obligation to act out of self-interest even though he or she might be naturally inclined to do so in most cases. Cf. L. Dumont, From Mandeville to Marx 61 (1977) ("[E]conomics escapes the fetters of general morality only at the price of assuming a normative character of its own.").

86. According to Smith's theory, while in the economic sphere the individual must act out of self-interest, in other spheres he or she must act out of sympathy. See A. Smith, The Theory of Moral Sentiments (1976). Notwithstanding these differences, however, Smith derives both the morals of the market and the morals of sympathy from a single moral vision predicated on utilitarian values.

87. Unger, supra note 5, at 625.

88. For a more comprehensive discussion of this point see Rosenfeld, Contract and Justice, supra note 27, at 827–32.

89. Promises to make a gift which are unenforceable as lacking consideration, on the other hand, are generally motivated by altruistic rather than self-interested concerns. Accordingly, consistent with Smith's analysis, such promises are less likely to promote the economic common good than promises purely motivated by self-interest.

90. Under this hypothesis, the proper function of contract law is to enforce exchange agreements motivated by self-interest. Consideration is a principal means to assure that contract fulfills its proper function, particularly in less developed markets where the subjective expression of self-interest by an agent is likely to be the best available evidence of that agent's self-interest. In fully developed markets where no single individual has a perceptible influence on the exchange value of commodities, however, an agent to a transaction may not always be the best judge of his or her own self-interest with respect to a given exchange transaction. Accordingly, contracts implied in law may be justified as a means to secure the promotion of an individual's self-interest where that individual is not in the position to be the best judge of his or her own self-interest.

91. Unger, for example, has argued that modern contract doctrine has been defined by vision and countervision, involving on the one hand freedom of contract and market values, and on the other, communitarian values and fairness. See Unger, supra note 5, at 616–33. Moreover, in the context of a conflict between moral

visions, law may well be more indeterminate and more incoherent than when it is firmly anchored in a single moral vision. Thus, it may be that consideration and contracts implied in law respectively embody conflicting moral visions, and that no valid internal connections could be drawn between these two legal doctrines. But in that case the failure is not with legal doctrine or legal interpretation, but with the lack of a unified moral perspective.

92. Another plausible hypothesis is that the moral vision that encompasses the morals of the market has become so eroded that contract law as a distinct and independent body of mutually consistent legal doctrines has disintegrated. This hypothesis is endorsed by the proponents of the death of contract thesis. See, e.g., P. Atiyah, The Rise and Fall of Freedom of Contract (1979); G. Gilmore, The Death of Contract (1974). Under this hypothesis the doctrine of consideration may seem incoherent but that would be because of the collapse of its moral foundation rather than because of any inherent problem with legal doctrine as such.

93. Thus, consistent with Fish's vision, there is a parallel between the appropriation by law as a practice (through incorporation and transformation) of materials from other practices such as morals and politics, and the appropriation by the practice of theory of legal materials such as legal doctrines as subject matters for evaluation.

94. Compare C. Perelman, The Idea of Justice and the Problem of Argument 16 (1963) (according to the principle of formal justice "beings of one and the same category must be treated the same way") with Trimble v. Gordon, 430 U.S. 762, 780 (1980) (Rehnquist, J., dissenting) (The equal protection clause of the Fourteenth Amendment does not require "that all persons must be treated alike. Rather, its general principle is that persons similarly situated should be treated similarly.").

95. Cf. Fallon, A Constructivist Coherence Theory of Constitutional Interpretation, 100 Harv. L. Rev. 1189, 1189–90 (1987) (the practice of constitutional interpretation recognizes the relevance of at least five types of arguments, including "value arguments" making claims about justice, morality or social policy).

96. See, e.g., id. at 1205.

97. This question has been at the heart of the affirmative action cases decided by the Supreme Court. See M. Rosenfeld, Affirmative Action and Justice: A Philosophical and Constitutional Inquiry, ch. 7 (1991) [hereafter Affirmative Action]; Rosenfeld, Decoding Richmond, supra note 2.

98. See Fallon, supra note 95, at 1205–06.

99. For a more extensive analysis of the relationship between the practice of philosophy and that of constitutional interpretation in the context of the equal protection clause, see M. Rosenfeld, Affirmative Action, supra note 97, at ch. 6.

100. See Weinrib, supra note 53, at 951.

101. Id. at 1014.

102. Id.

103. See id. at 1004–05.

104. Id. at 1011.

105. Id.

106. See supra text accompanying notes 59–60.

107. See Weinrib, supra note 53, at 980, 984.

108. Id. at 977.

109. See id.

110. See id. at 978.

111. Id.

112. Id. at 999.

113. Id. at 988.

114. Id. at 994.

115. Id. at 997.

116. See id. at 993.

117. See id. at 989.

118. See is. at 989.

119. See id. at 990.

120. See id. at 991–92.

121. Id.

122. Id.

123. Id. at 991.

124. Id.

125. See id. at 1009.

126. Id. at 1009–10.

127. See Brudner, supra note 15, at 1168–81. Since I agree, on the whole, with Brudner's incisive critique of Weinrib's formalism, I only concentrate on those shortcomings of Weinrib's theory that have a direct relevance to the specific concerns addressed by this article.

128. See id. at 1173.

129. Id. at 1178–81.

130. Just as in the context of a Smithian market economy where morals are not expelled from the marketplace (see supra text accompanying notes 84–86), a vision of corrective justice as applying exclusively to a regime of negative rights is not apolitical. Instead it is informed by the particular morals and politics that underly the free market economy.

131. It may be objected that in a feudal society distributions of benefits and burdens would not be conceived in terms of distributive justice. Even conceding this point, the fact remains that there is no *logical* impediment against a feudal conception of distributive justice such as the one outlined here.

132. It may be objected that from the standpoint of adjudication, both forms of justice must be viewed as backward-looking given the very structure of adjudication. Upon reflection, however, this objection misses the mark. Corrective justice seeks to recapture the past whereas distributive justice—whether oriented towards a past, present or future moment—construes all points in time upon which it focuses as presents looking into the future. As an illustration, consider the following example. A municipality has as a distributive rule that each of its adult members is entitled to be provided by government with housing having a market value of

$50,000, and a corrective rule that a victim of intentional wrongdoing is entitled
to full compensation in kind or in the market value equivalent of his or her loss
by the wrongdoer. Suppose now that *A* collected her $50,000 government subsidy
and invested $50,000 of her own money to have a $100,000 house built. After *A*
has moved into her new house, *B*, an arsonist, burns it to the ground. *A* could sue
B and obtain $100,000 in damages under corrective justice. In that case, the ju-
dicial objective would be to recreate as nearly as possible the moment preceding
the wrongdoing in a ritualized attempt to erase that act of wrongdoing. On the
other hand (assuming that *B* is destitute), *A* could bring an action to establish that
she is (distributively) entitled to a $50,000 housing subsidy (even though she has
already received such a subsidy in the past). In this latter case, applying legal
norms derived from distributive justice, the judge would have to focus on two past
moments: that of the destruction of *A*'s house by arson and the earlier moment in
which she received her original housing subsidy. But such judicial focus on the
past would not be for purposes of reinstating the past (as the judge in this action
does not seek to put *A* in the position to have a new $100,000 house similar to
the one she owned prior to the arson). Instead, it would be for purposes of determining whether these judicially framed past events give rise to a present entitlement to a future distribution.

133. For a discussion of the argument that the implementation of corrective or compensatory justice is necessary to buttress the achievements of distributive justice
in the face of violations of distributive entitlements, see M. Rosenfeld, Affirmative
Action, supra note 97, at ch. 1.

134. To illustrate these points, let us consider the example of a breach of contract.
Suppose that the buyer in a contract for the sale of goods refuses to pay the seller
after receipt of the goods in accordance with the terms of the contract. While it
seems obvious that corrective justice requires that the buyer compensate the seller
for the buyer's breach of contract, it is not self-evident what the measure of damages should be. Should it be the contract price? The market price of the goods?
Or, the "just" or "fair" price for such goods? Moreover, stipulation that the objective of corrective justice is the simultaneous wiping out of the wrongdoing of
the defendant and of the suffering of the plaintiff through an award of damages
does not suffice to establish the proper measure of damages. It might be interjected
that it is obvious that the contract price is the proper measure of damages, since
payment of the contract price as damages would put buyer and seller in the position in which they would have been absent any breach. Upon careful consideration, however, it should become apparent that the contract price only affords the
proper measure of damages if it is (distributively) just (or at least not unjust).
Thus, if under the applicable overall principle of justice, the market price of goods
is deemed just, then if the contract price in question happens greatly to exceed the
market price it would be unjust and could not provide the proper measure of
damages in the breach of contract case. Strictly speaking, in the latter case the
collection of that portion of the contract price which is in excess of the market
price would itself constitute wrongdoing calling for compensation. And in view
of the two wrongdoings involved—namely, the buyer's failure to pay for the
goods, and the seller's attempt to collect that portion of the contract price which
is in excess of the market price—corrective justice would require (as the simultaneous erasure of both wrongs) that the buyer defendant pay the market price of
the goods as damages to the seller plaintiff. In short, since the measure of damages
depends on what counts as a wrongdoing under a particular criterion of (overall)

justice, the relationships that come within the scope of corrective justice are clearly mediated, and the content of corrective justice is itself derived from substantive principles of justice inevitably grounded in politics. For an extensive discussion of the relationship between contract and justice, including the relationship between corrective or compensatory and distributive justice in the context of contract, see Rosenfeld, Contract and Justice, supra note 27.

135. See supra note 50 and accompanying text.

136. See, e.g., Schneider, The Dialectic of Rights and Politics: Perspectives From the Women's Movement, 61 N.Y.U. L. Rev. 589, 644–48 (1986) (discussing emergence of legal rights of battered women).

137. See supra text accompanying notes 108–09.

138. See supra text following note 129.

139. Id.; cf. Cornell, Institutionalization of Meaning, Recollective Imagination, and the Potential for Transformative Legal Interpretation, 136 U. Pa. L. Rev. 1135, 1162 n.95 (1988) ("Derrida brilliantly demonstrated the constitutive power of the past at the same time that he has also shown why the 'present' evaporates as an interpretive category, leaving us instead with the promise of the future implicit in a past never capable of being made present to itself.").

140. Corrective justice's propensity to (re)turn every here and now into a past is vividly illustrated by cases in which the plaintiff seeks *prospective* (compensatory) relief, such as those involving a petition for an injunction. Suppose a defendant places a crane in front of the plaintiff's house and declares that he intends to demolish the house. Plaintiff then sues defendant and seeks a preliminary injunction ordering the defendant not to destroy the house. In a sense, the judge who must decide the case, is asked to "restore" a status quo that has not yet been disrupted. Moreover, to the extent that the grant of the injunction must be predicated on a judicial finding of future likelihood of the threatened action by the defendant causing the plaintiff an irreparable harm (see J. Friedenthal, M. Kane and A. Miller, Civil Procedure 703 [1985], the judge must treat the here and now as if it were a past, and determine, based on his or her interpretation of the likelihood of future events, whether such present as past ought to be rewritten as if it had been already disrupted.

141. See supra text following note 24.

142. To avoid the sense of arbitrariness that follows from its seemingly *ad hoc* mode of operation, purely political justice may appeal to the precepts of some unwritten natural law. Given that for deconstruction, speech is a form of writing, it does not matter that natural law is not actually written law. Accordingly, depending on the actual circumstances involved, natural law may or may not be deemed to form part of a community's law. Where natural law is properly part of a community's law, and where political justice can be justified in terms of such natural law, political justice may be legitimately viewed as essentially reducible to legal justice.

143. See supra text following note 129.

144. Cf. Swann v. Charlotte-Mecklenburg Board of Education, 402 U.S. 1 (1971) (busing children for purposes of achieving racial desegregation of public schools is constitutionally permissible).

145. See supra notes 120, 121 and accompanying text.

146. For example, suppose there is a general consensus that distributive justice requires

the allocation of socially produced goods in proportion to each individual's subjectively felt needs. Under those circumstances, it seems perfectly natural to impose an ethical duty against claiming entitlements to goods which are not necessary to satisfy one's subjectively felt needs. But by the same token, it may be inadvisable to impose a similar legal duty, because of the severe difficulties or distasteful burdens—ie., the need to use lie detector tests to insure that claims do not exceed subjectively felt needs—which the requisite mechanism of external enforcement needed to sustain legal duties would inevitably have to produce.

147. The call involved here is, of course, the ethical call of deconstruction which involves a substantive ethical prescription, and which must be distinguished from ethics in general understood as a practice relying on internal constraints and sanctions.

5

Judgment After the Fall

Barbara Herrnstein Smith

MACINTYRE'S FALL AND JUDGMENT TYPOLOGY

It is a commonplace of traditional value theory that there are two fundamentally distinct types of evaluative discourse, one exemplified by statements such as "I like it," "I want to do it," or "I think so," the other by statements such as "It is beautiful," "It is right," or "It is true," the first expressing a subjective and merely personal preference (or desire or opinion), the second constituting an impersonal judgment of the objective value (aesthetic, moral, or cognitive) of something and thereby rightfully claiming universal validity. A key instance (and perhaps the founding one) of the distinction was developed by Kant in the opening pages of the *Critique of Judgement*.[1] A lay version of it is the familiar observation that, since one can say "It's good, but I don't like it" and "I like it though I know it's no good," it must be because we intuitively recognize and/or "our language embodies" a fundamental difference between personal feelings and objective value.[2]

These distinctions also operate crucially in Alisdair MacIntyre's *After Virtue*, a meditation on the alleged decline of moral discourse and practice in modern times.[3] Early in his first chapter, MacIntyre contrasts two kinds of reply to the question "Why should I do so-and-so?"

Reply #1 has a form such as *"Because I wish it,"* the "reason-giving force" of which, MacIntyre observes, is confined to "the personal context of the utterance."[4] It depends, he writes, "on certain characteristics possessed [by the speaker] at the time of hearing or otherwise learning of the utterance by [the listener]."[5] These confining contexts and characteristics are exemplified, in his discussion, by situations where the speaker is a police or army officer who has power or authority over the listener or where the listener loves or fears or wants something from the speaker. In contrast to this, the reason-giving force of Reply 2, which has a form such as *"Because it is your duty,"* is said by MacIntyre not to be so confined but, on the contrary, to be altogether unconditional, quite independent of who utters it or, he adds, even whether it is uttered at all. He continues:

> Moreover the appeal [of a statement such as "Because it is your duty"] is to a type of consideration which is independent of the relationship between speaker and hearer. Its use presupposes the existence of *impersonal* criteria—the existence, independently of the preferences or attitudes of speaker and hearer, of standards of justice or generosity or duty. *The particular link between the context of utterance and the force of the reason-giving which always holds in the case of expressions of personal preferences or desire is severed in the case of moral and other evaluative utterances.*[6]

According to MacIntyre, the emotive theory of value judgments, which he explains as the view that expressions such as "It is good" really mean "I like it and urge it on or recommend it to you,"

> is dedicated to characterizing as equivalent in meaning two kinds of expression which . . . derive their distinctive function in our language in key part from the contrast and difference between them. I have already suggested that there are good reasons for distinguishing between what I called expressions of personal preference and evaluative (including moral) expressions. . . .[7]

Therefore, he concludes, the emotive theory is really "a theory about the *use*—understood as purpose or function—of members of a certain class of expressions rather than about their *meaning*—understood as including all that Frege intended by 'sense' and 'reference.'"[8]

MacIntyre goes on to posit the remarkable hypothesis on which the major argument of *After Virtue* is subsequently constructed:

> Clearly the argument so far shows that when someone utters a moral judgment such as "This is right" or "This is good," it does not mean the same as "I approve of this; do so as well" or "Hurrah for this!" . . . [If it could be demonstrated] that in *using* such sentences to *say* whatever they *mean*, the agent was in fact *doing* nothing other than *expressing his feelings or attitudes and attempting to influence the feelings and attitudes of others* . . . [,] it would follow that the meaning and the use of moral expressions were, or at

the very least had become, radically discrepant with each other. Meaning and use would be at odds in such a way that meaning would tend to conceal use. We could not safely infer what someone who uttered a moral judgment was doing merely by listening to what he said. Moreover the agent himself might . . . be assured that he was appealing to independent impersonal criteria, when all that he was in fact doing was expressing his feelings to others in a manipulative way. How might such a phenomenon come to occur?[9]

How indeed? Or, rather, we might ask, in accord with what conception of language could the occurrence of any such phenomenon come to be *imagined?*

The significant features of that conception become clear as MacIntyre develops his "philosophical/historical" narrative, which goes as follows.[10] When all was well and there were still objective standards accepted by all the members of the *polis* (with a few exceptions about which nothing further need be said), moral discourse was such that there was always a dependable correspondence between (a) what moral expressions said and meant *in themselves,* and (b) what the people who *used* those expressions meant by them, and believed they were doing with them, and really did with them. In such a time, a listener could "safely infer" what someone was *doing* with a moral expression "merely by listening" to what that person *said.* And, in those good days gone, there was no confusion between expressions (or sentences) such as "I like it" and others such as "It is good."[11] The first, which *in itself* expresses some purely personal preference, was then *used* only to express purely personal preferences; the second, which presupposes impersonal standards and *in itself* embodies an appeal to them, was *used* only to appeal to such standards.

Now, alas, the story continues, all is schism and confusion: that which was once one and united is now many and fractured; those things which once corresponded and matched are now "discrepant" and "at odds"; and that which was once clear and dependable has become cloudy and shifting. Now what passes for morality is an "unharmonious melange of ill-assorted fragments,"[12] and there is no established way of deciding between conflicting claims. Now "'virtue' and 'justice' and 'piety' and 'duty' and even 'ought' have become other than they once were,"[13] so that "[m]oral judgments lose any clear status and the sentences which express them . . . lose any undebatable meaning."[14] Now people still *say* "It is good" and *think* they mean "It is good," but, without knowing it, they are really doing only what people used to do when they said "I like it" or "I want it," namely expressing their own feelings and trying to get other people to feel, do, or believe certain things. And everyone is deceived: listeners are deceived about what speakers are doing; speakers are self-deceived about what they themselves are doing; and moral philosophers are either deceived, complacent, or complicitous.[15]

MacIntyre wants to remind us what it was like before after-virtue, and is still like in a few places (he indicates specifically, "among . . . some Catholic Irish, some Orthodox Greeks and some Jews of an Orthodox persuasion, . . . in Scotland . . . [and in] Protestant communities in the United States, especially perhaps those in or from the South"),[16] and what, in our heart of hearts, the rest of us really wish it were like again. We reveal that we wish it by the very fact that we still *say* things such as "It is good," "It is right," and "Because it is your duty." For, even though we are *using* those expressions only to disguise from each other and from ourselves what we are really *doing,* that is, expressing our merely personal preferences and desires in manipulative ways, nevertheless, because those expressions *in themselves* embody impersonal appeals to objective standards, our very *use* of them "expresses at least an aspiration to be or to become rational in this area of our lives."[17]

The question that must be asked of this as of any other account of the Fall is not merely whether, with respect to every posited prelapsarian element, anything ever did or could happen that way but, no less importantly, whether, with respect to every deplored postlapsarian element, anything ever did or could happen otherwise. Thus, here, the significant questions would be whether expressions *ever* mean things "in themselves," whether anyone *ever* deduced motives directly from verbal forms, whether judgments could *ever* have undebatable meaning, and whether there is any use of language that does *not* try to get people to feel, do, and believe certain things.

The answer is, in every case here, no. What must be stressed is that no verbal form has meaning or force in itself—or ever did have, even before the Fall. Nothing is "in" the form. Everything is "in" the verbal agents themselves, specifically in their tendencies to produce certain verbal forms under certain conditions and to respond to them in certain ways: tendencies that are themselves the corporeally inscribed traces of the *differential consequences* of those agents' *prior* uses of, and responses to, those particular (which is to say, more or less similar) forms. Our verbal tendencies are, in other words, the products of our personal histories as verbal creatures. The general dynamics through which a listener comes to respond in some way to a so-called impersonal and unconditional (or "context-independent" or "objective") judgment such as "Murder is wrong," "*Es ist schön,*" or "Business is business" is no different from the dynamics through which he or she comes to respond to any other type of statement, including such explicitly "personal" and otherwise conditional, "context-bound," or "subjective" statements as "I am about to kill you," or "I just happen to find it appealing," or "For my money, business is business."

We are quite familiar by now with the idea that any utterance (or, of course, text or, in Derrida's sense, "writing") can, in principle, be "severed" from the conditions of its production, including the intentions and identity or other "characteristics" of the speaker. There is, however, no "type" of expression that is characteristically so severed, and none, even the most Mosaic or otherwise oracular in form (and even where evidently anonymous), the "force" of which operates with the sort of autonomy that MacIntyre claims as criteria for "evaluative (including moral) expressions." The alleged degeneracy and homesickness of contemporary moral thought cannot be exhibited in the disparity between "*the* meaning" or moral expressions and "*our* use" of them because there is not and cannot be any such disparity. Expressions such as "It is right," "It is good," and "Murder is wrong" cannot embody objectivist appeals *in spite of* how they are being used because, *aside from* how they are being used, there is no way for them to embody anything at all. To say that an expression has been "severed" from some "original" set of meanings is to say only that it has come to be *used* under a *different* set of conditions in relation to which it now "really means" something else.[18] Or, to put this another way, the notion of a disparity between the meaning and the use of a verbal form consists simply of privileging one set of conditions of usage over another. Commonly, as in MacIntyre's case, usages that were current at some earlier moment in the life of the community are privileged over later ones as more authentic, inherent, or proper—or perhaps it is here only earlier in the moral theorist's own life and, for that very reason, intuitively felt as more fundamental and (this being the crucial illusion in all such cases) as "embodied" in "the forms themselves."

The "force," "functions," and "claims" of *all* judgments and, indeed, of all statements (or "expressions") are conditional, contingent, and variable. To be sure, the ranges of conditions tend to become relatively confined and the variability relatively stabilized within particular verbal communities (that is, among groups of verbally interacting agents). But these confinements and stabilizations are the emergent effects of the interactive practices of the members of the community themselves; they are not the product of some essential/residual semantic "force" inhering in verbal *forms*. Moreover, plausible situations can always be specified in which forms that tend to operate one way under most conditions would, in fact, operate another quite different way. Thus, there are numerous, readily imaginable, circumstances under which an explicit "expression of personal preference," such as "It's just my cup of tea," could be replaced by an apparently "impersonal and objective" form, such as "It's absolutely the greatest ever," with very little difference in function, force, or claim—and, in those senses, "meaning." Indeed, the supposed binary distinctions between judgment types can always be observed to break down in verbal practice, for any verbal form can serve any discursive function—evaluative or other—under certain circumstances, and *each* of the two supposedly contrastive forms will, under some circumstances, serve the functions, operate with the force, make the claims, and, in those senses, have the meaning that, in classic axiological discourse-typology, are the distinguishing features of the *other* one.

As should be clear, the point of this analysis is not that there are *no* differences among the various verbal forms or discourse types dichotomized in traditional value theory: it is, rather, that there are multiple differences, that they are not only and always contrastive, that they include many that are not commonly cited, and that those commonly cited must be described otherwise. Not only can one not tell from its form alone what the force of an evaluative judgment is; one cannot tell whether an "expression" per se is evaluative at all. Any verbal form ("How odd!" "Is this the one you brought back from Rome?" "It's 10 o'clock, already—let's go," "Don't forget your umbrella") can, under some conditions, operate for a listener as a mark and sign of a speaker's "personal preferences," and there is a virtually unlimited range of forms ("cool," "the pits," "***," "XXX") through which someone can offer (and be understood to be offering) what is idiomatically termed an "objective" observation of the value of something or an "impersonal" estimate of its value for other people. Moreover, even such apparently simple and meager forms as appear in the examples just cited may be, for certain listeners, expressively and informationally quite subtle and specific: as, for example, when the listener has subtle and specific prior knowledge of the speaker's tastes, interests, and, especially, his or her verbal habits, or (as in travel guides or published film ratings) where the reader can interpret symbols such as "***" or "XXX" in accord with some more or less elaborate "key" that he or she has already learned. These cases, however, are not very different from those in which judgments are framed in more explicitly elaborated forms and, in fact, represent the ways that "expressions" of all "types" inevitably operate.

It was noted above that the particular lexical, syntactic, and modal form of the judgment (e.g., whether it is "Gee, you might try The Blue Moon Diner—all the fellows at the office go there" as opposed to "It's the best restaurant in town"; or "I think it's awful to hurt other people deliberately" as opposed to "Torture is wrong"; or, as in MacIntyre's examples of justifications, "Do it *because I want you to*" as opposed to "Do it *because it is your duty*") may be responsive to, and indicate to a listener, various subtle and specific circumstances. The circumstances thus responded to—and more or less effectively indicated to a listener—are by no means confined, however, to features of the objects or practices being evaluated or what is commonly and currently spoken of as the "referents" of an evaluative utterance. Indeed, what is crucially obscured by classic referential conceptions of "meaning" is the heterogeneity of the conditions that may be thus responded to and indicated, including the evaluator's specific social/political relationship to those he addresses and the general structure of motives that elicits and shapes his interaction with them—e.g., whether the speaker is someone's "superior officer" *or* her "lover," and whether he "fears" the listener *or* "wants something from" her, or whether the listener "fears" or "wants something from" him: differences of relationship and motive that MacIntyre obscures by lumping them together as contaminating or confining "personal" and "contextual" conditions in contrast to what he posits as the altogether "unconditioned" productions of putatively "genuine" moral judgments and justifications.

The formal features of a verbal judgment also respond to—and can indicate more or less well to a listener—such other subtle conditions as the speaker's beliefs concerning the extensiveness and stability of the circumstances under which his judgment would be applicable and his assumptions concerning the nature of his listeners' interest in his judgment. While it is unlikely that any of these conditions could be specifically articulated *as such* by the speaker or his listeners, they are nevertheless what both (or all) of them will have learned in learning, through prior verbal interactions with other people in their shared verbal community, the more or less recurrent conditions of usage of various verbal forms—which is, of course, why judgments (or any other types of utterance) have any "force" at all.

Because of other general aspects of communication that I cannot elaborate here, particularly those involving the inevitable disparities, differences, and asymmetries between what is "transmitted" by a speaker and "received" by a listener,[19] a listener cannot (and never could, even before the Fall) "infer" any of these matters—or anything else—"safely" from the form of a judgment. Non-identity, non-recovery, non-duplication, unpredictability, and uncontrollability are ineradicable structural features of all verbal transactions. To the extent, however, that certain verbal practices tend to occur with some regularity in a verbal community, we may observe certain *relative likelihoods*—matters of more-or-less and of statistical probability—in the formal features of value judgments offered under, and in response to, various conditions. For example, (and in the verbal communities with which most readers of this paper would be familiar), (a) the broader and more stable the range of conditions under which someone believes the judgment he offers would be applicable, (b) the more extensive the set of people for whom he believes it would be appropriable, (c) the more closely he believes his relevant interests, perspectives, expectations, assumptions, etc. coincide with those of his immediate audience, and (d) the more confident he is in his own beliefs concerning all these matters, the *more likely* it is that the judgment he offers will take the form of an "unconditioned" statement and hence appear to be an "impersonal" judgment appealing to "objective standards": "Simply great," "Simply false," "A beautiful shot," "The best novel she's ever written," "A vile, immoral act," etc. Conversely, (a) the narrower and/or more unstable he believes the range of applicability of the judgment to be, (b) the more confined and distinctive the set of people for whom he suspects it would be appropriable, (c) the more divergent he believes his personal interests, perspectives, expectations, etc. to be from those of his immediate audience, and (d) the more unsure he is of his ability to gauge any or all of these accurately, the *more likely* it is that he will qualify its utterance accordingly—phrasing it, perhaps, in highly guarded and conditional terms ("Great . . . for such-and-such people," "True . . . under such-and-such conditions," "Honorable . . . assuming such-and-such convictions," etc.) or, perhaps, framing it as a "merely personal" preference or opinion ("Well, anyway, *I* like it, . . . think so, . . . feel that way about ..," etc.).

Thus (and contrary to much "linguistic intuition" and Kant's apparent supposition),[20] when someone makes a formally unconditional and otherwise unqualified evaluative statement (*it's nifty, it's nauseating, es ist schön,* etc.), the fact that she does not name explicitly any limiting group of people need not imply that she is claiming universal validity for the judgment or takes the agreement of "everybody" to be the ideal condition of its appropriability. It may be and often is, rather, because she believes the defining features of the unspecified but nevertheless specific set of people for whom the judgment is likely to be

appropriable are already more or less accurately taken for granted by ⌉
her listeners: commonly enough as defining a set consisting of herself, ⌋
plus those listeners themselves, plus all other people *like* them in the
relevant respects (e.g., lovers of new wave music, students of cinematic
art, electronic engineers, communicants of the Catholic Church, professional people of means and leisure, etc.), but also quite often as
more or less inferable from the verbal/textual (and other) context of
the judgment (e.g., the book review section of *The New Yorker* as
distinguished from that of *Popular Mechanics,* or the current *Michelin
Guide to Italy* rather than a 1950 edition of *How to See Europe on
$5 a Day,* or the policy recommendations of a sociological study of
teenage pregnancy rather than a Vatican Encyclical). The speaker's
beliefs concerning what her audience assumes and infers may, of
course, be mistaken, but the possibility of error of that kind is an
ineradicable condition of all verbal transactions and does not undermine the appropriability of value judgments—or their "force," "validity," "truth value," or interest of any other kind—any more than that
of any other type of utterance.

Here, as elsewhere, the deconstruction of a classic dualistic distinction does not, as commonly feared and charged, yield a flattening,
collapse, or reduction: the undoing of the opposition of "subjective,
conditioned" and "objective, unconditioned" is not (as in Mac-
Intyre's—and other philosophers'—production of "emotivism")
equivalent to making all value judgments the expression of mere personal preference. Rather, the unsettling of pure, polarized extremity
opens the possibility—and recognition—of infinite internal differentiation: not "good, . . . true, . . . beautiful" (etc.) *either* "for myself
alone" *or* "for everybody," but, rather, "for myself plus these more or
less specific other people," or "though not for myself, yet probably for
these other people"—and, to be sure, *sometimes,* "perhaps only for
myself" and "for, as I insist and demand, everybody."

THE VALUE OF VALUE JUDGMENTS

"The work is physically small—18 by 13 inches—but massive
and disturbingly expressive in impact."

"She's a saint, but that's just my opinion."

"Yes, if you're looking for a teachable text; no, if you want the
most current research."

"Absolutely beautiful, though not, of course, for all tastes."

"Suggested Supplementary Readings"

"XXX"

Value judgments appear to be among the most fundamental forms of social communication and also among the most primitive benefits of social interaction. It appears, for example, that insects and birds as well as mammals signal to other members of their group, by some form of specialized overt behavior, not only the location but also the "quality" of a food supply or territory. And, creatures such as we are, we too not only produce but also eagerly solicit from each other both, as it might be said, "expressions of personal sentiment" (*How do you like it?*) and "objective judgments of value" (*Is it any good?*). We solicit them because, although neither will (for nothing can) give us knowledge of any determinate value of an object, both may let us know, or—and this will be significant here—at least *appear* to let us know, other things that we could find interesting and useful.

It is evident, for example, that other people's reports of how well certain things have gratified them, though "mere expressions of their subjective likes and dislikes," will nevertheless be interesting to us if we ourselves—as artists, perhaps, or manufacturers, or cooks—have produced those objects, or—as parents, perhaps, or potential associates—we have an independently motivated interest in the current states of *those people* or in the general structure of *their* tastes and preferences. Also, no matter how magisterially delivered and with what attendant claims or convictions of universality, unconditionality, impersonality or objectivity, any assertion of "*the* value" of some object or practice can always be unpacked as a judgment of its *contingent* value and appropriated accordingly: that is, as that speakers' observation and/or estimate of how well that object or practice, compared to others of the same (implicitly defined) type, has performed and/or is likely to perform some particular (even though unstated) desired/able functions[21] for some particular (even though only implicitly defined) subject or set of subjects under some particular (even though not specified) set or range of conditions.

Any evaluation, then, no matter what its manifest syntactic form, ostensible "validity claim," and putative propositional status, may be of social value in the sense of being appropriable by other people. The actual value of a particular evaluation, however, will itself be highly contingent, depending on such variables as the specific social and institutional context in which it is produced, the specific social and institutional relationship between the speaker and his listener(s), the specific structure of interests that motivates and constrains the entire social/verbal transaction in which the evaluation figures, a vast and not ultimately numerable or listable set of variables relating to, among other things, the social, cultural and verbal histories of those involved and, of course, the particular perspective from which that value is being figured.

We may take note here of the recurrent anxiety/charge/claim—I refer to it as the Egalitarian Fallacy—that, unless one judgment can be said or shown to be more "valid" than another, then all judgments must be "equal" or "equally valid." While I am suggesting here that no value judgment can be more "valid" than another *in the sense of an objectively truer statement of the non-contingent value of an object or practice* (for these latter concepts are seen as vacuous), it does not follow that all value judgments are equally valid. On the contrary, what does follow is that the concept of "validity" *in that sense* is unavailable as a parameter by which to measure or compare judgments. It is evident, however, that value judgments can still be evaluated, still compared, still seen and said to be "better" or "worse" than each other. The point, of course, is that their value—"goodness" or "badness"—must be understood, evaluated and compared *otherwise,* that is, as something other than "validity" in the objectivist sense. I shall return to the point below.

There is, of course, no way for us to be certain that our associates' reports of their personal likes and dislikes are *sincere,* or that the ratings and rankings produced by professional connoisseurs and local men and women of taste are, as we might say, "honest" and "objective." Indeed, we may grant more generally that any evaluation, aesthetic, moral, or otherwise, will be shaped by the speaker's own interests, both as a party to the verbal transaction in which the evaluation figures and in other ways as well. It may also be granted that, since value is especially subject-variable for certain classes of objects and practices (e.g., artwork, culinary preparations, erotic partners and activities), the appropriability of value *judgments* of such objects and practices may be correspondingly highly subject-variable. For these reasons, that is, because we do tend to learn that there's no such thing as an honest opinion and that one man's meat is the other's poison, we typically *supplement* and *discount* the value judgments we are offered "in the light," as we say, of knowledge we have from other sources: knowledge, for example, of the reviewer's personal and perhaps idiosyncratic preferences, or the judge's special interests or obligations and thus suspect or clearly compromised motives.

Or, rather, knowledge we *think* we have. For there is, of course, no way for us to be sure of the accuracy, adequacy, or validity of this supplementary knowledge either, and we may therefore seek yet further supplementary information from yet other sources: some trustworthy guide to travel guides, perhaps, or a reliable review of the reliability of film reviewers, or an inside tip on what tipsheet to buy. It is clear, however, that there can be no end to this theoretically infinite regress of supplementing the supplements and evaluating the evaluations, just as there is none to that of justifying the justifications of judgments, or grounding the grounds of knowledge of any kind—though, in practice, we do the best we can, all things considered . . . at least as far as we know these things, or think we know them. We need not linger over the epistemological regress here. What is more pertinent to observe is that, *in all the respects mentioned*, value judgments are not essentially different from "descriptive" or "factual" statements, and that their reliability and objectivity are no more compromised by these possibilities—or, for that matter, any *less* compromised by them—than the reliability or objectivity of any other type of utterance, from a pathetic plea of a headache to the solemn communication of the measurement of a scientific instrument.[22]

Though not *essentially* different, there are, nevertheless, *relative* differences of various kinds. That is, these types of discourse may be seen not as absolutely distinct by virtue of their radically opposed claims to "truth" or "objective validity," but as occupying different positions along a number of relevant continua. Thus, although the value of all objects and practices is to some extent subject-variable, the value of some objects and practices will be *relatively more uniform* than others among the members of some community—as will be, accordingly, the judgments concerning their value exchanged within that community. Similarly, although the conditions under which a particular judgment or report can be appropriated by other people are always to some extent limited, they will be *relatively broader* for some judgments and reports than for others. And, as I discuss elsewhere,[23] although fraud, exploitation and oppression are possibilities in any verbal interaction, their occurrence will be *relatively better controlled* by certain types of social and institutional constraints than others. Indeed, the familiar distinctions and contrasts among types of discourse that are at issue here—that is, between "merely subjective" and "truly objective" judgments, or between mere value judgments and genuine factual descriptions, or between statements that can and cannot claim truth-value—are no doubt continuously reinforced by the undeniability of just such relative differences which, however, in accord with certain conceptual operations perhaps endemic to human thought, are typically binarized, polarized, absolutized and hierarchized.

We may return here briefly to the Egalitarian Fallacy, that is, the idea that a denial of the possibility of objectively valid judgments commits one to the view that all judgments are "equal," "equally good," or "equally valid." As noted above, this is a strict *non sequitur* since, if one finds "validity" in the objectivist, essentialist sense vacuous, one could hardly be committed to accepting it as a parameter by which to measure or compare judgments, whether as better or worse *or* as "equal." What feeds the fallacy is the common assumption that "validity" in an objectivist, essentialist sense is the *only possible* measure of the value of utterances. (The Egalitarian Fallacy is thus another illustration of the more general rule that, to the dualist, whatever is not dualistic is reductionist; or, *If it's not distinguishable by my dualistic description of differences, then it's the same.*) What the present account suggests is that there are other parameters by which the value (goodness of badness) of judgments—and, indeed, of all utterances—can be measured and *conceived.*[24]

Value judgments may themselves be considered commodities—useful, appropriable, and thus valuable, in numerous ways. Moreover, some of them are evidently *worth more* than others *in the relevant markets.* Thus, the Michelin guides to Italian hotels, restaurants and altar paintings have, we might say, a well-attested reputation for objectivity and reliability, at least among certain classes of travelers. This is not, however, because there is, after all, just a little bit of objective—or universal subjective—validity to which some judgments can properly lay claim. On the contrary, it may be seen as a consequence of precisely those compromising conditions described earlier and summed up in the lesson that there's no such thing as an honest opinion: no judgment is totally unaffected by the particular social, institutional, and other conditions of its production, and none totally immune to the (assumed) interests and desires of its (assumed) audience—or, we could say, because it cuts both ways—*and that is the point*—no judgment is altogether *unresponsive to* those interests and desires. For, if we do not regard them as the regrettable effects of fallen human nature or as noise in the channels of communication or, in the terms of Jürgen Habermas's account, as "distortions" of the ideal conditions, "presupposed" by all genuine speech-acts,[25] then we may be better able to see them as the conditions under which all verbal transactions take place and which *give* them—or are, precisely, the *conditions of possibility* for—whatever value they do have for those actually involved in them.

To remark, as I have been doing here, the ways in which judgments have value without, in the traditional sense, truth-value is not to maintain that value is always high or positive, or positive for everyone. On the contrary, the value of any utterance—moral or aesthetic judgment, factual statement, mathematical theorem, or any other type—may be quite minimal or negative, at least for someone and perhaps for a great many people. For, as was stressed above, value always cuts both (or all) ways. An aesthetic judgment, for example, however earnestly offered, may—under readily imaginable social conditions—be excruciatingly uninteresting and worthless to some listener(s); or, conversely, though a factual report may be highly informative to its audience, it may—under readily imaginable political conditions—have been extorted from an unwilling speaker at considerable risk or cost to himself.

Such possibilities do not require us to posit any deficiencies of truth-value or breakdowns in the conditions that "normally" obtain in verbal transactions or are "presupposed" by them.[26] On the contrary, if anything *is* thus presupposed, it is precisely such negative possibilities. Or, to put this somewhat differently, the possibility of cost or loss as well as of benefit or gain is a condition of any verbal transaction for, in linguistic exchanges as in exchanges of any other kind, agents have diverse interests and perspectives, and what is gain for one may be, or involve, loss for the other.

It follows from the account of judgments outlined above that the conditions for "universally shared objective standards" would be achieved insofar as the members of a community approached total homogeneity and the community itself approached the status of a closed and static system, both immured from external interactions and secured against internal sources of instability. Since, in such a community, the conditions of judgment would be both unchanging and the same for everybody, there would be, in effect, no contingencies, all judgments would be, in effect, objective (though also, of course, for the same reasons, redundant), and normative authority would be located in a literally universal consensus backed up by the power of the entire community—except, perhaps, for a few unregenerately unassimilable malcontents.

It is doubtless the case the communal life presupposes shared goals and norms—or at least more or less congruous preferences and behavioral tendencies among its members and also routines of action, reaction, and interaction that are, at least in the long run, mutually and generally beneficial. It appears to be the characteristic belief of social critics who pursue the nostalgic mode that these are simple correlations or purely linear functions: that a community flourishes to the extent that consensus obtains among its members and that its norms are fixed and uniformly shared.[27] What this forgets, however, is that the well-being of any community is also a function of other and indeed opposed conditions, including the extent of the diversity of the beliefs and practices of its members, and thus their communal resourcefulness, and the flexibility of its routines and norms, and thus the community's capacity to respond to changing and emerging circumstances. For, of course, with the exception of Paradise and some other transcendental polities, no community *can* be immured from interactions with a changing environment, nor can the homogeneity of its members ever be taken for granted or conflicts among them ever be altogether prevented. Where *difference* continuously emerges, it must be either continuously negotiated or continuously suppressed, the latter always at somebody's cost and often enough, it appears, at, in the long run, considerable communal cost.[28] Given such conditions, it is perhaps just as well for "our society" that its norms are a "melange," that they constantly multiply, collide, and transform each other, that conflicts of judgment are negotiated *ad hoc,* and that normative authority itself is dispersed and recurrently changes hands, variously strengthening and becoming diffuse. And, given such conditions, it is perhaps also just as well that malcontents continue to be engendered and Falls continuously enacted.

I conclude with a brief, final glance at *After Virtue* and a question especially pertinent to this conference.

MacIntyre displays considerable disdain for the inauthentic—because merely "expedient"—types of legislative and judicial activity in which we engage in the absence of a genuine *polis*. Because contemporary secular society does not have and cannot hope to achieve consensus, its political processes are, he suggests, a sham. His example is the United States Supreme Court, the major function of which is not, he observes, to invoke a consistent set of principles but, rather, "to keep the peace between rival social groups adhering to rival and incompatible principles."[29] The observation is illustrated by the court's decision in the *Bakke*[30] case which, he notes, "both forbade precise ethnic quotas for admission to colleges and universities, but allowed discrimination in favor of previously deprived minority groups."[31] It would be "to miss the point," he remarks, even to try to figure out what consistent principles could be behind such a decision; for, in this as in other cases, the Supreme court "played the role of a peacemaking or truce-keeping body by negotiating its way through an impasse of conflict, not by invoking our shared moral first principles. For our society as a whole has none."[32] The point, it appears, is that genuine justice is not possible after the Fall; or, as MacIntyre goes on to say, "[w]hat this brings out is that modern politics cannot be a matter of genuine moral consensus. . . . Modern politics is civil war carried on by other means. . . ."[33] It would be worthwhile, I think, to consider the distribution of the social/political costs and benefits of the idea that postlapsarian politics is equivalent to civil warfare, that judicial decisions reached through negotiation and trade-off are inherently contemptible, that laws framed as "expedient[s] accommodated to special circumstances"[34] are hardly less so, and that the nature of political obligation "becomes systematically unclear"[35] where a government is only "a set of institutional arrangements for imposing a bureaucratized unity on a society which lacks genuine moral consensus. . . ."[36] Exactly what, we might ask, are the alternative forms of political process for which we should be holding out? And what should we be doing in the meantime?

APPENDIX

These related discussions of Kant's *Critique of Judgment* are adapted from *Contingencies of Value*, at 64–7.

Judgment Typology and Linguistic Intuition

Kant's initial acknowledgment of the variability of tastes—

> To one [man], violet color is soft and lovely; to another, it is washed out and dead. One man likes the tone of wind instruments, another that of strings. To strive here with the design of reproving as incorrect another man's judgment which is different from our own . . . would be folly. As regards the pleasant, therefore, the fundamental proposition is valid: *everyone has his own [sense of] tastes [ein jeder hat seinen eigenen Geschmack* (der Sinne)]. . . .[37]

—is only a foil to the major point and contrast that follows, itself set up by the observation that "everyone" would agree that, if "reproved" for not doing so, he *ought* to say not just "It is pleasant" but "It is pleasant *to me*." This is apparently an "ought" of linguistic propriety: that is, saying it would make explicit what is, according to Kant, presupposed by the use of the term *pleasant*. Or to put this another way, in not adding the first-person qualification, the speaker fails to make explicit the merely personal force (or reference or applicability) which, according to Kant, is involved in someone's saying that something is pleasant, as pointedly opposed to a judgment of "the beautiful" which claims not merely personal but objective—in the sense of universal subjective—validity:

> It would (on the contrary) be laughable if a man who imagined anything to his own taste thought to justify himself by saying: "This object (the house we see, the coat that person wears, the concert we hear, the poem submitted to our judgment) is beautiful *for me.*" . . . [For] if he gives out anything as beautiful, he supposes in others the same satisfaction; he judges not merely for himself, but *for everyone.* . . . Here, then, we cannot say each man has his own particular taste. For this would be as much as to say that there is no taste whatever, i.e., no aesthetical judgment which can make a rightful claim upon everyone's assent.[38]

What is notable in this passage is how much the force of the argument owes to presumed empirical facts about *linguistic* usage or convention, bolstered by what appears to be the tacitly universalized testimony of personal introspection or, as it might be called now, "linguistic intuition":

> Further, this claim to universal validity so essentially belongs to a judgment by which we describe anything as *beautiful* that, if this were not thought in it, it would never come into our thoughts to use the expression at all. . . . [39]

Although Kant's expressivist conception of the relation of language to thought may have prevented his recognition of it, the force of any appeal to linguistic propriety, usage or convention is, of course, itself historically and otherwise contingent. Thus, someone could always say: "Well, that may be what everyone meant by *schön* in 1790, at least in the salons of Königsberg, but hardly anyone means that anymore; these days nobody would laugh and only a handful of professors of philosophy would even be given pause if someone said, "You and your friends may not like my wife's poetry, but it's beautiful to me" or "This coat may be shabby and old-fashioned, but I've had it since my student days and it's beautiful to me." It is also questionable (though empirically indeterminable) whether, when people refer to something as "beautiful," it always or even typically does—or ever did—come into their thoughts that everyone ought to agree with them. Although it may be suspected that Kant was accurately reporting the implicit provincial universalism of the drawingroom conversation with which he was familiar, the point remains that the historicity of linguistic convention (and, thereby, of linguistic "intuition") and the contingency of usage deprive such observations of any epistemic authority or axiological force.

Consensus as Regulative Ideal

It is clear from the perplexity or inconclusiveness of the conclusion of the "Analytic of the Beautiful" that Kant recognizes the tautologous nature of the entire demonstration. The recognition is hedged and to some extent obscured, however, by the salvaging alternative left in its wake: that is, the suggestion that even if the claims of taste to universal validity cannot be ultimately justified, it may yet be Reason's labyrinthine way to have them *seem* justifiable so that a higher good, namely the institution of a perhaps illusory but nevertheless inspirational—and, therefore, properly regulatory—ideal of unanimity or consensus, can thereby be effected:

> Whether there is in fact such a common sense . . . or whether a yet higher principle of reason makes it only into a regulative principle for producing in us a common sense for higher purposes; whether, therefore, taste is an original and natural faculty or only the idea of an artificial one yet to be acquired, so that a judgment of taste with its assumption of a universal assent in fact is only a requirement of reason for producing such harmony of sentiment; whether the ought, i.e. [the claim and/or presupposition of] the objective necessity of the confluence of the feeling of any one man with that of any other, only signifies the possibility of arriving at this accord, and the judgment of taste only affords an example of the application of this principle—these questions we have neither the wish nor the power to investigate as yet. . . . [40]

Kant is able to salvage the otherwise thoroughly compromised claim of judgments of taste to universal validity by invoking the higher good that such claims serve. That invocation, however, only displaces one axiological question with another and leads into the usual infinite regresses. For one may always ask how high and how good that higher good is, and also *for whom* it is good at all. Is it—that is, unanimity, consensus, "the confluence of any one man's feeling with that of any other"—a good in itself? Is universal concordance self-evidently better than diversity, or even better in all cases than conflict? Is prior agreement indeed presupposed by human communication? And is it, as Kant does not question here, good for *everyone*? Or is it not the case, rather, that all these questions may be answered negatively and that the invocation of an ideally achievable consensus is not only not

good for everyone but tends inevitably to operate to the advantage of
the majority and those with *de facto* social power and to the disadvantage of the more "different," "idiosyncratic," "singular," and otherwise innovative and/or marginal members of any community? We
are evidently concerned here, however, not with logic but with social
politics or, perhaps, with the inseparability of the two.

NOTES

1. See the Appendix, Section A, infra, for discussion of the relevant passages in
   Kant's text.
2. The view or alleged view supposedly refuted is thus called, in Anglo-American
   philosophy, "emotivism." It is "alleged" because any account that questions the
   concept of objective value and, with it, the machinery of traditional axiology is
   commonly seen as, and said to be, "emotivist." The allegation illustrates the general tendency of objectivist thought to generate phantom heresies out of its own
   inversion. I discuss the latter point in Contingencies of Value, supra note 1, at
   150–84.
3. A. MacIntyre, After Virtue: A Study in Moral Theory (2d ed. 1984).
4. Id. at 9 (emphasis added).
5. Id.
6. Id. (emphasis added).
7. Id. at 13.
8. Id. at 13.
9. Id. at 13–14 (emphasis added).
10. I shall not be concerned here with the "historical" dimension of MacIntyre's nar-
    rative or its governing idea, namely that there has been a continual erosion of
    moral authority and moral consensus in Western thought and life beginning, it
    appears (MacIntyre's dating is vague and not altogether consistent), with the Ref-
    ormation and accelerating from the time of the Enlightenment. I would note, how-
    ever, that like many others who chart the Decline of the West along such lines, he
    underestimates the extent of the ranges and varieties of discourse and practice in
    any era, culture, or "community," and—especially through contrasts posed in
    such terms as "our predecessor culture," "the present age," and "modern life"—
    obscures crucial and relevant differences (e.g., those of class, gender, place, race,
    and historical experience) that cannot readily be seen as matters of degeneration,
    loss, failure, or fragmentation.
11. As can be seen in the passages quoted above, MacIntyre uses terms such as
    "expression" and "statement" in such a way that it is never altogether clear
    whether he is talking about abstract verbal *forms* or about particular *utterances*
    (of a certain form) produced in specific (hypothetical) contexts. Indeed, it appears
    that he does not recognize the difference or its significance for the questions at
    issue here.
12. A. MacIntyre, supra note 4, at 10.

13. Id. at 10.

14. Id. at 60.

15. According to MacIntyre, a few philosophers, such as G. E. Moore, have understood what modern people were really *doing* when they *said* "It is good," but those philosophers have tried only to make postlapsarian life more comfortable for the fallen by maintaining either that there never were any objective standards of wholesome moral discourse anyway, or that appeals to (such) so-called objective standards were always manipulative—hence, the emotive theory. See id. at 14–20. It should be observed that MacIntyre participates in the same dualism that produces both the standard axiological account and, as its self-inversion, the so-called emotive theory. Indeed, his "hypothesis" and its narrative development consists simply of the *temporalization* of that dualism. When the alleged emotivist allegedly says, "Since there are no objective standards, all judgments, including ostensibly impersonal ones, are nothing more than expressions of personal preference," MacIntyre says, in effect, "Since people *no longer* believe in objective standards, all judgments must *now* be—at heart, if not in form—nothing more than expressions of personal preference." Here, as elsewhere, the temporalization of a dualism yields a myth of the Fall.

16. A. MacIntyre, supra note 4, at 252.

17. Id. at 10.

18. MacIntyre writes of the "larger totalities" in which our moral concepts and their corresponding expressions were "originally at home" and of which they are now "deprived." Id. at 10. Yet, he fails to note the necessary corollary which is that if they remain available as concepts and continue to be used as expressions at all, it must be because they are now "at home" in *other* totalities. The latter may, of course, be more heterogeneous than those "original" ones, or coexistent now with more alternatives.

19. For further discussion, see Contingencies of Value, supra note 1, at 102–12, where, along with the entire telegraphic model of communication in which they have their place, the terms "transmitted" and "received" are seen to be fundamentally questionable.

20. See Appendix, Section A.

21. Having particular *effects* rather than performing particular functions is a more suitable unpacking in may cases.

22. The following summary of why, contrary to standard views of scientific method, the *replication* of a "finding" does not constitute a test of truth in science is relevant here:

> The problem is that, since experimentation is a matter of skillful practice, it can never be clear whether a second experiment has been done sufficiently well to count as a check on the first. Some further test is needed to test the quality of the experiment—and so forth. . . . The failure of these "tests of tests" to resolve the difficulty demonstrates the need for further "tests of tests of tests" and so on—a true regress.

> H. M. Collins, Changing Order: Replication and Induction in Scientific Practice, 2 (1985).

23. Contingencies of Value, supra note 1, at 106–10.

24. The force of J. L. Austin's insight that there are other measures, e.g., "felicity,"

has been all but lost in the objectivist appropriation of his work in so-called "speech act theory." It may be noted as well that Austin appreciated, though he did not pursue his own emphasis of it, the radical contingency of "truth":

> It is essential to realize that "true" and "false" . . . do not stand for anything simple at all; but only for a general dimension of being a right or proper thing to say as opposed to a wrong thing, in these circumstances, to this audience, for these purposes and with these intentions.

J. L. Austin, How to Do Things With Words, 144 (2d. ed. 1962).

25. J. Habermas, What is Universal Pragmatics? in Communication and the Evolution of Society (T. McCarthy trans. 1979). See Contingencies of Value, supra note 1, at 110–12, for further discussion of Habermas's conception of communication.

26. I am ignoring here the other parameters of goodness and badness—e.g., "comprehensibility," "syntactic well-formedness," "felicity," etc.—that are sometimes proposed, typically *in addition to* "truth-value," as required for or presupposed by effective (or, as in Habermas, "genuine") communication. Setting aside the serious questions of conceptualization and determination that might be raised concerning each of these criteria, one can grant that defects of roughly these kinds may occur where the speaker (e.g., one who mumbles, stutters, speaks "broken English" or produces malapropisms) would certainly be at a competitive disadvantage in linguistic transactions. Such criteria can be ignored here, however, since those who invoke them always consider them to be irrelevant to the specific kinds of negative value noted above. Thus, someone's evaluation of an artwork may be exquisitely well-formed, as well as earnest, but *still* excruciatingly uninteresting to her listeners, and a political prisoner's extorted report may be pronounced altogether felicitously and "accurately," so that it is readily understood and effectively appropriated by his questioners, but *still* at considerable cost to himself.

27. For other works in the same mode, see R. Bellah, R. Madsen, W. Sullivan, A. Swidler & S. Tipon, Habits of the Heart (1985); C. Taylor, Interpretation and the Sciences of Man, in 2 Philosophy and the Human Sciences: Philosophical Papers 15-57 (1985).

28. See Appendix, Section B, for further discussion of Kant's—and neo-Kantian—invocations of consensus as a regulative ideal.

29. A. MacIntyre, supra note 4, at 253.

30. Regents of Univ. of Cal. v. Bakke, 438 U.S. 265 (1978).

31. A. MacIntyre, supra note 4, at 253.

32. Id.

33. Id.

34. Id. at 254 (quoting A. Ferguson, Principals of Moral and Political Science, 144 [1975]).

35. Id.

36. Id.

37. I. Kant, Critique of Judgment, §7 (J. Bernard trans. 1951).

38. Id. at §7 (emphasis added).

39. Id. at §8.

40. Id. at §22.

6

In the Name of the Law
Samuel Weber

I

A Conference on Deconstruction and the Possibility of Justice can hardly avoid addressing the question of its own specificity: why *just* here, why *just* now? However general the issues addressed—justice, law, ethics—to reflect upon their relation to deconstruction is inevitably to pose the question of the *singular* configuration in which this reflection is taking place. Some five years ago, Derrida observed that the United States could be described as "that historical space which today, in all its dimensions and through all its power plays, reveals itself as being undeniably the most sensitive, receptive, or responsive space of all to the themes and effects of deconstruction."[1] At the same time, he cautioned against trying to find a single, authentic site for deconstruction:

> But is there a proper place, a history proper to this thing? I believe that it consists only in transference, and in the thinking through of transference, in all the senses this word acquires in more than one language, and first of all, that of a transference between languages. If I had to risk, God help me, a single definition of deconstruction, brief, elliptical, economical as a watchword (*mot d'ordre*), I would say without further ado: *plus d'une langue*, "more than one language," but also, "one language no more."[2]

In the light of this remark, the question of the particular conditions that have made a conference on "Deconstruction and the Possibility of Justice" itself possible, can be specified as one of a certain *transfer-*

ence: not just between different languages ("more than one language"), but also within each of them as well ("one language no more"). What seems characteristic of the transferential place and history in which deconstruction is engaged, is that the transfer *between* languages—be they so-called "natural" or national languages, or be they the discourse of individual "disciplines"—becomes dependent upon the transfers going on *within* their borders. Such "internal" transference tends to uncover "hidden articulations . . . within assumedly monadic totalities,"[3] and thus to open the possibility, and even the necessity, of elaborating new networks between areas in the process of turning themselves, as it were, inside-out.

In regard to language, the most pervasive instance of the "monadic totality" mentioned by de Man, is the *word.* Ever since *Of Grammatology,* Derrida has singled out the word, first theoretically, and then, more and more through his writing practices, as one of the foremost objects of deconstruction.[4] As an instance of such *intraverbal* transference, then, let us look briefly at one of the words we are here to discuss: *justice.*

If we consult the dictionary, beginning with *Webster's New Collegiate,* we discover not simply the usual multiplicity of definitions, but a diversity that seems to split single definitions in significant ways, as with the following: "The principle of rectitude and just dealing of men with each other; *also, conformity to it*; integrity; rectitude;—one of the cardinal virtues."[5] Other dictionary entries articulate different aspects of this split: justice is defined both as an ethical *principle,* and as the *institutional and practical realization* of that principle. Thus, the word can signify "[r]ightfulness; as, in the *justice* of a cause," but also "[t]he maintenance or administration of that which is just," including "merited reward or punishment."[6] Just is defined in terms of right, rightfulness, righteousness, but also as the implementation of this right, which in turn, entails not merely realization or application, but enforcement and sanction. This latter definition points toward another semantic dimension of the word, one that is not mentioned in *Webster's New Collegiate Dictionary,* but which, by contrast, occupies a prominent place in its French counterpart, *Le Petit Robert.* What the American dictionary describes as a matter of *organization*: "maintenance and administration" is defined in *Le Petit Robert* in terms of *power,* as the *"pouvoir de faire régner le droit,"* which might be translated as: "the power of imposing the rule of law."[7] This tendency to formulate questions of organization in terms involving the exercise of power also determines a phrase that has no precise English equivalent, since it precisely entails the fusion of these two aspects; that term is *pouvoir judiciaire*, and it is used, for instance, to define justice as an "organization of judicial power, the ensemble of institutions charged with administering justice in conformity with positive law."[8] In French, then, the gap within the interdependent meanings of a "single" word, between justice as an ethical principle, and justice as a legal institution, is not so much bridged as articulated by the word, "*pouvoir*," a word which tends to be missing from definitions of "justice" in *Webster's*. At the same time, however, *pouvoir* demarcates itself from *power*, precisely insofar as it retains the link between organization and force, by situating the latter in an institutional context. The phrase, *pouvoir judiciaire*, implies that the administration of justice entails the exercise of force, but also that such exercise in turn is inseparable from some sort of institutionalization. In short, there is a significant difference in speaking of justice as a judicial *system*, or as a judicial *power*.[9]

Thus, if it can be supposed that a certain tension between ethical ideals and political reality is always at work wherever the notion of justice is concerned, the manner in which such tension is articulated can be as different as the dictionary definitions we have just reviewed. In addressing such general topics as "justice," "law," and their "ethical relations," it would be easy to forget the singular tensions that traverse these terms and notions, and which in turn inevitably entertain specific relations to the dominant traditions of a language, a discipline, a nation. To do so would be to ignore the vigilance that deconstruction has consistently sought to maintain concerning the *singular* conditions under which *generalizing* practices are pursued. In *Mémoires* Derrida asserts that "it is impossible to understand American forms of deconstruction without taking into account the various religious traditions, their discourses, their institutional effects, and above all their academic effects."[10] The same, I suspect, holds for the very distinctive status of the law in this country. If, as Derrida observes, "contrary to what is so often thought, deconstruction is not exported from Europe to the United States," but instead "has several original configurations in this country,"[11] the "originality" of these "configurations" cannot be understood in isolation from the specific position of the law and of the judicial system (or power) in the United States. It is perhaps not entirely inappropriate, therefore, to begin by reviewing, briefly and schematically, one of the earliest and most astute attempts to define the singular status of the law and judiciary in America, that of de Tocqueville.

II

> There have been other confederations . . . republics . . . representa-
> tive systems [of government]; but I do not believe that, until now,
> any nation in the world has constituted the judicial system (le pou-
> voir judiciaire) in the same manner as the Americans.[12]

What de Tocqueville found most surprising in the American judicial
system was the fact that it retained the same formal traits as the European judiciary, while at the same time exercising a power unheard
of in Europe. In America no less than in Europe, de Tocqueville noted,
the judiciary is defined by three essential features. First, it is an *arbiter,*
and hence presupposes conflict: "[f]or there to be a judge, there must
be a trial." Second, its judgment must bear on *particular cases* and not
on *general principles.* A judge cannot "attack directly the general principle, and destroy it without having in view a particular case." Third,
courts can take action only when action is brought by others, i.e.,
"only when called (*quand on l'appelle*)" or, more literally, "seized,"
saisie.[13] What distinguishes the courts in America from those in Europe, therefore, is not their mode of action, but rather the way they
judge, and more specifically, the criterion upon which their judgments
are based. In contrast to their European colleagues, American judges
have both the right and the obligation "of basing their sentences (*ar-
rêts*) on the *constitution,* rather than on *laws.* In other words, they are
permitted not to apply laws that seem to them to be unconstitutional."[14]

It is this ability to appeal directly to the founding law of the body
politic, the constitution, that endows the judicial system in the United
States with unprecedented political power and that makes it a veritable "*pouvoir judiciaire.*" Not that a similar right does not exist in
France, but its exercise is far less general:

> In France, the constitution is equally the primary law, and judges
> have an equal right to take it as the foundation of their verdicts;
> but, in exercising this right, they could hardly avoid infringing
> upon another right more sacred than theirs: that of society, in
> whose name they act. Here ordinary reason must cede before rea-
> son of State.[15]

Whereas in France, "society," in whose *name* the courts judge, is identified with the state, and ultimately with the executive, in the United
States, the courts judge in the name of the law itself: the Constitution,

the "origin of all power," [16] without which there would be neither society nor state. In the deliberation of conflict, supreme authority is invested in a document which "dominates legislators no less than simple citizens. It is the primary law, and cannot be modified by a law." [17]

Since, however, that document cannot speak for itself, no more than can any text, the authority invested in it is transferred, as it were, to the instance charged with interpreting it, the Supreme Court:

> Never has a more immense judicial power been constituted by any other people. The Supreme Court is placed higher than any known court. . . . It is charged with the interpretations of laws. . . . One can even say that its prerogatives are almost entirely political, although its constitution is entirely judicial. Its sole aim is to see to it that the laws of the Union are executed. . . . In the nations of Europe, only individuals (*particuliers*) are brought before the courts; but one can say that the Supreme Court of the United States summons sovereigns before its bar . . . "[t]he State of New York against that of Ohio." [18]

The explanation of this unprecedented concentration of political power in the judiciary lies, according to de Tocqueville, in the "splitting of sovereignty" [19] characteristic of political confederations in general, and of the American Federation in particular. Conflicts that arise within parts of the sovereign body: between Federal and State government, between different states, between different branches of government, as well as between individual citizens, private associations and the government—all these require an instance situated outside of and above the fragmented, and hence often fractious institutions of government in order to be arbitrated. In no other system "are individual existences, which can struggle against the social body, larger and better able to resist the material force of the government" than in confederated peoples.[20] And hence, no other system has a greater interest in having a strong judiciary.

In face of the centrifugal tendencies of federated systems of government, then, the affirmation of the unity of the body politic is entrusted largely to an interpretive body, the Supreme Court:

> The president can fail without the State suffering . . . [t]he congress can err without the Union perishing . . . [b]ut if the Supreme Court ever comes to be composed of unwise or corrupt men, the confederation would have to fear anarchy or civil war.[21]

If, however, the Supreme Court is the most conspicuous institutional expression of the American judicial system, the influence of the judiciary, de Tocqueville remarks, far exceeds the administration of law and indeed affects American politics in general:

> What is most difficult of all in the United States for a foreigner to understand, is the judicial organization. There is, so to speak, no political event in which he does not hear the authority of the judge invoked; and from this he naturally concludes that in the United States, the judge is one of the foremost political powers.[22]

A certain "legal spirit" or mind, de Tocqueville observes, permeates American political life:

> the legal spirit (*l'esprit légiste*) is not restricted to the sphere of the courts; it extends far beyond. Lawyers . . . occupy the majority of public offices. They fill the legislatures, and head administrations; they exercise great influence upon the framing of the law and upon its execution. . . . There is practically no political question, in the United States, that does not sooner or later become a judicial question. . . . Judicial language becomes, in a certain sense, the popular language; the legal spirit, born in the schools and courts . . . infiltrates, as it were, all of society, down to its lowest ranks, and the entire people ends up by adopting part of the habits and tastes of the magistrates.[23]

What distinguishes "legal spirit" in its Anglo-American version from that found in France, according to de Tocqueville, is the use it makes of the past:

> The English or American lawyers looks for what has been done, the French lawyers for what was intended; the former seeks verdicts, the latter, reasons.
> When you hear an English or American lawyer you are surprised to see him so often citing the opinion of others, and hear him speak so little of his own, whereas the contrary is the case with us.[24]

In short, Anglo-American lawyers seek to found their deliberations and decisions on *precedents*; this, in turn, de Tocqueville argues, results in their being "increasingly separated from the people, finally constituting a class of [their] own. The French lawyer is only a scholar; but the English or American man of law resembles in a way the priests of Egypt; like them, he is the unique interpreter of an occult science."[25]

In this observation of de Tocqueville's may be found at least a partial explanation of how Anglo-American legal traditions may have contributed both to the relative receptivity deconstruction has encountered in America, as well as to a certain resistance. And this, not just because to those unfamiliar with deconstructive texts, they can seem often to be the work of "unique interpreters of an occult science." Like the Anglo-American lawyers described, deconstruction concerns itself more with "the opinions," or more accurately, with the writings "of others," than with ideas of its own. Indeed, deconstruction turns out to share at least *two* of the *three* traits through which de Tocqueville defines the judiciary: it comes only when called, and its concern, or occasion, is always tied to the particulars of that call: particular texts, questions, conflicts. In its manner of intervention, however, it distinguishes itself from that of the courts, and in particular from the Anglo-American legal tradition described by de Tocqueville. For if deconstruction responds to conflictual appeals, it is not with a view of arriving at a definitive verdict. In this sense, deconstruction does not arbitrate, nor set precedents.

To a society whose "constitution" depends in no small measure upon the rereading of a written text, in order for its authority to be reaffirmed in face of ever-changing conditions, deconstruction cannot but be both familiar and uncanny. As de Tocqueville remarks:

> It is surprising to observe the power (*puissance*) of opinion accorded by men to the decisions of the courts. This power is so great that it remains attached to the judicial form even after its substance has ceased to exist; it gives body to a shadow.[26]

In its peculiar way, deconstruction is called upon to address precisely the *power* to give "body to a shadow," and in so doing it raises the question of whether the two—body and shadow—can always be told apart. One particularly telling instance of this can be found in the writings of Paul de Man.

III

Writing of Paul de Man, Derrida has observed that "the thought of the law was always . . . rigorous, enigmatic, paradoxical, and vigilant, and I believe that it runs through his entire work."[27] The same could be said of Derrida's writing as well, as his essays on Kafka (*Before the Law*) and Blanchot (now collected in *Passages*) eloquently testify. If, however, I choose here to discuss the text that occasions the remark of Derrida just quoted—de Man's reading of the *Social Contract*—it is because it addresses the question of the law in a context similar to that we have been discussing: that is, in relation to the constitution and foundation of the body politic. "Body politic" is a term that Rousseau uses often, but which demonstrates, serves more to highlight a problem than to provide a solution. For although Rousseau repeatedly uses natural, organic metaphors to describe the formation and structure of society in the *Social Contract,* the main problem with which this text[28] is concerned can precisely not be satisfactorily articulated through the use of organic metaphors. The following passage, not cited by de Man, can help to indicate how Rousseau, in this essay, approaches this primary concern:

> The State or City being a moral person whose life consists in the cooperation and union of its members, has as its first and foremost concern its own preservation. . . . As nature gives each man absolute power over his limbs, the social pact gives the body politic absolute power over its members, and it is the exercise of this self-same power (*ce même pouvoir*) under the direction of the general will that bears, as I have said, the name of sovereignty.
>
> But since, outside of the public person, we must also consider the private persons of which it is composed, *and whose life and existence is naturally independent of it,* this matter demands a certain amount of discussion.[29]

In the first paragraph cited, Rousseau declares the power of the state "over its members" to be "absolute," since the relation of whole to part is said to be the same in the body politic as in the physical body; and yet, this "self-same power" ascribed to the (organic) whole, turns out, in the very next paragraph, to be not at all the "same" as that of a natural body, since unlike the latter, the "members" of the body politic have a "life and existence . . . naturally independent of it." In short, what is "natural" to the *organic* body, the dependence of individual organs upon the whole, is precisely not natural to the body politic. Moreover, the regularity with which this move recurs throughout the text indicates, de Man suggests, that the relation between individual and general in society cannot be construed in natural, organic terms, but that the radical heterogeneity of the two comprises the recurrent and determining problem of the *Social Contract.* Each time that Rousseau describes the utility and even necessity of a social pact and association through which individuals would subordinate their immediate, private interests to society in return for the protection and security furnished by the collective, he shortly thereafter acknowledges, explicitly or implicitly, that this necessity already presupposes what it is supposed to explain: the subsumption of the particular under the general will. In this context, one of the most symptomatic passages, upon which de Man comments, is Rousseau's account of how individuals come to opt for the general will:

> [W]hy is the general will always righteous (*droite*), and why does everyone always want the happiness of *each,* if it is not because there is no one who does not appropriate, in secret, the word *each* and who does not think of himself in voting for all? Which proves that the equality of right and the notion of justice that stems from it derive from the preference each gives to himself and consequently from the nature of man; [namely,] that the general will, to be true to itself, must be general in its object as well as in its essence; that it should have its point of departure in the whole in order to return to the whole, and that it loses its natural rectitude once it stoops to (*tombe sur*) an individual and determinate subject.[39]

In thus radically distinguishing the generality of the general will from all particularity and individuality, Rousseau renders the very notion of a "social contract" problematic: for how are two parties to "contract" with one another, if they can hardly establish *contact*? The individual who "votes" or opts for the good of all does so only by "secretly appropriating" the other, which is to say, by surreptitiously effacing its otherness. By this secret appropriation, "everyone" ceases to be a member of a whole and becomes just another individual. The general will, however, is no longer general once it is directed at, or by, an "individual and determinate subject." Given such noncommunication of individual and general, of private and public, it is difficult to conceive of how any contract or contact between them could ever arise, much less endure, except through what might be called synecdochal sleight-of-hand: the secret substitution of one individual for another, of "one" for "all."[31] Rousseau appears to concede as much at the end of the paragraph just quoted when he explains the inability of the general will to judge particular cases as resulting from the lack of a *tertium comparationis*: "[i]n judging of what is not us, we have no true principle of equity to guide us."[32] In cases of dispute or contention, where public and private interests clash, Rousseau admits that he can see "neither the law that should be followed nor the judge who should pronounce the verdict." It would be ridiculous to seek to in-

volve the general will in an altercation that involves partial interests.[33]
Rousseau sums up: [T]hus, just as a particular will cannot represent
the general will, the general will, in turn, cannot without changing
nature, become a particular will, it can *pronounce namely* (*prononcer
nommément*)[34] neither upon a man nor upon a fact.[35]

The general will cannot, namely, pronounce the names of individuals; which is to say, it cannot utter proper names. And yet, it cannot
exclude them either from its pronouncements. Within the argumentation of the *Social Contract,* it is this dilemma that will lead Rousseau
to the law, and through it, to the double necessity of "positive law,"
and of the "legislator."

In addressing this topic, Rousseau declares, he intends to "complete
. . . the foundations of" the theoretical "edifice."[36] With characteristic
aplomb, he once again introduces the problem by highlighting all of
its apparent insolubility:

> In order for each (*chacun*) to want what, according to the commit-
> ment of the social contract, he ought to do, it is necessary for each
> to know what he ought to want. What he should want is the com-
> mon good; what he should flee is public evil; but the State having
> only an ideal and conventional existence, its members have no nat-
> ural and common sensibility through which they would be imme-
> diately alerted [to what is useful or harmful]. . . .
>
> How then can individuals keep the community from evils that
> they can neither see nor feel except after the fact; how can they
> procure [public] good that they can judge only after its effect . . . ?
> Supposing them always submitted to the general will, how can this
> will manifest itself on every occasion?[37]

Since the whole people of a given state cannot be permanently assembled, and since "sovereignty cannot be represented,"[38] the task of
reconciling general and particular in the body politic would be impossible to accomplish, were it not for the "most sublime of all human
institutions":

> These difficulties, which would otherwise seem insurmountable,
> have been resolved by the most sublime of all human institutions,
> or rather by a heavenly inspiration that taught the people to imi-
> tate, down below, the immutable decrees of the divinity. . . . It is to
> the law alone that human beings owe justice and liberty. . . . It is
> this celestial voice that dictates to each citizen the precepts of public
> reason, and teaches him to follow the maxims of his own judgment
> and not to be incessantly in contradiction with himself. The laws
> are the driving force (*mobile*) of the body politic, only through

them is it active, [for] without laws, the State, once formed, is only a soulless body, it exists but cannot act, for it is not enough that everyone should be submitted to the general will; to be followed it must be known. From this results the necessity of legislation.[39]

As so often in this text, Rousseau, while ostensibly describing the reality of a phenomenon, gives an account of its "necessity," not, however, of its *possibility*. On the contrary, the recurrent gap between the two is the "*mobile*" of the *Social Contract*, the driving force that keeps its discursive machine moving. If the law is based on the "imitation" of divine "decrees," it is founded on a model that is itself not legislative. For, as Rousseau will state some pages later, "a decree [is] not an act of sovereignty, but of magistracy"[40]; it is not "a public act of the general will," with a general object, but that of a particular instance directed at particulars. By appealing to such "divine decrees," then, the decisive question, that of the *relation of general to particular in the law*, remains unanswered.

In a rigorous sense, this contradiction is incapable of being resolved. Rousseau acknowledges as much in describing the law as a "celestial inspiration," deriving from a transcendent sphere. Such recourse is incompatible with the self-reflexive conception that underlies the notion of a social contract and that determines political sovereignty to be the result of individuals "contracting with themselves."[41] But if this problem stubbornly belies the harmonious polity that the *Social Contract* seeks to theorize, the movement of the *text* suggests that the social "machinery" Rousseau is describing may more aptly be considered as an *institutionalization* of conflict, rather than as its resolution. This perspective emerges less from individual statements or propositions taken in isolation, than from the aporetical and problematic relations that they entertain with one another. In this context, it should not be forgotten that the body politic, as such, emerges only in response to a situation that Rousseau describes as follows:

[O]nce the needs of man come to exceed his faculties and the objects of his desires expand and multiply . . . the initial state can no longer continue, and human beings would perish if art did not come to the aid of nature. Now since man cannot produce new forces, but only unite and direct those that exist, he has no means of conserving himself other than collecting a sum of forces capable of overcoming the resistance [to self-preservation], putting them into play through a single driving force, bringing them jointly into action and directing them at a sole object. This is the fundamental problem to which the institution of the state supplies the solution.[42]

The "fundamental problem," to which the state is called upon to respond, and if possible to resolve, is that of providing individuals with
a *unified object of desire,* which in turn will allow them to "preserve
themselves," not merely in the physical sense, but in the moral one as
well. For it is only with the construction of a unified *object*—be it of
"need," "desire" or of "will"—that an equally unified *self, capable of
being preserved,* becomes *identifiable.* Left to its own devices, Rousseau implies, the asocial individual would tend to be dispersed by the
movement of desire and need. As de Man remarks, in a different, but
related context: "Unlike the 'individual,' who is always divided within
himself, the executive [or the state] is truly in-dividual, un-divided." [43]
On the other hand, to the extent that the state, or sovereign, is truly
individual, undivided, the question of its relation to the individual
remains open and unresolved.

It is this essential but enigmatic mediation between public and private spheres that the law is designed to establish. Although the form
and substance, subject and object of the law must, as Rousseau repeatedly emphasizes, be general, they must at the same time allow for
a certain particularization, for a certain applicability to individual
cases. Without which, the law would not be a law, but a maxim or a
saying of some kind. As de Man observes, "no law is a law unless it
also applies to particular individuals. It cannot be left hanging in the
air, in the abstraction of its generality." [44] In its irreconcilable duality,
the legal text, de Man argues, exemplifies the situation of texts in
general:

> Within the textual model, particularization corresponds to refer-
> ence, since reference is the application of an undetermined, general
> potential for meaning to a specific unit. The indifference of the text
> with regard to its referential meaning is what allows the legal text
> to proliferate, exactly as the preordained, coded repetition of a spe-
> cific gesture or set of gestures allows Helen to weave the story of
> the war into the epic. . . . The system of relationships that generates
> the text and that functions independently of its referential meaning
> is its grammar. To the extent that a text is grammatical, it is a log-
> ical code or a machine. . . . There can be no text without grammar;
> the logic of grammar generates texts only in the absence of refer-
> ential meaning, but every text generates a referent that subverts the
> grammatical principle to which it owed its constitution. [45]

The law of the law: the incompatible interdependency of general and
particular, is thus described as an effect of the text, of the paradoxical
operation of grammar and reference, of constative and performative

elements at work in all language. Similar considerations lead Derrida, in his reading of Kafka's parable, *Before the Law,* to define the law as "interdiction" (*l'interdit*): not that the law prohibits, "but that it itself is prohibited." The law interdicts itself by "interfering and deferring the 'ferance': relation, report, reference." [46] De Man, for his part, defines the aporetic structure that the text shares with the law as the result of a "double perspective," i.e.,

> as a generative, open-ended non-referential grammatical system and as a figural system closed off by a transcendental signification that subverts the grammatical code to which the text owes its existence. [47]

Remarking upon the general implications of this description, de Man observes that this " 'definition' of the text also states the impossibility of its existence." [48] But if the word "definition" is placed by him in quotes, it is also because the "definition" is rigorously applicable only to texts *in general. Particular texts,* by contrast, as his own readings demonstrate, do indeed have a certain mode of existence, even if it consists only in the singular configuration they trace of the general aporia. Indeed, perhaps this is what is most distinctive to texts: that they ex-ist *only* through a certain *singularity,* only *as* particular texts. The "impossible" law of the text would then fulfill itself, not through a logic or dialectics of self-negation, but rather by becoming the pretext for a certain *recounting* or *relating.* Perhaps this can explain, in part at least, the rather surprising reference, in the passage just quoted, to Helen: a "preordained, coded repetition of a specific gesture or set of gestures," common to the legal text and to texts in general, generates a story, or rather, generates the inscription of a story. And not just any story, but a story of "war," of desire, and of the limits of law. Nor is it a matter of indifference that the singularity of this story is signaled by the unexpected occurrence of a name that is both "proper" and feminine: Helen. As the cause of desire, "Helen" reminds us of that "fundamental problem which the institution of the State" is designed to solve. The naming of this particular name also recalls how an object of desire that is not "unified" can lead, not to the founding of states, not even simply to their undoing, but to the relating and recounting of that undoing in a story. In this sense, de Man remarks that the aporetic structure of the text (and of the law) "prefigures the allegorical narratives of this impossibility." [49]

The *Social Contact* is a strategically staged instance of such an allegorical narrative, whose strategy is manifest in the fact that it *does* what it describes. Taken statically, its individual arguments add up to a coherent whole just as little as do the individuals in the body politic. As de Man remarks, the edifice whose foundations are to be completed through the theory of a law, cannot stand:

> The text can be considered as the theoretical description of the State, considered as a contractual and legal model, but also as the disintegration of this same model as soon as it is put in motion.[50]

The decisive notion here is that of "motion." The model must be "put into motion," since, static and unmoved, it reveals itself to be tautological and redundant. But once it begins to move, it does not simply disintegrate, in the sense of dissolving; it transforms itself and permits something else to appear. A kind of "transference" takes place: in repeating itself, in revealing itself to be the illusory identificatory effect of repetition, it "gestures" towards other, more singular configurations and operations that do not entirely conform to the "binary logic" of whole and part. The retracing of such gestures and the necessity of their singularity is what deconstructive reading, such as that in which de Man *re-counts* the movements and mechanisms of the *Social Contract,* is *about*:

> it now operates to reveal differences where a metaphorical totalization had created the illusion of an identity, a delusive generality in such words as "man," "self," "people," or "State. . . ."[51]

To this list of nouns, we can now add: "law." Taking de Man's lead, let us retrace this process of "disintegration" at work in Rousseau's discussion of the law: the disintegration of the law making way for the law of disintegration, one whose repetitiveness, far from simply bringing back more of the same, allows unexpected differences to emerge. Rousseau introduces the chapter entitled "The End of Legislation" with the following remark:

> With the social pact we have given existence and life to the body politic; it must now be given movement and will through Legislation: For the original act by which this body is formed and united determines nothing about what it must do to preserve itself. This is the great object addressed by the science of Legislation.[52]

Here and elsewhere, the narrative discourse in which Rousseau's account is formulated makes it seem as if the "body politic" could *first* be "given existence and life" by the social contract, and only *then* receive "movement and will" through legislation. This semblance of sequentiality, however, is merely the temporalization (and temporization) of the very organic model that the text explicitly and repeatedly disqualifies. The body politic cannot be said to "exist" before it has a (general) will; it cannot be said to "live" before it can "move." "Preservation" does not follow upon the birth of the self: it constitutes it. Society must *reproduce* itself, must repeat itself, in order to *be*. But its reproduction/repetition does not add up to an integrated, self-identical state. The books do not balance. This imbalance is recounted in a narrative of origins which appears to establish a causal necessity; deconstructive reading recounts the imbalance of that recounting and thereby retraces it as the *allegorical transference of a non-sequitur*. But since it is allegorical, it follows that this non-sequitur does not simply replace the aporetical political state with the logical state of aporia. In the particular case at hand—Rousseau's discussion of the law—this translates as the fact that while its individual applicability does not follow from its generality, *at the same time,* and with singular insistence, something else ensues:

> [W]hen I say that the object of the laws is always general, I mean that the law considers subjects as a body (*en corps*), and actions by their genres or by their species, never a man in particular nor an action that is unique and individual. Thus, the law can very well mandate (*statuer*) privileges, but it cannot give them by *name* (*nommément*) to anyone; It can establish several Classes of Citizens, and even assign the attributions that will determine the rights of each of these Classes, but it cannot *specify that such and such* will be admitted to them; it can establish a Royal government and a hereditary Succession, but it cannot *elect a King* nor *name* a Royal family: in a word, any function relating to an individual object does not belong to the legislative power.[53]

For the law to preserve the body politic, it must function as the generality of the sovereign; in order for it to be legally effective, it must at the same time be applicable to particulars. To meet this dual exigency, Rousseau introduces the notion of *specification*: if the law must avoid concerning itself with "individual objects," it can, and indeed must address "species of actions." The law is now described not merely as the privileged manifestation of the general will, but also as that which *specifies* its object, the general good. But such specification can only articulate itself by virtue of an interdiction. The law is forbidden to pronounce proper names. Recalling the textual "model" suggested by de Man, one might describe the legal text as one which signifies, but which does not name. For it is in naming properly that language claims to enact singular reference. Thus, the law can establish general classes, assign them attributes, but "it cannot specify the admission of such and such," i.e. specify through the use of proper names; "it can establish a Royal government," but it cannot "name a Royal family" or choose a king by name. The first and foremost act of the law, then, is to prohibit itself from using proper names to define the object of its pre- and proscriptions. The more "proper," i.e. more individual and particular, the name, the less lawful the law. The law, in short, must be *anonymous*.[54]

And yet, despite this constitutive prohibition, there is one name that the law can and should use: that of the "people." In its application, the law must pronounce a proper name to assure its legitimacy. In the name of what people? "When the Law speaks in the name of the people," Rousseau observes, 'it is in the name of the people of today and not of the past."[55] But this people of today must, first of all, be determined by the past: for how else can it be determined just how this people will be constituted? The "people of today" is therefore determined by the laws of the past, but at the same time—which is therefore determined as a time of the past—this people of today is not bound by those laws: it is free to vote new laws that need not conform to those it has previously established.

In this context, de Man's assimilation of the law to the promise appears particularly significant. Laws, he argues,

> are future-oriented and prospective; their illocutionary mode is that of the *promise*. On the other hand, every promise assumes a date at which the promise is made and without which it would have no validity; laws are promissory notes in which the present of the promise is always a past with regard to its realization.[56]

Given Rousseau's insistence upon the fact that the sovereign cannot be bound by the law—which is tantamount to asserting, not merely that the people can *change* the laws, but that it has the right to *disregard* them[57]—the distinctive feature of sovereignty would be its right to *break* its promises, and its laws. Only by breaking its promises and laws, would the sovereign in principle be able to *keep* them, by affirming its constitutive right to *make* promises and laws.

Rousseau emphasizes, to be sure, that for the sovereign to exercise this right is for it to undermine the foundations of its existence (i.e. the social contract).[58] But the question still remains: What enables the sovereign to "make"—and this means to promulgate—a law in the first place? Viewed in terms of the general will, understood as the will of a "people," "the situation," as de Man points out, "is without solution. In the absence of an *état présent,* the general will is quite literally voiceless,"[59] for it is *so utterly entrapped in the present* that it can not raise that *présent* to the status of an *état.* The general will only presents itself when it is assembled; but since the assembly is always that of *today,* it is also gone tomorrow, like the "here and now" at the beginning of Hegel's *Phenomenology of Mind.* Or rather, it is not entirely gone, but different. Each successive moment can and must in principle be different from the preceding one. This is the temporal correlative of the body politic's inability to consolidate itself. The anonymous promises emitted by the general will in its assembled presence indicate that the future depends upon a present that in turn requires a certain past in order to legitimize itself.

This past is that of the lawgiver, whose place, Rousseau emphasizes, can only be extra-territorial. Accordingly, the gift of the law can have nothing to do with legislation, in the sense of ordinary lawmaking:

> It is neither magistracy, nor even sovereignty. This operation, which constitutes the republic, does not enter into its constitution. It is in a certain manner a particular and almost divine function, having nothing in common with the human realm: For if whoever commands men should not command the laws; similarly whoever commands the laws should not command men. . . . [Otherwise] he would never be able to prevent his particular views from affecting the sanctity of his work. . . . When Lycurgus wanted to give the Laws to his country, he began by abdicating sovereignty. It was the custom of most of the Greek cities to confide the drafting (*la rédaction*) of their [laws] to foreigners. . . . Whoever drafts the laws should therefore have no legislative power.[60]

The "particular function" of the lawgiver has to do with the fact that, despite his name—*Législateur*—he is not a *legislator* in the "proper" sense of the word. The *gift* of the law is very different from the *making* of it. It is a function of *framing,* which as such cannot simply fit within the frame. The problem, of course, is that it can also not be simply exterior to it. It is easier for Rousseau to describe what the lawgiver is not, than what he is. He cannot be a member of the sovereign people, since the people "cannot divest itself of the Supreme right," i.e. that of sovereignty. As a corollary, he can have no legislative power.[61] But if the giver of the law lacks all legislative power, his gift is anything but powerless. Indeed, without a certain power, there could be no gift at all.

This is precisely the enigma of the lawgiver: he gives what neither he nor anyone else has. Hence, the source of his gift, and its relation to the law, i.e. its "legitimacy," remain open questions. The noun, "legislator," provides an exemplary confirmation of de Man's remark concerning "the illusion of an identity, a delusive generality"[62] that attaches to certain words, and which functions to obscure differences and "relational properties."[63] It is the structure of such "relations" that is put in question by the singular "act" of the lawgiver: singular, since its addressee, the "people," can hardly be said to exist as such prior to the gift. It is this that distinguishes the gift of the law from the social contract it is called upon to consolidate: the former is described by Rousseau as an act of exchange, with the goal of profit: individuals cede their force and possessions in turn for the security, rights and property that only a community can guarantee. But the principle by which this community is constituted cannot be derived from the social contract understood in this sense. All such a contract can engender is its own, invented mirror-image *ad infinitum*: Individuals contracting with individuals, parts with parts, "each" taking his own interests for those of "all." Hence, the need for an act or an event radically different from the social contract. It is this that leads Rousseau to make the formation and survival of the body politic dependent upon the gift of a text, that "constitutes the Republic," but that itself "does not enter at all into its constitution."[64] Small wonder that de Man calls this gift is a "simulacrum," albeit an inevitable one:

> The metaphorical substitution of one's own for the divine voice is blasphemous, although the necessity for this deceit is as implacable as its eventual denunciation, in the future undoing of any State or any political institution.[65]

No doubt that the position of Rousseau here, in his derivation of the law, is therefore surprisingly close to the Hobbesian dictum: *autoritas, non veritas, facit legem.*[66] And no question, either, as de Man argues, that this recourse to divine authority undermines the explicit argument of the text, namely, that political sovereignty is the result of a reflexive, if "double" relationship of the political subject—the people—to itself. Rousseau's ironic dismissal of theories of the divine origin of "justice" applies as well to his own account of the gift of the law: "All justice comes from God, he alone is its source; but if we knew how to receive it from on high, we would need neither government nor laws."[67] What interests Rousseau, therefore, in his account of the lawgiver, is not the latter's unquestionable a-legitimacy, but rather the fact that his gift can nonetheless be effective in establishing a durable political community:

> prideful philosophy and blind partisan spirit . . . will continue to see [in such lawgivers] *only* fortunate impostors, but the true politician will admire in their institutions the great and powerful genius who presides over durable foundations (*establissemens*).[68]

Rousseau thus does not in the slightest dispute the fact that the lawgiver's appeal to divine authority is an *imposture:* what he contests is that this *alone* can explain the durable *imposition* of the law.[69] To understand how this imposition is possible, as well as certain of its implications, let us take another look at Rousseau's account of the enigmatic gift of the law.

The gift of the law is a gift only if it is accepted as such. Given the extra-territorial situation of the lawgiver, such acceptance must be brought about not by "prescribing anything to individuals," nor through "conviction," but rather through "persuasion."[70] It depends, therefore, on rhetoric. Although such persuasion seems inseparable from the extraordinary "soul" and "genius" of the legislator, a number of other factors are also alluded to. It is in this context that Rousseau himself introduces the notion of the *promise* (a fact that de Man, interestingly enough, does not discuss). Rousseau distinguishes between two kinds of promise: those said to be "purely gratuitous," and those which are "conditional." While declaring himself skeptical as to the existence of any truly gratuitous promises, Rousseau insists that in the case of the social contract, the promise to obey is always conditional. To accept the gift of the law means that "each individual promises to obey without reservation," but only under the condition that "it is for the welfare of all."[71] This is the logic of the exchange, of the social contract, and is therefore subject to all the unresolved (and unresolvable) problems already encountered: "The People is the sole judge" of the legitimacy of the laws, *but* it is also unable to distinguish reliably between the needs of some and the needs of all. "The laws are like pure gold that it is impossible to denature by any operation, and which the first test immediately restores to its natural form,"[72] *but* that natural form is inaccessible to the limited sensibility of individual citizens, etc. The "subterfuge" or "simulacrum" of which de Man speaks, can thus be defined, in the terms of the *Social Contract,* as that of a conditional promise whose conditions, however, are inaccessible.[73]

The problem of the law can be formulated, accordingly, as that of translating an unconditional (anonymous) promise into a conditional (nominal) one. It is hardly by accident, therefore, that Rousseau, in his discussion of the miraculous *gifts* of the lawgiver, includes among them the ability to translate, even where such is impossible:

> It was often the error of the sages to speak their own language to the populace instead of its; hence, they were neither heard nor understood (*entendus*). There are a thousand sorts of ideas that have only one language and that are impossible to translate to the People. Perspectives that are too general and objects that are too remote are equally beyond its scope.[74]

The translation of the legality of the law into a text that can be read by the People is clearly impossible, for all the reasons we have been discussing. It requires that metaleptic sleight-of-hand to which de Man calls attention, by which "the effect can become the cause . . . and men before the laws can become what they should become through them."[75] The linguistic operation, however, through which the rhetoric of metaleptic translation or transference *imposes* itself, is nothing other than the *recitation of a proper name* as the translation of an anonymous other, in which origin and end, individual and general converge in a "simulacrum" of identity.

For this reason, the lawgiver is not just a more or less talented ventriloquist, who "puts decisions into the mouth of the immortals in order to subjugate by divine authority those who are impervious to human prudence."[76] He does all of this, to be sure. But this in turn depends upon another gift: that of *speaking (in) their name*. If the lawgiver is "believed when he declares himself to be their interpreter,"[77] it is because of the force invested in this name, which, far from naming an individual, names nothing, if it is not the *proper name of anonymity* as such. It is the power of the name which imposes the law through an impossible translation that names the unnameable: the promise of a reference that would be both singular and universal, universally singular. In imposing its law, what is effaced is the very *impossibility* of the translation by which the anonymous is named improperly, but generically: as *People, Nation, State,* or *Sovereign.* The transference leaves its trace, however, in the interdiction of the proper name. The law *is* this interdiction, and at the same time, its *impropriety.*

It is this improper gift that lays down the law. As de Man concludes, although "the *Social Contract* has lost the right to promise anything . . . it promises a great deal."[78] The "great deal" that it promises is the *law of the proper name.* It has no *right* to that promise, but it does so anyway. It names: "State," "Sovereign," "People"—in the name of the Law. By so naming it provides the solution to the problem of the state: that of gathering the divergent needs and desires of individuals by presenting "one sole object."

It's a great deal. Even if, to quote de Man one last time, its "deceit is as implacable as its eventual denunciation"—which is to say, as implacable as its eventual de-naming. For what his reading of the *Social Contract* has demonstrated, is that no name has a right of its own. It's the law: the law of naming, of de-naming, and of renaming. Of enunciation, denunciation, and of a renunciation that would not just be abandonment, but a gift. Does one ever have the right to (refuse) a gift? Particularly one given in the name of the other?

But can we be sure we know what we are talking about, when we speak of accepting, or abandoning a gift "in the name of the other"? Towards the end of *Memoires,* Jacques Derrida takes his leave with a challenge, that bears upon this very question:

> Try and translate, in all of its syntactical equivocity, a syntagm such as "donner au nom de l'autre" or "une parole donnée au nom de l'autre." In a single sentence, it could mean in French, or rather in English: "To give to the name of the other" and "to give in the name of the other." Who knows what we are doing when we donnons au nom de l'autre?[79]

I want to take up the challenge and the question, by proposing the following translation—if indeed it can be called that—of the French phrase, *"donner au nom de l'autre"*: not just giving *to* the name of the other, nor just giving *in* the name of the other, but *giving in-to the name of the other.* In this act of ceding, which is at the same time one of bestowing—an act impossible ever to realize fully—deconstruction responds to the singular call of the anonymous other, not by laying down the law, nor even with a promise, but with something more like a suspended sentence.[80]

Giving in-to the name of the other—a great deal.

NOTES

1. J. Derrida, Mémoires: For Paul de Man 18 (C. Lindsay, J. Culler and E. Cadava trans. 1986). Some of the translations cited in this paper have been altered slightly for purposes of clarity.
2. Id. at 14–15.

3. P. de Man, Allegories of Reading 249 (1979).

4. Thus, Derrida initially articulates the difference between his notion of deconstruction and the Heideggerian *Destruktion* in terms of the status not just of a word, *Being,* but of the word as such:

> Doubtless, the meaning of Being is not the word "being" nor the concept of being, as Heidegger incessantly reminds us. But since this meaning is nothing outside of language or of the language of words, it is tied, if not to this or that word, to this or that system of languages (*concesso non dato*), at least to *the possibility of the word in general. And to its irreducible simplicity.*

J. Derrida, De la Grammatologie 34 (1967) (italics added). The motifs of the *signature* and of the proper name have emerged as focal points of Derrida's deconstruction of the word.

5. Webster's New Collegiate Dictionary 458 (1956) (based on Webster's New International Dictionary [2d ed. 1950]) (italics added).

6. Id.

7. Compare Webster's New Collegiate Dictionary, supra note 5, at 458 with Le Petit Robert 958 (1970). The translation of the *Petit Robert* definition offered herein assumes that "right"—*droit*—is the same as "law." Another problem of translation which, although it cannot be addressed explicitly in this paper, underlies—as problem—much of the following discussion.

8. Le Petit Robert, supra note 7, at 958.

9. In German, similar remarks could be made concerning the word, *Gewalt.* Which renders the title of Walter Benjamin's essay, *Kritik der Gewalt,* difficult, if not impossible, to translate into English. Derrida comments upon these difficulties in his discussion of Benjamin's text, published in this volume.

10. J. Derrida, supra note 1, at 16.

11. Id. at 14.

12. A. de Tocqueville, De la Democratie en Amerique 167 (1981) (translations offered herein will contain, on occasion, parenthetical references to the original texts cited, for purposes of clarification).

13. Id. at 168.

14. Id. at 169.

15. Id. at 170.

16. Id.

17. Id.

18. Id. at 225–26.

19. Id. at 244.

20. Id. at 227.

21. Id.

22. Id. at 167.

23. Id. at 370.

24. Id. at 367.

25. Id. at 367–68.

254 / In the Name of the Law

26. Id. at 213.

27. J. Derrida, supra note 1, at 8.

28. I will follow de Man's reading in concentrating primarily on the first version of the *Social Contract*, the so-called *Manuscrit de Genéve*. Page references herein are to 3 J.-J. Rousseau, Oeuvres complétes (B. Gagnebin & M. Raymond eds. 1964).

29. J. Rousseau, supra note 28, at 305–06 (italics added).

30. Id. at 306.

31. Rousseau's notion, that in the social pact "each individual contracts, in a manner of speaking, with himself," but "under a double relationship, namely as member of the sovereign toward private persons (*particuliers*) and as member of the State toward the sovereign" (Id. at 290), begs the question: that namely of the path by which the individual, given the limited immediacy of his private interests, comes to associate himself with *either* the sovereign *or* the state. Despite the narrative of origins in which Rousseau is engaged here, the question of the "social contract" has less to do with the founding of society, as a diachronic, determinate event, than with its structure or constitution, which, being aporetic, evokes what de Man calls "allegorical narratives." The latter have a function similar to that ascribed by Freud to "secondary revision" in dreams: that of dissimulating internal illogic behind a semblance of causal sequence.

32. Id. at 306.

33. This is undoubtedly why the judicial institution, as Rousseau conceives it, can not be "a constitutive part of the City," i.e., of the general will. Id. at 307, 454. See also J. Rousseau, Du Tribunat bk. IV, ch. 5.

34. As we shall see, "*nommément*," here and elsewhere in the text, applies to both the form and the content of the "pronouncement": it should be read, therefore, both as "namely" and as "by name," or "nominally." It applies both to the statement itself and to that which is being stated.

35. J.-J. Rousseau, supra note 28, at 307 (italics added).

36. Id. at 309.

37. Id.

38. "Sovereignty cannot be represented . . . it consists essentially in the general will, and will cannot be represented: it is the same, or it is other; there is no middle." Id. at 429.

39. Id. at 310.

40. Id. at 328.

41. Id. at 290.

42. Id. at 289–90.

43. P. de Man, supra note 3, at 265.

44. Id. at 269.

45. Id. at 268–69. It is perhaps worth noting here, in passing, that, contrary to widespread misapprehension, it is precisely the referential function of language which appeals most strongly to deconstruction, and to which it in turn appeals.

46. J. Derrida, Préjugés, in La faculté de juger 121 (1985). This text, as well as those of Kafka to which it refers, *Before the Law, The Question of the Laws, Spokesmen*

and *The Trial*, are all highly pertinent to this discussion of Rousseau, although I have no opportunity to deal with them explicitly here.

47. P. de Man, supra note 3, at 270.

48. Id.

49. Id. With this and other passages in mind, Neil Hertz, in an as yet unpublished paper, *More Lurid Figures*, discerns in the figure of Helen a "maternal" aspect associated both with the "law," that leaves itself "hanging," and with the narratives, to which it gives way. The fact that, as we shall see, the law is the condition of the reproduction and hence survival of the "body politic," would tend to confirm this reading. However, like Helen, the law does not simply nurture and preserve, it also subverts and destroys: itself no less than its "rule." And "to weave the story of the war into the epic," is not quite the same as *telling a story*. Perhaps the figure of Helen—or rather, of her *name*—can be read as a trace of what Neil Hertz finds "missing from de Man's critical account": the "thematization of the reader-critic's own fascination." Is anything more fascinating, and less thematisable, than finding oneself "preordained" to carry out a "coded repetition of a specific gesture or set of gestures"?

50. P. de Man, supra note 3, at 271.

51. Id. at 253.

52. J.-J. Rousseau, supra note 28, at 312.

53. Id. at 327–28 (italics added).

54. Having introduced the notion of "specification," and hence of *degrees* of generality and particularity, Rousseau is then able to distinguish on the one hand, "fundamental" or "political" laws, affecting the relation of "the whole to whole," but which pass by way of "intermediary forces," i.e. the branches of government, from "civil law," also designated as "particular Laws," since these concern the relations of the sovereign to individual citizens. "Criminal law" he considers "less a particular species of law than the sanction of all the others." The most important of all, Rousseau emphasizes, is that type of law "unknown to our politicians, but upon which depends the success of all the others," those by which "the force of habit" imperceptibly replaces "that of authority." Id. at 331.

55. Id. at 316.

56. P. de Man, supra note 3, at 273.

57. It should be noted that public deliberation that can obligate all subjects towards the sovereign . . . cannot inversely obligate the sovereign towards himself, and that consequently it is against the nature of the body politic that the sovereign should impose upon itself a law that it cannot infringe (*enfreindre*) . . . : It would then be in the situation of an individual (*particulier*) contracting with itself; whereby it is clear that there can be no species of basic Law binding upon the body of the People.

   J.-J. Rousseau, supra note 28, at 290–91. In the published version of the social contract, Rousseau adds that not only no "basic law" or constitution can bind the sovereign, but also that the same holds for the social contract itself. *Id.* at 362.

58. It is this paradox that will lead Carl Schmitt to his definition of sovereignty as the power of deciding upon the "state of exception" (*Ausnahmezustand*). See C. Schmitt, Politische Theologie 11 (4th ed. 1985).

59. P. de Man, supra note 3, at 273.

60. J.-J. Rousseau, supra note 28, at 313–14.

61. It is misleading to identify, as De Man does, "[w]hat Rousseau calls the '*souver-ain*'" with "the executive power," even after allowances for "historical hindsight" have been made. P. de Man, supra note 3, at 265. The power of the sovereign is above all that of legislating, for only the law, in its generality, is appropriate to the general will; the executive, by contrast, bears upon the particular conditions under which the law is to be implemented. Since, however, "the sovereign authority is by its very nature, only a moral person, whose existence can only by abstract and collective" (id.), it should rigorously be identified with none of the branches of government. Government, as Rousseau defines it, is "an intermediary body established between subjects and Sovereign to assure their mutual correspondence." J.-J. Rousseau, supra note 28, at 396.

62. P. de Man, supra note 3, at 253.

63. Id. at 249.

64. J.-J. Rousseau, supra note 28, at 313.

65. P. de Man, supra note 3, at 274–75.

66. T. Hobbes, Leviathan (1914, 1651). The tradition concentrated in this Hobbesian formula provides the point of departure for Carl Schmitt's theory of "decision" as an act that is structurally independent of and prior to all norms in the constitution of political bodies. Correlative to this is his notion of sovereignty as consisting in the power to suspend the constitution, a notion that Benjamin reinscribed (and transformed) in his *Origins of the German Mourning Play*. Schmitt's critique of all normative juridical thinking, is pertinent to many of the issues raised here.

67. J.-J. Rousseau, supra note 28, at 326.

68. Id. at 317–18 (italics added).

69. This is also the perspective from which Lacan approaches the question of the law in psychoanalysis. Lacan's formulations often echo this passage of Rousseau, as for instance in Subversion of the Subject and Dialectics of Desire:

> Let us proceed from the other conceived as the site of the signifier. No statement of authority has in this respect any guarantee except for its utterance as such . . . [w]hich we formulate in saying that there is no metalanguage that might be spoken, or, more aphoristically, that there is no Other of the Other. The legislator (the one who claims to erect the law) who presents himself in order to make up for this (*qui se présente pour y suppléer*) does so as an imposter; but not the Law itself, no more than he who acts on its authority (*celui qui s'en autorise*).

J. Lacan, Ecrits 813 (1966). For an English translation of this work see J. Lacan, A. Sheridan trans. 1977.

70. J.-J. Rousseau, supra note 28, at 316.

71. Id. at 315.

72. Id.

73. Such inaccessibility becomes the most manifest trait of the law in the writings of Kafka.

74. J.-J. Rousseau, supra note 28, at 316.

75. Id. at 317.

76. Id.

77. Id.

78. P. de Man, supra note 3, at 276.

79. J. Derrida, supra note 1, at 150.

80. The motif of the *suspended sentence* characterizes the German Baroque Mourning Play, according to Walter Benjamin: "One can . . . speak of the trial of creation, which accusation (*Klage:* literally, complaint, lament; also charge) against death—or against whomever it may be—is relegated to the books only half finished, at the end of the play. Its resumption (*Wiederaufnahme*) is thus inscribed in the mourning play." W. Benjamin, Ursprung des deutschen Trauerspiels 148 (1963). If sentence is suspended not merely in its execution, but in its very enunciation, it is because the chief defendant in the "trial of the creation" is none other than the proper name itself: "The mournful feels itself recognized through and through by the unrecognizable. To be named—even when the namer is like unto the Gods, and blessed—always retains, perhaps, a hint of mourning." Id. at 254. The suspended sentence is also Benjamin's "response" to the decisionism of Carl Schmitt; in a world such as that of the Baroque Mourning Play, decisions are as necessary as they are impossible, as the antinomical figure of the Baroque Sovereign demonstrates: Tyrant and Martyr in one.

7

Forms

Charles M. Yablon

The papers that have preceded me have all been extremely original and interesting.

I must provide the missing Derridean supplement.

I must be boring.

This is not difficult for me. I am a lawyer.

I know many boring things.

Many very, very boring things.

I must be boring. I must bore. But in another sense, to bore is to dig, to probe under the surface, to uncover that which has been hidden, to view that which has not previously been seen.

In that sense, the papers that have preceded me have been very boring indeed, and I may truthfully say that I hope I may be only half as boring as those who have preceded me.

I have chosen as my topic a boring thing. A boring lawyer's thing. It is a blank summons in a civil action based on the forth set form in Form 1 of the Appendix of Forms as issued pursuant to Rule 4 of the Federal Rules of Civil Procedure. It is a form, and like a Platonic Form, it is perfect of its type. All other federal court summonses, the thousands of summonses served on human beings every day in this country, partake of the form of this summons, are based on the form of this summons, are judged by the form of this summons. A summons that does not follow the form of this summons is a poorly drafted summons, a defective summons. Perhaps it is not a summons at all.

This is a form. It has no substance. It is filled with blanks. It is unsigned. It has no names, no places, no times. It is for no one. But it is not for no one. It is for you.

AO 440 (Rev. 5/85) Summons in a Civil Action

United States District Court

—————————————— DISTRICT OF ——————————————

SUMMONS IN A CIVIL ACTION

        V.

CASE NUMBER:

TO: (Name and Address of Defendant)

YOU ARE HEREBY SUMMONED and required to file with the Clerk of this Court and serve upon

PLAINTIFF'S ATTORNEY (name and address)

an answer to the complaint which is herewith served upon you, within _____ days after service of
this summons upon you, exclusive of the day of service. If you fail to do so, judgment by default will be taken
against you for the relief demanded in the complaint.

———————————————————— ————————————————————
CLERK   DATE

————————————————————
BY DEPUTY CLERK

"You are hereby summoned." Here, by this summons, this form, you are hereby summoned. The statement is true. It cannot be false. The written statement "You are hereby summoned" proves itself. If you seek to dispute it, you acknowledge its call to you, and thereby prove that you have indeed been summoned. You have been summoned, and cannot dispute it.

The statement is not a statement of fact, but an act of summoning, yet also a statement describing the act of summoning. You are hereby summoned. Who has summoned you? The form does not say. Surely not the plaintiff, the one who has sued you. The plaintiff, like you, is a subject of this document, not its author. When the blank spaces are filled in in some lawyer's office, the plaintiff's name will sit uncomfortably just above yours in the caption of the case. It will be neither larger nor smaller than yours and will be separated from your name merely by the interposition of the printed "v." That letter "v." is a part of the form. It is the part of the form which places you two, plaintiff and defendant, literally and figuratively, on opposite sides.

You are hereby summoned. Who has summoned you? Is it the Clerk, or the Deputy Clerk, whose titles appear below two signature lines at the bottom of the page? The Clerk will not sign this summons. It will be stamped with merely the form of her signature. The Deputy Clerk will not, as a matter of law, sign the document, even if she writes her name on the bottom line. The Deputy Clerk merely acts for the Clerk, who does not act at all, but merely has someone else stamp her signature on the summons. The summons is signed by no one. It is written by no one. But it summons *you*.

"You are hereby summoned . . ." You are "required to serve." Service is now required of you. You have been called, you have been summoned, and now you must serve. You have been drafted. Like an unwilling recruit, you must appear at a time and place not of your own choosing, swear an oath, file papers. You have been drafted by a document.

You have been accused. Statements have been made against you. Your wrongful actions have been observed. They have been recorded. They have been written down. The writing that contains them will be attached to the summons. It is called a complaint. It is complaining about you.

You are required to file and serve an answer to the complaint. It is not enough merely to answer, you must *serve* an answer. You have been summoned. You must serve. An expectation has been created. An answer must be served to serve the expectation. After all, there are rules.

The summons never mentions the rules. Never refers to them or tells you what they are. The rules are not a subject of the summons. They are not cited or discussed. If the rules were stated, you might read them. They could be opened to discussion. They could be interpreted. The rules might turn out to have more than one meaning. They might not tell you what to do.

The summons does not tell you the rules. The summons is a thing issued pursuant to the rules. It tells you what to do. The rules are not stated. The rules are not open to discussion. Yet when you read the summons you know there must be rules, because the summons is all about the things you *must do*.

"You are hereby summoned and required to file with the Clerk of this Court and serve upon plaintiff's attorney [whose name and address are to be typed in] an answer to the complaint which is herewith served upon you, within [a certain number of] days after service of this summons upon you, exclusive of the day of service."

You are required to file. You are required to serve. You have a certain number of days, carefully counted, exclusive of the day of service. Expectations have been created. They are waiting for your answer. The summons presumes, without ever stating them, the existence of clear, mandatory, determinate rules, time deadlines, rules for counting, expected actions, forbidden actions. The first unstated message of the summons is: There are rules and you must obey them.

There are rules but you do not know them. You are required to file and serve an answer. Not merely answer, not say "get lost" or "leave me alone" or "the complaint against me is a tissue of lies." You must file an answer with the Clerk of the Court. You must serve an answer upon plaintiff's attorney. The rules require a special kind of answer. You must answer according to the rules. You must serve your answer upon plaintiff's attorney, whose name and address appear prominently in the center of the summons. It is plaintiff's attorney who has written the complaint. It is plaintiff's attorney you are required to serve. Obviously, plaintiff's attorney knows the rules.

Plaintiff's attorney knows the rules and you do not. You need help. You need someone who knows the rules. You cannot answer for yourself.

You cannot answer for yourself, and you do not have much time. The number of days you have before you must file and serve your answer is specifically set forth in the summons. Your days are numbered, exclusive of the day of service. Your days are numbered. You cannot answer for yourself. The second unstated message of the summons is: "Get a lawyer, fast."

But surely a mere document cannot wield such power over you. You are free to ignore it, resist it, answer any way you want, say "to hell with the rules," tear up the summons. You may be punished for such disobedience but you can still assert your freedom from the rules.

You can tear up the summons. You can refuse to serve. But you cannot be free of the rules. The rules contemplate that you might tear up the summons. The rules anticipate that you might refuse to serve. Such actions are still subject to the rules.

The rules contemplate their own disobedience. The summons expects you may fail to live up to expectations. You are expected to serve, but you may fail. If you fail, you are still subject to the rules.

"If you fail to do so, judgment by default will be taken against you for the relief demanded in the complaint." If you fail, judgment will be taken against you. Who will render judgment? Again, the summons provides no names. No one will render judgment. No one will act. But someone will be acted upon. Judgment will be taken. Against you.

This judgment is not a gift provided by a fair and enlightened judiciary. This judgment will not be given by anyone. This judgment will be taken. Against you. By default. It will be triggered by your fault, your failure to meet expectations. You may wish to have your refusal to answer be interpreted as an act of defiance, of resistance to the rules, a grand gesture of protest. But is has already been interpreted, before it has ever occurred, as merely a default, a failure to make service, a non-event. Under the rules your action will be interpreted as a default, because default is an action contemplated by the rules. You have not resisted. You have not protested. You have merely defaulted. You have failed to meet expectations. Judgment will be taken against you. Not maliciously. Not vindictively. Not because of your actions. But merely because you failed to act, according to the rules. The rules define your actions even as you seek to defy them. The third unstated message of the summons is: "You are not free to resist."

As the preceding discussion has, I think, indicated, the language of the summons is indeterminate on a number of levels, but that does not mean that it lacks meaning. Quite the contrary, as Robert Cover, and I think Derrida as well, would remind us, the indeterminacy of legal language must be used as a way of revealing and analyzing the power exerted and pain inflicted by legal processes, not as a way of denying that power and pain. Second, indeterminacy, particularly in a Derridean context, does not reflect a lack of meaning, but an overabundance of meaning, of denotations and connotations, of words that mean many things at once, of words that remind us of other words, of things that are said and things that are unsaid. Words in context, like the context of a summons, are not malleable putty that can mean anything we desire. Rather, they are brittle, like a pane of glass presenting a single face to the world, but with tiny cracks of alternative, even opposing meanings, that can shatter and break up the dominant understanding. A summons is a routine legal form. It is also an instrument of power and pain. That is the indeterminacy that gives it meaning.

Part Three

Comparative Perspectives on Justice, Law and Politics

8

On the Margins of Microeconomics

David Gray Carlson

Inside the economy of classic price theory is—another economy! But not the economy of supply and demand that price theory sets out to domesticate. The underground economy—where the work is really done—is hidden. It is, in Derrida's words, "a war economy." [1]

This paper applies Derrida's ideas to the price theory. What follows, then, is a grammatology—a deconstruction. As a result of this deconstruction, price theory, which *presents* itself as the law of the perfect market, will be shown to be founded on—as it must be founded on—an imperfect market. This imperfect origin of the perfect market occurs because opportunity costs (a vital element of the marginal cost of production) point to another market, which points to another market, and so forth. At least as a matter of origin, one of these other markets must once have been an imperfect market. This origin in market imperfection betrays price theory's purpose—the reconciliation of private gain with public good as a necessary property of contract exchange. Such a reconciliation depends on perfect markets everywhere, all the time.

Deconstruction is an equilibrium theory of what Derrida calls the general economy of *being*. [2] Determinate being, in precritical thinking, is taken as self-evident—unmediated by thought. Concepts are conceived as eternal and self-standing. In Jacques Derrida's terminology, such beings are assumed to be *present*, and this faith in the self-subsistence of concepts is described as a "philosophy of presence."

Philosophy of presence works by suppressing the other by force or violence, even while denying that this violence occurs. What appears to be a whole is covertly an economy. But this suppression can be disrupted from within the very paradigms of a philosophy of presence. This disruption is what Derrida calls moving "from restricted to general economy"[3]—a move this paper hopes to make with regard to price theory.

In Derrida's terminology, microeconomics is the restricted economy, and the disrupted microeconomics the general one. This general economy "is the one that shows how metaphysics's eternal attempt to *profit* from its ventures is based upon an irreducible *loss*, an 'expenditure without reserve' without which there could be no idea of profit."[4] That is to say, the restricted economy claims a profit—the unified whole—but does so only by concealing a loss—the loss of the Other that is violently suppressed. In a restricted economy, the insolvent theoretician promises more than he can provide.[5] In microeconomic parlance, the restricted economy has failed to internalize its costs.

Derrida's famous neographism[6] "différance" misspelled with an *a* and pronounced (in French) precisely like "difference," is a portentous concept for microeconomics. Derrida writes:

> this discreet graphic intervention [the errant "a"], which neither primarily nor simply aims to shock the reader or the grammarian . . . , this graphic difference (*a* instead of *e*), this marked difference between two apparently vocal notations, between two vowels, remains purely graphic: it is read, or it is written, but it cannot be heard. It cannot be apprehended in speech, and we will see why it also bypasses the order of apprehension in general. It is offered by a mute mark, by a tacit monument, I would even say by a pyramid, thinking not only of the form of the letter when it is printed as a capital, but also of the text in Hegel's *Encyclopedia* in which the body of the sign is compared to the Egyptian Pyramid. The *a* of *différance*, thus, is not heard; it remains silent, secret and discreet as a tomb: *oikesis*. And thereby let us anticipate the delineation of a site, the familial residence and tomb of the proper in which is produced, by *différance*, the *economy of death*. This stone—provided that one knows how to decipher its inscription is not far from announcing the death of the tyrant.[7]

Translated into the context of this paper, the market imperfections I will locate inside (but on the margins of) price theory are the *archèwriting*, a "discreet graphic intervention." This intervention cannot be heard from the perspective of logocentrism. It bypasses this particular "order of apprehension." This intervention is signalled by the letter *a* which (when *capital*ized—i.e., reduced to "present value") resembles a pyramid—a tomb. Thus, capital intervention spells the death of price theory *qua* theory, a death foretold in the etymology of the word "economy," derived as it is from *oikos* (household), which is akin to *oikesis* (tomb).[8] The real economy in microeconomics, then, is an *economy of death*. All of this is inscribed on the tomb that the *a* of différance represents, a tomb, incidentally, that is memorialized on the back of every dollar bill turned out by the United States Treasury Department. The tyranny whose death is foretold is, of course, that of microeconomics whose will to power works to suppress its origin in death. Every dollar bill, with its pyramidal symbolism, encases the eye of a radically other god that stares out at those who would theorize in a totalizing way about how the dollar might circulate. This eye of god winks at microeconomics from the *a* of différance—the trace upon which our economy truly depends.

THE MARKET'S RHETORICAL FUNCTION

It is my thesis that modern American price theory—the type that describes a perfect market—is a philosophy of presence. It works by banishing time. Time is itself a market imperfection. Furthermore, price theory's perfect market must originate in market imperfections. Thus, at the same time price theory defines and banishes imperfections, it cannot do without them. It implicitly relies on imperfections for its origin. The self-betrayal of the perfect market occurs at a marginal point, and it occurs through a palpable act of deferral. There is a certain irony here. Since Marshall, price theory has celebrated marginality and has made the margin the center of its attention. Thus, both competitive and oligopolistic prices are determined by the marginal cost of production. There is a sense in which classic price theory is already attuned to deconstruction's program of bringing the margin back into the center. Yet the margin I want to identify is at the margin of these margins. The irony comes from the fact that price theory constantly defers the very margin which is supposed to govern the domain of price theory.

It is always a first step in deconstruction to construct the very thing to be deconstructed. This moment is always a dangerous one, because it is possible that one deconstructs a straw man—a theory that no one holds or defends. Perhaps for this reason, Derrida sticks to texts of living or once living human beings, rather than some abstract set of connected ideas that no one has asserted.

Similarly, I would like to let George Stigler's classic textbook, *The Theory of Price*,[9] to stand in for price theory generally.

In Stigler's work, price theory has at its center—in a very heliocentric sense—perfect markets.[10] Perfect markets are considered natural and authentic. Perfect markets correspond to "speech" in Derrida's system. Market imperfections are the hated fall from grace. Economic theorizing therefore consists of "taming" data that do not conform to the vision of the perfect market. These imperfections correspond to what Derrida would call "writing." [11] From Stigler's viewpoint, imperfections are unnatural, just as to Saussure or Levi-Strauss (as described in Derrida's work), writing threatens authenticity.

Needless to say, this is not how Stigler conceives of his project. Stigler is quite aware of the embarrassing other-worldliness of perfect markets. The perfect market is nevertheless defended from the charge of utopianism because of its predictive power in our world.[12] The example chosen to illustrate this power is as follows:

> To maximize his utility, the buyer searches for additional prices until the expected saving from the purchase equals the cost of visiting one more dealer. Then he stops searching and buys from the dealer who quotes the lowest price he has encountered.[13]

Notice that this theory—involving search costs—focuses on an individual who has expectations. One expectation is the cost of one more visit to a store. The other is the expectation of what saving will be discovered there. If the first exceeds the second, no further visits will occur. Instead, the customer will visit the store known to have the lowest price.[14]

Stigler imagines three objections by a noneconomist. First, the noneconomist will deny that people maximize this thing called utility.

> He will say that people typically do not maximize anything—that the consumer is lazy or dominated by advertisers or poor at arithmetic. And indeed there are consumers who not only suffer from these disabilities but are also downright confused. Why attribute to them the cold-blooded, logical approach of a well-built modern computer?
>
> Second, what precisely is the cost of canvassing one more seller? All one has to do is to drive over to another dealer and talk to him for a few minutes. How can a monetary value be placed upon these actions—which are pleasant for some people and distasteful to others?
>
> Finally, does not the economist merely say . . . that the buyer will visit as many dealers as he visits—no more, no less. The rule does not say whether he visits one or every seller[15]

Stigler's "basic reply" to these imagined attacks: price theory "enables us to predict how consumers (and markets) will behave."

Stigler (somewhat carelessly) describes how this theory might generate testable propositions in the world.

> The cost of searching out one more price varies . . . But it will vary much less among commodities than the gain from a 1 percent saving in price varies among commodities.[16]

One can quarrel with this assumption that searching for an automobile costs the same as searching for, say, a rare herb or chemical. There is a certain vision that Stigler obviously has in mind—given a standard kind of consumer good that is listed in the Yellow Pages and are familiar and comfortable to consumers, the cost of searching for commodities is uniform. Stigler equates searching with visiting stores—and whether the customers wants cars or washing machines, the cost of a visit is uniform. His assumption drastically limits the amount of commodity acquisition to which a theory is addressed. Let us note that implicit-but-unnecessary assertoric limitation and move on:

> On an automobile, 1 percent is now perhaps $75 or $100; on a washing machine, 1 percent is perhaps $4 or $6. So any person, the theory predicts, will search more for low prices when buying an automobile than when buying a washing machine. A person who enjoys shopping may visit ten automobile dealers and three appliance stores; one who does not enjoy shopping may visit three automobile dealers and one appliance store—but in each case the consumer will search longer before buying the automobile. This is a testable implication, and if the facts contradict the prediction, the theory underlying the proposition is wrong.[17]

Although this is still off the path of my basic purpose, one can complain of a certain nonsequitur here. Stigler's theory initially predicted when a given consumer would visit a store. Now he thinks that the theory predicts that more visits occur for cars than for washing machines, because—given a stipulated percentage price variation—the car differential can finance more visits than the washing machine differential. Stigler also has ignored an equilibrating relation between searches and prices. If indeed car prices are very close together, searching for cars is deterred, compared to searching for washing machines. Therefore, it is highly possible that washing machines generate more shopping than cars.[18]

The prediction that Stigler makes is "that the range of prices of washing machines quoted in a city's retail outlets will vary more (relative to their average) than the prices of automobiles."[19] And, sure enough, Stigler has data that show car prices varied 1.72 percent in 1959, while washing machines varied 3.42 percent in 1955.

Stigler scolds us for suspecting that, though billed as a prediction, the whole exercise was cooked from the beginning and must be demoted to mere explanation—that is, Stigler, had two facts before him, and the theory is offered to unify the facts. Stigler denies this:

> It may be said that the facts were already known and all the economist has done is make out a fancy explanation for them . . . This objection is not factually correct: the theory was contrived first and the facts then sought. But it is not necessary for the reader (economist or noneconomist) to decide whether I am telling the truth. The real reply is that there are infinitely many sets of data that can be used to test the predictions. The reader can go out in his city and collect prices of automobiles and washing machines or (since this general theory applies to all homogeneous goods) prices of houses and paring knives.[20]

We can accept this point—explanation and prediction certainly entwine themselves and are merely different temporal relations between fact and theory. Whether theory came first and fact later, or vice versa, theory constitutes the unity of disparate facts. It is the nature of this unity that concerns us here. The unity can be described as follows—the facts are inconsistent with the premises of a perfect market. They must therefore be "tamed" by reference to a perfect market, to show that the theoretic core stays intact. Viewed this way, perfect markets can be analogized to a center that exerts a gravitational pull. The stray facts that Stigler has presented have spun off the gravitational center of the perfect market. Stigler then struggles to find the imperfections that connect the facts to the theoretic core.

Now if, as I maintain, this theoretic core can be shown to be a metaphysical impossibility—that the center flies apart of its own accord—does this destroy the cultural power of price theory? Undoubtedly not. All economists know that a perfect market has no empirical validity whatsoever, and if it has no metaphysical coherence either, such a blow cannot deliver more damage upon price theory than its well-acknowledged empirical failures already have. In either case, economists defend the facial implausibility of the theory with its predictive success:

> When we assume that consumers, acting with mathematical consistency, maximize utility, therefore, it is not proper for someone to complain that men [sic] are much more complicated and diverse

than that. So they are, but if this assumption yields a theory of behavior which agrees tolerably well with the facts, it should be used until a better theory comes along.[21]

Thus, Stigler sounds open and tolerant of other theoretic cores and invites competitors to present theories that better unify the facts. We can be skeptical of this tolerance, however, because microeconomics presents an infinite opportunity to defend the theory from the facts, merely by finding some disturbing cause to which is attributed the theory's failure. This opportunity for fudging is betrayed in the following qualification:

> If the right element in the diverse situations has been isolated, the theory will work: it will yield predictions better than those which can be reached with any alternative theory.[22]

The infinite opportunity to protect the theory from the facts occurs in the phrases "right element" and "isolated." Thus, when theories fail to predict the fact, a microeconomist can save the theory by finding the disturbing cause that re-establishes the unity between fact and theory.[23]

If predictive power, as supplemented by the infinite fudging in case of predictive failure, can protect the theory from empirical attack, likewise we can expect that metaphysical incoherence will not interrupt the practice of microeconomics. This is because microeconomics is fundamentally poetics, not science—bricolage rather than engineering.

The poetics that price theory pursues is the fusion between libertarian individualism and utilitarian altruism. In price theory, selfish persons, by pursuing their own ends, are shown to serve the public good. This portrait rationalizes private, seemingly destructive behavior with the production of happiness in the world. A kind of *geist*—an invisible hand or the cunning of reason—is shown to transcend individual calculation in favor of the community. Yet this *geist* can only do its work in the other-worldly perfect market. Indeed, "perfection" is nothing but the conditions under which public and private good can be reconciled.[24]

It is precisely this myth of perfection that I intend to disrupt, if I can, in the next section of this paper. The source of this disruptive principle is seemingly innocent. It is the requirement that the marginal cost of production include compensation for opportunities foregone by investing in marginal production in the market at hand. This opportunity cost must be a positive amount in order to justify a market exchange at the competitive price. And yet this opportunity cost depends upon the existence of economic rents in some other market. If that other market—and all other markets—were governed by the competitive price, market exchanges could not originate themselves— not without some oligoplistic intervention.

Stigler writes, "the cost of any productive service in producing *A* is the maximum amount it could produce elsewhere." [25] It is the myth of this "elsewhere" to which I now turn.

MARGINAL COST

The normative goal of market economics is to equate supply and demand. When supply is constricted below demand, prices (in a free market) are supposed to rise. The naive account is that such a rise in prices creates a deadweight loss to society. A more sophisticated account views a rise in prices as only contingently bad and hence contingently good. According to this account, society loses from rising prices only if (a) the consumer who is priced out of the constricted commodity chooses to spend instead on another commodity that was subject to less market dysfunction than the original commodity was, or (b) the consumer who will pay the higher price is forced to withdraw funds from a market that is less competitive than that of the original commodity. If, for example, Commodity *A* was price competitively at $10 but has now gone to $12 because of restricted supply, society actually benefits from the oligopolistic behavior if those consumers who are priced out of the market are driven to choose a product which has $2 or more of price-marginal-cost differential. This follows because society will now more efficiently allocate resources between Commodity *A* and Commodity *B*.[26] Similarly, suppose the consumer decides to stay in the market for Commodity *A*. The consumer therefore withdraws $2 from a market in which there exists more than $2 of differential between price and marginal cost. Society then benefits because it once again better allocates resources between Commodity *A* and Commodity *B*. Or, to say the same thing in different words, a rise in prices has no normative consequence, standing alone. Only if those prices disrupt optimal distribution of commodities does price change become significant.[27]

To avoid the empirical burdens of second-best distortions, it is absolutely necessary for the armchair economist to assume that all other markets are always competitive. Similarly, they assume that all productive inputs in the production curve they are studying can be obtained for the competitive price. These assumptions assure that competitive pricing in *their* model appear to be efficient. The existence of economic rents anywhere else in the economy means that competitive pricing in any given market is only contingently efficient.[28]

The universal banishment of economic rents means that all prices must equate with the marginal cost of production. In order for competitive pricing to be achieved, microeconomists have a very specialized notion of marginal cost.

Formally, marginal cost is the difference between total cost at n units of production and total costs at n + 1 units of production.[29] This formula tells us nothing about what a cost is. The allocation of costs to production is essentially an *a priori* proposition—one that depends on political, controversial, and historically contingent material. For example, if an excise tax applies, that tax must be part of the marginal cost of production, because that tax shows up in

$$TC^{(n+1)} - TC^n = MC$$

Another cost that is less intuitively included in the above formula is the cost of opportunities foregone elsewhere. For example, suppose we redefined MC to exclude opportunity costs, so that the cost of materials, piecemeal labor and excise taxes were the only difference between $TC^{(n+1)} - TC^n$. This definition of marginal cost would be inadequate for the proposition that supply (marginal cost) ought to equal demand, though it would be adequate to describe exchange in general, if we do not wish to account for production (as in Arrow's Theorem).[30]

A crude numerical example becomes necessary. Suppose that a producer projects that if she produces 100 widgets, TC = $900, but if she produces 101 widgets, TC = $909, because she calculates that the raw materials (seemingly her only expense in producing the marginal widget) will cost $9. Furthermore, the marginal cost of each widget is $9, so that the producer has a perfectly elastic supply curve. Marginal cost of $9 inadequately equates supply with demand. If the price demanded is $9, the manufacturer receives zero compensation for producing the 101st item. A profit maximizing the manufacturer expects a return on the investment of $9. Not getting it, the manufacturer prefers to deposit $9 in her next best opportunity—manufacturing doodads at $9.45. It so happens that doodads also require $9 worth of materials (or we have mathematically equated x units of widgets with y units of doodads to produce that result). Also, we assume there are no entry costs into doodads and no exit costs from widgets. In order to induce production of the 101st item, the price of widgets must rise to $9.45, because, at anything less, the manufacturer does better making doodads than she does making widgets.

If all manufacturers face identical cost of raw materials and the identical alternative investment opportunity, no manufacturer will produce the widget that our principal manufacturer has declined to produce, until such time as the price rises to $9.45. Furthermore, if the cost of the raw materials is a flat $9 at all levels of production, not only will the producers fail to replace the widget foregone. No manufacturer will produce a widget at all. In this exercise, time is suppressed. Widgets are produced, sold, and consumed instantaneously—in no time at all. Hence, if the marginal widget cannot be produced, neither can any widget exist.[31]

Supply cannot equal demand at $9. In order for manufacturers with equal raw material costs and equal alternative opportunities to produce the extra widget (or *any* widget, if the $9 cost is constant at all levels of widget manufacture), the market must reimburse the manufacturers for the opportunity foregone. Stated otherwise, in order for supply to equal demand, supply (marginal cost) must be defined to include the opportunity foregone as a *cost*. Therefore, the competitive price of widgets, the price that describes when the manufacturer produces the 101st widget, must reimburse the widgeteer for the 45 cents foregone because the widgeteer gave up the opportunity to manufacture doodads.

There is nothing natural or inherent behind the inclusion of opportunity cost as one of the marginal costs of production.[32] Opportunity cost is thrown in simply because supply-and-demand curves will not operate to predict the termination of production without this concession. And yet opportunity cost is the downfall of a coherent marginal theory of price. As we shall see a little later, it contains the contradiction that must be suppressed for modern price theory to sustain itself.

This too must be said about opportunity costs. They are the only real cost that exists, in price theory. Recall that the perfect market banishes time. Production, exchange and consumption all occur simultaneously. Hence, buyers are always in the habit of financing production. It is as if buyers of widgets brought the necessary $9 in inputs with them to production. What the producers offer is not ownership of inputs, because any propertyless producer can look to the buyers to supply the inputs—instantaneously. What the producers do is to control the process of production, such that they have the right to recover their opportunity costs. Hence, in our example, the $9 may drop from our discussion. We need speak only of the 45 cents the producer requires to supply widgets rather than doodads.

Now it should be apparent that this universal opportunity cost resembles a gigantic oligopoly in opportunities. Monopoly theorists are well familiar with the critique of ordinary oligopolies. Because an oligopoly represents a shared economic rent, oligopolists have an incentive to cheat on each other by increasing production and sneaking it to the market at a lower price. By doing so, a cheating oligopolist may gain a larger share of the economic rent for herself than the oligopoly provided. But if the oligopolist is discovered, competition breaks out. The price quickly (instantaneously, in a perfect market) reverts to the competitive level. But it does not go below the competitive level, because otherwise *all* production in that market will cease altogether.

There is another way to view the oligopoly. Suppose, instead of enforcing the oligopoly by monitoring whether members were sneaking goods to the market to grab a larger share of economic rents, the oligopoly simply enters into an agreement with every other producer in the world to raise *their* prices so that every producer earned economic rents. When this universal oligopoly becomes perfect, then what was once economic rents become transformed into opportunity costs.

A universal oligopoly of opportunities changes economic rents into marginal costs. It changes oligopoly into competitive pricing. But this is still not enough to prevent a market crash if any producer has any surplus wealth. If there is any surplus wealth anywhere, the producer who owns it has the incentive to plow it into production. This in turn has the effect of increasing production and upsetting the equilibrium. If the equilibrium is upset in one market, the opportunity costs in that market have been lowered. Simultaneously, *all* opportunity costs have been transformed back into economic rents. Competitive pricing now demands an across-the-board price cut. In our widget market, the opportunity cost of 45 cents has lowered for widgets, doodads and everything else in the world.

Hence, it is yet another feature of the perfect market that there must be no savings and no investment. Rather, every penny of the opportunity costs earned in production must be spent in consumption.

What ought to be apparent now is that a disequilibrium between consumption and production brings the universal opportunity cost down. Meanwhile, prices can never go up. Recall that in the perfect market, buyers finance production and, as we have just seen, there can be no accumulated wealth. Because of instantaneous financing with no debt service charge—time does not exist in perfect markets—the cost of all inputs could be deleted from the formula. All that matters is the bare opportunity cost. This cannot go up, unless economic rents exist somewhere to draw producers out of the market at hand and into the market with rents. But competitive pricing eliminates the possibility of economic rents, so that the possibility of an increase in opportunity costs is also eliminated.

On the other hand, it must be admitted that if an eternal equilibrium is asserted, with opportunity costs already in place, perfect markets will never dissolve.[33] So conceived, perfect markets are a dead thing, nothing we wish to emulate. Instantaneous movement is no movement. For real human beings to approach the perfect market is to approach death itself.

ORIGINS

In the above discussion, it is conceded that if a perfect market maintains itself, but only at the expense of its historicity. Things happen instantaneously in perfect markets—in no time at all. Perfect markets are a Uchronia. These criticisms make clear that a perfect market is metaphysically impossible.

It is also possible to show that such a market must have its origin in market imperfections and hence is dependent upon them for its existence. If so, then it can be said that a perfect market is dependent for its existence on market imperfections.

Let us revert back to the beginning of organized society, before a single contract exchange took place. Let us impose on this society the norm of competitive pricing. Under what conditions can there be a trade between two persons for different commodities?

In this society, suppose Fred is tall and can gather apples, while Barney is short and can grub for roots better than Fred. It will still pay for a trade to occur because Fred's labor is embodied in surplus apples (and Barney's labor is embodied in surplus roots). Each must charge the other the marginal cost of production, as governed by the next best opportunity to another market. But now, the only alternative production to roots or applies is leisure.[34] How much is leisure worth? Each side is able to say subjectively whether each would rather have the other's surplus instead of leisure. If this leisure has a positive value, it constitutes the opportunity cost of providing labor.[35] As a result, it is possible to have production consistent with pricing at marginal cost.

This account of the first contract exchange substitutes purely subjective preference for objectively determined opportunity costs. Up to now, opportunities were defined by markets. No one was allowed to say, "I choose to charge more because I don't care to invest time or resources in anything else. I'd prefer to be unemployed." If anyone were allowed to say this, marginal cost would be purely subjective. That is, *any* price, no matter how high, would always be the competitive price because a producer could always define for herself what marginal costs are by claiming she'd prefer leisure over gauging the public with high prices.

For example, suppose IBM were a monopolist and, in violation of our competitive pricing policy, simply declared that it would charge a monopoly price. When challenged by the government, IBM then responded, "We will hold our productive resources idle unless we are given freedom to charge what we want. We prefer leisure as the next best opportunity to charging the monopoly profit." If IBM were allowed to boycott the market because leisure were its next best opportunity to charging a monopoly price, then *all* economic rents could be reformulated into marginal cost, and the microeconomic critique of monopoly power would break down.

For this reason, opportunity cost must be a purely objective standard. That is, a person's time and labor is valued by *others*, not by the producer/owner of the labor. Neither Fred nor Barney can be allowed to *declare* the subjective value of his labor or other inputs. This is not to say that Barney cannot have leisure, or that Fred must work twenty-four hours a day. Similarly, a consumer good that *could* be productive need not mandatorily be moved into production. Competitive pricing only requires that *if* an asset *is* moved into the productive sector, it must be priced at its marginal cost of production as valued objectively by others. This must be so in order to maintain the critical bite that supply-and-demand curves do have. Otherwise, price theory surrenders the consumption-production distinction, a distinction every bit as important to price theory as is a positive opportunity cost.

If the perfect market has an origin, then it is in subjective choice not governed by anything so objective as prices in other markets. Yet this origin in pure subjectivity belies what perfect markets represent themselves to be—an objective ideal against which historical markets might be compared.

TIME

Time and presence have a double relation. In the present, time is banished, and but time also moves. At one moment, presence suppresses past and future and in this sense does not move. A concept is a philosophy of presence in the sense that it denies all movement. Yet, in the present, as we observe things in motion, we experience movement as presence, to which the other sort of presence is inadequate.

Price theory replicates this double relation with time. Several references have already been made to this phenomenon. In price theory things happen *instantaneously*. Goods are instantly produced, distributed and consumed. For example, sales do not occur sequentially. If they did, one moment's sale would not affect all the prices of a commodity. Instead, it is stipulated that, in the absence, of price discrimination, all prices for the commodity are the same. This is because all sales occur instantaneously and simultaneously. Things that happen instantaneously happen in *no time at all*.

Alternatively, time is frozen in the form of a *rate* of production. In equilibrium, the rate of production stays constant; there is "no tendency to change until supply or demand conditions change."[36] Although a rate is supposed to subsume a time, it effectively banishes it by sublating it into a fixed quantity.

Time is the enemy of a perfect market. If time is introduced into the model, then goods can never be priced at the competitive level. The ability of one producer to rush a commodity to market before any other constitutes a moment of monopoly price. If a producer is the only one in the market for even a moment, then buyers are led to compare a higher price now versus the lower price when the market imperfection is cured. Time becomes a negative commodity in competition with the commodity that is present in the marketplace. Consumers may pay to avoid losing it or may choose to wait and take the lower price later.[37]

Although time is the enemy of the perfect market, it is also its friend, in the sense that time can provide an originary economic rent and hence a positive opportunity cost. In other words, in the negative market for time, in which buyers will pay producers to save time, producers can earn a positive economic rent. Therefore, in such a market, the producer becomes originally justified in a timeless perfect market to charge a positive price. But the contradiction is that the "other market"—the market for commodities at a future time—is in history while the classic perfect market is not. A theorist who wishes to save the timeless perfect market by reference to time must assert that this market for time is not an instantaneous one, but the perfect market to be saved—by definition timeless—is outside of that dynamic universe of time.

Thus, opportunity cost enjoys an identity with time, and time enjoys an identity with the disrupting trace. Both must be suppressed in a successful philosophy of presence. On this reading of price theory, *history* is the opportunity by reference to which price theory—an ahistoric philosophy of presence—can save itself.

CONSEQUENCES

This paper has shown that a policy of competitive pricing can be consistently applied for all commodities only in a timeless universe that denies its own origin in pure subjectivity. As a result, price theory does not present a "deep normative structure" of how the world should be run. Microeconomic price theory has failed on a theoretic level to show that market exchange is or could be an unambiguous utilitarian good. The utilitarian poetics of reconciling private selfishness and public good have failed. The two cannot be perfectly reconciled in a historic market transaction.

This is not to say that we should abandon market activity. It is simply to say that market activity can be defended only according to a different poetics—a poetics that conceives of itself as *bricolage* and not *engineering*. I, for one, rather like the bustle of market activity, but I am not prepared to say that each and every market exchange is a good thing. Nor am I able to explain exactly why it is that markets have done so well for the American standard of living. This is merely my intuition—an intuition that is, of course, the product of the same market economy I seek to defend. It is far less clear that Dante or the Ayatollah Komeini would have the same assessment of American economic history and its influence on culture. Whatever merits the American market system has, those merits are historically situated and not logically compelled.

NOTES

1. J. Derrida, Disseminations 5 (B. Johnson trans. 1981).
2. J. Derrida, Writing and Difference 255 (A. Bass trans. 1978).
3. Id. at 251–77.
4. J. Derrida, Margins of Philosophy 209 n. 2 (A. Bass trans. 1982).
5. J. Derrida, The Postcard 388–89 (A. Bass trans. 1979).
6. Margins of Philosophy, supra note 4, at 3.
7. Id. at 3–4.
8. Id. at 8 n. 8 (translator's note).
9. G. Stigler, The Theory of Price (4th ed. 1987).

10. The following comments by Derrida describe precisely the status the perfect market enjoys in microeconomics:

> Thus it has always been thought that the center, which is by definition unique, constituted that very thing within a structure which while governing the structure, escapes structurality. This is why classical thought concerning structure could say that the center is, paradoxically, *within* the structure and *outside it*. The center is at the center of the totality, and yet, since the center does not belong to the totality (is not part of the totality), the totality *has its center elsewhere*. The concept of centered structure . . . is contradictorily coherent.

Writing and Difference, supra note 2, at 279.

11. Id. at 267 ("*This*—major—writing will be called *writing* because it *exceeds* the *logos* . . .).

12. Stigler also learned early to hedge his bets and admit that the perfect market might not be completely knowable:

> The minimum assumptions for a theoretical model [of the perfect market] can be stated with precision only when the complete theory of that model is known. The complete theory of competition cannot be known because it is an open-ended theory; it is always possible that a new range of problems will be posed in this framework, and then, no matter how well developed the theory was with respect to the earlier range of problems, it may require extensive elaboration ins respects which previously it glossed over or ignored.

Stigler, Perfect Composition, Historically Contemplated, in Microeconomics: Selected Readings 183 (E. Mansfield ed. 1971). Yet, in practice, Stigler proceeds *as if* the theory were closed and complete.

13. Stigler, supra note 9, at 2.

14. See id. at 241 ("A popular strategy, at least with economists, is to continue to search until the expected gain from another search is less than its cost"). Although Stigler does not say so, "price" here would have to be defined as the cost of the item to be purchased plus the cost of going to and from the store. On this definition, the customer will *not* choose the item with the lowest price by a retailer.

15. Stigler, supra note 9, at 2.

16. Id.

17. Id.

18. Notice another limiting assumption. The aesthetic pleasure of shopping for cars and appliances is precisely identical, so that unit of search between the two commodities can be directly compared. If this is wrong, the proposition is *not* testable. But again, let's pass by this further limiting assumption and pretend that Stigler's theory is indeed testable in the real world.

19. Id.

20. Stigler, supra note 9, at 5 (footnote omitted).

21. Id.

22. Id.

23. This is the theme of M. Blaug, The Methodology of Microeconomics (1980).

24. Stigler, supra note 9, at 83.

25. Id. at 112.

26. This misallocation has been called "Pareto Resource Misallocation." See Markovits, The Causes and Policy Significance of Pareto Resource Misallocation: A Checklist for Micro-Economic Policy Analysis, 28 Stan. L. Rev. 1 (1975); Markovits, A Basic Structure for Microeconomic Policy Analysis in our Worse-Than-Second-Best World: A Proposal and Related Critique of the Chicago Approach to the Study of Law and Economics, 1975 Wis. L. Rev. 950.

27. Harberger, Monopoly and Resource Allocation, in Microeconomics: Selected Readings 206 (E. Mansfield ed. 1971).

28. This message has been well understood since at least 1956. See Lipsey & Lancaster, The General Theory of the Second Best, R. E. Stud. Dec. 1956.

29. See Stigler, supra note 9, at 183 ("Marginal cost is defined as the increment in total cost divided by the increment in output with which it is associated").

30. See C. Dyke, Philosophy of Economics 110–13 (1981).

31. This is so when the marginal cost curve is perfectly elastic. If the curve is upward sloping (as when economy of scale is exceeded) production would occur at $9, though it would be instantaneously produced, sold and consumed. Furthermore, an upward sloping supply curve implies that a flat price reserves economic rent for the producer. For this reason, the flat pricing of a commodity is itself not competitive, when the supply curve is not equally flat. In case of rising marginal cost curves, efficiency demands that there be perfect price discrimination against suppliers. That is, efficiency demands price controls on each unit on the rising supply curve, so that all economic rents are eliminated. We must assume that each input is paid the Marginal Physical Product with respect to that input (Euler's Theorem), or

$$\sum_{i=1}^{\infty} = a_i \frac{\delta Q}{\delta a_i}$$

This assumption guarantees, essentially, that in this situation,

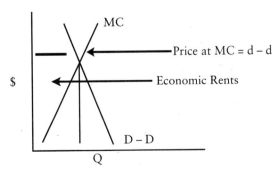

these economic rents cannot be charged to the producer by her suppliers. See A. Chiang, Fundamental Methods of Mathematical Economics, at 407 (1974) ("Economically, this property means that under conditions of constant returns to scale, if each input factor is paid the amount of its marginal product, the total product will be exactly exhausted by the distributive shares for all the input factors, or, equivalently, the pure economic profit will be zero"); Stigler, supra note 9, at 157 ("if each productive factor is paid at the rate of its marginal productivity, the payments to the factors will exactly equal total product").

32. There may be *moral* arguments for reimbursement of opportunity cost. For example, the scholastics justified interest on loans on the basis of *lucrum cessans*—a gain foregone by the lender on an alternative investment. M. Blaug, Economic Theory in Retrospect 30 (4th ed. 1985). But there is nothing natural or required of such conclusions.

33. This is Stigler's assumption. See Stigler, Perfect Competition, supra note 12, at 182 (perfection competition denotes "that a resource will obtain equal returns in all possible uses").

34. "Leisure is the economist's name for nonmarket work, and historically it has been applied to both arduous labor and utter indolence within the household." Stigler, supra note 9, at 102.

35. Id. at 100.

36. Id. at 178.

37. See id. at 103 ("the cost of a good is its price *plus* the value of the time spent in the queue").

9

Hermeneutics and the Rule of Law
Fred Dallmayr

That society has a rule-governed character is a standard sociological axiom: in fact, every continuous human enterprise or activity—whether individual or collective—is assumed to be rule-governed in some sense. Without this feature of rule-governance, the assumption goes, individual and social behavior is bound to lapse into randomness and radical contingency. While plausible on a high level of generality, the assumption is beset with major difficulties—which have been recognized increasingly in recent decades. Ever since Wittgenstein's observations on "rule-following," it has been acknowledged that the application of rules cannot in turn be strictly rule-governed—without conjuring up an infinite regress of stipulated rules (for their own application). More importantly, the range of rule-governance itself has been contested in philosophical and social-theoretical literature, especially through the introduction of a sharp contrast or dichotomy between regular and irregular or between normal and abnormal practices and contexts. While the application of rules in normal settings is manageable though complicated, rule-governance entirely breaks down in irregular conditions or in the hiatus between rule-governed discourses or "paradigms." Thus, to mention only one example, Richard Rorty in *Philosophy and the Mirror of Nature* distinguishes sharply between "normal" and "abnormal" discourses—a distinction which in his presentation coincides with the opposition between epistemology and hermeneutics or between "commensuration" and "conversation." While normal discourse, in his view, is conducted "within an agreed-upon set of conventions about what counts as relevant contribution," the abnormal variant is practiced by someone "who is ignorant of these conventions or who sets them aside."[1]

The problems surrounding rule-governance are not restricted to a narrowly academic level. Directly or indirectly they affect one of the most time-honored and revered ingredients of Western culture—traceable at least as far back as Plato's *Laws*:[2] the doctrine of the "rule of law." According to a powerful tradition of Western political thought, good government or the ideal regime is defined by rule-governance, namely, as a "government of laws and not of men." This doctrine, in turn, is not simply an accidental political bias but rather linked with central premises and hierarchical postulates endemic to Western civilization: particularly the rule of reason over arbitrary will, of universal principle over particular circumstances, and ultimately of idea over matter. Given this cultural-historical background, questions concerning the status of rule-governance are bound to have a deeply unsettling effect by touching the fiber of political and intellectual life; hence the unease and suspicion engendered by contemporary trends fomenting such questions—especially trends associated with "hermeneutics" and "deconstruction." In Rorty's distinction (noted above), hermeneutics stands as the antithesis to "systematic" and epistemic knowledge—although elsewhere he has differentiated more carefully between a normal or ordinary hermeneutics and a more radical or "extraordinary" type (bent on dislodging familiar rules or conventions). The latter nuance is basically discarded by Stanley Rosen in his recent study entitled *Hermeneutics as Politics*. Taking the side of epistemic knowledge and rational rule governance, Rosen views hermeneutics (in its predominant strands) as an invitation to arbitrariness and thus as a pacemaker to intellectual and political disorder.[3] In the following, I intend to explore not so much the relation between hermeneutics and politics in general but the impact of the former on that dimension of political life traditionally thematized as the rule of law. In a first step, I want to retrieve and recount the chief facets of this dimension as it has been articulated in the history of Western political thought. In a second step, I turn to the recent ascendancy of hermeneutics, with a main focus on legal hermeneutics or the intimate connection between interpretation and jurisprudence. By way of conclusion, I review the effect of hermeneutics on rule-governance, with an eye toward finding a path between normalcy and abnormality or between convention and invention.

I

Given its prominence in Western culture, the rule of law has occasioned a considerable amount of literature and commentary; for present purposes I can only highlight some main facets of its historical trajectory. One point which needs to be noted in this account is the unstable meaning of the phrase; like the notion of "reason," rule and law are themselves the targets of continuous interpretation and reinterpretation. Thus, in classical Greek thought, legal rule-governance was ultimately tied to a higher rule governing the cosmos in which human reason was meant to participate—which is a far cry from the modern conception of law as an outgrowth of human rationality or an innate natural faculty of reason. In Plato's political philosophy, public lawfulness was linked either with the philosopher's special insight or else settled institutional arrangements; but rule or law was never merely an abstract norm but a complex web of relationships attentive to concrete situations and diverse modes of proper conduct (or natural "right"). With some modifications this view was shared by Aristotle whose notion of good government, as differentiated from "bad" regimes, was predicated on the prevalence of justice seen as an equitable and nonrepressive way of life transgressing selfishness. In the Roman republic, lawfulness largely approximated this concrete form of equity; with the expansion of the Roman empire, however, law in the sense of rational rule-governance was increasingly elevated above loyal contingency and broadened into a universal maxim. In Stoic thought, human law was designed to reflect ultimately the universal *logos* or "flame" of reason, a flame whose sparks were assumed to be more or less equally distributed among all human beings.[4] The conception of a universal principle, and its juxtaposition to local contingency, were continued in the medieval distinction—familiar from Thomas Aquinas but more widely accepted—between universal "natural law" and local "human law," a distinction which in turn was premised on the difference between reason and will and between universalism and particularism.

The theme of law, however, exceeds philosophical speculation. In medieval Europe, rule-governance was most prominently anchored and institutionally secured in the *Magna Carta* of 1215, particularly in the section stating that no one (or no "freeman") could be deprived of property except in accordance with the established "law of the land."[5] During subsequent centuries the clause developed into a bulwark against absolutism and into the pacesetter of a steadily expanding and solidified rule of law. Under the Stuarts and during the Civil War period, the rule was championed by lawyers and parliamentarians against both royal and military claims to absolute power; speaking for a rising middle class anxious for peace and prosperity, James Harrington in his 1656 work *The Commonwealth of Oceana* defined good government (and particularly British government) as an "empire of laws and not of men."[6] While still contested in Harrington's time, lawfulness or rule-governance was the motto of the post-revolutionary settlement and generally emerged as the mainstay of modern liberalism or liberal regimes. According to John Locke, lawfulness was characteristic both of man's pre-civil condition in the "state of nature" and of organized civil society—with lawfulness being a synonym here for the dictates of natural or unaided human reason. In terms of his *Second Treatise*: "The state of nature has a law of nature to govern it which obliges everyone; and reason which is this law teaches all mankind (who will but consult it) that, being all equal and independent, no one ought harm another in his life, health, liberty or possessions." Lawfulness and rule-governance were not set aside but rather supplemented and reinforced in civil society, namely, through the enactment of positive laws backed up by legal magistrates. Holding that the "great end of men's entering society" was in the enjoyment of life and property, Locke argued that the central instrument or means for reaching this goal was "the laws established in that society." Accordingly, he proclaimed it as the central task and as "the first and fundamental positive law" of all commonwealths to institute or establish a legislature or "legislative power"—an institution which was to be not only "the supreme power of the commonwealth" but "sacred and unalterable in the hands where the community have once placed it."[7]

Although insisting on the supremacy of lawmaking over all types of royal or executive prerogative, Locke was by no means ready to condone an unlimited or arbitrary prerogative. In the *Second Treatise*—which basically stipulated the parameters of liberal-parliamentary government—civil legislation was hedged in by several safeguards or restrictions. First, although installed as supreme authority in the commonwealth, the legislature's power "is not nor can possibly be absolutely arbitrary over the lives and fortunes of the people"—the chief reason being that the rules of the state of nature prescribing equal liberty do not cease to exist in civil society but are only corroborated by positive enactments; hence, "the law of nature stands as an eternal rule to all men, legislators as well as others." The second safeguard derived from the obligation of the legislature to enact only general or universally applicable laws and not rules tailored to particular circumstances or contingencies. Being the representative or mouthpiece of the collective good or of the combined interests of all members of society, the legislature—Locke argued—"cannot assume to itself a power to rule by extemporary, arbitrary decrees, but is bound to dispense justice and decide the rights of the subject by promulgated standing laws and known authorized judges." The prohibition of arbitrariness and legal particularism was the central pillar of good governments as articulated in the *Second Treatise*: "Absolute arbitrary power, or governing without settled standing laws, can neither of them consist with the ends of society and government." Summarizing his thoughts on lawmaking and lawfulness, Locke arrived at an eloquent formulation of the rule of law—a formulation echoing through the subsequent history of the doctrine. Legislators, he wrote, "are to govern by promulgated established laws, not to be varied in particular cases, but to have one rule for rich and poor, for the favorite at court and the countryman at plow." The laws enacted by the legislature were designed ultimately for no other end but the common "good of the people." [8]

The circumscribed or rule-governed character of legislative authority was enhanced in the eighteenth century through the doctrine of the division and tensional "balance" of governmental powers—a doctrine commonly attributed to Montesquieu's *Spirit of the Laws*[9] (although rudiments of the idea antedated this work). In the French context, lawfulness or rule-governance was a main pillar of Enlightenment thought, a legacy which was fully preserved by Rousseau (despite his presumed proclivity for revolutionary turbulence). Like Locke, it is true, Rousseau was no advocate of a separation or balanced division of powers, but accorded supremacy to the lawmaking or legislative authority. Moreover, in the figure of the "Legislator" he made room for an extraordinary or extra-normal dimension or creative political invention transgressing settled conventions. Nevertheless, once a commonwealth or republic was inaugurated, Rousseau insisted firmly on the need for lawfulness and the prevalence of general and established laws representing the collective interest of all citizens or the "general will." As he wrote in *The Social Contract*, the general will "cannot relate to any particular object" or circumstance but only the body politic at large or the people as a whole. When the people in its entirety or viewed as a collective body "makes rules for the people as a whole," it is "dealing only with itself" and not with an isolated part or fragment. Accordingly, he noted, the matter concerning which a rule is made "is as general as the will which makes it. And this is the kind of act which I call a law." Underscoring the distinction between universalism and particularism or between rational rule-governance and arbitrariness Rousseau added: "When I say that the province of the law is always general, I mean that the law considers all subjects collectively and all actions in the abstract, it does not consider any individual man or specific action." Continuing this train of thought, *The Social Contract* went so far as to equate state or *polis* with lawfulness or the rule of law: "Any state which is ruled by law I call a 'republic,' whatever the form of the constitution; for then, and then alone, does the public interest govern and then alone is the 'public thing' or *res publica* a reality." [10]

In large measure, French Enlightenment thought and British parliamentary liberalism set the pattern for American republicanism and constitutional government. Even prior to the establishment of the national government, various colonial or state charters reflected the combined impact of this legacy. Particularly noteworthy in this regard is the constitution of Massachusetts of 1780. In addition to containing a lengthy list of individual rights or liberties, the document provided for the separation of the powers of government into legislative, executive, and judicial branches—and this for a clearly stated purpose, namely, "to the end it may be a government of laws and not of men." [11] The federal constitution inaugurated in 1787 reflected a similar inspiration. Suspicious of any arbitrary power, including the absolute supremacy of the legislature, the founders adopted the principle of separated powers, though hedged in by complicated checks and balances. Moreover, going beyond Locke's vague safeguards, they proclaimed the Constitution itself as the supreme law of the land, a law even binding on Congress. As Alexander Hamilton stated in *The Federalist*: "No legislative act, . . . contrary to the Constitution, can be valid. To deny this, would be to affirm, that the deputy is greater than his principal; that the servant is above his master." By subordinating legislative acts to the Constitution as the supreme law of the land, Hamilton also shifted the accent from congressional supremacy to that branch of government specifically entrusted with the maintenance and interpretation of the supreme law: the judicial branch. "If it be said," he added, "that the legislative body are themselves the constitutional judges of their own powers, and that the construction they put upon them is conclusive upon the other departments, it may be answered, that this cannot be the natural presumption." It was more reasonable or rational in Hamilton's view to suppose "that the courts were designed to be an intermediate body between the people and the legislature, in order, among other things, to keep the latter within the limits assigned to their authority. The interpretation of the laws is the proper and peculiar province of the courts." [12]

With the shift of accent to the courts, Hamilton's comments implicitly inaugurated or anticipated the principle of "judicial review," which was to become a mainstay of the rule of law in America. He continued: "A constitution is, in fact, and must be regarded by the judges, as a fundamental law. It therefore belongs to them to ascertain its meaning, as well as the meaning of any particular act proceeding from the legislative body." In normal circumstances the presumption was in favor of the congruence or concordance between foundation and specific enactment, between the general and the particular law. However, in case of an "irreconcilable variance" between the two— Hamilton insisted—"the Constitution ought to be preferred to the statute, the intention of the people to the intention of their agents." [13] Although foreshadowed in Hamilton's statements, judicial review of congressional enactments was not actually exercised or implemented until some fifteen years later in Justice John Marshall's famous 1803 ruling in *Marbury v. Madison*.[14] In this decision—renowned for its subtlety and shrewdness—Marshall clearly subordinated legislative acts of any kind to the higher law of the Constitution. "The question whether an act, repugnant to the Constitution, can become the law of the land," he argued, "is a question deeply interesting to the United States; but, happily, not of an intricacy proportioned to its interest." [15] To decide the question it was only necessary, in his view, to recollect and recognize certain "well established" principles, particularly the principle that the government of the United States was one of separate and limited powers, with a written constitution explicitly designed to safeguard these limitations. "Certainly," Marshall added, "all those who have framed written constitutions contemplate them as forming the fundamental and paramount law of the nation, and consequently the theory of every such government must be, that an act of the legislature, repugnant to the Constitution, is void." [16] More specifically, it was the duty of the judicial branch represented by the highest court to implement this theory and to invalidate unconstitutional acts. Invoking the language of Harrington and the Massachusetts charter, Marshall concluded that "[t]he government of the United States has been emphatically termed a government of laws, and not of men." [17]

As inaugurated by such classical formulations of the Enlightenment period, rule-governance developed into a central pillar of liberal and constitutional government during the nineteenth century. This development, however, was not entirely smooth or free of theoretical and political complications. By solidifying into a doctrine, rule-governance or the rule of law also underwent a subtle change: namely, in the direction of a steady formalization and legalization—although this trend was more pronounced in Continental Europe than in the Anglo-American context. In earlier formulations, law and lawfulness were still closely linked with notions of the common good and thereby with broader substantive concerns. Thus (as indicated), Locke saw legislative power circumscribed by demands of the collective good, while Hamilton viewed the written constitution as expression of the will of the people as a whole (as contrasted with congressional authority). Formalization during the nineteenth century was chiefly evident in the association of rule-governance with formal state structures, an association epitomized by the notion of the "law state" or "state of law," better known under the German and French labels of *Rechtsstaat* and *état de droit*. In the French setting, the idea of the *état de droit* was first articulated by such liberal thinkers as Guizot and Benjamin Constant and subsequently adopted and fleshed out by jurists during the Third Republic. In German thought, the concept of the *Rechtsstaat* was anticipated in Kant's stipulation that the function of the state be restricted to the realization of law or the "idea of law" (*Rechtsidee*)— as distinguished from welfare and police functions. This initiative was carried forward, with variations, by a string of liberal philosophers and jurists ranging from Friedrich Julius Stahl over Robert von Mohl to Rudolf Gneist. In his 1830 work *Philosophy of Right*, Stahl offered a purely formal definition of the rule of law as embodied in the "law state" (*Rechtsstaat*): namely, by distinguishing the latter rigorously both from the traditional "patrimonial" state—where law was the tool of monarchs or princes—and from popular-democratic conceptions of state and law as emanating ultimately from popular will.[18]

While undoubtedly entailing cognitive benefits, formalization from the beginning was beset with theoretical as well as political quandaries and aporias—which were bound to come to the fore with the passage of time. On the political level, the distinction between *Rechtsstaat* and popular-democratic government was evidently problematical, especially in an era of growing democratization (whether under nationalist or socialist auspices). In an unusually forthright manner, the conflict or tension has been pinpointed by Gottfried Dietze in his study *Two Concepts of the Rule of Law*. Dietze observed: "Democratism threatens constitutionalism, for democracy, like other forms of government, contains the germ of degeneration into a state of might, arbitrariness, and injustice."[19] As can readily be seen, the formulation pits rule-governance against popular rule, lawfulness against political power, and reason against (arbitrary) will—without sufficiently exploring how law can govern independently of politics and reason without an element of willing. Although generally favoring constitutionalism over "democratism," Dietze in the end argued in favor of a balance between the rule of law and public power centered in the state, or between the "law state" (*Rechtsstaat*) and "state law" (*Staatsrecht*). As he pointed out, the tensional balance was already implicit in the phrase "rule of law" itself, given that the accent in the phrase could be placed either on "rule" or on "law." To the extent that the latter term was accentuated, the political dimension of the phrase remained opaque or underdetermined. On the other hand, if the "ruling" character of law was highlighted, the dividing line from public power was blurred: "Since the rule of law is a rule of men, in so far as in the last analysis it is determined by men, it approaches the 'rule of men' quite closely."[20]

As propounded by Dietze, tensional balance had a precarious status—not only politically (the focus on state power), but also and more importantly for theoretical or philosophical reasons. As it happens, the rift between rule-governance and politics or between reason and willing has been intensified in our century to the point of antithesis and complete incommensurability. From the perspective of logical positivism, reason was stylized into a capacity of formal (logical or linguistic) analysis, a capacity applied in an extrinsic manner to empirical reality of the contingent data found in the world. Adapting this outlook to the field of jurisprudence, Hans Kelsen developed a completely formal or "pure" theory of law, a theory in which legal rules were linked in a strictly deductive nexus and basically independent from (or only extrinsically related to) social and political life. In Kelsen's view, legal normativity was self-grounded or self-grounding (by being anchored in a basic norm or *Grundnorm*), while normlessness was identified with the abyss of irrational contingency and abnormality. Embracing the opposite side of this theoretical antimony, Carl Schmitt extolled the political grounding of normative or legal systems, the fact that such systems are ultimately generated and maintained by a sovereign political power or will. Defining politics or "the political" as the demarcation between the normal and the un-normed, between the familiar and the alien (or between friend and foe), Schmitt identified sovereignty with the capacity to decide on the "state of exception," that is, on issues exceeding rule-governed normalcy. As formulated by these jurists and their respective disciples, the issue of rule-governance and politics defied rational settlement and basically ended in aporia. Nowhere was this aporia more keenly perceived than in Franz Neumann's celebrated study on *The Rule of Law*, subtitled *Political Theory and the Legal System in Modern Society*. In this study Neumann distinguished sharply between two conflicting poles of public life: namely, between politics and legality or, in his terms, between "state sovereignty" and the "rule of law." As he wrote: "Both sovereignty and the Rule of Law are constitutive elements of the modern state. Both however are irreconcilable with each other, for highest might and highest right cannot be at one and the same time realized in a common sphere." [21] Far from being mutually complementary, sovereignty and rule-governance were exclusive of each other, and "[w]herever an attempt at reconciliation is made we come up against insoluble contradictions." [22]

Going beyond the extrinsic relation between power and rule-governance, Neumann's study carried the conflict or aporia into the concept of law itself. As he pointed out, it was necessary to recognize a "dual notion of law," one in which law is refracted into a "political" and a "material" dimension. Under the political rubric was encompassed "every general norm and every individual command imputable to the state, whether just or unjust, convenient or inconvenient." [23] From the political vantage, every decision of the sovereign state organ had to be viewed as legal; accordingly, law "is only *voluntas* and not *ratio*" (a phrase reminiscent of the Hobbesian dictum that *"auctoritas non veritas facit legem"*). By contrast, law in its material dimension referred to "such norms of the state as are compatible with defined ethical postulates, whether such postulates be those of justice, liberty or equality, or anything else." [24] Seen from this angle, law or lawfulness was equivalent to rational normativity, since "the essence of norms is the reasonable principle (*logos*) which it embodies" [25] and which is "wholly transparent to the speculative intelligence." [26] What remained excluded from this principle and thus "opaque to reason" were only the "accidents" of its realization, and these were only an "inevitable imperfection" and by no means a constitutive feature of the rule of law. Ultimately, the gulf yawning between rational transparency and political power could not be bridged—as little as it was possible to reconcile normal rule-governance and sovereign intervention in the legal fabric: "Not every *voluntas* is therefore in correspondence with the demand of a certain *ratio*. Material law and absolute sovereignty are clearly mutually exclusive." [27]

II

Neumann's study has justly been acclaimed as one of the most perceptive accounts of the complexities surrounding the rule of law; yet, despite its subtlety, the book hardly pressed issues far enough. Even when pursued or transplanted into the conception of law itself, the initial aporia persisted: the "political" and "material" dimensions of law remained extrinsically related and thus ultimately incommensurable. Actually, however, the situation is still more complicated and entangled: at a closer look, rule-governance and politics, *ratio* and *voluntas* seem more intricately correlated or interlaced. This aspect can be perceived through a glance at the concrete operation or functioning of rule-governance. In the prevalent view (shared by Neumann), rule-governance or the "rule of law" means first of all that the law can be known independently of circumstances as a purely rational proposition, and furthermore that the rule is the same for all or applied in the same manner to all individuals (in a given jurisdiction) or at least to all individuals placed in the same circumstances. At this point, however, a hermeneutical problem—or rather a host of problems—arises. For, one may ask, how can the law or its content be fully known apart from any contextual concretization—given that the law can never exhaustively stipulate its range of application? Moreover, how can the "sameness" of the rule of the sameness of its application be grasped apart from interpretation—given that the individuals and concrete situations are never entirely identical or exchangeable? As we know already from Aristotle, sameness and difference in human conditions are not simply empirical facts or amenable to apodictive cognition, but rather depend on insightful judgment and comparison, that is, on some degree of artful imagination.

Questions or quandaries of this kind are not novel discoveries but endemic to the history of Western thought—from Greek and Roman jurisprudence down to the present time. In a particularly acute and provocative manner these questions were at the forefront of Nietzsche's iconoclastic inquiries. As he remarked on numerous occasions, "sameness" of circumstances is not simply an empirically ascertainable fact but depends on perspective and contextual framework; differently phrased: instead of being the work of nature, sameness and difference derive basically from human interpretation. Applying this thought to physics and the so-called "laws of nature," Nietzsche stated in *Beyond Good and Evil:*

> One will forgive, I hope, an old philologist who cannot desist from the malice of pointing his finger at poor interpretation. But really, that "conformity of nature unto law" of which you physicists talk so proudly as if . . . that lawfulness is the result only of your *explication de texte*, of your bad philology.[28]

Without great difficulty, a similar argument could also be directed at the notion of a "conformity" of human beings unto law, that is, at legal rule-governance in the social domain. Pursuing a radically anti-positivist path (opposing all modes of simple givenness), Nietzsche in the end arrived at an agonal perspectivism, that is, a view of reality as refracted into a multitude of conflicting construals and interpretations. As he wrote in a letter of 1888: "The basic presupposition that there is a correct interpretation at all—or rather *one* single correct one—seems to me to be empirically false. . . . In a word, the old philologist says: there is no single beatific interpretation." [29]

Quite apart from Nietzschean perspectivism, issues of interpretation cannot rigorously be exiled or segregated from normative rule-governance; in fact, the more normativity is formalized and elevated above contingencies, the more its content appears in need of interpretive retrieval and assessment. In our century no one has more clearly perceived and articulated this nexus than Hans-Georg Gadamer. In his *Truth and Method*, Gadamer discussed and underscored the intimate and not merely extrinsic relationship between rule-governance and concrete-contextual interpretation. Reviewing the philosophical literature on hermeneutics, the study noted a progressive tendency during the last century to privilege the cognitive grasp of texts over concrete-practical exegesis, that is, the aspect of rule-knowledge over rule-application; in traditional terminology, the development meant the downgrading and erosion of the *"subtilitas applicandi"* in favor of semantic understanding and explication. Attributing this tendency to a mentalist or privatizing bent, Gadamer's own view of hermeneutics sought to recover the interdependence and mutual implication of these interpretive components. As one should note, recovery of application in his case was not synonymous with a turn to "applied science"—as if practical exegesis was somehow posterior to, or derivative from, a prior rule-knowledge; on the contrary, the point was precisely the impossibility of their neat segregation. As Gadamer observed: "In the course of our reflections we have come to see that understanding always involves something like the application of the text to be understood to the present situation of the interpreter;" [30] accordingly, we are compelled to move beyond the nineteenth-century view by regarding semantic perspicacity and practical exegesis as a comprehensive or "unified process." In this process, different interpretive components are not merely extrinsically conjoined or collated; instead, "we consider application to be as integral a part of the hermeneutical act as are understanding and interpretation." [31]

Guided by these considerations Gadamer turned his attention to the history or genealogy of hermeneutics, and particularly to its origins in philology, theology, and jurisprudence. As he noted, these disciplines were marked by their inability rigidly to separate cognitive from practical concerns. The original close connection linking philological with legal and theological hermeneutics, he wrote, derived from

> the recognition of application as an integral element of all under-standing. In both legal and theological hermeneutics there is the essential tension between the text set down—of the law or of the proclamation—on the one hand and, on the other, the sense arrived at by its application in the particular moment of interpretation, either in [a] judgment or in preaching.[32]

Neither theology nor jurisprudence in his view were able to distance or stylize their respective texts into a set of objective propositions amenable to a purely "scientific" or value-neutral analysis. Just as the meaning of Scriptures could not properly be grasped and transmitted except in the mode of practical exegesis, so a legal text or statute was not merely there "to be understood historically, but to be made con-cretely valid through being interpreted."[33] The linkage of understand-ing and praxis, *Truth and Method* added, was not restricted to the disciplines of jurisprudence and theology but carried implications for hermeneutics in general and broadly for the status of the humanities or human sciences. If these observations are correct, Gadamer wrote, "then we [confront] the task of redefining the hermeneutics of the human sciences in terms of legal and theological hermeneutics."[34] Given the close connection between law and jurisprudence and social or public life, the study even spoke of the "exemplary significance of legal hermeneutics" for the humanities and a proper conception of interpretation as such.[35]

While stressing the nexus of understanding and praxis, Gadamer did not deny the possibility of a certain distantiation of texts within limited confines and for specific purposes. Thus, commenting on Em-ilio Betti's classificatory distinction between the legal historian and the practicing lawyer or jurist—that is, between the cognition and the application of the law—he readily admitted a difference of accent and concern, stating:

> The jurist understands the meaning of the law from the [vantage of] the present case and for the sake of this present case. As against this, the legal historian has no case from which to start, but he seeks to determine the meaning of the law by considering constructively the whole range of its application.[36]

Despite this concession, however, Gadamer strenuously resisted the segregation of concerns, that is, the opposition between an "objective" meaning of the law available to the historian and a merely contingent or particular meaning superimposed on the law by the practicing jurist in a given case. Countering Betti, he considered it inadequate to say that the historian's objective was simply to "reconstruct the original meaning of a legal formula,"[37] while the jurist's task was to "harmonise that meaning with the present living actuality" (*Lebensaktualität*).[38] In reality, neither the historian nor the jurist could fully extricate himself from a lived or practical engagement with the law. According to *Truth and Method*, even the most meticulous legal historian could not help but approach a statute or legal text from a given field of experience and thus perform a certain kind of application. The legal historian, we read,

> is apparently concerned only with the original meaning of the law, the way in which it was meant and the validity it had when it was first promulgated. But how can he know this [meaning]? Can he know it without being aware of the change in circumstances that separates his own present time from that past time?[39]

That is, can the legal historian know this meaning without mediating in some way the past with the present? This kind of mediation, however, was precisely the labor undertaken by the practicing judge or jurist. Thus, Gadamer insisted:

> The hermeneutical situation of both the historian and the jurist seems to me to be the same in that when faced with any text, we have an immediate expectation of meaning. There can be no such thing as a direct approach to the historical object that would objectively reveal its historical value [its sense or status]. The historian has to undertake the same task of reflection as the jurist.[40]

Throughout *Truth and Method*, Gadamer's emphasis was on correlation and mediation—of text and application, of past and present, of understanding and pre-understanding. The assumption was by no means that of a smooth convergence or coincidence of elements, or of a harmony accomplished without practical and reflective labor; in fact, the study repeatedly spoke of tension or "tensional relationship" (*Spannungsverhältnis*). Ultimately, this tension or mediating labor was the hallmark of the "hermeneutical circle" in which interpretation is always already enmeshed—which does not cancel the task of clarification or the distinction between better and worse modes of understanding. Apart from other customary antinomies, hermeneutical mediation was particularly designed to undercut the traditional subject-object dichotomy familiar from Cartesian and Kantian philosophy. "Inasmuch," Gadamer wrote, "as the actual object of historical understanding is not events, but their 'significance,' it is clearly not a correct description of this understanding to speak of an object existing in itself, and approach of the subject to it."[41] Such a description thoughtlessly tore asunder what was basically correlative and mutually implicated in hermeneutics: "The truth is that there is always contained in historical understanding the idea that the tradition [handed down to] us speaks into the present and must be understood in this mediation—indeed, as this mediation."[42] Seen from this vantage, legal hermeneutics was not really a "special case" but, on the contrary, was "fitted to restore the full scope of the hermeneutical problem and so to retrieve the former unity of hermeneutics, in which jurist and theologian meet the student of the humanities."[43]

III

Since the publication of *Truth and Method*, hermeneutics and interpretation theory have entered on a broad scale into the field of jurisprudence, both on the Continent and in America. Increasingly, students of law and practicing jurists have come to acknowledge the operation of a "hermeneutical circle" in their work and inquiries—although the notion seems more congenial to common law practitioners than to adepts of statutory and civil law. To be sure, the impact of hermeneutics is not restricted to the somewhat subdued and circumspect version formulated by Gadamer. Partly under the influence of Nietzsche (and also of legal theories of the Weimar period), a more aggressive and conflictual variant has entered the legal domain, a variant generally hostile to the role of precedents. Following in the footsteps of a radical perspectivism, interpretation is sometimes described as the work of a constructive or constitutive praxis—in traditional terminology: of the faculty of application (*subtilitas applicandi*) virtually exempt from the demands of understanding and explication. Occasionally, the interpreter is assigned a nearly sovereign power over texts, a power reducing meaning to performance and convention to invention. Against this background, the issue of the present pages comes starkly into view: the precarious status of the rule of law in our time. On radical-perspectivist premises, an inescapably human and political factor seems to enter the law or legal practice—in a manner jeopardizing a central theme or intent of Western political thought. For, with the intrusion of politics, the rule of law is in danger of collapsing into the very "government of men" which originally it was meant to forestall. This danger conjures up a host of related worries: Does law here not become a captive or instrument of arbitrary caprice, of the whim of particular interpreters? Are we not witnessing here the triumph of power over law, of *voluntas* over *ratio* (which the hermeneutical circle had hoped to obviate)?

The triumph of radical or "deconstructive" *voluntas* is precisely the target of Rosen's critique in *Hermeneutics as Politics*. In Rosen's view, the entire thrust of modern thought—of which postmodernism is only the most recent offshoot—points in the direction of a downgrading of objective reason in favor of arbitrary praxis, of cognitive truth in favor of spontaneity. Inaugurated by Enlightenment philosophy and German idealism this development gathered momentum in Nietzsche and finally culminates in contemporary hermeneutics (labeled "the characteristic obsession of postmodernism"). In the course of a trend spanning two centuries, he writes, "theory (the contemplation of truth) is replaced by interpretation (a perspectival fiction, masquerading as a theory). All thinking is then interpretation." According to *Hermeneutics as Politics*, the recent turn to interpretation is only the latest twist or "last convulsion" in the death throes of modernity and its celebration of willfulness: "If we grant at the outset that human existence is nothing more than self-interpretation, or in other words that to be is to be interpreted, then understanding becomes, if not a convulsion, the dance of signifiers in the ballroom of our semantical imagination." For Rosen, the political import of hermeneutics derives from its complicity with power politics, its more or less overt endorsement of a Neitzschean will to power. Far from generating a new kind of political order, however, this endorsement only underwrites the subversion of order, just as deconstruction is only a camouflage for destruction. "Edifying hermeneutics," he concludes,

> is the exoteric doctrine of the will to power, an instrument of the cunning of reason, a stage in the dialectical self-destruction of bourgeois civilization. In political terms, edifying hermeneutics (and perhaps even unedifying hermeneutics) is an expression of middle-class fear of the violent and repressive nature of truth.[44]

Although prompted by a genuine concern, Rosen's reaction is no doubt farfetched and excessive—particularly if focused on hermeneutics. For, the corrosive effects feared by Rosen clearly obtain only if interpretive praxis is entirely sundered from understanding and explication, that is, if exegesis is cut off or removed from the cultural and political context in which interpreters are at best participants but not sovereign masters. Attentiveness to this contextual bond is a central feature of historical and textual hermeneutics, especially in its Gadamerian version. As previously indicated, hermeneutical mediation in his view is precisely a means for bypassing traditional antinomies, in particular the bifurcation between subject and object, text and application; from this vantage, questioning the objective givenness of a text or law is not equivalent to the simple acceptance of interpretive caprice. As Gadamer writes, with reference to legal interpretation seen as the concretization of law in a given case:

> [T]he creative supplementing of the law that is involved [here] is a task that is reserved to the judge, but he is subject to the law in the same way as every other member of the community. It is part of the idea of a legal order that the judge's [decision] does not proceed from an arbitrary and unpredictable whim, but from the just weighing up of the whole [situation in context].[45]

According to *Truth and Method*, the nexus of text and exegesis is operative in different modes in philological, theological and legal settings; the common ingredient, however, is that textual meaning only discloses itself in concretely engaged interpretation which, in turn, remains embedded in a social fabric of understanding. Thus, Gadamer adds:

> We can then, bring out as what is truly common to all forms of hermeneutics that fact that the [meaning] to be understood finds its concrete and perfect form only in interpretation, but that this interpretive work is wholly committed to the meaning of the text. Neither jurist nor theologian regards the work of application as [involving an emancipation from] the text.[46]

Hermeneutical mediation comes to an end whenever one party arrogates to itself a sovereign prerogative, that is, the capacity to determine the meaning of legal and other texts unilaterally in a binding fashion. At this point, mediation is replaced by the stark antithesis between text and praxis, between law and politics—an antithesis which typically is resolved through the absorption of law by power, of reason by sovereign commands. Differently phrased: understanding gives way to a kind of "state of nature" remediable only through absolute fiat. This alternative is fully recognized by Gadamer in his stress on the shared meanings of a legal community. Where such a shared fabric is lacking, he observes, where—as in the case of royal absolutism—"the will of the absolute ruler is above the law," stated simply, "hermeneutics cannot exist" (legal or otherwise). For, in this case, the ruler can assign to his words meanings entirely departing from common understandings or practices. In terms of jurisprudence, the point here is not to interpret the law in such a way that the particular case is decided properly or justly in accordance with the "legal meaning" of the law. Instead, "the will of the absolute ruler [who] is above the law" can effect or implement his preferences or views of justice "without regard for the law—that is without the effort of interpretation." Needless to say, these observations can be extended beyond the range of royal absolutism to any kind of sovereign privilege—whether the latter be claimed by an intellectual elite, a radical party, or a class.[47]

While acknowledging exceptional circumstances, Gadamer's hermeneutics cautiously avoids a Hobbesian scenario by insisting on the cultivation of shared meanings and a shared public space as a premise of interpretive praxis. It is hardly an accident that, in *Truth and Method*, the comments on legal hermeneutics and its significance are directly preceded by a section dealing with the "hermeneutical relevance of Aristotle"—a section presenting the Aristotelian conception of practical-moral judgment (or "*phronesis*") as dependent upon learning experiences garnered in a shared moral way of life (or "*ethos*"). As in the case of jurisprudence, practical judgment is embedded in and nurtured by historically transmitted understandings and beliefs—although the latter can be refined, sharpened, and even creatively be modified in a given instance or application. Similar Aristotelian underpinnings can also be found in Emilio Betti's theory of interpretation, despite the obvious differences between his position and Gadamer's. Pointing to the inevitable incompleteness and elusiveness of rule-governance, Betti assigns to jurisprudence, and particularly to practical legal exegesis, the task of functioning as an "organ of community consciousness"—though not an organ subservient to the currents of public opinion. As he notes, such a function is starkly at odds with an empiricist (or logical-empiricist) construal in which text and interpretation, rational rule-governance and legal praxis are sundered and where practicing jurists are treated as "isolated atoms uprooted from the holistic context of which they are a part." What is chiefly neglected in this construal is the intimate nexus between interpretation and the common beliefs (or common sense) of a community and the fact that jurists are not so much autonomous masters as representative participants in a shared way of life. Echoing Aristotelian teachings, Betti exhorts jurists not to place their trust exclusively in statutory clauses or conceptual formulas but to nurture a common moral sense, that is, a "sensitivity and understanding for the legal *ethos* (of their community) including the future-oriented demands of society." [48]

For contemporary readers, Gadamer's and Betti's notion of shared meanings or a shared way of life may seem excessively benign, if not entirely misleading. From both a Marxian and a Nietzschean vantage, social life is not so much a consensual abode but rather an embattled arena marked by profound rifts or contradictions and by a more or less overt struggle for power. In post-structuralist terminology, meanings circulating in the public realm are basically contested and permanently contestable notions—with efforts at stabilization typically seen as a camouflage for subtle modes of dominance. As noted above, contemporary jurisprudence is not alien or averse to agonal-conflictual models—sometimes to the point of encouraging a radical rupture between law and politics, between rule-governance and interpretive praxis. As it seems to me, this tendency needs critical assessment. While serving as a corrective to a placid consensualism, agonal contestation in my view cannot entirely cancel (Gadamerian) hermeneutics, at least in its guiding intent. At this point, it may be advisable to recollect another conflictual model which is not so much extrinsic as crucially endemic to understanding and lawfulness: Hegel's notion of the struggle for recognition. In this model, shared meanings and public reason are not so much the premises as rather the outgrowth which remains fragile and always dependent on concrete-historical learning experiences. Hegel's notion, I believe, contains a lesson for the rule of law in an age of political instability and social dislocation. Taken by itself or as a purely deductive system, rule-governance cannot sustain a community but rather provokes as its supplement the rule of power (or the "government of men")—just as abstract reason invites the inroads of private caprice. On the other hand, while not reducible to rational maxims, public life can and should be pervaded by a common reasonableness or a reasonable common sense, a sense preventing lawlessness and engendered precisely at the intersection of concrete agon and mutual recognition. This sense, I take it, is at the core of the Greek view of *ethos* and also of the Hegelian concept of *Sittlichkeit* (construed in a non-idealist fashion).

Expressed in mundane-political terms, courts and lawyers cannot maintain lawfulness or the rule of law in a society rent by deep ethnic, economic or other fissures or where there is a widespread sense of corruption, unfairness, and inequity. Only by remedying or healing these fissures through concrete engagement (or a struggle for recognition) is it possible to restore the common reasonableness which is the nourishing soil of legal rule-governance. On a cross-cultural or international level, only concretely shared learning experiences and not abstract edicts, I believe, can overcome or counterbalance the ingrained "state of nature" between feuding nation-states. By the same token, present social-political conflicts cannot be set aside by appeal to a common "tradition" or a shared consensus presumably operative in the past; contrary to a facile reading of Gadamer's work, tradition is not a compact formula capable of overriding present (and expected future) agonies. If, as Hamilton argued, the Constitution is the expression of the common sense of the people (as distinguished from more circumscribed legislative power), then this sense cannot be frozen or congealed at a given moment in a manner silencing subsequent generations or subjecting them to a rigid ancestral cult. In this case, too, hermeneutical mediation surely must do its work—by linking past and present understandings without granting sovereign mastery to "original intent" (or any other isolated intent or preference); for, such privileging would stylize the Constitution into an abstract document removed from the labor of interpretive praxis, thereby undercutting the productive, often agonally sustained continuity of public reasonableness of *Sittlichkeit*. As Hegel remarked in the *Philosophy of Right*, public *Sittlichkeit* manifests the mediation of the objectively given law and the subjective autonomy of the interpreting agent or citizen. "The unity of the subjective with the objective and absolute good," he wrote, "is *Sittlichkeit* or ethical life; in it we find reconciliation as it accords with the concept (of goodness)." And he added: "Law and (subjective) morality cannot exist independently, but must have the ethical (*Sittliche*) as their support and sustaining ground." [49]

NOTES

1. R. Rorty, Philosophy and the Mirror of Nature 315–16, 320 (1979). In social-theoretical literature, the same dichotomy surfaces in the contrast between "structure" and "event" as articulated by structuralist and post-structuralist writers. On this contrast see the comments by Michel Foucault and several interviewers in M. Foucault, The Foucault Reader 55–56 (P. Rabinow ed. 1984), especially the statement: "[A] whole generation was long trapped in an *impasse*, in that following the works of ethnologists, some of them great ethnologists, a dichotomy was established between structures (the *thinkable*) and the event considered as the site of the irrational, the unthinkable, that which does not and cannot enter into the mechanism and play of analysis at least in the form which this took in structuralism." Id. at 55.
2. See Plato, Laws (R. Bury trans. 1984).

3. S. Rosen, Hermeneutics as Politics (1987). For the distinction between ordinary and extraordinary hermeneutics, see R. Rorty, supra note 1, at 320–21, 360.

4. On classical Greek thought see L. Strauss, Natural Right and History (1953); see also A. MacIntyre, After Virtue: A Study in Moral Theory 121–45 (2d ed. 1984). Regarding the transition from Greek to Hellenistic and Stoic thought compare Foucault's comments: "You can see, for instance, in the Stoics, how they move slowly from an idea of an aesthetics of existence to the idea that we have to do such and such things because we are rational beings—as members of the (universal) human community we have to do them." M. Foucault, supra note 1, at 354. In lieu of an "aesthetics of existence" I would prefer talking of a move from a "virtue ethics" to a deontological ethics. The notion of rule-governance is thematized by Foucault under the label of *mode d'assujettissement.*"

5. See W. Jennings, Magna Carta and Its Influence in the World Today 44–47 (1965).

6. See J. Harrington, The Common-Wealth of Oceana (1656).

7. J. Locke, Of Civil Government: Second Treatise 5–6, 109 (1955).

8. Id. at 110–14, 119.

9. See C. Montesquieu, The Spirit of the Laws (T. Nugent trans. 1949).

10. J. Rousseau, The Social Contract 81–82 (M. Cranston trans. 1968).

11. See A. Grimes, American Political Thought 108 (1955).

12. See The Federalist No. 78 (A. Hamilton).

13. Id.

14. 5 U.S. (1 Cranch) 137 (1803).

15. Id. at 176.

16. Id. at 177.

17. Id. at 163.

18. See F. Stahl, Die Philosophie des Rechts nach Geschichtlicher Ansicht (1830–37); see also R. von Gneist, Der Rechtsstaat (1872).

19. G. Dietze, Two Concepts of the Rule of Law 48 (1973).

20. Id. at 10, 48. Regarding the danger of democratic "degeneration" Dietze quoted the statement by Carl J. Friedrich: "Democracy threatens constitutionalism; tending toward permissiveness, it contains the seeds of the realization of man's lust for power, arbitrariness, and injustice."

21. F. Neumann, The Rule of Law: Political Theory and the Legal System in Modern Society 4 (1986).

22. Id. Compare H. Kelsen, Pure Theory of Law (M. Knight trans. 1967); C. Schmitt, The Concept of the Political (G. Schwab trans. 1976); C. Schmitt, Political Theology: Four Chapters on the Concept of Sovereignty (G. Schwab trans. 1985).

23. F. Neumann, supra note 21, at 45.

24. Id.

25. Id.

26. Id.

27. Id. Intermittently, the study made a feeble attempt to escape the sketched anti-

nomy. Thus, opposing Schmitt's radical decisionism, Neumann argued that "the abnormal cannot be the unique and essential element in a definition" (of law). Id. at 26. He also invoked a formula coined by Hermann Heller: "The normless will of Schmitt fails equally to solve the problem as the will-less norm of Kelsen." Id. at 27. See H. Heller, Die Souveränität, Ein Beitrag zur Theorie des Staats- und Völkerrechts (1927).

28. F. Neitzsche, Beyond Good and Evil 25 (M. Cowan trans. 1955).

29. The letter is quoted in J. Granier, Perspectivism and Interpretation, in The New Neitzsche: Contemporary Styles of Interpretation 197 (D. Allison ed. 1985).

30. H. Gadamer, Truth and Method 274–75 (1975) (In the above and subsequent citations I have altered the translation slightly for purposes of clarity.).

31. Id. at 274–75.

32. Id. at 275.

33. Id.

34. Id. at 277.

35. Id. at 275–77, 289.

36. Id. at 290.

37. H. Gadamer, supra note 30, at 291. The reference to Emilio Betti relates to E. Betti, Teoria Generale della Interpretazione (1955).

38. Id.

39. Id. at 292.

40. Id.

41. Id. at 293.

42. Id.

43. Id.

44. S. Rosen, supra note 3, at 7, 9, 87, 193. The notion of edification is borrowed from Rorty. See R. Rorty, supra note 1.

45. H. Gadamer, supra note 30, at 294.

46. Id. at 297.

47. Id. at 294.

48. E. Betti, supra note 37, at 858–60, 864. The above passages are translated from the German edition of this text (published in a single volume), E. Betti, Allgemeine Auslegungslehre als Methodik der Geisteswissenschaften 659–60, 664 (1967).

49. G. Hegel, Philosophy of Right 259 (T. Knox trans. 1967) (translation slightly altered).

10

Laying Down the Law in Literature: The Example of Kleist

J. Hillis Miller

> ... *die Wahrscheinlichkeit nicht immer auf* ,
> *Seiten der Wahrheit ist.*[1]

Can a work of literature lay down the law? What would it mean, for literature and for the law, to say yes to that proposition? Shelley in his "A Defence of Poetry" said, notoriously, that "poets are the unacknowledged legislators of the world."[2] Can we take that seriously, or is it just hyperbolic poetic license? To ask this another way, is a work of literature ever a speech act that inaugurates a new law? If a work of literature may sometimes posit law, does this happen when the work is written or only later on when it is read? If the latter, does the work have to be read justly to be efficacious or may it just be read? What kind of law might a poem or novel make statutory? If a work of literature lays down the law, does it do so only in its original language, or does its legislative power continue in translation? Does the whole work legislate, or just some particular, perhaps detachable, part? This is like asking whether the whole marriage ceremony is necessary to marry the couple, or whether only certain words in it, such as "I pronounce you man and wife," work performatively.

The first quarter of Heinrich von Kleist's "Michael Kohlhaas,"[3] the story by Kleist which serves as the focus for this discussion, was first published in part in a periodical in 1808,[4] two years before the whole story appeared in the first volume of Kleist's collected stories.[5] Was that fragment, from the point of view of legislative power, like a marriage ceremony broken off after only part of it has been performed? To ask these subsidiary questions is to see how unlikely or even absurd it is to suppose that a work of literature might in any practical or literal sense "lay down the law." A work of literature may conceivably have inaugural originality, but not, it would seem, the universality of law, the demand made by a law on all people within its jurisdiction to obey it or suffer the consequences.

That works of literature reflect the law and may even, in part at least, be determined by the legal conditions in a given country at a given time cannot be doubted. Brilliant recent studies have been published in this area.[6]

Nor can it be doubted that recent theoretical developments in law, especially so-called "critical legal studies," have been decisively influenced by literary theory. This relation is by no means straightforward. Some work in Critical Legal Studies has, so it seems to me, conflated "reader response" criticism with what is sometimes called "deconstruction" to produce a new and clearly productive amalgam that is not quite faithful to either of its progenitors. There is no reason to be dismayed by this. It is an example of the transformative torsion that occurs when theoretical "approaches" are transferred from one discipline to another, or from one language or country to another. "Deconstruction in America" is not the same thing as deconstruction in France, Germany, Japan, or the People's Republic of China. Deconstruction in the law is not the same as deconstruction in literary study, and in both areas it is plural rather than singular. In any case, there is no doubt that legal thought has appropriated recent literary theory.

Moreover, law and literature, and their respective elaborately institutionalized disciplines, overlap in a number of ways. Literary theory attempts to derive general laws from particular cases or to apply general law to the reading of particular cases, just as "real" law depends in manifold ways on assumptions about what makes a narrative good or plausible and about the proper legal procedures for moving from a particular story to legislation or to a court decision that is quasi-legislative. As legal scholars well know, there are disquieting implications for the law in recent work suggesting some fundamental unreadability in narratives generally. In criminal cases, for example, the just application of the law depends on getting a story straight about what happened, just as major Supreme Court decisions depend on the presupposition that it is just to move from the contingent details of a specific case such as *Roe v. Wade*,[7] at bottom a particular story about particular people, to a judgment of constitutionality that decisively effects the lives of millions of people. The Supreme Court, as we say, "legalized abortion," and it seems likely to "illegalize" it once more, with the help of state legislatures.[8] The appeal to precedent in law means, most often, the appeal to an agreed-upon narrative or particular cases, often agreed upon only after lengthy and expensive litigation.

Both law and literature depend on resolving (or tacitly avoiding) the vexed question of the validity of example, or, in traditional rhetorical terms, the validity of synecdoche, part standing for whole. This issue is not absent from the present essay. How could I be justified in drawing general conclusions about whether literature lays down the law on the basis of a single, perhaps eccentric, example? The institutions of both law and literature are determined by complex assumptions, often "unwritten laws," about what makes a good argument or a proper narrative. It is instructive for someone from within one institution to move momentarily within the unfamiliar and sometimes even seemingly absurd conventions of the other.

Finally, it cannot be doubted that some works of literature contain thematic reflections about law or dramatizations of legal topics that add something irreplaceable to our understanding of law. An example is Shakespeare's *The Merchant of Venice* or his *Measure for Measure*, or, as I shall try to demonstrate here, the stories of Kleist.

My question is a different one. A precondition for asking it is accepting all three of the relations of law and literature I have named: the reflection by literature of law; the influence of literary theory on legal theory, and vice versa; and the presentation within literature of insights into the law that do more than reflect the legal situation of the time. I ask, rather, whether a work of literature can in any sense be conceived to be lawmaking, that is, can literature inaugurate or establish law? Can literature not only preserve the law or break it, but posit a new law? I shall investigate this question, in its relation to the other three connections of law and literature, through a reading of Heinrich von Kleist's "Michael Kohlhaas."[9]

All Kleist's remarkable stories, not to speak of his plays and many of his anecdotes and short works, contain thematic elements involving the law—often disturbing and paradoxical elements.[10] The question of doing or not doing justice was a fundamental topic for Kleist. He was fascinated by the impingement of various kinds of law on individual human experience: divine law, civil or human law, moral law, physical law (for example, the "law" of causality), and aesthetic law (for example, the millenial assumptions, going back at least to Aristotle, about what makes a shapely and coherent narrative, and therefore about the relation of narrative to truth). Legal studies and literary studies, as I have said, share the need to set up rules for the interpretation of narrative in order, among other uses, to establish guilt or innocence in criminal cases by getting a story straight or to decide, for example, whether Shakespeare's *Macbeth* is a tragedy in the same sense as is Sophocles's *Oedipus Rex*. Readings of Kleist's strange and unsettling stories have played an important part in recent demonstrations of the extreme difficulty, perhaps impossibility, of doing that.

The stories are unsettling in part because they show people decisively effected by erroneous but plausible stories told about them when they were haled before the law. The empirical data, that everyone agrees on, can be put together this way or that way, and there is a disastrous tendency for the data to be put together erroneously, through malice, by accident, or just by application of normal assumptions about probability—"Wahrscheinlichkeit." [11]

Part of what is unsettling is the way the reader is engaged in the same activity of "reading" that is shown in the story to be so difficult and so likely to lead to catastrophe when it is done wrong. When we read one of Kleist's stories, we are reading a story about the disastrous legal consequences of story-telling and story-reading.

Kleist was also fascinated by the possibility of conflicts among various jurisdictions, the conflict, for example, between divine and human law, or between the laws of physical causality and the requirements of plausible concatenation imposed traditionally on storytelling, or between the incongruent jurisdictions of adjacent or superimposed domains, as in the conflicts between Saxony law, Brandenburg law, the law of the Holy Roman Empire, and Protestant or Catholic church law in "Michael Kohlhaas." Kohlhaas is subject to all these laws, and if one does not condemn him, another will.

Kleist's concern for the law can be exemplified in any of his stories. *The Marquise of O—* turns on the question of a rapist's obligations to his victim (and, uneasily, vice versa). The next to the last act of violence in the sequence of violent acts that makes up *The Foundling* is precipitated by a decree from the government giving the protagonist's property to his wicked foster son. The strange last episode, in which the protagonist is ultimately hanged without absolution by papal decree, is determined by a law in the papal states "forbidding a criminal to be executed without his first receiving absolution." [12] In hanging Piachi without absolution, the Pope breaks a knot in the law by breaking the law, in order to preserve the legal system. In *The Earthquake in Chile* a great earthquake briefly suspends, in an idyllic interlude, the implacable operation of social, civil, moral, and ecclesiastical law. All these laws return with a vengeance in the final scene, instigated by a Judgment Day sermon in the cathedral following the earthquake. In *The Duel* a pure woman is accused of fornication, on the basis of apparently irrefutable circumstantial evidence. God, so it seems at first, confirms her guilt in a *holy trial by combat*. [13] The story involves laws of various sorts throughout. In one way or another, most of Kleist's works, like the ones I have mentioned, explicitly involve the law.

No story by Kleist, however, is more dominated by legal questions than "Michael Kohlhaas." It is Kleist's earliest, and by far longest, story and the first to display his characteristic narrative innovations. The subtitle is (*Aus einer alten Chronik*) (*From an Old Chronicle*)[14] Indeed many of the chief events of the story, including the unlikely-sounding interview of the eponymous hero with Martin Luther,[15] are based on "Nachricht von Hans Kohlhasen, einem Befehder derer Chur-Sächsischen Lande. Aus Petri Haftitii geschriebener Märckischer Chronic."[16] The events in question occurred around 1540 in Saxony and Brandenburg. Kleist could with some justice claim that he did not invent or inaugurate anything. He was just telling it like it was, obediently following his historical sources, submissive to their law.

On the other hand, one episode, the anecdote of the fulfillment of an unlikely prophecy, comes from another source, a work of fiction, and the crucial intervention of an old gypsy fortune-teller appears to be Kleist's invention. Moreover, Kleist apparently made up other events and episodes, as well as most of the circumstantial details of conversation and behavior, along with many, but not all, of the proper names. Even the hero's name is changed from Kohlhasen to Kohlhaas, and from Hans to Michael, the latter presumably to suggest associations with the destroying Archangel Michael. Kohlhass is twice in the story called a "Würgengel [avenging angel]."[17]

Uniquely Kleist's own, finally, are the brutal violence, the laconic abruptness with which episode follows episode, the decisive role of unlikely happenstance, and, most of all, the telling of the story with the distinctive Kleistian rapidity of staccato tempo and rhythm. This abruptness is imaged in the stories themselves by frequent references to lightning bolts or by episodes in several of the stories in which someone's brains are dashed out. This new rhythm, it could be argued, is Kleist's most novel invention, something not encountered in any other narrative mode before or since. It is as distinctive, say, as the style of a sonata by Domenico Scarlatti. It is therefore inimitable. One could not imagine someone else writing a "Kleist story." The imposture would be immediately evident.

As is characteristic of fictions claiming to justify themselves with the prior authority of history, the claim by Kleist only to be following sources is a cover for a high degree of inventive originality. The "*aus*" in the subtitle must be taken to mean not only "from" but "out of" in the sense of "going far away from," as Kohlhaas goes out of Brandenburg into Saxony in the opening episode of the story. The story, as I shall show, has much to do with the crossing of borders from one jurisdiction to another. Kleist in "Michael Kohlhaas," it might be said, continually crosses from history to fiction without saying so. Without signalling the transgression in any way, he moves repeatedly from the safely grounded and lawful realm of history into another realm under the jurisdiction of a law the story itself establishes, without prior ground.

On the other hand, the distinction between inaugural fictions and representative recapitulation of historical events will not hold. A fiction is worthless, from the point of view of laying down the law, if it does not somehow take hold. To work it must get itself institutionalized, "legalized," sanctioned, guaranteed, in some community of readers. "Rewriting history," even in the sense of getting given historical events into a form accepted by the community as "right at last," may have decisive performative, statute-making power in that community. A current example is the role in the women's movement of the rewriting of history to include more of the role of women in making history, including literary history.

Nevertheless, the reader concerned with the potential lawmaking power of literature is made uneasy by a story like "Michael Kohlhaas." It is impossible to tell from any markers within the story itself where history stops and fiction begins, although the subtitle implicitly claims that it is all history, taken "from an old chronicle." [18] This claim is repeated within the story, for example in one notation about the Elector of Saxony: "Where he actually went, and whether in fact he arrived in Dessau, we shall not attempt to say, as the chronicles which we have compared [aus derin Vergleichung wir Bericht erstatten] oddly contradict and cancel one another on this point [auf befremdende Weise, einander widersprechen und aufheben]." [19] This makes it sound as if Kleist has scrupulously followed his sources, even refraining from choosing between them when they contradict one another. This is an ironically fictitious claim, though one that has been made often enough in fictions masquerading as history. Kleist's story would be very different if it contained only that for which he had historical authority.

Even without that anxiety, the story is disturbing enough. The horse dealer Michael Kohlahaas was "einer der rechtschaffensten zugleich und entsetzlichsten Menschen seiner Zeit [one of the most upright and at the same time one of the most terrible men of his day]." [20] He was in every way admirable: quiet, law-abiding, an excellent husband and father, hard-working, "das Muster eines guten Staatsbürgers [the very model of a good citizen]." [21] "But," as the narrator says, "his sense of justice [Rechtgefühl] turned him into a brigand and a murderer." [22] That sense of justice, the reader is told a little later, "einer Goldwaage glich [was as delicate as a gold balance]." [23] The image of the delicate balance is not casual, since the story turns on Kohlhaas's demand for equity and recompense. He wants back exactly what he has lost. He has a refined sense of equivalences and is a connoisseur of differences. Or, rather, he will not accept equivalences at all. For Kohlhaas, only the same is the equal of the same. He is a strict literalist in his sense of justice. He does not want recompense, for example money or other horses, for what has been done to his horses. He wants the same horses returned to him in just the condition in which he left them.

Kleist's word "Rechtgefühl [sense of justice]," used twice, is more than a little ominous. It does not name a willingness to obey external law but a scrupulous inner measuring scale by which Kohlhaas evaluates on his own the justice or injustice of what someone does. He tries people's actions "vor der Schranke seiner eigenen Brust [before the bar of his own conscience]."[24] The Protestant Reformation of Kohlhaas's day was promulgated through an appeal to the priesthood of all believers and to the independence of each person's spiritual witness and power to read the Bible. Luther's most revolutionary act, it could be said, was to translate the Bible into German. Kohlhaas's inner sense of justice may, in a given case, measure things differently from the way lawyers, judges, courts, and other legal authorities measure them. He lives under a double jurisdiction, one external, one the call on him of something other than any external law, just as Kleist's story, "Michael Kohlhaas," makes its call on its readers from a place and according to a law that may not be assimilated into any previous law.

The story tells of just such a conflict between two jurisdictions. When Kohlhaas is crossing the border from Brandenburg to Saxony one day with a string of horses he means to sell in Leipzig, he is illegally detained at a castle on the border for lack of an imaginary pass. Two black horses from his string are kept behind, ostensibly as gage, when he is allowed to proceed. Kleist stresses the contingency and irresponsibility of this injustice. It is not a concerted plan by the castellan, steward, and Junker of the castle; it just "sort of happens." When Kohlhaas returns several weeks later with legal proof that the pass is not necessary, he finds that his once plump and glossy blacks are skinny and dull, scarcely able to stand on their feet. They have been worked nearly to death in the fields. The groom he has left behind to care for the horses has been robbed, beaten, and driven from the castle. The rest of the story describes the extraordinary escalation of Kohlhaas's attempts to get just recompense for the damage done to him.

Just recompense, to Kohlhaas, means return of the groom's stolen possessions, payment of the groom's medical expenses, and, most of all, the return of his horses just as they were. He demands that they be fattened by the lord of the castle, the Junker Wenzel von Tronka. "Those are not my horses, your worship!" he cries to the Junker. "Those are not the horses which were worth thirty gold gulden! I want my well fed and healthy horses back!"[25] Justice is not done to him by the courts of either Saxony or Brandenburg, in part because influential people in both capitals are related by blood or marriage to the Junker von Tronka. Family loyalty is stronger than the law, and subverts it. The authorities at Dresden and Brandenburg dismiss his suit. They tell him to fetch his horses from Tronka Castle and forget about the whole incident. Finally, his wife is mortally injured by an over-zealous bodyguard when she tries to press the suit on his behalf in a personal appeal to the Elector of Saxony in Berlin.

After burying his wife, Kohlhaas takes the law into his own hands. Later, during an interview with Luther, Kohlhaas justifies his actions by saying, "I call that man an outcast [verstoßen] . . . who is denied the protection of the laws [der Schutz der Gesetze]! . . . whoever denies me it thrusts me out among the beasts of the wilderness [den Wilden der Einöde]; he is the one—how can you deny it?—who puts into my hand the club that I defend myself with."[26] Kohlhaas here claims that he has been put back into a state of nature, and therefore is justified in initiating a new social contract.

Kohlhaas draws up "einen Rechtsschluß [a decree]" that, "kraft der ihm angeborenen Macht [by virtue of the authority inborn in him],"[27] demands that the Junker fatten the blacks with his own hands in Kohlhaas's stables. When the Junker refuses to do this, Kohlhaas gathers followers, burns Tronka Castle, and kills the steward, the castellan and their families, but not the Junker, who escapes. He then sets himself up with an increasing band of armed men as an independent force seeking the Junker to wreak vengeance on him. He scourges the countryside. He sets fire to Wittenberg and then Leipzig, punishing them for harboring the Junker. He and his men are seemingly invincible. All attempts to capture him fail. Only the intercession of Martin Luther, in a strange interview based on historical fact, but going beyond historical documentation in its circumstantial detail, persuades Kohlhaas to lay down his arms, accept amnesty from the Elector of Saxony, and seek justice again through the court at Dresden. In the end justice is done to him, the Junker is given a prison sentence, the black horses are returned to Kohlhaas as fat as ever, along with full compensation for the damages to him and his groom. But Kohlhaas is at that same moment executed by judgment of the Emperor of the Holy Roman

Empire in Vienna. The latter considers himself not bound by the amnesty. The legal authorities support him in this. Kohlhaas's crime is "Verletzung des öffentlichen, kaiserlichen Landfriedens [breach of the peace of the Empire]." [28]

As is so often the case in Kleist's stories and plays, the verdict repeats the crime. [29] If it is unjust for Kohlhaas to have "einen Scheffel Hafer . . . gescheut [made a business of a bushel oats]," [30] as the proverb he cites has it, if it is wrong to burn down the castle, kill all those people, pillage the countryside, set fire to two cities, over an affair of two black horses, it seems also unjust to execute him for what is legally defined as no more than a breach of the Emperor's peace. Neither punishment fits the crime. Both are incommensurate. It would not take a delicate gold balance to see that something is amiss in both cases with the scales of justice.

Kleist's way of telling the story stresses the mortal irony of the double ending. The day of Kohlhaas's execution, the day when he "was to make atonement to the world for his all-too-rash attempt to take its justice into his own hands [sich selbst in ihr Recht verschaffen zu wollen]," [31] is also, as the Elector of Brandenburg tells him as he is led to the scaffold, "der Tag, an dem dir dein Recht geschieht! [the day on which justice is done you]." [32] "Look here," he says, "I am giving you back everything that was taken from you by force at Tronka Castle, which I as your sovereign was duty bound [schuldig war] to restore to you: the two blacks, the neckerchief, gold gulden, laundry—everything down to the money for the doctor's bills for your man Herse. . . ." [33] With one hand the law makes him full recompense; with the other it deprives him of his life. The story makes it clear that Kohlhaas would never have got justice in the affair of the blacks if he had not taken justice into his own hands and so earned himself the headsman's axe. The scales of justice do not balance. From the point of view of the law, justice has been done. The law has been maintained and fairly administered. The authorities can sleep with good consciences. From Kohlhaas's point of view, he has lost everything, at the very moment he has regained everything he has lost.

How can we read this story justly, do it justice? One curious fact about "Michael Kohlhaas" is already evident. Even more than with most works of fiction, it seems necessary to repeat the story in order to talk about it, "read" it, analyze it, and evaluate it. Much of the "criticism" of Kleist's stories is limited to this point. [34] An example is the introduction by Greenberg to the English translation cited here. If "Michael Kohlhaas" is inaugural, original, and inventive, perhaps culpably so, if it lays down its own new Kleistian laws of storytelling, in defiance of traditional laws of the relation of narrative to history or of probability to truth, the story's effect on its readers seems to be a compulsion to tell the story over again. We must repeat the crime, if crime it is, in the effort to account for the story, to do it justice, to assimilate it into what is already known about literature and into conventional ways of rationalizing literature, just as in the story the highest authorities seem compelled to do again in a new form what Kohlhaas has done. They do this in an effort to heal the breach of the peace he has caused, to reassert their jurisdiction and justify their authority.

This compulsion to retell suggests an answer to the question posed earlier about how a work of literature might not only be original, invent something unheard of before, but also proliferate itself as a universal law. The story tends to disseminate itself and to compel its readers to do again what it does, just as Kohlhaas's demand for justice turns into widespread injustice, if that is the right word for it. This injustice expands not only in what he is led to do, but also in what he leads others to do. This is an ironic and exceedingly disquieting version of Kant's formulation of the categorical imperative, in the *Grundlegung zur Metaphysik der Sitten*: " . . . ich soll niemals anders verfahren, als so, *das ich auch wollen könne, meine Maxime solle ein allgemeines Gesetz werden.*" (" . . . I should never act in any other way than in such a manner *that I could also will that my maxim should be a universal law.*")[35]

But how does it happen in the story (as opposed to *with* the story) that Kohlhaas's initial demand for justice in the matter of his two horses escalates to a universal juridical, political, and moral level? The series of "decrees" Kohlhaas issues shows how a universal new law is implicit in his initial and stubbornly maintained demand for justice from the courts on the basis of his own private and exceedingly delicate "Rechtgefühl." The German word for "decree," "Rechtsschluß," sounds stronger to an English-speaker than its English equivalent. It suggests establishing a right or laying down a right.

For Kohlhaas, one "Rechtsschluß" leads rapidly to more and then quickly to the revolutionary establishment of a new order of law. Speaking first in the name "of the authority inborn in him," Kohlhaas is soon claiming in the "Kohlhaas Manifesto [Mandat]" that he is "waging righteous war [einem gerechten Krieg]" on the Junker Wenzel von Tronka.[36] He demands support from all citizens of Saxony "on pain of death and the certain destruction by fire of everything they [call] their own."[37] In a seemingly inevitable crescendo, this becomes in his second manifesto a definition of himself as "einen Reichs- und Weltfreien, Gott allein unterworfenen Herrn [a free gentleman of the

Empire and the world, owing allegiance to none but God]." On this basis he invites "all good Christians" to join him.[38] He issues yet another manifesto when he sets fire to Leipzig. In this he describes himself as "a viceroy of the Archangel Michael [einen Statthalter Michaels, des Erzengels], come to punish with fire and sword, for the wickedness into which the whole world was sunk, all those who should take the side of the Junker in this quarrel."[39] Kohlhaas's final manifesto, issued from the captured castle of Lützen, where he has established his command, is to "summon the people to join with him to build a better order of things."[40] It is signed from "the Seat of Our Provisional World Government [*Weltregierung*]."[41] Now when he goes forth "a large archangelic sword [is] borne before him on a red leather cushion ornamented with gold tassels, while twelve men with burning torches [follow] after."[42] This is appropriate for someone who, like his namesake the Archangel Michael, wields fire and sword as his chief instruments of destruction.

The reader will see the mad logic of this rapid expansion from the particular and parochial to the universal. Though Kohlhaas's quarrel is only over a pair of horses, as soon as he appeals from the judicial system of Saxony to his own private sense of justice, he has in effect renounced his citizenship and challenged the legitimacy of the courts. He has implicitly declared himself the leader of a revolutionary new world government, with its own new code of laws and other appurtenances of state: rulers, legislators, courts, universities, and the rest. Though the appeal from the public courts to the bar of his own breast is not apparently violent, it implicitly possesses the violence of all inaugural positing of new law and the legitimazation of a new state. Kohlhaas's appeal to his innate sense of justice in the affair of the two horses implies the establishment of not just a single new law or provisional court but of a revolutionary new world order. The initial limited demand contains its own implicit universalization. It contains also within itself the possibility of all the violent acts Kohlhaas and his men commit. The appeal to a justice that is private and at the same time universal, a law above the law, is intrinsically violent, even when that appeal is performed in the most non-violent way, for example, by passive disobedience or peaceful assembly.

Kohlhaas's proclamation of a new world order takes the usual form of such proclamations, whether they are successful or not. Though his decrees and manifestoes would create, performatively, the new people and the new law in the name of which they speak, his declarations speak as if that law and the people brought together under the rights it establishes already exist and are merely described, constatively, in his proclamation. Declarations of independence do not take responsibility for what they do. They speak in the name of a pre-existing people and pre-existing rights that in fact they create by performative fiat.[43] "We hold these truths to be self-evident,"[44] but they were not "self-evident" before our founding fathers enunciated them, in a speech act that was not just a statement of pre-existing fact.

Kohlhaas's new declaration of the rights of man, however, is an infelicitous performative. The context and circumstances are not right. His proclamation is not ratified by a new contract and a new constitution. That this might happen is what the authorities in Saxony fear and what leads them to treat him with such violence. Some similar fear, it may be, has motivated the authorities who have put down so ruthlessly the pro-democracy movement in the People's Republic of China. It began as a few students hanging posters and meeting to make speeches, but soon a million citizens were rallying and there were posters everywhere.

At the moment of Kohlhaas's greatest military success, Luther intervenes to persuade Kohlhaas "in den Damm der menschlichen Ordnung zurückzudrücken [to return within the confines of the social order]."[45] In a notice posted all over the Electorate, and then in an interview, he accuses Kohlhaas of being both "filled with injustice [Ungerechtigkeit] from head to foot," and "a rebel and no soldier of the just God" for daring to take justice into his own hands.[46] Kohlhaas's reply, as I have said, is that he has been "denied the protection of the laws" and, therefore, is cast out of the community of the state in which he lives, and so is justified in setting up his own state.[47] But Kohlhaas does not really mean that he had been returned to a state of nature, outside all laws. He means that the courts of Saxony and Brandenburg do not mediate the law for him, that law he carries in his own breast. He is therefore justified in setting up a new law and a new social order in which justice in the name of the law will be done to him. Luther replies that no one has denied him the protection of the laws, that he should forgive his enemies, take back the horses, thin and worn as they are, and fatten them himself. No one but God has the right to declare the Elector unjust for denying his suit. In the end Kohlhaas agrees to disband his army, accept amnesty, and press his suit again before the courts of Saxony with Luther's sponsorship. Nevertheless, he stubbornly refuses to budge on the main point. "[L]et judgment [*die Erkenntnis*] be pronounced as is my due," he says, "and let the Junker fatten my pair of blacks."[48]

This interview with Luther is profoundly ironic. Only a few years earlier this same Martin Luther had nailed those theses to the church door in Wittenberg and had uttered his "Ich kann nicht anders [I cannot do otherwise]." Luther has himself behaved just as Kohlhaas is behaving. He has defied all civil and ecclesiastical authorities. He has appealed beyond them to a higher justice. On the ground of that justice, he has established on his own something even more important than a new state, a new church.

Luther's revolution has been a success. In two decades his new church has been institutionalized and accepted by certain states as legitimate. Luther himself wields great political as well as spiritual power. Nevertheless, he sternly refuses to Kohlhass the right to act as he himself has acted, though, curiously enough, in his message to the Elector of Saxony he more or less accepts the argument that he has refused to countenance in his interview with Kohlhaas. ". . . as a matter of fact," the narrator reports him as writing,[49] "the wrong done Kohlhaas had in a certain sense placed him outside the social union [außer der Staatsverbindung]; and in short, so as to put an end to the matter, he should be regarded rather as a foreign power [eine fremde . . . Macht] that had attacked the country (and since he was not a Saxon subject, he really might be regarded as such) than as a rebel in revolt against the throne."[50] The complicated jurisdictional situation of the time is not entirely different from the situation in the United States today. In the United States, too, a crime that crosses state borders may be subject to the laws of one or the other of the states or of federal law. In the United States, too, it may take much litigation to decide in which court a defendant should be tried. Kohlhaas seeks justice from Saxony and then from Brandenburg. He is ultimately condemned by a high court of the Empire, on the technicality that the amnesty grant by Saxony does not bind the Emperor's court.

But to define Kohlhaas as a "foreign power" is to put him in a sense outside any of these laws. Or rather it is to subject him either to the laws governing warfare between states or to the conventions of those delicate diplomatic negotiations between states that keep the peace, often by endless inconclusive discussions. Such discussions, strictly speaking, are outside the laws of any state. They are in a sense unlawful, or they are subject only to international law or to the unwritten laws of diplomacy, since they are governed by the laws of neither of the states that engage in the diplomatic negotiations. What is concluded by diplomacy must be ratified separately in each state in order to become effective. Walter Benjamin compares the conventions of diplomacy to those unwritten laws that govern discussions within families. For him, both these realms are outside the "violence [*Gewalt*]" that characterizes state power and law.[51]

Though Luther is willing to argue that Kohlhaas is in a sense a foreign power, he is wholly unwilling to let him define himself as the justified emissary of God's vengeance. He refuses to hear Kohlhaas's confession and administer him the Sacrament unless he will forgive his enemies and give up taking private vengeance. Nevertheless, the possibility that Kohlhaas really is the viceroy of the Archangel Michael, sent by God to punish a wicked people who have a corrupt judicial system, hovers over the story as a faint possibility, just as Kleist plays ironically with similar possibilities of divine intervention in his other stories. Kohlhaas compares his unwillingness to forgive to Christ's: "even the Lord did not forgive all his enemies." [52] As the narrator says of the sack of Tronka Castle: "Der Engel des Gerichts fährt also vom Himmel herab [In such a fashion does the angel of judgment descend from heaven]." [53] A lot hangs on how the reader takes the "also" or "in such a fashion" in this sentence, as it also does when Kant says I should act in such a fashion ("also") that the maxim drawn from what I do could be made a universal law for all mankind.

What is the difference between Luther and Kohlhaas? Is it no more than the difference between a successful and an unsuccessful revolution, one that gets itself institutionalized and legitimized, and one that ends, like most revolutionary attempts, with the execution or imprisonment of the insurrectionist? Kohlhaas's revolution may be justified but unsuccessful. On the other hand, if Kohlhaas is not an emissary from God, he is creating an entirely unjustified issue over a small matter. He has made a business of a bushel of oats. He should submit himself to the law of the country he lives in or does business in and take whatever judgment the court hands down.

How would we decide about that fine line between a Luther and a Kohlhaas? Should we let history decide? Suppose the South had won the Civil War in the United States? Would that retroactively make the South's cause more just? Somehow it does not make sense to let the contingencies of history decide matters of justice. On the other hand, if Kohlhaas *is* a second Archangel Michael, a viceroy of God sent to punish those who do not administer the law rightly, then what he does is not revolutionary, original, or originary at all. He is a keeper of the law, a preserver of it, neither a breaker of the old law, nor a present-day Moses, Lycurgus, or Christ who institutes a new law, fulfilling and cancelling the old. He does not set up a law unheard of before, the basis of a novel world order, original and inaugurative, without precedent.

The same thing can be said of Luther. He claimed not to be founding a new religion but to be reforming a corrupt Christendom by returning to an old, traditional, and entirely authorized Christianity. The Reformation returned the same to the same. The fact that Lutheranism has been so thoroughly institutionalized and merged into state power by the time Luther has his interview with Kohlhaas indicates how little truly initiatory the Protestant Reformation was. Luther is, by 1540, an instrument of the established civil order, at least as he is presented by Kleist, but also as he is presented in standard historical accounts.

Here is the paradox inherent in the idea of the laying down of a new law, whether as a political act described in a work of literature or as a law-positing act performed by the work of literature itself: In order to work it has to appeal to precedent. It cannot authorize itself. It has to claim merely to describe and reinforce pre-existing rights and laws. And in order to work it must be institutionalized after the fact, legitimated by the elaborate machinery of society, inscribed in statutes and rules, with some kind of police for their enforcement and an agreed and publicized code of sanctions. In order to be socially effective, a work of literature must be canonized, surrounded by a complex context of editions, reviews, commentary, pedagogical traditions, and so on. But as soon as either Michael Kohlhaas, the man, or "Michael Kohlhaas," the story, is authorized from the past and institutionalized for the future, he or it is no longer novel, unheard-of, or original, but homogeneous to what already has been legislated. He or it does not lay down a new law but confirms an old one. The story of Kohlhaas as told by Kleist admirably exemplifies this contradiction.

So far I have been talking primarily about events or themes described in the story. What about the working of the story itself, as a historical event, a text written by Heinrich von Kleist at a certain time and place and published under certain circumstances, then later on published and republished, translated, and commented on, until finally it fell into my hands and under my eyes as reader? I have said that the paradox inherent in the idea of laying down a new law applies not only to the political acts described in a work of literature, for example Kohlhaas's insurrection and execution, but also to the law-positing act performed by the work, for example, by this story. How can that claim be defined, understood, and justified?

In order to do so, I turn to a crucial episode in "Michael Kohlhaas" not so far discussed, the episode of the gypsy fortune-teller. This episode is an allegory of the working of the story. It shows that the story is not descriptive or constative, but performative. Or rather, it shows that the story performs by describing or telling, since, strictly speaking, within the terms of traditional speech act theory, there is nothing performative about Kleist's story. "Michael Kohlhaas" does little more than narrate, in a dry, terse, economical, chronicle-like style, events that are said to have occurred in history. Its intention does not appear to be at all performative, but purely epistemological, to get the facts right, to tell it like it was. Such judgment as the narrator passes on Kohlhaas is ironic through and through. It expresses the collective judgment of the time more than the evaluation to which the story itself leads the reader: "And now the fateful Monday after Palm Sunday arrived, on which Kohlhaas was to make atonement to the world for his all-too-rash attempt to take its justice into his own hands." [54]

The story of the improbable fulfillment of the gypsy woman's prediction about a roebuck is borrowed and modified by Kleist from an almost forgotten novel, Friedrich Maximilian Klinger's *Der Kettenträger*,[55] read by Kleist in 1801.[56] The main part of her story, however, seems to have been Kleist's addition to history. It is a fabulous element that intervenes decisively into the life-story of the historical Kohlhaas as Kleist tells it. Several motifs characteristic of Kleist's storytelling come together in this episode: the ironic hint of signs indicating God's inscrutable judgment; the working of exceedingly improbable coincidence in human life; the performative function in human history of messages, letters, notes, papers, decrees, manifestoes, court judgments—writing of all kinds. For Kleist, such writings do not simply describe, communicate, or inform. They make something happen. An example is the way Kohlhaas's failure to get justice from the courts is mediated by documents. The law's delay, the interminable "process" that keeps postponing Kohlhaas's suit—throwing it out of court, telling him to give it up—works by way of papers and documents, never by that direct face to face confrontation Kohlhaas cannot obtain until it is too late and he has put himself outside the law by taking the law into his own hands.

The first of these motifs, the possibly supernatural sign, appears early in the story when "ein ungeheurer Wetterschlag [a huge lightning bolt]" and "ein plötzlich furchtbarer Regenguß [a sudden fierce downpour of rain]" [57] stop Kohlhaas just as he is about to burn down the cloister where von Tronka's aunt is Abbess and has been harboring von Tronka. Are we to take this seriously as a manifestation of God's judgment on Kohlhaas? Is it the sign of the abrupt intervention of eternity into time? The text does not allow the reader to decide with certainty. There is the lightning bolt. You can read it anyway you like.

The second motif, coincidence or improbable happenstance, pervades the whole episode. Kohlhaas encounters the gypsy woman by sheer accident, though the encounter is decisive for his fate. He just happens to be in the market town of Jüterbock when the gypsy woman is telling the fortunes of the Electors of Saxony and Brandenburg, who just happen to have met there to transact some business. She predicts good fortune for the Elector of Brandenburg, but bad fortune for the Elector of Saxony. She refuses to tell the latter what that bad fortune will be, but writes down on a little piece of paper "the name of the last ruler [of his house], the year in which he shall lose his throne, and the name of the man who shall seize it for himself by force of arms."⁵⁸ For some mysterious reason, never explained, she gives the paper to Kohlhaas, who has joined the curious crowd around the fortune-teller. She tells him it is an amulet that will save his life. Kohlhaas does not read the paper until the last moment of his life. The narrator says, somewhat obscurely, that he refrains "for various reasons."⁵⁹ The paper unread has, in a way, more power. Once Kohlhaas knows what it says, then he will have the power, and with it the responsibility too, to tell it or not to tell it, as his conscience directs. As long as he has not read it, he can use his ability to read it or not read it as an additional weapon.

That what she has predicted for both Electors will infallibly come to pass is guaranteed when "the pledge for the truth of everything she said"⁶⁰ is improbably fulfilled. The roebuck does come to meet them in the market place, just as she said it would, even though the Elector of Brandenburg has the deer slaughtered for the table to prevent the fulfillment of the prediction. A huge butcher's dog takes the carcass from the kitchen and drops it at their feet. As the Elector of Saxony says, in a sentence that recalls the earlier lightning bolt: "The lightning [Blitz] that plummets from a winter's sky is no more devastating than this sight was to me."⁶¹

Later on, it just happens, by an exceedingly unlikely coincidence, that the Elector of Saxony encounters Kohlhaas as he is being taken in chains to be tried before the High Court at Berlin. Until then the Elector has not known the identity of the man to whom the gypsy gave the paper, nor has he been able to find him. The Elector suffers a stroke when Kohlhaas explains to him how he got the paper he keeps in a lead capsule around his neck. The Elector becomes obsessed by his awareness that Kohlhaas has the paper that will tell him his future. Tormented by a desire to know what the future is, he tries every available expedient to get the paper from Kohlhaas, promising him freedom and a full pardon, and trying to get his execution postponed, all to no avail.

Most improbably of all, the Elector's Chamberlain just happens to choose the actual gypsy woman, who just happens to look marvelously like Kohlhaas's dead wife and to have the same name, when he takes an old woman from the streets at random to impersonate the real fortune-teller and persuade Kohlhaas to release the paper. A propos of this even the narrator utters the words I have taken as an epigraph for this paper: "probability is not always on the side of truth."[62] Kleist justifies this event by a solemn appeal to history, but the event in question, we know, is fictitious: "something had happened here which we must perforce record but which those who may wish to question are perfectly free to do."[63] "I cannot help it," Kleist in effect says; "this is the way it happened." This is like Luther's "Ich kann nicht anders." But this is *not* the way it happened. The appeal from Aristotelian laws of probability in *mimesis* to the higher authority of what actually happened in history is rather an appeal from Aristotelian poetics to a new Kleistian poetics based on improbable but veracious contingency.

The gypsy woman betrays her charge from the Chamberlain and tells Kohlhaas to keep the paper. On the day of his execution, she sends a message warning him that the Elector intends to dig up his body after he is executed in order to get the paper. Kohlhaas retaliates, just before he is beheaded, by looking the Elector in the eye, unsealing the paper, reading it through, and then swallowing it. The Elector promptly falls down unconscious in a fit. The story ends with the report that the Elector of Saxony returns to Dresden "shattered in body and soul,"[64] while Kohlhaas's children are made knights, and his descendants flourish. He is universally respected by the people for his respect for a law that is superior to all positive, institutionalized laws. To that law he alone has access, through his "Rechtgefühl."[65] As for the fulfillment of the gypsy woman's prophecy, "what happened subsequently," says the narrator in his laconic way, "must be sought in history [in der Geschichte nachlesen muß],"[66] (literally "must be read after in history").[67] The gypsy woman's political and personal prophecy echoes the oracle of Apollo, who, in *Oedipus Rex*, tells Laius his son will kill him. It echoes also the witches' prophecy in *Macbeth*. To hear such predictions, in literature if not in life, is to know that, however improbable they are, they will inevitably come to pass, down to the last detail. Such prophecies are performative rather than merely constative. Prophecies are something like promises. They say: "This will happen, I promise you."

What is the reader to make of this episode? Why did Kleist not tell the reader what was the fulfillment of the prophecy? Why did he add just this fiction to his historical sources? The added episode of the gypsy fortune-teller is a fiction smuggled into history that radically changes the meaning of that history. It is an admirable allegory of the relation to history of both Michael Kohlhaas and "Michael Kohlhaas," both the man and the story. The addition signals the transformation of history into literature, that is, into a collocation of words that has its own power to intervene performatively into history at the later date when it is written, published, and read. By "literature" here I mean any retelling, since even the driest after-the-fact chronicle will have "literary" or rhetorical elements that make it effect something in its own time and later on, whenever it is read.

Kohlhaas's establishment of a new world government to get justice over an affair of two horses is like Kleist's writing of this strange story. Each is an abrupt interruption of the course of history, political history in the one case, literary history in the other, and, by way of the latter, in however small a way, political, ethical, and social history. Kohlhaas would initiate a new state law. The story would initiate new ideas of narrative probability and truth, and implicitly, by way of that, new codes for everything in society that depends on narrative, such as, for example, the pleading of cases before the law.

"Michael Kohlhaas" is without recognized power or authority. It is not a sacred text, nor even a work as central to the established canon of Western literature as are, say works by Goethe and Schiller, though "Michael Kohlhaas," rather surprisingly, has a curious kind of canonicity in German-speaking countries. It has been read and studied in detail by generations of German and Swiss schoolchildren at what we would call the Junior High School level. The story is read as a model of elegantly correct German prose style, but also, inevitably, as an ideological model. A recent radio play was modeled on the story. A bookstore in Berlin is called "Kohlhaas & Company" and has a black horse as logo. Michael Kohlhaas, I am told, has been invoked recently in Berlin during the spectacular transformations of East Germany, haled as a complex model of resistance and political courage, though the story can also be read as a warning against the temerity of taking the law into one's own hands. Read in one or another of these ways, embedded in the immediate making of history, "Michael Kohlhaas" is a work that works. It performs.

The story tells the reader the likely outcome of such a performative fiat. Kohlhaas's revolutionary gesture is quashed. He is executed. The pre-existing law closes around him. He leaves scarcely a ripple on the surface of European history. He is better known through Kleist's fictitious story about him than through any conspicuous effect he has on the course of history. The episode of the fortune-telling paper, however, informs the reader that Kohlhaas is the bearer of history. He carries the future within himself and will have a decisive effect on it. But that future remains unknown until it happens. Only Kohlhaas reads the paper. He carries its secrets to the grave. The separation of his head, that knows the secret future, from his body, that incarnates the script on which the future is written, expresses with savage irony the separation between doing and knowing. The future he carries in himself remains unreadable, impossible to codify or institutionalize. What will happen will happen. On the fated day the last member of the Elector's family will be deposed, his throne seized by force of arms. Kohlhaas, like the avenging Archangel Michael, will have helped bring this about by deflecting the course history would otherwise of taken.

In the same way, Kleist's story, too, posits a new law, but this law is also unreadable in the sense that it resists theory. The effect of reading the story cannot be rationally predicted. The story cannot be satisfactorily assimilated into the institution of literary study or study of the social effects of literature. Insofar as the story is explained, rationalized, theorized, and accommodated into the general enterprise of accounting for literature, or made lawful, its own inaugural heterogeneous law is obliterated, forgotten. That law, nevertheless, goes on working every time the story is read, just as Kohlhaas's revolutionary lawmaking power vanishes when he is executed and yet goes on operating from "beyond the grave" in the fulfillment of the gypsy woman's prophecy, in the example of an exigent sense of justice he has left behind, and even in the flourishing of his progeny.

"Michael Kohlhaas" does what it tells. It establishes the law of the absence, unavailability, or failure of the law. In it an affront to the law is repaired by a repetition of an affront to justice. The same thing may be said of the performative effect of the story itself. Insofar as it fails to account for the events it tells, in the sense of making them reasonable, telling them justly, or "justifying" them, making them square, as when we speak of a "justified margin," it is a performative that does not perform. Or what it does is to bring to light the failure of narrative to serve as the handmaiden of the law by making the grounds of just law fully perspicuous. The story enunciates the law of the unreadability of that law in the name of which all particular laws are promulgated and justified.

Like Michael Kohlhaas, literature lays down the law. That new law is socially and historically effective, but always in unforeseen, unpredictable ways, whenever "Michael Kohlhaas" is arraigned before the bar of justice each reader carries in his or her own breast. The story's effects are always unreadable before the fact. In order to find out the performative effect of literature in history, we must read that effect afterwards in history itself.

The legislative power of a literary work cannot be read in the work itself. Nevertheless, it commands and institutes. It brings something "other" into history, even in papers, like this one, that attempt to explain the work rationally. The lawmaking power of the work carries over even into commentary that tries to explain it. Though it is impossible to tell whether the story speaks with the authority of the law above all laws or whether it just happens, as a natural fact, it makes law and enforces it, like a Kleistian lightning bolt.

NOTES

1. "[P]robability is not always on the side of truth." H. von Kleist, Michael Kohlhaas (As einer alten Chronik), in 2 Sämtliche Werke und Briefe 96 (H. Sembdner ed. 1961) [hereafter Kohlhaas Chronik]; H. von Kleist, Michael Kohlhaas (From an Old Chronicle), in The Marquise of O—and Other Stories 175–76 (M. Greenberg trans. 1960) [hereafter Kohlhaas Chronicle].

2. P. Shelley, A Defence of Poetry, in Shelley's Critical Prose 3, 36 (B. McElderry, Jr. ed. 1967).

3. Kohlhaas Chronik, supra note 1, at 9; Kohlhaas Chronicle, supra note 1, at 85.

4. The first quarter of Michael Kohlhaas was published in 6 Phöbus (June 1808; issued in November).

5. H. von Kleist, Michael Kohlhaas, in I Erzählungen 1–125 (1810).

6. One example is an admirable book by Brook Thomas exploring the legal contexts of nineteenth-century American literature. B. Thomas, Cross-Examinations of Law and Literature: Cooper, Hawthorne, Stowe, and Melville (1987).

7. 410 U.S. 113 (1973) (striking down Texas law which made it a crime to procure an abortion except to save the mother's life and upholding a woman's constitutional right to terminate her pregnancy).

8. See generally Webster v. Reproductive Health Serv., 109 S. Ct. 3040 (1989) (reformulating legal framework established in Roe, 410 U.S. 113, in order to uphold several provisions of Missouri laws regarding abortion, thereby permitting the states increased latitude in this area).

9. Kohlhaas Chronik, supra note 1; Kohlhaas Chronicle, supra note 1.

10. For example, Der Findling, Das Erdbeben in Chili, Der Zweikampf, Der Zerbrochne Krug, über die allmähliche Verfertigung der Gedanken beim Reden.

11. See Kohlhaas Chronik, supra note 1, at 96.

12. H. von Kleist, The Foundling, in The Marquise of O—and Other Stories 229 (M. Greenberg trans. 1960).

13. H. von Kleist, The Duel, in The Marquise of O—and Other Stories 285, 318 (M. Greenberg trans. 1960).

14. Kohlhaas Chronik, supra note 1, at 9; Kohlhaas Chronicle, supra note 1, at 85.

15. See 2 Sämtliche Werke and Briefe 895–96 (H. Sembdner ed. 1961) [hereafter Sämtliche].

16. Schöttgen & Kreysig, III Diplomatische und curieuse Nachlese der Historie von Ober-Sachsen und angrentzenden Ländern (1731).

17. Kohlhaas Chronik, supra note 1, at 54; Kohlhaas Chronicle, supra note 1, at 134.

18. See supra note 14 and accompanying text.

19. Kohlhaas Chronik, supra note 1, at 99; Kohlhaas Chronicle, supra note 1, at 179.

20. Kohlhaas Chronik, supra note 1, at 9; Kohlhaas Chronicle, supra note 1, at 87.

21. Id.

22. Id.

23. Kohlhaas Chronik, supra note 1, at 14; Kohlhaas Chronicle, supra note 1, at 93.

24. Id.

25. Kohlhaas Chronik, supra note 1, at 15; Kohlhaas Chronicle, supra note 1, at 94.

26. Kohlhaas Chronik, supra note 1, at 45; Kohlhaas Chronicle, supra note 1, at 125.

27. Kohlhaas Chronik, supra note 1, at 31; Kohlhaas Chronicle, supra note 1, at 111.

28. Kohlhaas Chronik, supra note 1, at 94; Kohlhaas Chronicle, supra note 1, at 174.

29. P. de Man, Allegory of Reading, in Allegories of Reading (1979). The observation comes in passing during a reading of Rousseau's Profession de foi:

> A text such as the Profession de foi can literally be called "unreadable" in that it leads to a set of assertions that radically exclude each other. Nor are these assertions mere neutral constations; they are exhortative performatives that require the passage from sheer enunciation to action. They compel us to choose while destroying the foundations of any choice. They tell the allegory of a judicial decision that can be neither judicious nor just. As in the plays of Kleist, the verdict repeats the crime it condemns. (Id.)

De Man shows the way the temptation of "theism," in the Profession de foi, is at once condemned as intellectually foolish and at the same time shown to be in some form inevitable. The text demands that we pass judgment on what it says and about what it says, while showing that such judgment is necessarily groundless. My reading of Kleist's allegory of justice in "Michael Kohlhaas" also sees the situation of the reader as analogous to that of the protagonist, but while not denying the rigor of the narrow place in which Rousseau's Profession de foi, de Man's essay, and Kleist's "Michael Kohlhaas" in their different ways put their readers, I glimpse the possibility of a new justice and a new taking of responsibility for acts and judgments made in this narrow place. If we must judge and act, we must also say of these acts and judgments, as Kohlhaas and the signers of the Declaration of Independence in different ways did of what they had done: "Yes, I did it, and I take responsibility for it, even though it was unjust in the sense of not being based on an ascertainable prior ground of justice within the political order I inhabited. I declare my act and judgment to be the basis of a new justice." A work of literature lays down the law, I am arguing, in a manner analogous to these acts and judgments.

30. Kohlhaas Chronik, supra note 1, at 47; Kohlhaas Chronicle, supra note 1, at 127.

31. Kohlhaas Chronik, supra note 1, at 100; Kohlhaas Chronicle, supra note 1, at 179–80.

32. Kohlhaas Chronik, supra note 1, at 101; Kohlhaas Chronicle, supra note 1, at 181.

33. Id.

34. See, e.g., Mann, Preface to H. von Kleist, The Marquise of O—and Other Stories 5 (M. Greenberg trans. 1960) [hereafter Marquise of O]; M. Greenberg, Introduction to Marquise of O, supra, at 27.

35. I Kant, Grundlegung zur Metaphysik der Sitten, Werkausgabe 28 (J. Miller ed. 1982). This sentence and its surrounding context in Kant are discussed in J. Miller, Reading Telling: Kant, in The Ethics of Reading 13, 26 (1989). This paperback edition of 1989 rectifies an error in translation in the first edition.

Hardy E. Jones defines Kant's idea of the relation between moral agency and lawmaking in a way that parallels my thoughts about "Michael Kohlhaas," the story, and Michael Kohlhaas, the person. H. Jones, Kant's Principles of Personality (1971). For Kant, says Jones,

> a person is a moral agent with an autonomous will by virtue of his lawmaking capacity—his power of self-legislation. Kant says that rational agents are subject to laws arising from their own self-legislating wills: they are required to obey only those rules of which they themselves are sources. This is something which is essential to their freedom and without which they could not be rightly regarded as morally responsible beings. (Id. at 131)

I owe this citation to Paul Privateer. Jones, in the passage I cite does not signal, as Kleist does, the social disorder or violence that might follow if each citizen were to obey only laws of which he or she was the source, nor does he signal what is problematic about that word "source." What faculty or agency within me is the source of the laws I establish with my "self-legislating will"? Kant's books of moral philosophy are attempts to answer this question, or rather to explain why it cannot be answered, why we cannot ever confront the moral law within us face to face, though its imperative command over us is categorical.

36. Kohlhaas Chronik, supra note 1, at 34; Kohlhaas Chronicle, supra note 1, at 114.

37. Id.

38. Kohlhaas Chronik, supra note 1, at 36; Kohlhaas Chronicle, supra note 1, at 116.

39. Kohlhaas Chronik, supra note 1, at 42; Kohlhaas Chronicle, supra note 1, at 121.

40. Kohlhaas Chronicle, supra note 1, at 121.

41. Kohlhaas Chronik, supra note 1, at 41; Kohlhaas Chronicle, supra note 1, at 121.

42. Kohlhaas Chronicle, supra note 1, at 123.

43. Jacques Derrida has written brilliantly on this paradox of a performative masking as a constative statement in two essays: J. Derrida, Declarations d'Independence, in Otobiographies (1984) and J. Derrida, Admiration de Nelson Mandela ou Les lois de la réflexion, in Psyché: Inventions de l'autre 453(1987).

44. The Declaration of Independence, ¶ 2 (U.S. 1776).

45. Kohlhaas Chronik, supra note 1, at 42, Kohlhaas Chronicle, supra note 1, at 122.

46. Kohlhaas Chronik, supra note 1, at 42–43; Kohlhaas Chronicle, supra note 1, at 122–23.

47. Kohlhaas Chronicle, supra note 1, at 125.

48. Kohlhaas Chronicle, supra note 1, at 127.

49. The actual letter Luther sent has not survived. It is lost to history.

50. Kohlhaas Chronik, supra note 1, at 49; Kohlhaas Chronicle, supra note 1, at 129.

51. The work of diplomacy, says Benjamin, "wie der Umgang von Privatpersonen [like the intercourse of private persons]" is "jenseits aller Rechtsordnung und also Gewalt [beyond all legal systems and therefore beyond violence]." Walter Benjamin, Zur Kritik der Gewalt, in Metaphysisch-geschichtsphilosophische Studien 195 [hereafter Kritik]; W. Benjamin, Critique of Violence, in Reflections 293 (Jephcott trans. 1978) [hereafter Critique].

52. Kohlhaas Chronicle, supra note 1, at 128.

53. Kohlhaas Chronik, supra note 1, at 32; Kohlhaas Chronicle, supra note 1, at 112.

54. Kohlhaas Chronik, supra note 1, at 100; Kohlhaas Chronicle, supra note 1, at 179–80.

55. F. M. Klinger, Der Kettenträger (1796).

56. The evidence for this is a letter from Kleist to Wilhelmine von Zenge of 22 March 1801. See Sämtliche, supra note 15, at 635.

57. Kohlhaas Chronik, supra note 1, at 35; Chronik Chronicle, supra note 1, at 115.

58. Kohlhaas Chronik, supra note 1, at 92; Kohlhaas Chronicle, supra note 1, at 172.

59. Kohlhaas Chronik, supra note 1, at 86; Kohlhaas Chronicle, supra note 1, at 166.

60. Kohlhaas Chronik, supra note 1, at 93; Kohlhaas Chronicle, supra note 1, at 172.

61. Kohlhaas Chronik, supra note 1, at 93; Kohlhaas Chronicle, supra note 1, at 173.

62. Kohlhaas Chronicle, supra note 1, at 175–76.

63. Kohlhaas Chronik, supra note 1, at 96; Kohlhaas Chronicle, supra note 1, at 176.

64. Kohlhaas Chronicle, supra note 1, at 183.

65. Benjamin observes that the "great" criminal characteristically commands such paradoxical respect and admiration from the people. He is the law-breaker who nevertheless reveals something essential about the violence involved in all law-making, even if his punishment is accepted as necessary to maintaining law and order. Kritik, supra note 51, at 35; Critique, supra note 51, at 281.

66. Kohlhaas Chronik, supra note 1, at 103; Kohlhaas Chronicle, supra note 1, at 183.

67. In the body of this paper my lips must remain sealed, since the meaning of the story depends on the fact that the Elector's future is not revealed there. In this footnote, however, separated from the body of the paper as neatly as Kohlhaas's head is separated from his body, I append the following: The Elector of Saxony from 1532 to 1547, that is, at the time of the story, was John Frederick I, der Grossmütige or the Magnanimous (1503–1554), the last Elector of the Ernestine branch of the house of Wettin. He was wounded and taken prisoner by Charles V's victorious army at the battle of Muhlberg (April 24, 1547). Though a sentence of death was not carried out, in the capitulation of Wittenberg, May 10, 1957, the Elector renounced the electoral lands to his second cousin, Maurice, duke of

Saxony from 1541, of the Albertine line of Wettins. Presumably the gypsy woman's prophesy contains these facts. As the Elector fears, he himself is the last of his line to rule Electoral Saxony. My source, by the way, the Encyclopaedia Britannica, says nothing at all about Kohlhaas in the entry for John Frederick I, much less about the gypsy woman. 13 Encyclopaedia Britannica 38 (1966). There is a three volume biography of John Frederick I I have not yet seen. Ich muss es nachlesen.

11

Statistical Stigmata

Henry Louis Gates

> The True utterance is like the brand of beer
> that commands 95 percent of the market and
> the false like the brand with only 5 percent.
> Richard Posner[1]

> A system-grinder hates the truth.
> Ralph Waldo Emerson[2]

I

One measure of the success of the law and economics movement on the right is the extent to which the techniques of economic analysis— the models of rational choice—are seen, on the legal left, as tainted.[3] If there is a baby in the murk of its bath water, the consensus seems to be that it has long since drowned. Mark Kelman, for example, argues that the law and economics account simply *is* liberal social theory, in its most exhaustively worked out form, and he treats it as a *reductio ad absurdum* of liberal social theory (meaning, I think, social choice theory).[4] Yet if we restrict ourselves to the *descriptive* dimension of these programs, there seems to be no reason why the apparatus cannot lend itself to progressive ends. In the liberal tradition, one could cite Bruce Ackerman's enlistment of the Coase Theorem in the service of legal activism; for while its apparent prescription for judicial non-intervention has no force outside its explicitly counterfactual conditions (perfect knowledge, perfect rationality, zero transaction costs), the extended causal horizons suggested by its application point to a much broader way of reconstructing the judicial 'facts of the matter."[5] And while we decry the use of the Kaldor-Hicks test in Reagan-decreed cost/benefit analysis,[6] we might remember that Lord Kaldor was himself a socialist and advisor to the Labor Party. Obviously, it's in the gap between "is" and "ought" that politics hides out.

In what follows, I want to try to explore the intersection of "race" and "statistics" in a way that takes neither term for granted. Statistical conceptions of both race and racial discrimination have become central in the policy sciences, in economic social theory, and in the economic analysis of law and its theory of "statistical discrimination."

(From Richard Posner's perspective, for example, much racial discrimination may have a positive social benefit.)[7] But rather than responding to the lawyer-economist with a reflexively apotropaic gesture—the rhetorical equivalent of garlic and wolfsbane—I want to look at the "probabilistic turn" in which racial identity comes to be rewritten as a statistical property: for it is the same probabilistic turn that undergirds the so-called "ethical basis" of wealth maximization.

II

Few revolutions in thought had the social impact of what is now called the "probabilistic revolution." Nineteenth-century Europe saw not only what Ian Hacking calls "an avalanche of printed numbers," but the proliferation of statistical societies, statistical congresses, and national statistical bureaus. The new statistics spawned the sanitary movement (which, as Hacking says, "increased life expectancy more than anything in history"), and was intimately connected with the condition-of-England debates and movements of social reform.[8]

But the trail of the serpent is over all.[9] As Ian Hacking has observed, "[t]he first discussion of human kinds was made at exactly the moment when statistical/classificationary social science began, which was also the moment when our idea of the normal was beginning to enter human consciousness."[10] At first blush it seems paradoxical: you might suppose that a sophisticated understanding of human variation would blur and destabilize the tidy divisions of humanity generated by eighteenth-century anthropology.[11] But statistical reason is double-edged in this regard.

This can be seen in the work of Adolphe Quetelet, a pioneer and popularizer of "moral statistics," who perhaps more than any one else helped institutionalize the social-statistics movement and keep it on track. As a theorist, Quetelet's great contribution was the claim that human variation, social/behavioral as well as physical, can be interpreted as variations from an objective mean, distributed according to a law of errors, rather like a pattern of holes on a dart board. The law of errors (or accidental causes) explains the pattern of variation. For Quetelet, it is a "general law that applies to individuals as well as peoples and that rules our moral and intellectual qualities no less than our physical qualities, [a law] that dominates our universe and seems destined to spread life through it."[12] But what these variations are variations *from* is Quetelet's new creature, *l'homme moyen*, The Mean or Average Man. Quetelet, a supporter of a "Laplacian social science, arrives at the same conception as the critics of Laplace: the order of things according to natural kinds. . . . [Quetelet] not only notes the existence of natural classes as a *fact,* as Venn did, he elevates it to the status of *law* that governs the universe." [13] (For Quetelet, a statistical regularity was itself a social law.)

You might expect from all this that the law of errors would take the place of racial classification, as a sort of explanation for human variation. Instead, it served as a technique for racial retrieval, though by introducing a statistical model of race rather at odds with the anthropological one. A chapter in Quetelet's 1849 book, *Theory of Probabilities,* is subtitled: "Each race of men has its particular type." [14] He writes:

> Each people presents its mean, and the different variations from this mean, in numbers which may be calculated a priori. This mean varies among different people, and sometimes even within the limits of a single country, where two people of different origins may be mixed together. [15]

For "men of different races . . . have different laws of development." And he explains how you can use the law of errors to ascertain the existence of distinct racial types with a cluttered intermixed population. "The law of possibility has then this new advantage, that it assists in the resolution of a problem very interesting in anthropological respects." [16]

Seventy years later, the practitioners of biometrics followed Quetelet's example of its logical conclusion and disposed altogether of the anthropological or "ideal-type" model of racial classification in favor of the statistical one. As Nancy Stepan writes, race then became "a populational and statistical concept. . . . The unit with which the anthropologist must therefore deal, said Pearson, was not the racial type, nor the individual, but a 'statistically representative sample of race.' " [17]

Despite its success in colonizing both the social and natural sciences, however, the rise of probabilism was fraught with a number of conceptual ambiguities (though I'll have to pass over some of the most important). To many, there appeared to be a gap between probabilistic and causal investigations. The elimination of that gap was part of a general trend away from viewing statistical laws as secondary or phenomenal, supervening on some other causal structure (the reductionist view), to a conception in which statistical law had automony (the non-reductionist view).

There was also an equivocation between probability as a measure of belief, an index of uncertain information, and as an objective property in the world. Any face of the die is equipossible in a roll. But for the German statistician Jakob Friedrich Fries, its outcome is already determined in nature. Equipossibility is a condition of our knowledge.[18] In current terms, this is the distinction between objective and subjective or epistemic probability.[19] Note that epistemic, or so-called subjective, probability goes hand-in-hand with a reductionist view of statistical laws as superintending on other mechanisms, while an objective or realist account of probability pretty much ordains the non-reductionist view.

Where you stand on that question will also effect where you stand on the question of single-case probabilities—that is, whether or not you think they exist. Jakob Friedrich Fries argued in the 1840s that "statistical laws apply only to the mass, and are without significance for individuals."[20] He was vigorously (and successfully) challenged on this. His challengers asserted that it made no sense to talk about laws applying to groups if they didn't apply to individuals. And I'll return to the issue of single-case probability in the litigation of racial discrimination a little later.[21]

III

Before I consider statistical discrimination as theorized in conservative policy science, however, I want to consider the evidentiary use of the statistics of discrimination. For in both cases, administrative costs take precedence over justice.

I want to look briefly at the 1987 Supreme Court decision in *McCleskey v. Kemp.*[22] The background to the case, in a nutshell, is as follows. In the state of Georgia, a black man kills a white man, and is sentenced to death. At this time, one of the most comprehensive and sophisticated studies ever conducted on judicial sentencing, the Baldus study, shows an enormous racial disparity in capital sentencing in the state of Georgia: those who kill whites are eleven times more likely to be condemned to death than those who kill blacks. Even after extensive statistical analysis—controlled for 230 possible nonracial variables—the odds for a capital sentence for a white-victim crime is 4.3 times greater than for a black-victim crime. As a sentencing factor, race ranks with prior conviction for rape, armed robbery, and even murder.[23] The race factor here isn't merely statistically significant, it is, as you might think, downright determinative.

Armed with this massive statistical body of evidence, McCleskey seeks habeas corpus relief on the grounds that there was a constitutionally impermissible risk that race "played a significant role in the decision to sentence him to death." [24]

The Baldus study was scrutinized and hailed by various prominent statisticians, including representatives of the National Academy of Sciences, as among the most sophisticated empirical work ever done on criminal sentencing. The experts agreed that the Baldus study proved that capital sentencing in Georgia is a discriminatory process.

Federal District Court Judge Owen Forrester had a different opinion. In his view, the Baldus study simply did not represent good statistical methodology. He protested that its findings were "arbitrarily structured little rinky-dink regressions . . . [which] prove nothing other than the truth of the adage that anything may be proved by statistics." [25]

Forrester's basic objection to the Baldus statistics was that the information it collected "could not capture every nuance of every case." [26] This is true enough. On the other hand, as an appeals brief noted, "[b]y insisting on a standard of 'absolute knowledge' about every single case, [Judge Forrester] implicitly rejected the value of all applied statistical analysis." [27] Obviously you wouldn't need these statistics under conditions of perfect knowledge.

Pace Judge Forrester, the higher courts each accepted the internal validity of the Baldus statistics—or affected to. The issue became one of its judicial relevance.

The appeals court argued that the statistical evidence was irrelevant: that McCleskey needed direct evidence showing that he himself was the victim of discrimination. According to the court, "[n]o single petitioner could, on the basis of these statistics alone, establish that he received the death sentence because, and only because, his victim was white." [28] Thus the statistical evidence cannot be determinative in any given case.

There are two ways of reading this interpretation of the evidence. Perhaps the court is establishing a higher standard of certainty for the statistical evidence than any other sort (even fairly direct evidence—say, the fact that a juror is heard murmuring something suitably discriminatory—would leave open the counterfactual possibility that the defendant would have been sentenced to die anyway). But perhaps the court simply failed to apprehend the force of statistical evidence in the first place. [29]

The same logical incoherence afflicts the Supreme Court's decision. [30] Again, the Court assumed, for the sake of argument, the validity of the Baldus statistics; then said there was no evidence concerning discrimination in the *McCleskey* case. But if you recognize the force of statistical argument, as I suggested, you can't hold both positions. The Baldus statistics are evidence—albeit rebuttable evidence—relevant to the disposition of the *McCleskey* case. (For Justice Powell, it did not constitute "exceptionally clear proof"; but the standards he established were so high it is doubtful that the prosecutors in capital sentences always met them in securing the convictions.)

It should be clear that in distinguishing starkly between statistical and causal investigations, the court recapitulates a nineteenth-century confusion about the meaning of "moral statistics." For a Court that finds that "[t]he magnitude [of a statistical regularity] cannot be called *determinative* in any given case"[31] remains entrapped in a pre-modern problematic; an episteme whose demise has been placed (prematurely, as *McClesky* suggests) at the last quarter of the nineteenth century.

One of the signs of constitutional retrenchment in the Supreme Court is an increasing insistence, in civil rights cases, on a finding of discriminatory intent, rather than discriminatory effect. After *Mc-Cleskey*, it looks doubtful whether statistical evidence—no matter how strong—can ever constitute clear and compelling evidence of purposeful discrimination in the eyes of the Supreme Court. In fact, we could go further and say that this is precisely the strategic function of the "purposeful": as a test that would eliminate from consideration evidence that is statistical in nature and, subsequently, predictions that are probabilistic in nature. (Incidentally, Randy Kennedy has noted that *"no defendant in state or federal court has ever successfully challenged his punishment on grounds of racial discrimination in sentencing."*)[32]

Probability functions in the place of ignorance. It is because the infinitude of "microaggressions" (as Delgado has it)[33] constitutive of racism defy positivist verification that statistical regularities become important. It would not be too much to say that the statistical regularity uncovered by the Baldus study, in effect, functions like a rule; a rule governing judicial sentencing.

Powell's explicit position is that of someone who rejects the idea of single-case probability. Under the Court's logic, it doesn't make sense that McCleskey's chances are worse than another's; indeed, it doesn't make sense to quantify his chances at all.

And as we've seen, this tension between individual contingency and general probability, so vexing for Powell, is woven through in the history of statistical reasoning in the nineteenth century. Like the English statistician Robert Leslie Ellis in the 1840s, Powell sees contingency as located at the level of individuals; and he distinguishes absolutely between causal and statistical investigation.[34]

What we see in these court decisions is a profound discomfort with applying statistical laws to individual events. Yet when we are discriminated against, we are discriminated against not as individuals, but as tokens of a type, as representatives of a class; and judicial remediation must assume the same form. Here's what marks the distinction Alan Freeman makes between the "perpetrator perspective" and the "victim perspective"[35]: the perpetrators are always individuals, while the victims constitute a class, a collectivity, a statistical genus.[36]

IV

Few exercises in applied ethics have so captured the popular imagination as the one that made its debut in the *Washington Post* a few years ago.[37] It was the famous case of the jewelry store, the buzzer, and the black face at the door. (The jewelry store owner is a Bayesian who believes [or knows; depending on how you set it up] that blacks are much more likely than whites to rip him off, to the degree that he would rather forgo a potentially profitable transaction with a black customer than expose himself to that risk.) And of course, this isn't just a hypothetical case. Patricia Williams has written movingly about her experience of being denied entry at a downtown Bennetton shop while Christmas shopping one weekend.[38]

Looking at some of the evidentiary principles enunciated in *McClesky*, we might speculate about the possible disposition of the fictitious case, *Williams v. Bennetton*.[39] Suppose, having decided to seek legal remedy, she tries to bolster her case by collecting statistics about the store's patterns of inclusion and exclusion by race. Say it turns out that the owner, seasoned by bad experience, refuses entry to people he doesn't like the look of, and the people he doesn't like the look of include almost all blacks, though it is not restricted to blacks (scruffy whites fare poorly, too). The first judge rejects the data as useless: it doesn't capture the nuances of every case, he points out. The owner has clearly used his discretion in responding to subtleties that these "rinky-dink regressions" can't capture. Further along, your statistics are treated more politely. The Supreme Court tells you: these general patterns are interesting in the abstract; but we need clear and compelling proof that the racial factor was determinative in *your* case. It seems they want you to meet the counterfactual test of proving that you would have been admitted had you been white. The court thus conjures up the specter of an imaginary white Patricia Williams to trump the legal claims of the real (black) one.

But is it even clear that the Bayesian shopkeeper who systematically excludes blacks (as bad risks) can be held guilty of "purposeful discrimination" in any event? Not if purposeful discrimination must involve a "conscious intent to harm blacks," [40] since racial characteristics here are merely a surrogate for less perspicuous ones. (The judicial test of "purposefulness" might be whether blacks were excluded qua blacks or qua members of a high risk group.)

In fact, our Bayesian shopkeeper provides a paradigm case of statistical discrimination as discussed in the law and economics literature. "In recent times," Judge Posner asserts, ". . . the most important factor responsible for discrimination probably has been information costs." [41] Such discrimination is rational because it is efficient: race is merely an inexpensive surrogate or proxy for other undesirable characteristics. Contrary to popular belief, then, such discrimination— which is, in his view, most discrimination—is likely to be *reinforced* by contact. (For Judge Posner this would explain the salience of racism in the South, where there's contact between the races. At long last— an economic interpretation of the old saying: familiarity breeds contempt.) Hence "the 'balancing' approach sometimes used in constitutional cases might, if honestly followed in racial cases, result in upholding many instances of racial discrimination on efficiency grounds, even if distributive effects were also weighed in the balance." [42]

Nevertheless, given its current illegality, Posner does take pains to suggest an approach to remedy. He asks,

> [w]hat is the appropriate remedy in a job discrimination case in which a violation has been ajudged? If the employer has discriminated against blacks, he should, in my judgment, be required to pay the damages of any black person against whom he has discriminated (perhaps doubled or trebled to facilitate enforcement where damages are small). This type of judgment both compensates and deters and seems preferable to an injunctive remedy requiring the employer to hire a specified number or percentage of blacks. . . . Such an injunction . . . operates as a capricious and regressive tax on the white working class. Moreover, *many of the blacks who benefit from the decree may not have been discriminated against by the firm,* and many of those discriminated against may not benefit from the decree. [43]

Note that when Posner speaks of a "capricious tax on the white working class," Posner speaks of a harm incurred by an entire genus; but
when he speaks of blacks, he doesn't allow that the whole class of
them is damaged by these discriminations. Rather, he shifts abruptly
to the individual level—the land of contingency.

Posner's view has strange consequences. An employer who, as it
were, hangs a "Whites Only" sign on the front door and thereby en-
sures that only whites apply, in Posner's view, damages no one and has
no incentive to change his ways. His liability increases with the number of blacks who actually apply and are turned away. If the employer
actively seeks out individual whites in order to fill vacancies (rather
than advertising for applicants), against which black has he discriminated?

Posner is discomforted by a remedy in which blacks, other than the
individual black who was discriminated against, might benefit. I do
not share his worries on that score. But Posner's view of discrimination as a discrete intersubjective action clashes with another intuition.
Even if I'm not personally turned away from a diner—for I know I
won't be seated—I am disadvantaged by not being able to eat there.

To accommodate these intuitions, we might think about a more
generous application of the probabilistic turn I sketched earlier. As
I've said, it turns out that every mainstream theory of probability today makes room for objective, and therefore single-case, probability.
And that much suggests another approach to the issues.

V

I want to try to frame the ethical issue—following a suggestion
made by K. A. Appiah—as one of *probabilistic harm*.[44] We might
frame the question: can you harm people by decreasing their chance
of getting some good?

If you think of single-case probabilities as objective features of a
person, then a change in your chance of getting some good is an objective change in your position. And it may be right to compensate
you for that change—even if there's no manifest harm done (now—
or ever). (Contrarily, if you don't believe in single-event probability,
then you won't be able to recognize any harm as having been done to
someone unless manifest harm occurs.)[45] In considering the offense
when we expose people to "reckless disregard," for instance, Appiah
would have us pose the question: is it that we risk putting them at
harm; or harm them by putting them at risk? If the latter, you could

presumably recover damages on normal damage theories. In any case, the idea seems familiar: along the lines of suing for exposure to asbestos—even if you don't actually get a disease from it. Damages, actual or consequential, are conventionally considered compensation for direct or indirect injury; you need to prove the harm. But if you think of change to single-case probabilities as itself a kind of harm, then there *is* an actual damage. Of course, the only access we have evidentially to the actual damage will almost always be statistical evidence about the chances (which involves looking at groups of people—it can't be found by looking strictly at you).

Now, this realist interpretation of probabilistic harm avoids the Court's mine-field of "purposeful discrimination." By reconstructing the impact of statistical discrimination as an issue of liability—and of damages—it side-steps the whole vexed issue of intent.[46] For our legal economists, negligence is a *technical* question—subject to the Learned Hand calculus[47] or a problem for a Chicagoan's slide rule. Recasting statistical discrimination in these terms—as harmful changes in objective probabilities—brings us to a new problem: law-and-economics techniques could, in principal, be used on behalf of radical judicial remediation. (Probably too radical: the challenge, presumably, would be coming up with constraints on the principle's application.)[48]

Justice Holmes's preference for having liability lie where it falls—that is, allowing it to be borne by the victim in the absence of compelling reasons not to—may have been justified on the basis of administrative costs, but it's not an attractive solution in the case of demonstrated discrimination. (And while strict liability fails to excuse people who had good intentions, as Jules Coleman[49] reminds us, the victims have good intentions, too.) Given the notion of probabilistic harm, furthermore, there could be no Posnerian scruple about an injunction benefitting someone other than the actual victim. For even if a given candidate hadn't applied, her chances of getting the job would have been lower than equity requires, and that *is* a kind of harm, on this analysis.

A final irony. The explicit linchpin of what Posner proposes as the "ethical basis of wealth-maximization" is the principle of compensation *ex ante*. Subject, perhaps, to some constraints about foreseeability, the principle obviously serves to confer moral legitimacy on laissez-faire capitalism: whatever happens, you were paid for it (i.e., you received compensation *ex ante*), and therefore you have consented to it. Compensation *ex ante* is of course probabilistic: but on my realist interpretation, compensation *ex post* can be too. In fact, the realist interpretation of probability helps us make sense of the very idea of compensation *ex ante*.[50] Conversely—and more important for my purposes—the probabilistic structure of compensation *ex ante* provides a different way of conceiving of compensation *ex post*.

Start with this question of compensation *ex ante*: precisely *what* does it compensate you for? You might say, in loose parlance, that you're being compensated for accepting risk, which certainly *sounds* as if risk (a change in objective probability) is a harm for which you deserve compensation. This realist interpretation of Posner's principle of compensation *ex ante* as consent—the linchpin that joins the normative and descriptive aspect of his program—makes it just a special case of compensation for probabilistic harm. The Posner principle of compensation *ex ante* should thus *support* the probabilistic claims for compensation *ex post* to the class of targets singled out by statistical discrimination regardless of whether they have been manifestly victimized as individuals.[51]

VI

The project I've been haphazardly conducting is perhaps best described as perverse. Granted, educing larger contradictions in the discourse of the systematizers is a venerable hobby in humanistic disciplines. But some may object to my interest in smaller contradictions: isn't this the intellectual equivalent of what the State Department calls "constructive engagement"?

Perhaps at stake are competing claims for the tradition of philosophical radicalism, indeed, the very origins of political economy (neither of which can be extricated from the intellectual developments I sketched earlier).[52] I worry that in the course of a necessary critique of economism, some critics have conceded too much by accepting Posner (he is my synecdoche) as *terminus ad quem* of political economy as such. And I take some solace in the fact that many of the most powerful and original new arguments for realism have emerged from the radical tradition.[53]

It would be a mistake, though, to see the return to naturalism as a countertrend to the postmodernist (and now somewhat tired) exaltation of indeterminacy. The theoretical claims of indeterminacy neither rule out nor determine any politics in particular. If the hoary and suspect distinction between theory and practice is marked anywhere, it is in the distinction between the contingent real and the indeterminate imaginary. Plainly, the simple affirmation of indeterminacy cannot stanch the very human pain of racial stigmata. Statistical they may be:

they bleed just the same. Those utopian discourses of postmodernism do play an important role for us. Only remember: while they speak of dawn, the rest of us still dwell in the twilight of probability.

NOTES

1. R. Posner, Economic Analysis of Law 544 (2d ed. 1977).

2. R. Emerson, 3 Journals 523 (1870).

3. It is a familiar, and plausible, objection that the allure of law and economics reflects a misguided craving for scientificity, uncomplicated by questions of value. But it is one thing to deny economics' explanatory privilege; another to insist (like some who are captivated by the hermeneutic model) on its irrelevance. That neither discourse can be simply mapped onto the other doesn't mean the juxtaposition is without value. Both inhabit a nomological rhetoric; and economics, too, is a "kind of writing."

   In her recent book, *Contingencies of Value,* Barbara Herrnstein Smith points out the ways in which the divide between disciplinary economics and the "humanistic" disciplines might seem to be imperiled: from one side, as economic analysis grows more nuanced and complex, it looks increasingly humanistic; from the other side,

   > [those in] humanistic disciplines explore with increasing subtlety the complex ways in which *economic* dynamics, at every level of analysis, condition the production and reception of artworks and, more generally, condition the value of all cultural objects and practices. It may appear, then, that a deconstruction of the double domain of value is at hand. Perhaps it is. Since, however, the distinction between humanistic studies and disciplinary economics is implicated in more fundamental conceptual and ideological oppositions and is clearly a highly charged and to some extent self-defining distinction on one side, there is no reason to think this will happen easily or soon.

   B. Herrnstein Smith, Contingencies of Value 129 (1988). Certainly her book is exemplary of how to negotiate fruitfully between the two registers.

4. See, e.g., M. Kelman, A Guide to Critical Legal Studies 115–26 (1987). For a synoptic critique of the foundations of such social theory that combines analytic and historicist perspectives, see N. Hartsock, Rational Economic Man and the Problem of Community, in Money, Sex, and Power: Toward a Feminist Historical Materialism 38–54 (1983).

5. See B. Ackerman, Reconstructing American Law 46–55 (1984).

6. See Markovits, Duncan's Do Nots: Cost-Benefit Analysis and the Determination of Legal Entitlements, 36 Stan. L. Rev. 1169 (1984) (citing President Reagan's Executive Order No. 12,291, prohibiting federal agencies from making new regulations that do not pass a cost-benefit test).

   Nicholas Kaldor had, of course, specific plans for the surplus generated by the potential-Pareto superior move. The application of the criterion in some law and economics is fraught with a telling ambiguity, however. Legal economists usually describe Kaldor-Hicks superiority as requiring that a move produce enough wealth that the winner has more than would be needed to bribe the loser into acquiescence. But if what's at stake is buying the victim's consent (rather than some other criterion of objective compensation), then a proposal that purports to be free of distributive consequences has, in fact, a distributive agenda. See Polinsky, Probabilistic Compensation Criteria, 86 Q. T. Econ. 407 (1972). For the principle of the diminishing marginal utility of money makes the poor easier to bribe than the rich. (Note that while Posner's ethic of wealth-maximization is designed to work independent of utilities, part of its explicit justification is as a serviceable proxy for utility.) The question whether to give more attention to allocative efficiency or distributive impact will always be one of ethical judgment.

7. "Laws forbidding employment discrimination are costly even when applied to employers who in fact discriminate." R. Posner, The Economics of Justice 360 (1981). "In recent times, however, the most important factor responsible for discrimination probably has been information costs." Id. at 362. Under a "balancing" approach, "many instances of racial discrimination [would be upheld] on efficiency grounds, even if distributive effects were also weighed in the balance . . . [those who think otherwise] may be in for a rude shock." Id. at 363.

8. See Hacking, Was There a Probabilistic Revolution 1800–1930? in 1 The Probabilistic Revolution 45–55 (1987). Hacking, perhaps the leading historian of the rise of probabilism, concludes that the multitude of institutional and social changes in gear with a series of conceptual innovations justifies talk of one "big" revolution, just not in the Kuhnian sense of the term (i.e., no particular intellectual development was of Kuhnian magnitude). Incidentally, the rise of probabilism subtends the whole array of philosophic traditions; for a discussion of probabilism in the Hegelian tradition, see Michael Heidelberger's wide-ranging essay, in 1 The Probabilistic Revolution, supra, at 117–156 (and the references cited therein).

9. See Putnam, The Trail of the Serpent is Over All, in The Many Faces of Realism 16–22 (1987) (a section of the book containing an evocative description of nominalism). I am grateful to K. A. Appiah for drawing my attention to this material.

10. I. Hacking, A Tradition of Natural Kinds (April 14, 1989) (unpublished paper for the Oberlin Colloquium).

11. See Gates, Critical Remarks, in the Anatomy of Racism 319–29 (D. Goldberg ed. 1990) (tendentiously surveying this tradition of enlightenment anti-essentialism).

12. See Krüger, The Slow Rise of Probabilism: Philosophical Arguments in the Nineteenth Century, in 1 The Probabilistic Revolution (1987) at 76 (hereafter Slow Rise of Probabilism) (quoting M. A. Quetelet, Du Système Social et des lois qui le régissent, at IX, 16). He notes that the law of errors was "already seen as an element of universal order somewhat earlier, e.g., by Fourier."

13. Id.

14. M. A. Quetelet, Letters addressed to H. R. H. the Grand Duke of Saxe Coburg and Gotha, on the Theory of Probabilities, as Applied to the Moral and Political Sciences 94 (O. Downes trans. 1849). (The book originally appeared in French in 1846.)

15. Id. at 96.

16. Id.

17. N. Stepan, The Idea of Race in Science: Great Britain 1800–1960 at 135 (1982).

18. Slow Rise of Probabilism, supra note 12, at 68.

19. See M. Resnik, Choices: An Introduction to Decision Theory 62–75 (1987) (discussing the classical [objectivist], frequentist, and subjectivist interpretations of probability).

20. See Porter, Lawless Society: Social Science and the Reinterpretation of Statistics in Germany, 1850–1880, in 1 The Probabilistic Revolution 359 (1987).

21. See infra text accompanying notes 39–43.

22. 481 U.S. 279 (1987).

23. See Kennedy, McCleskey v. Kemp: Race, Capital Punishment and the Supreme Court, 101 Harv. L. Rev. 1388, 1395–1400 (1988).

24. Id. at 1388.

25. Id. at 1400 n.45.

26. Id. at 1400 (quoting McCleskey v. Zant, 580 F. Supp. 338, 356 [1984]).

27. Id. at 1400 (quoting Brief Amici Curiae for Dr. Franklin Fisher, Dr. Richard O. Lempert, Dr. Peter W. Sperlich, Dr. Marvin E. Wolfgang, Professor Hans Zeisel & Professor Franklin E. Zimring at 3, McClesky v. Zant, 580 F. Supp. 388 [N.D. Ga. 1984], rev'd en banc sub nom. McCleskey v. Kemp, 753 F.2d 877 [11th Cir. 1985], aff'd, 481 U.S. 279 [1987]).

28. *Kemp*, 753 F.2d at 877, 896.

29. For further consideration of the role of statistics in law see Zeisel, Statistics as Legal Evidence, in 15 International Encyclopedia of the Social Sciences 246 (1968).

30. McCleskey v. Kemp, 481 U.S. 279 (1987).

31. McClesky, 753 F.2d at 897 (emphasis added).

32. Kennedy, supra note 23, at 1402 (emphasis in original). He observes that "[w]hen the Court announced in Washington v. Davis, 426 U.S. 229 (1976), that discriminatory purpose constituted the *sine qua non* of equal protection claims, it stated as an important justification the need to limit the intrusiveness of federal judicial remedies." Id. at 1414 (citations omitted). Policy considerations thus determine the outcome of fact finding, an approach Kennedy describes as "ridden with pernicious vices." Id. at 1415.
    Of course, the courts haven't invariably rejected statistical evidence. In Title VII litigation statistical evidence is normally invited by the "disparate impact model" (which, in contrast to "disparate treatment," typically examines whether facially neutral employment practices with discriminatory effects are justified by legitimate business reasons). But disparate impact cases standardly involve a collective plaintiff, and do not award damages, aside from back pay.

33. See Delgado, The Ethereal Scholar: Does Critical Legal Studies Have What Minorities Want? 22 Harv. C.R.-C.L.L. Rev. 301, 309 n.50 (1987).

34. See Slow Rise of Probabilism, supra note 12, at 69; cf. Daston, Rational Individuals Versus Laws of Society: From Probability to Statistics, in 1 The Probabilistic Revolution 301 (1987).

35. See Freeman, Legitimizing Racial Discrimination Through Antidiscrimination Law: A Critical Review of Supreme Court Doctrine, 62 Minn. L. Rev. 1049, 1052–57 (1978).

36. See Seltzer, Statistical Persons, 17 Diacritics 82 (Fall 1987) for a fascinating discussion on the role of typicality in both later nineteenth-century American social thought and literary practice.

37. Wash. Post, Sept. 7, 1986 (Magazine), at W13.

38. Williams, Ideology as Style, in Some Consequences of Theory (J. Arac & B. Johnson eds. 1990) (delivered at the 1988 English Institute).

39. My concern here isn't how the court would actually handle the hypothetical case—which has significant differences from *McCleskey,* so that doubtless many other doctrines and precedents would come to the fore—but merely to extend one of the lines of reasoning present in the *McCleskey* decision. (Powell cited features specific to the treatment of the discretionary powers of judicial sentencing in calling for impossibly high standards of proof).

40. Kennedy, supra note 23, at 1420.

41. R. Posner, supra note 7, at 362.

42. Id. at 363; see supra note 1. The absurdity of Posner's presumption that most racial-discriminators are acting rationally is pointed up even with mainstream economics. See D. Kahnemann, P. Slovic & A. Tversky, Judgment Under Uncertainty: Heuristics and Biases (1982) demonstrating that people simply aren't Bayesians (or, at least, are extremely bad ones).

43. R. Posner, supra note 7, at 360–61 (emphasis added).

44. See K. A. Appiah, Probabilistic Harm (July 1989) (unpublished manuscript). I stress that the author is not to blame for my casual misappropriation of his analyses.

45. I wonder if courts have sometimes employed overly subjectivist categories, like "psychological damage," as surrogates for probabilistic harm in cases involving exposure to risk or the increased probability of future harm. (Given two plaintiffs in an otherwise identical position, you might wonder why someone who is psychologically frail should be entitled to greater damages than someone blessed with emotional fortitude and mental equanimity.)

46. To be sure, the legal economists aren't very big on intent in any event; Posner says the distinction between intentional and unintentional torts is essentially trivial. And once you introduce the Posnerian principle of probabilistic compensation as *consent,* intent, as such, becomes pretty elusive.

47. United States v. Carroll Towing Co., 159 F.2d 169 (2d Cir. 1947).

48. A fascinating and wide ranging proposal (which I unfortunately encountered only after having prepared this paper) to quantify tort damages according to evidential probability is Makdisi, Proportional Liability: A Comprehensive Rule to Apportion Tort Damages based on Probability, 67 N.C.L. Rev. 1063 (1989). Makdisi actually considers and rejects "the concept of damages for mere exposure to the risk of harm without actual harm occuring" (id. at 1065 n. 4), though he does not give these cases the analysis that I consider above (and according to which actual harm *has* occurred in such instances). It is clear, however, that administrative costs are likely to constrain greatly the concept of probabilistic harm in awarding damages.

49. J. Coleman, Markets, Morals and the Law (1988).

50. Posner's construction of compensation *ex ante,* as consent has been widely criti-

cized. See, e.g. R. Dworkin, A Matter of Principle 275–80 (1985); J. Coleman, supra note 49, 115–22.

51. Of course, there remains the problem of payment-in-kind. If an injury can be probabilistic, then perhaps damages can be probabilistic too—meted out simply as an increase in the probability of receiving some good. We need another principle here!

52. I mean the grouping and trajectory described in Elie Halévy's classic, E. Halévy, The Growth of Philosophical Radicalism (M. Morris trans. 1955).

53. In the "critical naturalism" that Marxist philosopher Roy Bhaskar has proposed, for example, we find an anti-positivist and anti-reductionist approach to social knowledge. As he argues, "to investigate the limits of naturalism is *ipso facto* to investigate the conditions which make social science, whether or not it is actualized in practice, possible." R. Bhaskar, Reclaiming Reality 67–68 (1989). Bhaskar has charted out his vision of critical naturalism in these books: A Realist Theory of Science (1975), The Possibility of Naturalism (1979), and Scientific Realism and Human Emancipation (1986).

12

Rights, Modernity, Democracy
Agnes Heller

I

Modernity is a breakthrough in the process of deconstructing (in the sense of the German term *Abbauen*) the "natural artifice" which for millennia has secured the survival of the human race. All great civilizations, from ancient Egypt to Mexico through medieval Europe, represented a version of a socio-political arrangement which alone was able—until the emergence of modernity—to integrate men and women into an organized whole, beyond the pale of a village community and the sheer natural ties of blood-relationships. A few attempts have been made to deconstruct the "natural artifice" in order to set up an alternative arrangement, the best known example being Athenian democracy. Until very recently, however, all of them failed.

I have termed the pre-modern socio-political arrangements as versions of the "natural artifice." "Natural" here stands for "arrangement by nature" (*physis*) in the Aristotelian interpretation of the concept. Whatever is common to all socio-political arrangements, exists "by nature." The term "artifice" is the counterpoint of the term "natural." What is natural to the pre-modern perception is no longer natural to the modern one. Modern imagination begins to emerge when the "natural" appears artificial, a man-made construct which can be deconstructed.

A virtually infinite variety of arrangements are possible within the general mode of the natural artifice. What is common in all of them is decisive for us moderns alone. For the non-moderns, it was the difference of the distinct natural artifices that mattered. Not even the early moderns aimed at the deconstruction of the natural artifice; rather, they attempted to streamline, modify, or perfect it. The deconstruction of one element was followed by the deconstruction of several others with increasing speed, until the aim of an *alternative* socio-political arrangement appeared on the horizon. The acceleration of deconstruction is such that when it slows down, at least in the so-called Western world, the process is perceived to have stopped.

If we follow Aristotle's theory that arrangements common to all political bodies and societies, which are otherwise completely different in kind, exist "by nature," we can easily identify "natural arrangements" with the sole exception of the project of modernity. I use the term "the project of modernity" because in the actual, and very short, story of modernity, a few vestiges of the ancient arrangements still survive, and, in some cases, remain well-entrenched. For all practical purposes, the modern arrangement is utterly unnatural. In spite of the radical deconstruction of the alternative arrangement, modernity has not yet proved its ability of a *longue durée* survival. Modernity may or may not endure in the future. It is an open-ended arrangement, an experiment. Modernity can become an alternative social arrangement, and as such "natural," under two conditions.

First, modernity may succeed in becoming a "natural artifice" just as the one it had so successfully deconstructed. In other words, it may become a natural arrangement in the Aristotelian sense (existing "by nature," one shared by each and every culture), accommodating at least as many versions of completely different concrete socio-political arrangements and cultures as the first "natural artifice" did.

Second, and this follows from the first, the longevity of the "experiment" of modernity depends on whether it can generate the mechanisms for cultural-ethical reproduction, and, more importantly, the human motives for this reproduction.

The modern world is frequently described as non-traditional, in contrast with the traditional, pre-modern world. The juxtaposition makes sense on some counts, but not on others. Because the natural artifice of pre-modern arrangements is the so-called time-honored tradition, the deconstruction of this tradition is perceived as radically anti-traditional. Further, the modern world is open-ended, therefore tradition has lost the power of absolute justification. Yet it is equally true that the modern world exhibits a hitherto unprecedented ecstatic relation to "tradition as such" (that is, to several different kinds of tradition, not just one of them). Modernity has been simultaneously moving toward establishing its own traditions. Modernity appears as the executioner of all traditions only where one equates tradition with the natural artifice of pre-modernity. Whenever cultural models have been disentangled from their original socio-political settings, moderns eagerly rush to reinterpret and assimilate them into their new, and still unnatural, alternative socio-political arrangements. That traditional assets are sometimes treated as museum pieces is another matter and it is outside the framework of this paper.

In his celebrated book *After Virtue*,[1] Alasdair MacIntyre makes the apposite observation that traditional ethical (moral) terms are used out of their original context in modernity. He adds that, having been severed from their original setting, these terms no longer make sense. True enough, most of our ethical terms were born out of the pre-modern arrangement, though Greek enlightenment inspired their philosophical interpretations. (As a result of the latter, these terms may be disentangled from their original setting more easily than certain other concepts.) Free-floating cultural traditions gain a new meaning, however, within the framework of the new essential socio-political and cultural patterns. It may well be true that we misunderstand these ethical terms, or that we cannot understand them without adopting an imaginary position in the arrangements of the "natural artifice" of pre-modernity. But this is not a "truth" for us, for it neither edifies nor provides us with an essential insight. MacIntyre's statement draws its pathos from the underlying assumption that modern men and women will be unable to rearrange those ethical terms in their completely different setting even after a considerable interpretive modification. MacIntyre is not the only one who mistakes deconstruction for destruction. For him, as for many others, modernity, this unnatural arrangement, is by definition barren. The deconstruction of "natural artifice" is believed to go with the destruction of tradition as a whole: of all beliefs, convictions, certainties, morals, religions, and meaningful ways of life. If one presupposes, as I do, that deconstruction is not destruction, but rather a radical rearrangement of forms of human cooperation and the mechanisms of problem solving, the circumstance that traditional ethical terms are free-floating and sometimes out of context, is not the foreboding of doom. One may still cherish the trust that sooner or later, they will be rearranged within the socio-political universe of symmetric reciprocity.

What was, after all, that initial socio-political arrangement "by nature"? First and foremost, it meant the rule of a single male. In 99 percent of all human cultures known to us (and this may still be a quantitative understatement), this single male ruled uncontested. In society, that is, within the family, in the *oikos*, this was the case even during the very short periods of republican or democratic constitutions, in which a few males, rather than one, ruled in the political arena. The natural artifice is the arrangement of asymmetric reciprocity. Its world is hierarchically organized. The members of each cluster are equals among each other and unequal, that is, higher or lower, in relation to the members of other clusters. One already belongs to a social cluster in the womb; the newborn's destiny is written upon the cradle. The famous teleological determination of virtues appertains to hierarchy and asymmetry. We may well be equals before God, but in this vale of tears we must live up to our own particular virtues, duties and destinies—those of the perfect master or the slave, of the nobleman or the serf, or of the obedient wife—according to the hierarchy of ends. This arrangement sometimes works fairly well.

In deconstructing this "natural artifice," modernity has embarked on a unique historical experiment. Human coexistence is now to be renegotiated. In the prudent discussion of "the social contract" or a "new covenant," the early moderns found the apposite allegory of this renegotiation. The term "contract" is awkward, evoking unhappy associations, yet is grasps the most crucial aspect of modernity. *Symmetric reciprocity* is the new arrangement, affecting all levels from the family to political decision making through the relationship of cultures, peoples and states.

The well-known predicament of modern men and women, their contingency and their contingency awareness, appears here in a more positive light. Because their destiny is not ready-made at birth, nothing is written upon their cradle They cannot become what they are in the old fashion, by being guided by their own, socially determined *telos*, but only by choosing themselves. Symmetric reciprocity, as the main constitutive element of modern society, does not exclude a hierarchy resulting from the division of labor. It merely asserts that men and women are not thrown into its network at birth, but that they enter into such a division later, potentially (although not really) by their own choice. Actual inequality and formal equality are not contradictions. One is born equal and becomes unequal. One is born free and can become unfree. Monarchy is the natural rule in a world of asymmetric reciprocity. Yet, sporadically, other political arrangements can be accommodated. One assumes that democracy is the natural rule in a world of symmetric reciprocity; one cannot exclude, however, the success of other political arrangements. In our age, totalitarianism has emerged as an alternative political answer to modernity.

Tyranny is less dangerous in a society of asymmetric reciprocity than it is in our society. In an asymmetric society, the hierarchy of the estates, the whole socio-political pyramid, protects the single person against the tyrant. No such protection exists within the arrangement of symmetric reciprocity. Total control and the totalization of the entire socio-political universe can only come about here.

It is too early to assess the success of the new arrangement compared with the old. The new is pregnant with great promise, but it also could give birth to unpredictable dangers. Even if modernity survives and symmetric reciprocity takes democratic forms by opening access to political decision making, action and rule for everyone concerned, the world may still end up spiritless, lacking in culture, void of subject and deprived of meaning. However, these questions of the gravest importance are beyond the horizon of the present line of inquiry.

It is essential to distinguish between the concept of natural *law* and that of natural *right*. In his discussion of natural rights in pre-modern times, Leo Strauss, in *Natural Right and History,*[2] merges "natural law" and "natural right" theories in order to contrast both to historicism. I am convinced, however, that the historical circumstance in which historicism came to be opposed to both concepts is not a sufficient reason to identify them.

Natural law concepts are very well placed in the framework of the "natural artifice." If all customs, as well as social or political institutions that happen to be shared by all integrations, exist "by nature," one can easily draw the conclusion that the common aspect of socio-political arrangements is that they are what they are by the "law of nature." Like all legitimizing devices, the conception of "natural law" too allows for a critical use, as can be seen in the case of Antigone. One can have recourse to this device in claiming justice. In other words, certain well-defined rights derive from the law of nature. But the old concept of natural law cannot be used as a tool for deconstructing the natural artifice itself, unless "natural law" is interpreted in the light of so-called "natural rights," because the idea of "human rights," this archetype of natural rights, upsets the time-honored balance of asymmetric reciprocity by challenging it head-on.

Hegel dismissed the natural right theory as a fiction[3] in order to replace it with yet another fiction. But Hegel's argument deserves closer scrutiny. In terms of this argument, statements such as "man is born free" or "all men are born free" are not only false, but they are also guilty of reasserting the ontology of the old "natural law." In the old theory, Hegel ruminates, free men are free because they are thus born, slaves are slaves also because they are thus born, and the like. In stating that we are all free because we all are thus born, we entrench ourselves in a false ontology. In fact, we are not born free but we can nevertheless become free; this is the truth of our age, Hegel contends.

However, statements such as "all men are born free" need not be unmasked as fictions, because they are meant to be fictions (or metaphors). Their ontological character is illusory. *They are ethical and political principles.* they are *not theoretical,* but rather pure practical principles. The first part of Rousseau's famous dictum gains its political weight from its counterpoint contained in the second part: "Man is born free and everywhere is in chains."[4] It is not an explanatory, but rather a politico-rhetorical device. The Kantian distinction between regulative and constitutive theoretical principles on the one hand, and regulative and constitutive practical principles on the other, was a sophisticated philosophical rendering of actual ethical and political practices. The famous principles of the Declaration of Independence, which, in terms of the text, were held to be self-evident truths, illuminate how such principles are used practically, both in regulating action and constituting a new socio-political arrangement, in other words, a constitution.

The same aspects of "natural right" theories which were criticized by Hegel could also be considered a credit on several counts. First, "natural right" theories use pre-modern devices ("man is born such and such") in order to upset the pre-modern *status quo ante;* and this is indeed a debit. It can be transformed, however, into a credit if it is well done. Deconstruction, from ancient sophism through post modern practices, prefers to upset time-honoured ideas, customs and ideologies from within, and on their own grounds, without using any further presuppositions. Yet "human (natural) right" theories do not stop at this stage. The moment they use rights as an *arche,* they take an external position. And at this point we again face Hegel's disapproval. Principles are empty Oughts, he contends, if they have no actuality. And, indeed, if men are everywhere in chains, the "self-evident truth" that men are born free, has no actuality at all. By way of conclusion, one can only utter the seemingly empty sentence that men *ought* to be free.

Without entering this complex and rhetoric-ridden debate, I am inclined to credit again the "human (natural) right" theory with at least an inkling of two great intuitions. First, the claim that men ought to be what they are, namely free, is a streamlined reformulation of the Aristotelian attempt to unify *physis* and *nomos.* This time, however, the unity is based upon an arrangement of symmetric reciprocity; this is the line of division between the "natural artifice" and modernity.

Second, the theory suggests that agreement and disagreement in theo-retical-speculative matters and agreement/disagreement on the practi-cal plane can be entirely separated from one another. The significance of this second grand intuition needs to be explored in some detail.

Let us recapitulate Rousseau's logic: all men are born free, yet they are everywhere in chains. They ought to be free (unity of *physis* and *nomos*). Obviously, here Ought is not inferred from Is. The sentence "all men are born free" is a value statement. The second sentence comes closer to a statement of fact: "they (men) are everywhere in chains." Whether or not this statement of fact is true is irrelevant from the normative point of view. As far as the norm is concerned, men simply should be what they by nature are, namely, free. One can con-tinue to discuss the truth content of the statement "men are every-where in chains." One can first dismantle its rhetoric, and figure out afterwards who is free and who is unfree, what makes some freer than others, under what condition can people be freer than they now are and the like. One can also continue to disagree on all points. To cut a long story short, the recognition of the diversity of opinions is built into the original stance of the human right concept. Philosophers, being for the most part uneasy with open-ended dialogues, did what they could to hide before the public eye this "blot on the escutcheon"; the permissiveness, the pluralism and the practical liberalism which are inherent in the concept of human right.

The value-statement "all men are born free" is both descriptive and expressive. We hold it to be a self-evident truth that all men are born free. It is precisely because of this shared conviction that men are, indeed, born free. Put bluntly, if this self-evident truth is universally held, then the status of all men will be one of "freely born." Because they are "freely born," all human beings will have an equal status from the moment of their birth. This sentence is simply the expression of the new socio-political arrangement, and this is precisely why it can serve as the best means, as well as the best battle cry, for deconstruct-ing the old.

Those who challenge the truth-content of that self-evident truth—"all men are born free"—on the grounds of the unequal distribution of wealth, pinpoint a burning social issue but misunderstand the state-ment they believe to undermine. Among the free-born men of Athens, some were rich and others poor, some were the offspring of good fam-ilies, others came from families of ill repute. But they were all born free, whereas others were born slaves. The famous battle-cry has spelled out the absolute difference between the natural artifice and the new (modern) arrangement. Slavery is an anomaly in modernity, whereas the unequal distribution of wealth is not. The latter is the matter which needs to be addressed within the framework of the new arrangement, and it is to be addressed in different ways within different forms of life.

If some (not all) people are freely born, their freedom is determined by the very existence of those born unfreely. What they can do that others cannot is what "being born freely" means. If every human being is freely born, the concrete contents of having been freely born disappears. Freedom becomes an abstraction, an empty possibility. This is why the question of what freedom is needs to be raised. The answers to this question are practically infinite, and they are eminently practical. Modernity is about the concretization of "freedom."

Every form of life in modernity is, by definition, the concretization of the abstract possibility of having been born free. This is not meant as a predictive, but rather as an analytical statement. There is no longer a "social pyramid." The modern world is flat because it is symmetrical. This is precisely why modern values can be universal. The universality of a value is a perfectly simple thing. It means that the opposite of the value cannot be chosen as a value. Freedom is certainly such a universal value, since no one is publicly committed to unfreedom as a value. The value of life also comes close to attaining a universal status.

At the moment of their conception, universal values became the main objects of enthusiasm. This is the story of the French Revolution and Kant's philosophy. The idea of Freedom still triggers enthusiasm, particularly in the moments of liberation. But where modernity is taken for granted and when it has reached its adequate political form (one or another type of democracy), enthusiasm recedes, and the work of concretisation of the universal value(s) takes off.

Rights are the institutionalized forms of the concretization of universal values (both of the value of freedom and of life). They can be substantive or procedural. Allegorically speaking, they can establish frameworks for action, negotiation and much else, as they serve as road signs for steps taken in the direction of the further "concretisation" of values.

Right-language is, and should be, the *lingua franca* of modern democracy which, in contrast to the ancient model, includes liberalism. Right-language cannot achieve full meaning if it is spoken from the position of the "natural artifice." Symmetric reciprocity is the condition of the mastery of this language. But right-language cannot be a mother tongue. The mother tongue is the lingo of forms of life. More forms of life give rise to greater differences and more mother tongues.

354 / Rights, Modernity, Democracy

Yet right-language is not a second language and it is certainly not an artificial one. One learns it together with the mother tongue, but it is spoken only if the occasion so requires.

Let me emphasize once again that modernity is a newborn and that modern democracy is still in its first experimental stage. We do not know how things are going to develop, but we can voice certain concerns. Should right-language be raised to the status of a mother tongue, no real difference could be accommodated in the modern world. Life would not merely be uniform, but also void of creative imagination. In addition, it would be a life without community and immediacy. And the converse also seems true: if right-language will not be generally spoken as a *lingua franca*, modernity might easily go down into the history books (if still there will be any) as yet another misguided and miscarried experiment of the *homo sapiens*.

III

Rights are formal and abstract, but not in the same way or to the same extent as universal values are. They always include a substantive element ("freedom for what, in what, to what" and the like). These substantive elements are inherited from our ancestors. Referring to rights means to claim something that is due, which is justice. The concept of rights stems from the concept of justice, but they are different in kind.

In my book, *Beyond Justice*,[5] I have distinguished between two main types of justice: static justice and dynamic justice.

Static justice is the perfect case of what I have termed the formal concept of justice: the norms and rules which constitute a human cluster, should be applied consistently and continuously to each and every member of that cluster. Members of the same cluster are constituted as equals by the very norms and rules which apply to them, while members who belong to different and interrelated clusters are constituted as unequals, given that different norms and rules apply to them. If clusteral norms are applied continuously and consistently, everyone gets what is due to him or her. Since rules and norms define with a certain precision what is due to whom, no conflict arises about the conception of distributing of honors, things, services. Conflict arises only about their actual distribution. People do not claim "rights" in claiming what is due to them; rather, they claim satisfaction.

In the case of dynamic justice, certain norms and rules themselves are declared unjust. The claimants or contesters want a "new deal," a new set of norms or rules to be substituted for the old ones. Insofar as they aim at delegitimizing actual norms and rules, they have recourse to values, in particular, to those of freedom and life. Normally, delegitimizing claims do not play the first fiddle. The matter is decided by violence or, at best, by negotiations backed by force.

In modernity, dynamic justice has become an everyday phenomenon. Since daily life cannot be the territory of constant street fights, alternative solutions have been sought for, and dynamic justice proved to be a fertile heritage. Delegitimizing and legitimizing claims alike began to play the role of the first fiddle in the process of conflict solving.

The same story can also be recounted in reverse. Once it has become a self-evident truth that all men are born free, everything that is due to free persons is due to all persons. What is due to free persons traditionally? First, maximum protection of the law, if there is any; second, access to communal-political decision making, if the latter is common practice. Hence, if everyone is born free, everyone has to be equal before the law and receive maximum protection under the law. Furthermore, everyone needs to have equal access to institutions of political and communal decision making. Yet equal and maximum protection under the law and equal access to power are never completely realized. Old wounds begin to ache again, and completely unforeseen problems emerge. Apart from everything else, basic political and legal categories are the main training ground of hermeneutics. What seems to be a fair amount of protection, equality or political power today, will appear ridiculously unsatisfactory tomorrow. Interpretation guided by dynamic justice becomes a matter of course, a daily practice.

Whenever men and women argued on behalf of alternative rules and norms, they had recourse to values such as freedom and life. Since dynamic justice is a matter of course and needs to be constantly practiced, it has to take institutionalized forms. The procedure of having recourse to values such as freedom or life, also requires that certain basic patterns be followed. It is the right-language that provides these patterns.

Thus, right-language performs a double task. It is the major vehicle of deconstructing the natural artifice from the standpoint of symmetric reciprocity. It is also the language of conflict management within the socio-political arrangement of symmetric reciprocity. In the first capacity, it has an air of nobility around it. In the second capacity it is but a tool, an equation, having a purely instrumental value. And yet it is in this second capacity that right-language can become natural in the ancient sense, that is, as something common to all cities, states, and all peoples. Ancient travellers from Herodotus to Marco Polo knew that wherever they visited so-called "civilized" countries they would meet persons born to rule and others born to obey. They merely had to find out who was born to rule and who born to obey, and, further, the forms of ruling and obeying. Under a possible natural arrangement of symmetric reciprocity, cultures may well differ from each other to the same extent as China differed from Venice, in Marco Polo's time. The "only" difference now would be that the truth that all men *and women* are born free, would be taken as self-evident in each of them.

IV

Alasdair MacIntyre, in his latest book *Whose Justice? Which Rationality?*[6] played out the best, and, as far as I can see, the only unbeatable trump-card against liberalism in general, and against right-language in particular. MacIntyre argues that by emphasizing difference or in subscribing to total cultural and epistemological relativism, one merely reconfirms all fundamental claims of liberalism. As long as one believes in a community of discourse, where discourse is conducted according to neutral, impersonal, tradition-independent standards, every concrete language can be translated into this common language. This is one way of easily accommodating each and every difference. When this illusion is abandoned by post-Enlightenment persons, all everyday worlds are treated as distinct and unique examples of pragmatic necessities and every framework of all-embracing belief that extends beyond the realm of pragmatic necessity will be regarded as unjustified. Post-Enlightenment liberals view the order of traditions as a series of masquerades. Theirs are the internationalized languages of modernity, "the languages of everywhere and nowhere."[7] An absolutistic language alone, the language of a particular form of life which claims full rightness and truth for itself, presents a *not merely philosophical but also social* alternative to an all-encompassing liberal universe.

I think this is a correct assumption. Every view and each form of life can be accommodated by liberalism except "absolute absolutism." Absolutists claim that only the particular kind of truth they acknowledge is true, only the kind of action they recommend is proper, virtuous, or right, whereas all alternative views and practices are either untrue or wrong. Absolutism finds an easy accommodation within liberalism; moreover, liberalism itself frequently takes an absolutistic shape. "Absolute absolutism" makes the same statements as absolutism, yet it denies (to repeat: not merely philosophically but also socially) the right of others (other absolutists and relativists alike) to make a similar claim for the truth and rightness of their own theory or practice. This is why "absolute absolutism" cannot be accommodated by sincere liberalism. In addition, "absolute absolutism" is the language of the "natural artifice," whereas right-language is one of the major tools of deconstructing this artifice.

I coined the term "sincere liberalism" in order to juxtapose it with "insincere liberalism." Liberalism becomes insincere if it pretends to be able to accommodate "absolute absolutism." Just recently, in the wake of the Rushdie affair, we witnessed a less than edifying display of insincere liberalism. A liberalism which maintains that because all cultures are unique and need to be respected in their uniqueness, one must be "understanding" toward the specificity of exterminating ideological enemies. Tactful tolerance towards the call for ideological murder is not liberalism but simply a bad joke. Right-language is, as a rule, drab and commonsensical. Yet sometimes courage is needed to talk this language, and the need for the old enthusiasm may recur. Readiness to display the old-fashioned enthusiasm is one of the major characteristics of sincere liberalism. In a political context, sincere liberalism is democratic liberalism.

It is difficult to remain true to sincere or democratic liberalism as long as one juxtaposes right-language with historicism. Philosophy as a merely speculative enterprise can produce marvels with transcendentalism. However, speaking the "right-language" is not a theoretical, but rather a pragmatic, practical, and judgmental exercise. Here transcendental deductions are not conclusive. On my part, I have recommended the introduction of the historical dimension into speculations about so-called universals on the theoretical-philosophical plane; but this issue is extraneous to the concerns of the present paper. Put briefly, right-language need not present itself as *the* rational language of the human race beyond space, time, and history; neither should it make a (fraudulent) plea for total impartiality. Commitment to right-language does not need to be combined with the belief that rational argumentation leads to the victory of the best argument without any other conditions having been met. Since right-language is not the embodiment of *logos*, those who think that it needs to become the *lingua franca* of our age, are not logocentrist. Making the recommendation for right-language is a very general commitment to the modern world as the world of symmetric reciprocity. Right-language can be termed

a historical and conditional universal (it is conditional because absolute absolutists do not speak this language). No commitment to any
concrete form of life is implied in speaking the right-language as the
lingua franca; but a commitment to rejecting several forms of life is
certainly implied. Democratic liberalism can embrace all metaphys-
ico-ontological claims, all kinds of sciences, creeds, vocations, plays,
eccentricities. But it cannot shelter all practical (political and ethical)
institutional arrangements, practices, judgments, and exercises. In the
same fashion as natural (human) right theories once deconstructed the
old "natural artifice" in the political theatre of the West, so does right-
language continue to deconstruct systems of asymmetry, whether they
reappear in traditional forms or assume a certain new, streamlined
shape. From totalitarianism to patriarchy, from group discrimination
to all kinds of institutionalized subservience, right-language now continues to challenge all principles, institutions, and arrangements of
asymmetric reciprocity.

V

Rights are first and foremost vehicles of conflict resolution, although they also contribute to the emergence of certain conflicts and
to their expression. Let me briefly illustrate the situation in which the
right-language needs to be spoken and how the language works
through a model.

Let us assume that there are thousands and thousands of different
cultures on our planet. Let us also assume that each of them speaks a
mother tongue which is untranslatable into the mother tongue of any
other. They are all unique. One culture is pluralistic, the other is not,
one is individualistic, the other communitarian. They subscribe to different scientific paradigms, religions, artistic practices. One form of
life values a work-ethic, the other prefers leisure; one of them culti-
vates monogamy, the other promiscuity. Actions which are regarded
as completely rational within one form of life will be viewed as entirely irrational in the other.

Let us further assume that there are certain conflicts between those
cultures; we may reasonably assume this much on the basis of historical experience. Conflicts can be solved by violence, force, negotiation
and discourse. In order to negotiate and to conduct a discourse, a
common language must be spoken. Since each culture in our model
speaks only its own language, and since this language cannot be translated into any other, negotiation and discourse are by definition ex-

cluded. What remains is violence and force. Put bluntly, in the case of a conflict, the stronger exterminates or enslaves the weaker. With a few exceptions, this is the way intercultural conflicts were solved in pre-modern times. Moral exhortation apart, this solution is no longer feasible, at least in the long run. Due to the modern development of industrial technology, both war and control have become total. If men and women who inhabit entirely different cultures do not want to commit collective suicide, they must embrace the two remaining alternatives: negotiation and discourse. In order to negotiate or to conduct a discourse, they need to talk to one another. In order to talk to one another, they need a common language. No culture can superimpose its own language on all others. Given their complete differences, other cultures would not accept the offer (absolute absolutism). What remains is to invent a *lingua franca* spoken by every culture as its second language. It is not necessary that the whole mother tongue of each culture should be translated into this *lingua franca,* only the portion that enables citizens of each and every culture to address their conflicts in practical terms, to seek a solution together. This is how to invent the right language.

But right-language is never the starting point. These cultures first need to have something in common without which they cannot possibly invent right-language as their *lingua franca.* What they first need to have in common is the arrangement of symmetric reciprocity; or, as a minimum condition, they all need to accept as a self-evident truth that all human beings are born free.

Theoretically, we have maneuvered ourselves into a circle. But in practice, there are no circles; there are no pure models either. There is no "yes" or "no," only "more" or "less."

Although moving in circles is the headache of theory, not of political practice, a formidable problem remains which causes a headache in both theory and practice. The assumption that all cultures, in themselves unique, of our pure model can address their conflicts in the language of rights does not imply that they can also solve their problems by using this language. Insofar as they can, we are speaking in terms of rational compromise. Yet, sometimes two rights are on a collision course. If this happens, intercultural discourse has to address the very "language of rights" in order to provide a new scheme of interpretation. Intercultural discourse can be conducted with the mediation of an interpreter. All cultures in a discourse situation can make reference to their own values as ones embedded in their own form of life. The aim of such a discourse is consensus on an entirely new intercultural arrangement. I have described such a discursive procedure in my books *Radical Philosophy*[8] and *Beyond Justice,*[9] and space does not allow for recapitulating it in this context. Yet what needs still to be emphasized is the very condition of the possibility of such a consensus *which is a higher order consensus prior to the discourse.* At this point, it does not suffice to subscribe to freedom as a value and to the self-evident statement that all men are born free. A culture must necessarily accept that freedom is the highest (supreme) value. We are thus back at the circle, though on a higher level.

The age of philosophy of history confronted us with the choice between everything or nothing. Everything became nothing. But nothing did not become everything, only something. Rights are far from being everything—but they are certainly something.

NOTES

1. A. MacIntyre, After Virtue (1981).

2. L. Strauss, Natural Right and History (1953).

3. G. Hegel, Philosophy of Right (T. Knox trans. 1942).

4. J. Rousseau, The Social Contract (C. Sherover trans. 1984).

5. A. Heller, Beyond Justice (1987).

6. A. MacIntyre, Whose Justice? Which Rationality? (1988).

7. Id. at 395–96.

8. A. Heller, Radical Philosophy, 106–33 (1984).

9. A. Heller, supra note 5, at 138–52.

13

Algorithmic Justice
Alan Wolfe

> *Julius stopped in front of his friend. "Listen,*
> *Rupert. If there were a perfectly just judge I*
> *would kiss his feet and accept his punishments*
> *upon my knees. But these are merely words*
> *and feelings. There is no such being and even*
> *the concept of one is empty and senseless. I tell*
> *you, Rupert, it's an illusion, an illusion."*
> *"I don't believe in a judge," said Rupert, "but*
> *I believe in justice. And I suspect you do too,*
> *or you wouldn't be getting so excited."*
> *"No, no, if there is no judge there is no justice,*
> *and there is no one, I tell you, no one."*[1]

If there are no metanarratives, is justice possible? With the exception of religious belief—to which it is often compared[2]—the quest for justice invariably has involved grand stories that take people beyond the concerns of the material world into considerations of the transcendental. The just act, the just person, and the just society have been viewed as possessing an otherworldly nature, as if only heroic action on the part of heroic actors could achieve, or even approximate, them. Plato's stories may be, in Geertzian language,[3] "thick," while Rawls' are "thin," but neither points toward standards directly observable in the everyday course of social practice, lying, as they are, either hidden in shadows or behind a veil of ignorance.

Those philosophical dispositions known as postmodernism, poststructuralism, and deconstruction[4]—in questioning whether there exist any standards of meaning, evaluation, taste, truth, or morality outside of the specific ways we make contingent rhetorical arguments about such contested terrains—lead inexorably to the conclusion that no transcendental metanarratives of justice can exist. To be sure, skeptics such as Stanley Fish would claim, this does not mean that no standards of justice are possible, just as Barbara Herrnstein Smith argues that the absence of any uncontested aesthetic standard does not mean that objects of art cannot be assigned value.[5] Such arguments instead try to show that the standards we develop for such matters as justice and truth are the products of specific language games, conventions, shared normative understandings or community practices, due to change when new contingencies arise from whatever source, including pure happenstance.

There seems little question that the air admitted to discussions of law through the windows opened by postmodernism has been refreshing. Perhaps interpreters of texts will never again be quite so certain in insisting that certain conclusions—including ones dealing with the lives and liberties of real people—follow directly and automatically from materials written down generations ago. But the epistemological skepticism introduced by the overlap between law and literary criticism does not resolve fundamental issues involved in the quest for justice so much as it alters their focus. If meaning does not exist in texts but instead if the interpretations brought to those texts by readers, what we require, instead of a theory of the text, is a theory of the reader.

People read the texts that other people write. (Although the structure of DNA has been compared to a text, to date I have not seen any efforts to deconstruct the texts of living species besides our own; similarly, non-living species, such as computers, can generate texts which humans, if they wish, can deconstruct, but machines do not seem capable of putting into any interpretative context the instructions given to them.) Moreover, not all people read and write. Infants do not, and neither do the illiterate nor the brain dead. The capacity to read and write is a potential, something that can only be undertaken by a self: a mature, socialized human individual who has grown up in a society and possesses the tools of culture given to her by that society.[6] No adequate theory of readers is possible without a sociological theory of the self, without some notions, coming perhaps, from writers like Mead, Schutz, Garfinkel, or Goffman—which seek to define the self, not as found in nature (for in nature there are no selves) but only as the product of society and its dynamics.[7]

Sociological theory since the nineteenth century has been premised upon one or another form of philosophical anthropology. Theorists may differ in how they claim humans to be a special and unique species, but it is common to all the great thinkers in the sociological tradition that humans do have special capacities and that these capacities are a product of the way they organize their artificial environments. Since interpretation, at the very least, assumes that human beings can be reflective agents who can assign meaning to texts—including those texts by which their affairs are regulated—and adjust the meanings they find in those texts to meet the contexts and contingencies within which they find themselves, contemporary philosophical skepticism ought to find itself in historic continuity with the philosophical anthropology of sociological theory. And yet it does not. "Essentialism" runs against the grain of the contingency and relativism so characteristic of these philosophical tendencies, since, in assigning fundamental qualities to the human species, it assumes that at least some things are certain and exist in spite of the interpretations we give them. Indeed the distinction between nature and culture which lies at the heart of sociological theory, according to theorists like Herrnstein Smith, needs to be disarmed "of its ideological power. . . . With respect to human preferences," she writes, "nothing is uniform, universal, natural, fixed, or determined in advance, either for the species generally, or for any specific individual, or for any portion or fraction of the species, by whatever principle, sociological or other, it is segmented and classified."[8]

In short, postmodern philosophical perspectives are not only not neutral toward the way sociologists have defined the self, but actively hostile. Foucault's description of man as an historically contingent creation about to be washed away from the sand by the next epistemological wave hovers over nearly all such contemporary approaches to knowledge.[9] In the heady Nietzschean atmosphere of contemporary thought, talk of the self verges close to humanism—only humans, remember, have selves—and that particular combination of naivete and arrogance alleged to be characteristic of Enlightenment thought. From a postmodernist perspective, one is led to address such apparently human matters as desire and need without positing the existence of autonomous human agents, as, for example, again in the case of Herrnstein Smith—who coins the phrase "desired/able" in order to indicate

> that the valued effect in question need not have been specifically desired (sought, wanted, imagined, or intended) as such by any subject. In other words, its value for certain subjects may have emerged independent of any specific human intention or agency and, indeed, may have been altogether a product of the chances of history or, as we say, a matter of luck.[10]

Smith's concern is with the process of evaluation, with the way in which we establish standards of aesthetic judgment. But the question raised by her denial of human agency can be raised for theories of justice as well, since conceptions of justice always involve questions of evaluation. Indeed the stakes involved in developing a theory of human agency are higher when we discuss justice than when we discuss taste, for one can imagine people living in the absence of any transcendental standard of the latter—although I am not sure I would want to—but it is almost impossible to imagine them, at least in human form, living in the absence of the former. Yet legal theorists at-

364 / Algorithmic Justice

tracted to postmodernism are as reluctant as literary theorists to acknowledge the existence of an autonomous self; Thomas Heller, for example, discussing the indeterminacy of the law, points out that it "does not arise because the standpoint of the human individual is in some way privileged or central. Rather, indeterminacy is an element of the grammar of complex systems or a feature of the observation/system relationship." [11]

The minimal condition for a theory of justice is that we find a justification or legitimation for constraint. Other participants in the intellectual division of labor, especially economists, may argue for freedom, although it is not too difficult to perceive that the market is a prison as well as an opportunity.[12] Law talk, by contrast, is always explicitly about regulation, the intellectual problem at hand being one of understanding—and in some cases trying to change—rules that make possible life in groups. Note that even those most committed to a skeptical epistemological stance in no way deny the constraints involved in thinking about law; their point is simply that those constraints have no ultimate justifications, only local, contingent, and socially constructed ones. Given that there will be constraints, we can judge a theory of judgment by the legitimacy of the standards it establishes for restraining our actions. The postmodernist reply that there are *no* non-contingent standards is useless; for even the most radical versions of postmodern theory, as we have seen, still presuppose a human ability to interpret the contexts in which people find themselves. If we accept that minimal philosophical anthropology as our non-contingent standard, the question we can ask is: how, in the absence of *both* a theory of texts *and* a theory of people, can postmodern theories of justice legitimize obedience to rules in such a way as to make those who are subject to such rules better interpreters of the rules that rule over them?

Epistemological skeptics imagine two ways by which human affairs will be regulated if we deny the possibility of any standards of justice outside the purely contingent and local. One was suggested by Thrasymachus—the first postmodernist—and is repeated, in more elegant form, by Foucault and those inspired by him. Everything being power, the only antidote to oppression is a transformation in the relations of power. Appeals to justice, from such a perspective, are naive and self-defeating, a lingering symptom of wooly-headed humanism. One might just as well ask an earthquake to stop rumbling as ask holders of power to bind their actions in accord with some pre-existing standard of justice. Replace all justice discourse by power discourse and then we can begin to talk about who makes the rules and how. "Does might make right?" Stanley Fish asks. "In a sense the answer I must give is yes, since in the absence of a perspective independent of interpretation some interpretive perspective will always rule by having won out over its competitors." [13] Or, more epigrammatically, "the gun is always at your head." [14]

It seems doubtful that an approach emphasizing the ubiquity of power and force in human affairs could generate an account of justice that takes cognizance of human interpretative capacities, although someone may come up with an argument to that effect. The conventional response, in this case, seems like the correct one: if all knowledge reflects the power of contending forces, then the way to constrain individuals is not to rely on persuasion but coercion. Fish, who believes that persuasion—e.g., rhetoric—is coercion, consequently holds that human agents have strikingly little freedom in these matters: "In the end we are always self-compelled, coerced by forces—beliefs, convictions, reasons, desires—from which we cannot move one inch away." [15] The theory of the self associated with any such answer to the quest for justice is a theory asserting that there can be no self, or at least not a very autonomous one.

As an alternative to the justice-lies-in-the-interest-of-the-stronger kind of argument, there is another way to think about constraint contained within postmodern approaches to legal regulation, and it is the one on which I want to focus in this paper. There being no truths or standards outside the operation of a system, this way of thinking argues, then the rules that structure the system lie within the system. Each system is governed by its own laws, and such laws have as their goal the reproduction of whatever system in which they are found. The inspiration for such ways of thinking about rules comes, not from the grand tradition of Western metanarratives about justice, but instead from cybernetics, information theory, economics, population ecology, quantum physics, cellular autonoma, linguistics, sociobiology, artificial intelligence, DNA, and chaos theory. I will call such conceptions of justice *algorithmic*. They offer a different solution to the nihilism that seems to lie within deconstruction. We do not, if we follow such an approach, have to conclude that because there are no metanarratives there are no rules. Rather we can govern our affairs and at the same time avoid privileging any one version of the good by imagining our rules to be self-referential to that activity, whatever it is, in which we find ourselves engaged.

Although algorithmic notions of the good avoid the stark view of coercion inherent in arguments that equate knowledge and power, they are even less charitable toward the possibility of an interpretative and autonomous self. Algorithms are rules designed to be followed with as little interpretive variation as possible. They may help explain how computers function and how species other than our own regulate their affairs, although, as I will try to show, there is a strong case that even in those cases non-algorithmic rule-following is more important than researchers, at first, realized. They can, however, only be applied to human affairs if we accept the notion that humans are precoded rule-followers. Yet if humans are following instructions algorithmically, then they will have no interpretive capacities, will be unable to read texts, will not be able to supply meaning to documents that can inherently have no meaning, and, as a result, will be subject to a fate of following rules without any input into how those rules are formulated and applied. Surely that is a conclusion that postmodernists would wish to avoid at all costs.

At one level, postmodernists certainly do wish to avoid such a conclusion; Fish, for example, finds in Chomskian linguistics an almost complete algorithmic system, a formalism of truly nightmarish dimensions.[16] One alternative to Chomsky, of course, would be to develop a kind of sociolinguistics—such as that associated with ethnomethodology in sociology—in which meaning would be understood as what human speakers provide in the contexts within which their conversations took place.[17] But a move in this direction is a move toward the self, constituting a step back up the slippery slope of essentialism that we have just, in turning to postmodernism, slid down. Postmodern theories of justice, I will argue, faced with a choice between making a commitment to a theory of the self demanded of their interpretive face and relying on algorithmic conceptions of rule following associated with their skeptical face, tend to adopt the latter. Sometimes this is explicit, such as in the case of Niklas Luhmann, Gunther Teubner, and others attracted by cybernetics and information theory.[18] At other times the move toward algorithmic justice is more reluctant, opting not for "hard" algorithms, such as those associated with artificial intelligence and Chomskian linguistics, but instead for "soft" algorithms associated with the automatic and "natural" following of the rules of a practice. Still, hard or soft, what characterizes algorithmic justice is a lack of appreciation for the rule-making, rule-applying, rule-interpreting capacities of human beings and an emphasis instead on the rule-following character. The price postmodernism pays for its flirtation with algorithmic conceptions of justice is a very high one:

the denial of liberation, play, and spontaneity that inspired radical epistemologies in the first place.

II

To provide legitimacy for the enormously difficult task of coordinating our actions toward common goals without relying on force, a conception of justice must *mean* something to those who will be governed by its imperatives. Yet meaning is precisely what texts cannot possess according to much of the philosophical inclination under discussion here. Texts nonetheless contain words. Do those words convey anything if they do not convey meaning?

At least for some thinkers working within postmodern philosophical assumptions, texts, if not capable of conveying meaning, *are* capable of conveying information. It ought to be immediately clear that information and meaning are not only not the same thing, but that they can work at cross purposes. (American voters, for example, have more information than ever before about the candidates for whom they vote, yet seem to cast votes that are less meaningful than ever before, understood in the sense of making sense of how they behave.) Meaning is a macro-phenomenon that involves making larger sense out of smaller bits, while information, especially in the computer age, reduces larger complexity into smaller, and presumably more manageable, units. If we accept one distinction between symbols and signs—that the former work top down and the latter bottom up[19]— then symbols can have meaning, while signs convey information.

From the standpoint of a theory of communication, information has remarkable properties, ones that have been seized upon by theorists to develop information processing machines of great potential. When it was discovered that certain phenomena found in nature, such as the structure of DNA, were also understandable as an information processing mechanism, the possibility of a unified theory of cognition began to seem possible. Surely a number of human activities, such as language, could be understood as the reduction of complexity through information processing, and, since thinking was believed to take place in its own language,[20] it was a short step to the conclusion that the human brain was also an information processor. Once that insight was accepted, then all human activities—including not only how we speak, but how we write poetry, compose music, make our laws, conduct our economic activities, and everything else—could be understood to be governed by similar dynamics. The unified theory of cognition promised by the information processing model, in other words, offered to unify, not only what we understand to be the sciences, but to link the sciences together with both the social sciences and the humanities.

What is often called postmodernism is fascinated by the potential of information processing. This is certainly true of the inventor of the phrase, Jean Francois Lyotard, who has a tendency to take extreme, and rather dubious, positions vis-a-vis the capabilities of information processing, such as suggesting that artificial intelligence will be capable of translating from one "natural" language to another, that computers could "aid groups discussing metaprescriptives by supplying them with the information they usually lack for making knowledgeable decisions," and that data banks will serve as "nature" for postmodern individuals.[21] But the fascination with information processing is not just a Lyotardian quirk. The writings of Deleuze and Guattari, for example, are filled with images of machines that program other machines in ever-recurring fashion, down to the notion that the structure of desire takes the form of a binary system.[22] It may well be the case that the tendency to attribute to information all the capacities that one has stripped from meaning characterizes many thinkers who believe that knowledge is defined by relationships among signs, rather than by reference to any "reality," including symbols containing meaning, standing behind the signs themselves.

Information theory is usually thought of in connection with developments in cognitive science, mathematics, linguistics, decision theory, and rational choice theory—all of them closer in spirit to the epistemological certainty and rationalistic clarity that postmodernism rejects. Yet the matter is clearly more complicated than that. The two intellectual giants who created the framework for postmodernism and deconstruction—Nietzsche and Saussaure—were both attracted to cybernetic notions of self-regulating systems because the rules governing such systems made it possible for the relationships between things to keep them suspended in air without being either ground down to a reality beneath them or tied to a reality above them.

The case of Nietzsche is particularly instructive in this regard given the importance that he has assumed in the law and literature debates.[23] But it is not the Nietzsche whose perspectivism is so attractive to critical legal scholars that is important here, but instead the Nietzsche of *Zarathustra*. In speaking of the metamorphosis of the lion into the child in one of his early speeches, Zarathustra introduces the image of a "self-propelled wheel," preparing the way for his later discussion of the eternal recurrence—images and concepts quite similar to the ideas of Goedel, Escher, and Bach which have been found to be compatible with the age of information machines.[24] Moreover, even if we do not accept the notion of the eternal recurrence as a cosmology—which Nehamas, in defending Nietzsche asks that we do not—we can still accept it not as a "theory of the world but a view of the self."[25] Nietzsche's somewhat mysterious references to the notion that if we could live our lives over again we would live them in exactly the same form as we have can, therefore, be read as a kind of *gedankenexperiment* designed to show that the world is still possible without selves that can be defined by essential, non-contested, features.

A fascination with eternal recurrence, with the notion that automatic processes can generate exactly similar responses over and over again, would seem to characterize all those thinkers who are skeptical of the possibility of autonomous, choosing, selves. Considering the importance attached to notions about the death of the author associated with Barthes—let alone the Derridean suspicion of there being anything outside the text—self-recurrence takes on a special fascination in the literary culture inspired by postmodernism, recognizing in Borges, for example, the postmodernist *par excellence*.[26] One ought not to be surprised, consequently, that postmodernist thought, which is so inspired by Nietzsche, can also overlap so significantly with the "self-propelled wheels" now known as Turing machines or computers. What they all have in common is a distrust of the active self and, as a result, an attraction to algorithmic imagery. Writing about artificial intelligence, for example, Sherry Turkle points out that:

> If mind is a program, where is the self? [AI] puts into question not only whether the self is free, but whether there is one at all. . . . In its challenge to the humanistic subject, AI is subversive in a way that takes it out of the company of rationalism and puts it into the company of psychoanalysis and radical philosophical schools such as deconstructionism. . . . Artificial intelligence is to be feared as are Freud and Derrida, not as are Skinner and Carnap.[27]

From this perspective, the contrast between the rationalism of cognitive science and the irrationalism of postmodernism and deconstruction takes a backseat to their common attitude toward the non-autonomy of the self.

The extreme representative of the common ground shared by information theory and literary postmodernism is Michel Serres, who has incorporated all the reference points for information theory—entropy,

Maxwell's demon, the second law of thermodynamics, Claude Shannon, and Boltzmannian quantum physics—into a theory of the origins of language. Information theory allows Serres to develop a theory of communication without there necessarily being any communicators. In contrast, for example, to Habermas, who specifies two parties to a communication (and who, in so doing, inspires heavy-handed critique from Lyotard),[28] Serres shows how language may be possible without knowing anything about its origins:

> I know who the final observer is, the receiver at the chain's end: precisely he who utters language. But I do not know who the initial dispatcher is at the other end. I am confronted indefinitely with a black box, a box of boxes, and so forth. In this way, I may proceed as far as I wish, all the ways to cells and molecules, as long, of course, as I change the object under observation.[29]

As might be expected, Serres's theory about the origins of language has little to do with the notion of an autonomous self.

> There is only one type of knowledge and it is always linked to an observer, an observer submerged in a system or in its proximity. And this observer is structured exactly like what he observes. . . . There is no more separation between the subject, on the one hand, and the object, on the other. . . . [30]

As Serres's remarks would seem to indicate, communication is possible within the terms of information theory, but interpretation is not. Information can only be transmitted, not read. The act of reading, by bringing an interpreting self in confrontation with a text, can only be viewed, from the perspective of information theory, as noise. Although one may argue that Serres's approach provides "a unique example of the possibilities opened up by bringing literary culture and scientific thought into play with one another,"[31] it is hard to see how. Hence Paulson, who wants literary critics to take information theory seriously, winds up concluding that even though literature, as an artifact of culture, may only be a form of noise, still "[w]hat literature solicits of the reader is not simply reception but the active, independent, autonomous construction of meaning."[32] Without ever explicitly suggesting so, Paulson's study suggests that although there are strong similarities between deconstruction and information theory, the former at least allows for readers, even if it does not theorize much about them, while the latter does, and can, not. In pushing information theory to its logical conclusion, these efforts make clear why a purely algorithmic approach to communication is inappropriate to the texts that human beings write and read: meaning exists when human selves attribute characteristics to the symbols around them, while information requires only relationships between signs irrespective of whether there exist selves reading into those signs anything whatsoever. Surely the attraction of information theory is its promise that it can bypass the problem of meaning in a philosophical culture where meaning has become so problematic. In doing so, however, it renders the readers of texts into passive receivers of information as if they were computer programs or DNA molecules. Recent developments in both artificial intelligence and biology suggest, more than ironically, that the notion of an algorithmic transmittal of information is not only of little relevance to humans, but also not completely characteristic of what takes place either in machines or in other living species.

The recent history of artificial intelligence ("AI"), in fact, constitutes a major attack on the notion of algorithmic rule-following. Although a number of starts were made in AI research that were non-algorithmic in nature—including Frank Rosenblatt's notions of perceptrons and the expert systems approach adopted by Newell and Simon[33]—the early decades of work in AI were inspired by efforts to represent the real world in machines through the device of giving machines programs written as precisely as possible.[34] If the software instructions were precise enough, the argument ran, then whether the von Neumann architecture of a central processing unit actually modelled the way human brains worked was irrelevant. It turned out, however, that the scripts and frames proposed by researchers such as Minsky and Schank to represent the real world were so brittle in nature that the limits of a purely algorithmic approach to artificial intelligence were quickly reached.[35] As one critic pointed out, the problem with such an approach was that for the machine to know anything, it first had to know everything.[36] Machines, in short, could clearly be programmed to follow rules, but whether such rule-following constituted intelligence in anything like the way that quality is generally understood was another matter. Intelligence, at least in human form, is, according to two neurobiologists and one mathematician, non-algorithmic in nature; human brains work, not by following rules, but by recognizing realities in the larger world and thereby incorporating experience and context into the thinking process.[37]

The failure of "software" approaches to AI were hailed in some quarters of the artificial intelligence community, especially among those who believed that the proper way to design machines was not by creating software programmed with precise instructions, but literally by designing machines to resemble the presumed architecture of human brains. Connectionist, neural net, or parallel data processing models—as they came to be called—did not begin with the assumption that memory could be stored in a CPU, to be accessed through instructions in the form of rules. Instead networks of electrical charges were constructed in such a manner that machines could "learn" by using the strengths between connections to narrow down a problem until a solution was found that was correct, or at least, less incorrect than a series of possible solutions that were rejected.[38] Precision—what I have been calling, following Nietzsche, eternal recurrence—was sacrificed in such approaches for the flexibility introduced by allowing machines to "settle in" to solutions.[39] Algorithms, in short, already found to be inappropriate to humans, were similarly found to be inappropriate to machines.

Purely algorithmic understandings of information transmittal have received a blow from another quarter: that of the process by which DNA sends instructions through its replication and thereby makes possible species development. The roughly parallel discoveries of realizing Turing machines of great power and the uncovering of the structure of DNA presented an irresistible challenge to sociobiologists in particular: genes present information in the form of instructions which determine the trajectory by which a species evolves. As Richard Dawkins put the matter, "We are survival machines—robot vehicles blindly programmed to preserve the selfish molecules known as genes."[40] So convinced was Dawkins of the appropriateness of the computer metaphor to the evolutionary process that he developed a software program that would enable the user to trace the patterns of many different evolutionary possibilities by specifying relevant features at the beginning of the process in order to understand how even very slight flaws in the transmission of messages (such as those contained in DNA) create fantastic variation over enormous periods of time.[41]

One should, therefore, note that both the two leading representatives of sociobiological thinking—Dawkins on the one hand and Edward Wilson on the other—found that a purely algorithmic understanding of genetic transmission ultimately could not explain the speed of human evolutionary changes. Dawkins, for example, after spending an entire book discussing selfish genes, concluded that the day of the gene was passed; in the future, cultural transmission—represented in what he called memes (from *mimesis*)—would take over and, being superior, drive out genetic transmission entirely.[42] Meanwhile Wilson, together with Charles Lumdsen, rejected the analogy with computers completely, on the grounds that the memory capacity of human brains would have to be larger than we can imagine to contain all precoded instructions sufficient to account for human evolution.[43] Instead Lumsden and Wilson argued for what they called "gene-cultured coevolution,"[44] a process by which the biological and the social share in determining the course of human evolution. They introduced a distinction between primary and secondary epigenetic rules as a way of recognizing that the latter allowed for the possibility of autonomous minds affecting the course of evolutionary development,[45] an important concession, but one that still left open the possibility of third-order epigenetic rules (and others beyond that) in which mind was understood to play even a greater role than they were prepared to admit. Their concessions to their critics, in short, were probably not enough to explain how evolution took over and produced such enormous variation in the development of our species in such a remarkably short (by evolutionary standards) amount of time. Algorithmic understandings of evolutionary dynamics, in any case, have been found as problematic in biology as they have been in computer science.

Perhaps the information processing model associated with these sciences is flawed, even in areas where, unlike with humans, it had been expected to work. If so, then there may be reason to question some of the assumptions of information theory. Oyama, for example, has argued that the notion of self-reproducing feedback loops so essential to information theory is a metaphor developed because the existence of computers provided the relevant imagery. But one would be incorrect, in her view, to adopt a preformatist attitude toward information, that is, to conclude that information always exists before the means developed for its transmission are imagined. "The developmental system," she writes, "does not have a final form, encoded before its starting point and realized at maturity."[46] We need to conceptualize the transmission of information, rather, as developmental, as a process that adds something to the process in the course of its evolution rather than spinning around within the same already existing information. Oyama's arguments, of course, are not a refutation of information theory, and one may still argue, as some biologists do, that life itself is "autopoietic" in the sense that "living beings are characterized in that, literally, they are continually self[re]producing."[47] Still the possibility that self-recurrence may not be a characteristic found in nature does raise the question of whether it is a helpful way to think about society, since society is generally held to be populated by human agents whose actions can alter purely algorithmic codings.

Two conclusions, then, can be reached about the search for the perfect algorithm. One is that if there are perfect algorithms, they are incompatible with the notion of freely choosing autonomous selves. Systems, not their components, have autonomy in a purely algorithmic world, just as, in some of the more mechanistic views of sociologist like Durkheim and Parsons, social structures, not individuals, determine consequences.[48] At the same time, however, we have also seen that even if imaginable in theory, a perfectly algorithmic system is in practice far more difficult to realize than at first understood. Algorithmic machines are too brittle to resemble human intelligence. Genetic transmission of information, especially in the case of humans, takes place over time periods far too short for algorithmic principles to be able to explain them. Information theory, far from providing the basis for a unified theory of cognition, may be highly limited in its applications to relatively contrived situations. The search for the perfect algorithm is both futile and self-defeating.

III

If algorithmic notions are as problematic as they seem, even in areas such as artificial intelligence and genetic transmission, they seem even less likely to be of use in such human and social activities as reflecting on justice (or knowledge, morality, and taste). They do, nonetheless, possess one feature which makes them attractive to postmodernist thinkers: their denial of the possibility of autonomous human agency overlaps with the suspicion of humanism and the negation of the self so characteristic of Derrida, Lacan, Barthes, Foucault and other influential thinkers. Hence although algorithmic thinking is highly formalistic and anti-interpretative, many contemporary theorists cannot avoid the temptation to introduce algorithmic conceptions into their arguments.

Perhaps the most interesting example of the power of algorithmic imagery is the effort by Barbara Herrnstein Smith to make a case against any non-contingent standards of evaluative judgement. For Herrnstein Smith, the Western humanistic tradition has sought standards of "transcendence, endurance, and universality"[49] in its evaluation of literary works, but her own personal relationship to Shakespeare's sonnets convinces her instead that "everything is always in motion with respect to everything else."[50] If value is therefore never a fixed attribute of any particular product under evaluation, how do certain cultural products come to be seen as worthy, while others are assigned to the dust bin of culture? Herrnstein Smith relies on economics for an answer: each of us has a personal economy of needs and resources. "Like any other economy, moreover, this too is a continuously fluctuating or shifting system, for our individual needs, interests, and resources are themselves functions of our continuously changing states in relation to an environment that may be relatively stable but is never absolutely fixed."[51]

Markets, then, play a role in the creation of literary standards, and not only in the narrow economic sense of money. But the important question is what kind of market this is: are we talking of the kinds of rigged and fixed markets which radical critics since Marx believe drive capitalist societies or instead the purely automatic, homeostatic markets envisioned by eighteenth-century liberals? For Herrnstein Smith, it is clearly the latter: markets are interesting to her because they work independently of the desires of the agents in the market.[52] Like contemporary rational choice theorists, Herrnstein Smith argues that self-interest drives everything we do: "We are always, so to speak, calculating how things 'figure' for us—always pricing them, so to speak, in relation to the total economy of our personal universe."[53] But unlike rational choice theorists, Herrnstein Smith does not believe that "we" do this calculating consciously and as autonomous choosers:

> Most of these "calculations," however, are performed intuitively and inarticulately, and many of them are so recurrent that the habitual arithmetic becomes part of our personality and comprises the very style of our being and behavior, forming what we may call our principles or tastes—and what others may call our biases and prejudices.[54]

Since we find in Herrnstein Smith's account a picture of the market which is far more invasive than anything found in writers like Gary Becker and Richard Posner who see markets everywhere, we do not wonder that algorithmic conceptions of self-regulating systems come to dominate her account of how standards of taste become established. So much is in motion at such speeds that the only possible regulation of the whole process is automatic regulation, or what Herrnstein Smith calls an "evaluative feedback loop":

> Every literary work—and, more generally, artwork—is thus the product of a complex evaluative feedback loop that embraces not only the ever-shifting economy of the artist's own interests and resources as they evolve during and in reaction to the process of composition, but also all the shifting economies of her assumed and

imagined audiences, including those who do not yet exist but whose emergent interests, variable conditions of encounter, and rival sources of gratification she will attempt to predict—or will intuitively surmise—and to which, among other things, her own sense of the fittingness of each decision will be responsive.[55]

Not surprisingly, therefore, Herrnstein Smith finds attractive any way of thinking that emphasizes algorithmic processes. In the course of her discussion, she touches on the possibility that human brains may be cognitively hard-wired in predetermined ways;[56] criticizes the Habermasian notion of rational communicative standards on the ground that we speak, as we spend, only out of self-interest, so that honesty in speech, if it ever exists, is the product of a Mandevillian lack of intention;[57] adopts information theory as the model for an epistemology in which "what is traditionally referred to as 'perception,' 'knowledge,' 'belief,' . . . would be an account of how the structures, mechanisms, and behaviors through which subjects interact with—and, accordingly, constitute—their environments are modified by those very interactions"[58]; uses information theory to explain that evaluative classifications exist so that "energy need not . . . be expended on the process of classification and evaluation each time a similar array is produced"[59]; argues that often such classifications are "fixed in the DNA"[60]; and relies on Brownian motion and Nietzsche's "play of forces" to criticize any who suggest an "overall, underlying, or ultimate governing outcome toward which each instance of human productive-acquisitive *or* consummatory-expenditure activity (all making, getting, and spending, we might say) is directed. . . ."[61]

Most illustrative of all, however, is Herrnstein Smith's account of why certain products of culture have entered our canon. In answering this question, she is not only more economistic than the most committed rational choice economist, she is also more taken with genetic theories of evolution than most sociobiologists. Artistic texts survive the way species do: "These interactions are, in certain respects, analogous to those by virtue of which biological species evolve and survive and also analogous to those through which artistic choices evolve and are found " 'fit' or fitting by the individual artist."[62] Evolutionary feedback loops allow Herrnstein Smith to resolve the question in aesthetic theory proposed by Hume: why do we consider Homer great? The answer is not that Homer survived because he was great but that because he survived he is considered great. "Nothing endures like endurance."[63] Images of eternal recurrence combine with Durkheimian functionalism to explain the secret of Homer's success:

Repeatedly cited and recited, translated, taught and imitated, and thoroughly enmeshed in the network of intertextuality that continuously *constitutes* the high culture of the orthodoxly educated population of the West (and the Western-educated population of the rest of the world), that highly variable entity we refer to as "Homer" recurrently enters our experience in relation to a large number and variety of our interests and thus can perform a large number of various functions for us.[64]

Although Barbara Herrnstein Smith is not writing about justice but about evaluation, her analysis demonstrates the linkage between the position that there are no non-contingent standards in the world and the need, consequently, for automatically functioning regulatory mechanisms. When we turn to writers who are directly concerned with justice, we find exactly the same linkage. The clearest example is Luhmann, who finds in cybernetics and information theory an answer to the question of what makes society possible. Luhmann wants to understand how societies—which are not only enormously complex, but are also, in their modern form, more complex than ever before—reproduce themselves through time. Arguing, in a tradition that goes back to Mandeville and Adam Smith, that no conscious direction can ever guide a system so complex, Luhmann turns to methods by which systems reduce their complexity. Computers, of course, reduce complexity by dividing all information into bits that can be expressed as zeros and ones. So, argues Luhmann, do legal systems. A legal system can exhaust the entire realm of the possible through the legal/illegal dichotomy. That distinction, in a sense, constitutes the "hardware" of a legal system. In order for the system to take a decision in a specific case, "software" programs access the system, feeding back into the "memory" and thereby creating new rules that anticipate future programs.[65]

For Luhmann, the dynamics of specific cases introduced into the system continuously redefine the binary codes, interacting again with new programs in ways that resemble eternal recurrence. The whole system, he argues,

is a matter of a specific technique for dealing with highly structured complexity. In practice this technique requires an endless, circular re-editing of the law: the assumption is that something will happen, but how it will happen and what its consequences will be has to be awaited. When these consequences begin to reveal themselves they can be perceived as problems and provide an occasion for new regulations in law itself as well as in politics. Unforeseeable consequences will also occur and it will be impossible to determine if and to what extent they apply to that regulation. Again, this means an occasion for new regulation, waiting, new consequences, new problems, new regulation and so on.[66]

"Autopoietic law" thereby, according to Luhmann, avoids many of the problems faced by other philosophies of law. It explains how a legal system can change, for example, as well as provides a way of thinking about the law that guarantees its autonomy from other systems.

Luhmann's theories about the law overlap with postmodernism because autopoietic systems are non-hierarchical. Being circular in their dynamics, they avoid privileging any one set of legal norms over any other; as Luhmann expresses it, "There can therefore be no norm hierarchies," or, somewhat more self-reflectively, "legal forms are valid because they are valid."[67] But if legal scholars turn to autopoietic theories of justice out of a generalized commitment to principles of equality, they may find the equality not worth having. Since notions of self-regulation come primarily from biology on the one hand and artificial intelligence on the other, any legal system designed by such principles cannot incorporate specifically human capabilities, such as the possibility that autonomous human subjects can interpret the instructions given to them out of their history and contexts. For if the agents ruled by laws can interpret laws, then automatic self-regulation no longer exists. Any conception of justice that might emerge from such a system would have to be just in the way ant colonies are just or the evolution of different species of worms is just or computer programs are just. Justice would thus be defined as having reached some kind of stable equilibrium that makes possible the continued reproduction of the system. What justice could not be, under such a conception of law, is a quality that enhances a specific human capacity to bring meaning to situations and contexts in order to guide them toward any purpose defined by a community of autonomous actors.

Stanley Fish's reflections on the law illustrate the dynamics of algorithmic justice in a slightly different way than Luhmann's. Fish is well known for his insistence that standards do not transcend the particular points of view of the communities that interpret them. Whether he is correct or not is not the point on which I want to focus. I want to argue instead that by introducing the term "community,"[68] Fish is under a certain obligation to talk sociology: to discuss what a community is, how its members act, what relationship exists between individual needs and community concerns, and other typical concerns of sociological theory. After all, an enormous emphasis is being placed by Fish's approach on the practices carried out by human agents, including not only judges, but professors of law and literature, readers of texts, and, presumably, all those affected by the legal decisions which in turn are affected by how judges and legal intellectuals make their arguments.

Surprisingly, however, questions involving sociological practice play relatively little role in Fish's writings. Consider his answer to the question of why we ought to be concerned about the interpretation of legal texts in the first place. For Fish the overlap between law and literary criticism is the result of a glitch in democratic theory: the existence of judicial review, which in enabling judges to overrule democratic decisions in the name of fidelity to an earlier text, builds counter-majoritarian tendencies into our political system.[69] Yet why do we have constitutional texts, and procedures for reviewing them, at all? Surely both the Constitution and the practice of judicial review illustrate a larger sociological problem: one identified quite clearly by the rational choice philosopher Jon Elster in his discussion of Ulysses and the Sirens. Constitutions, as Elster argues, deal with the problem of binding, the ways in which one generation attempts, like Ulysses tying himself to the mast, to make it possible for the next generation not to be seduced by the temptations of immediate gratification and self-interest.[70] Judicial review, by contrast, grows out of the recognition that the bonds, if tied too tightly, result in bondage. Far from being a quirk in the system, judicial review exists as part of a dynamic process by which societies continuously reform themselves and their institutions over time to insure a balance between the contradictory goals of adhering to foundation norms and allowing for change. As is the case with so many other aspects of legal practice, judicial review makes it necessary to pose a host of questions about the agents doing the review: who reviews the founding document? What standards of practice ought to guide them? Are they freely choosing agents or part of a larger social structure? What qualities of mind do they have? What qualities of mind ought they to have? To not address sociological questions about the nature of real people in discussing the interpretation of legal texts is like discussing the plot of Ulysses without reference to the character of the man who tried to save his ship and his men.[71]

Although the question of how human beings follow practices thus assumes great importance for Fish, his analysis of what a practice means is to quote a pitcher for the Baltimore Orioles. Like Dennis Martinez, who just throws a ball to get the batter out without thinking about ultimate goals, an agent "need not look to something in order to determine where he is or where he now might go because that determination is built into, comes along with, his already-in-place sense of being a competent member of the enterprise." [72] Agents, in Fish's view, are part of a performative chain, not one, to be sure, of the automatic transmittal of information without consciousness, but nonetheless one that works automatically and without requiring autonomy and self-judgement. There is no autonomy in this view, or, more precisely, all autonomy lies with the historical events that determined the patterns of a practice. Individuals, being "deeply situated," [73] just follow rules, rules which themselves are so deeply situated that individuals may not, and probably are not, aware that they are following them. " 'Be the best you can be,' " Fish writes in response to Dworkin, "finally means nothing more than 'act in the way your understanding of your role in the institution tells you to act.' " [74]

Since agents naturally follow the rules determined by their roles in the institutions that define their practices, little would be amiss if Fish were to focus on those institutions themselves. After all, if the members of a professional subcommunity developed through some kind of democratic practice an agreed-upon set of norms, little would be wrong in expecting that each of them would then bind themselves to the rules that defined their practice. Yet, no subcommunity can possibly develop such standards fairly without agreement upon larger normative and procedural issues, such as that their decisions will be made by majority rule, that the practices to which they adhere will not violate Judeo-Christian beliefs, that their behavior will be guided by law, etc. In other words, the development of a theory about how agents act is intimately linked to a discussion of the larger, normative standards of the society (not just the subcommunity) in which agents practice. If there are norms viewed as just in the society and practices viewed as procedurally correct in the professional subcommunity, then agents can follow rules naturally, or even algorithmically, without violating their autonomy.

The problem, of course, is that Fish believes that transcendental standards of just or moral behavior can not exist. Within the confines of that argument, the failure to look beyond the automatic and natural following of the rules of a practice becomes a serious matter indeed. As he often points out, Fish is neither an anarchist nor a nihilist. Quite the contrary. Like many thinkers attracted to algorithmic imagery, he imagines structures that are so tightly organized as to make anarchism impossible. For this reason, Fish, for all his distaste for formal algorithmic thinking, concludes with a position not all that distinct from Chomsky's. To be sure, the rules of transformational grammar work in such a way that the personal proclivities of the speaker are irrelevant, whereas the rules of thumb of a practice depend very much on the idiosyncracies of the person engaging in the practice.[75] Yet in both cases particulars are embedded in generals, in the one case the rules of grammar, in the other "the individual who is always constrained by the local or community standards and criteria of which his judgement is an extension."[76]

IV

Those skeptical of the possibility of any transcendental standard of justice posit that none of the theories we may have about justice—both of the transcendental and anti-transcendental sort—matter. Even the most skeptical, such as Fish, do, however, believe that theory talk matters, even if theory does not.[77] But what if theory talk *is* theory? It would be under the assumptions I have been making in this paper. To be sure, there is no such thing as a view from nowhere,[78] universally valid, from which we can deduce standards of justice that bind our actions for all time. Yet purely contingent understandings of what binds us together, being contingent, cannot bind, or at least bind what we need to be bound. Already existing interpretative subcommunities, which by definition share normative standards, are not the ones that need grand narratives about justice, but instead communities seeking to answer questions such as these: how do we resolve our disputes with one another and make those resolutions binding? How do we aim to make our resolutions as fair as possible to the parties to the conflict? How does a community exist in time, passing on the rules by which it regulates its affairs to those who did not participate in the original making of such rules? What do we expect from newly admitted members of our community in return for their membership in the community? Who makes the rules? Who follows them? Who questions them? Who changes them? Social justice exists when diverse communities can be knitted together because, whatever their other differences, the one thing they require is some normative consensus, however vague, about the purposes that define their society.

Faced with the dilemma of how we can develop standards of justice that are more than contingent and local but less than universal and permanent, we rely on the minimal philosophical anthropology that even postmodernism, indirectly, concedes. Since we are all members of a larger community governed by a text and the interpretations of that text we bring to it, we seek standards of justice that recognize and allow us to develop our capacity as readers and interpreters. Those who do what Fish calls theory talk are engaged in the process of sharpening and refining the standards by which real human beings interpret texts. They are setting an example, using their powers as thinkers and writers to create provisional standards of justice, recognizing that these are socially created rather than found in nature or theology, and that, because these standards are recognized as minimally transcendental, we expect that they will, before changing, last for a considerable period of time—say across two generations—and, during that time, be accepted as generally binding.

If that is the case, then the most likely place to find a standard of justice lies, after all, in the major texts that frame talk about theory—the Constitution, decisions of the important courts, and articles in law reviews and similar outlets that debate both specific laws as well as standards of interpretation. From such a point of view, writers like Fish, by engaging in theory talk, contribute to theory. What they say matters a great deal and, moreover, matters in a transrhetorical way, just as I believe that what I am saying, while rhetorically presented, also involves more than rhetoric. One embarks, Fish claims, on a slippery slope down the anti-formalist road: once you question formalism's first assumption, you have no choice but to question them all. Yet, as I have tried to show in this paper, there is a road back up the slope again. Once we understand that whatever permanence and universality we lose in any transcendental standard of justice is more than compensated for by the recognition that the transcendence we get, however temporary, is a product of our own efforts, we require a sociological theory of the self to put back into people and their efforts and practices the meanings about justice that we have, rightly, stripped away from texts.

The failure of postmodern theorists of justice to develop an adequate philosophical anthropology dealing with the capacities of human selves undermines much of the strength of its critique of intentionalism and other problematic theories of interpretation. The notion that truths are not embedded in texts in such a fashion that we can divine what to do simply by reading the words is a profound idea. In turning the question of justice back to us, to those who read and interpret texts, postmodernism makes possible a self-governing political community capable of interpreting its rules for the benefit of its members. But that potential can only be realized, not by denying humanism, but by welcoming it, by recognizing that what makes us human is our ability to shape and interpret rules according to the contexts in which we find ourselves. If that means that we have to accept at least some minimal transcendental standards and distinctions—that, for example, there is a difference between nature and culture, that humans do have special abilities, that the socially constructed can be transcendental without necessarily being permanent—then this is a small price to pay for gaining control over the rules that we simultaneously make and follow. Why bother to argue that the rules are not made by God or nature only to argue instead that, however they are made, our only choice is to follow them rather than remake them through all the practices in which we engage?

NOTES

1. I. Murdoch, A Fairly Honorable Defeat 218 (1970).
2. S. Levinson, Constitutional Faith 9–53 (1988).
3. C. Geertz, Thick Description: Toward an Interpretive Theory of Culture, in Interpretation of Cultures 3–30 (1973).
4. There are obvious differences between these terms, as the polemics between Derrida and Foucault indicate. Nonetheless, for purposes of the argument presented here, all these approaches are suspicious of transcendental standards of justice that can be embodied in texts like constitutions and thereby can be linked in this presentation—contingently, of course.
5. S. Fish, Doing What Comes Naturally: Change, Rhetoric, and the Practice of Theory, in Literary and Legal Studies (1989); B. Herrnstein Smith, Contingencies of Value: Alternative Perspectives for Critical Theory (1988).
6. For a study of the impact that the ability to write (and, by implication, the ability to read) has on the structure of society, see J. Goody, The Logic of Writing and the Organization of Society (1986). The capacity of our reading material to link us together in a society sharing a moral framework is emphasized in W. Booth, The Company We Keep: An Ethics of Fiction (1988).
7. For a conception of the self close to the one I am discussing here, see C. Taylor, Sources of the Self (1989).
8. B. Herrnstein Smith, supra note 5, at 78.
9. M. Foucault, The Order of Things: An Archaeology of the Human Sciences 387 (1970).
10. B. Herrnstein Smith, supra note 5, at 193.
11. Heller, Accounting for Law, in Autopoietic Law: A New Approach to Law and Society 307 (G. Teubner ed. 1988).
12. For relevant demonstrations of this point see, e.g., Lindblom, The Market as Prison, 44 J. of Pol. 324 (1982); Preston, Freedom, Markets, and Voluntary Exchange, 78 Am. Pol. Sci. Rev. 959 (1984); West, Authority, Autonomy, and Choice: The Role of Consent in the Moral and Political Visions of Franz Kafka and Richard Posner, 99 Harv. L. Rev. 384 (1985).

13. S. Fish, supra note 5, at 10.

14. Id. at 520.

15. Id.

16. Id. at 315–20.

17. See, e.g., Schegloff & Sacks, Opening Up Closings, in Ethnomethodology: Selected Readings 233–64 (R. Turner ed. 1979).

18. See the bulk of the essays in Autopoietic Law: A New Approach to Law and Society, supra note 11. One of the exceptions, the arguments of which overlap to some degree with those here, is Rottleuthner, Biological Metaphors in Legal Thought, in Autopoietic Law: A New Approach to Law and Society, supra note 11, at 97.

19. See, for a typical account, H. Pagels, The Dreams of Reason 192–94 (1988).

20. J. Fodor, The Language of Thought (1975).

21. J. Lyotard, The Postmodern Condition 4, 51, 67 (1984).

22. See, e.g., G. Deleuze & F. Guattari, Anti-Oedipus: Capitalism and Schizophrenia 14 (1977).

23. Levinson, Law as Literature, in Interpreting Law and Literature: A Hermeneutic Reader 155–73 (1988); for an argument that Levinson has misapplied Nietzsche's ideas about how texts can be interpreted, see Weisberg, On the Use and Abuse of Nietzsche for Modern Constitutional Theory, in id. at 181–92.

24. D. Hofstader, Godel, Escher, and Bach: An Eternal Golden Braid (1979); F. Nietzsche, Thus Spoke Zarathustra, in The Portable Nietzsche 139 (1954).

25. A. Nehamas, Nietzsche: Life as Literature 150 (1985).

26. Foucault's *The Order of Things,* which ends with the image of man being washed away in the sand, begins with a discussion of a passage from Borges. M. Foucault, supra note 9, at xv. Poe and Roussel, two other novelists fascinated with the entrapping imagery of machines, are also important literary sources for postmodernist speculations.

27. Turkle, Artificial Intelligence and Psychoanalysis: A New Alliance, 117 Daedalus 241, 245 (1988).

28. J. Lyotard, supra note 21, at 60–67. Lyotard also has strongly critical views toward Luhmann, yet, at least with respect to their joint fascination with cybernetics and the reduction of complexity, they share more than he is prepared to admit. See N. Luhmann, The Differentiation of Society (1982).

29. Serres, The Origin of Language: Biology, Information Theory, and Thermodynamics, in Hermes: Literature, Science, Philosophy 82 (1982).

30. Id. at 83.

31. W. Paulson, The Noise of Culture: Literary Texts in a World of Information 31 (1988).

32. Id. at 139.

33. A Newall & H. Simon, Human Problem Solving (1972); F. Rosenblatt, Principles of Neurodynamics (1962).

34. Even the simplest instructions imagined in the Turing machine, however, can, from Wittgensteinian premises, be understood as something more than the simple

following of a rule. See on this point Shanker, Wittgenstein Versus Turing on the Nature of Church's Thesis, 24 Notre Dame J. of Formal Logic 615 (1987).

35. R. Schank & R. Abelson, Scripts, Plans, Goals, and Understanding (1977); Minsky, A Framework for Representing Knowledge, in Mind Design 95 (J. Haugeland ed. 1981).

36. I. Rosenfield, The Invention of Memory 112 (1988).

37. The neurobiologists are I. Rosenfield, id. at 144–45, and G. Edelman, Neural Darwinism 44 (1987). The mathematician is R. Penrose, The Emperor's New Mind 405–18 (1989).

38. For various approaches, see P. Churchland, Neurophilosophy: Toward a Unified Science of the Mind-Brain (1986); Foundations (Parallel Distributed Processing: Explorations in the Microstructure of Cognition No. 1, 1986); S. Grossberg, Neural Networks and Natural Intelligence (1988); C. Mead, Analog VLSI and Neural Systems (1989); Churchland & Sejnowski, Perspectives on Cognitive Neuroscience, 242 Science 741 (1988).

39. Although PDP approaches are less attracted to the kinds of eternal braids discussed by Hofstadter, they resonate with postmodern themes in another way. Like deconstruction, connectionist approaches to AI believe that meaning does not lie behind any text but only emerges, if it exists at all, as a relationship between signs. As D. A. Norman puts it, "I believe the point is that PDP mechanisms can set up almost any arbitrary relationship. Hence, to the expert, once a skill has been acquired, meaningfulness of the relationships is irrelevant." Norman, Reflections on Cognition and Parallel Distributive Processing, in Psychological and Biological Models 531, 544 (Parallel Distributed Processing: Explorations in the Microstructure of Cognition No. 2, 1986).

40. R. Dawkins, The Selfish Gene ix (1976).

41. R. Dawkins, The Blind Watchmaker (1986).

42. R. Dawkins, supra note 40, at 205–14. Dawkins does not address the issue of whether memes reproduce themselves less algorithmically than genes. He does write, however, that "[t]he computers in which memes live are human brains." Id. at 211. Since, as we have seen, human brains are believed to function non-algorithmically, the shift from genetic to cultural transmission would seem to indicate a less algorithmic process.

43. C. Lumsden & E. Wilson, Genes, Mind, and Culture 332 (1981).

44. Id. at 19–34.

45. Id. at 53–58.

46. S. Oyama, The Ontogeny of Information 23 (1985).

47. H. Maturana & F. Varela, The Tree of Knowledge 43 (1987). As might be expected Maturana and Varela are fascinated by ideas of self-recurrence, using a drawing from Escher to make their point. Id. at 25.

48. "The division of labor does not present individuals to one another, but social functions." E. Durkheim, The Division of Labor in Society 407 (1964). Interesting enough, theorists in artificial intelligence, stumped by how essentially dumb bits of information can be linked together into something smart called intelligence, utilize images strikingly similar to Durkheim's: "Each mental agent by itself can only do some simple thing that needs no mind or thought at all. Yet when we join

these agents in societies—in certain very special ways—this leads to true intelligence." M. Minsky, The Society of Mind 17 (1986).

49. B. Herrnstein Smith, supra note 5, at 28.

50. Id. at 15.

51. Id. at 31.

52. There are occasions in her text, however, where Smith takes the opposite tack and argues that markets are rigged: "The linguistic market can no more be a 'free' one than any other market, for verbal agents do not characteristically enter it from positions of equal advantage or conduct their transactions on an equal footing." Id. at 111.

53. Id. at 42.

54. Id. at 43.

55. Id. at 45.

56. Id. at 101.

57. Id. at 108–09.

58. Id. at 95.

59. Id. at 122.

60. Id.

61. Id. at 144.

62. Id. at 47.

63. Id. at 50.

64. Id. at 53.

65. N. Luhmann, Ecological Communication 64–66 (1989).

66. Id. at 66.

67. Luhmann, The Unity of the Legal System, in Autopoietic Law: A New Approach to Law and Society, supra note 11, at 21, 23.

68. S. Fish, Is There a Text in This Class? (1980).

69. S. Fish, supra note 5, at 338–39.

70. J. Elster, Ulysses and the Sirens (rev. ed. 1984).

71. Although I am in strong disagreement with his moral philosophy, I am in agreement with MacIntyre that it is impossible to understand Greek conceptions of virtue without discussing the matter of character. A. MacIntyre, After Virtue (1981).

72. S. Fish, supra note 5, at 388.

73. Id. at 387.

74. Id. at 391.

75. Id. at 317.

76. Id. at 323.

77. Id. at 14.

78. T. Nagel, The View from Nowhere (1986).

14

Conditions of Evil

Reiner Schürmann
(translated from the French by Ian Janssen)

In philosophy it is advisable to state where and how one begins. One popular way of beginning appears in meta-remarks often heard and read such as this: "If I argue that X, then the result will be undesirable; therefore I shall argue that Y." This amounts to an acknowledgment, touching in its candor, that the starting point is desires, and the argument their legitimation.

Desires, however, are as notoriously unreliable as they are inescapable. They make one argue the maximization of now this, now that preference. One may suspect imagination at work as some object of desire gets promoted to the rank of ultimacy.

In what follows I shall try to examine a certain maximizing strategy in philosophy, as well as what after Kant may be called an "expanded way of imagining." In such maximization and such expansion, imagination will prove incongruously turned against itself. In its *arraying* strategy it posits standards more normative than which nothing can be desired, while in a *disarraying* counterstrategy it lets itself be given singulars. These discrepant workings may shed some light not only on the origin of desirable standards, but also on what common opinion explains as violation of just such standards: namely, evil.

The general title chosen by the organizers of this conference[1] mentions "the politics of transformation." In attempting to spell out conditions of evil, I have been guided by the ambition to learn more about certain sufferings that the West has inflicted upon itself before the middle of this century. The natural metaphysician in us might pick up those conditions—a plural not to be effaced—with one shovel and treat them summarily as negation of standards.[2] It seems to me that one can sort out that shovelful and in the process gain some precision both about ultimates and about the way they allow for the possibility of evil.

Such sorting out goes not without pains. On the one hand, it has to deal with collective and individual hysteria, with leaders of formidable efficacy, with long lasting hatreds and short memory, with vendetta conventions and sham treaties, economic depression or boom, etc. Assortments of this kind may help explain mini-chains of events (perhaps the electoral victory of 1933). They hardly yield an understanding. On the other hand, trying to sort out conditions of the large-scale pathologies of our century, it is difficult to avoid entering precisely the sphere of standards, values, and the like. What may be gathered there is the fallout from principles betrayed: democracy, human rights, freedom . . . Of course values and principles were betrayed. But what intelligibility about conditions does one gain from bemoaning a sellout? Concerning the first part of the title chosen by the organizers, I draw this conclusion for my purposes: attempting to think politics of transformation, it is advisable to stay clear not only of neo-positivist management of facts, but also of paleo-idealist assertion of standards.

As to its second part, "The Limits of Imagination," the incongruous strategies of imagination mentioned—positing standards, letting singulars be—will allow one to follow a road other than positivist, idealist, or of some pragmatic in-between. The starting point in philosophy may then not be simple, as the natural metaphysician's impetus toward norms keeps asserting itself in all experience and as singulars ask to be let-be. The task that I wish to describe consists in expanding thinking beyond, or outside, normative theticism, toward *diasozein ta phainomena:* toward remaining faithful, while giving thetic desire its due, to singulars as they show themselves.

DIFFERING ULTIMATES

If it is agreed that philosophy can do more than plead interests, be they libidinal or institutional, where and how to begin cannot remain optional. Here are some criteria that help keeping clear of both the instrumentalization of thinking and its speculative disconnection from phenomena. A starting point that neither abandons ordinary experience nor trans-substantiates it into the extraordinary will have to be looked for in something everyone is familiar with, however poorly; it will have to be a knowing[3] that is not episodic, not contingent; a knowing whose seat is everydayness; from which other experiences and types of knowledge arise; and which does not in turn depend on some more primary knowing. To avoid making argumentation minister unwittingly to desires, one will have to grasp irreducible traits in

everydayness and put them to the test of a historical-systematic investigation. Let us call such an inquiry into conditions a *phenomenology
of ultimates*. Why phenomenology and what ultimates remain to be
seen. To the claim, voiced right and left, that we need norms in order
to understand, judge and act, a phenomenologist's response has always been and should be: To learn what is to be done, no more is
needed than insight into ultimate conditions of what shows itself to
ordinary experience.

Ethics, then, does not belong to philosophy, no more than to imagining some politics of transformation. On the other hand, inasmuch
as expanding imagination—that is, thinking—bears upon ultimates,
such expansion is philosophy's essential task.

To attempt a non-ethical, non-moral, discourse about evil, one may
mimic the Gnostics' question (mimes being experts in demythologiz-
ing) and ask: How did evil enter the world? Such a discourse begins
not with some narrative of a primordial fall, but with a certain primal
scene with and through which it has to work. The scene is the conflict
of heroic and democratic laws in fifth century Athens, as represented
on stage by Aeschylus and Sophocles. Agamemnon slits Iphigenia's
throat *in the name* of what is called "values": nation (more than the
polis, less than the state), army, honor of course, plus perhaps Greek
expansionism and the Ionian colonization . . . One cuts, so as to promote a common name capable of setting the law. But by the same
slitting, Agamemnon also cuts himself off from the law of the Atrides.
He decides for one clear cut law: *for* the one at Aulis, *against* the one
at Mycene where other obligations would have compelled him to cut
and decide differently. At Aulis, his public function inserts him into a
world that bestows on him a meaning as head of the armies. Yet also
at Aulis, the undeniable allegiance—yet an allegiance denied—to the
family lineage singularizes him as well. The allegiance to his blood
line expels him in advance from the world of weapons and battle
ships, the world that in sacrificing his daughter he extolls as unequivocally normative. Knowing the expulsion and singularization that accompany clear cut normativity makes any univocal meaning meaningless. That knowing, made explicit, is tragic knowledge.

Here then are ultimates that we know, however poorly, in everyday
experience: the *maximization* of some name fixing our bearings and
contextualizing a world; but also, incongruously conjoined with it,
the *singularization* within any such constituted world, which results
from the pull of other actual worlds to which I belong.

How did evil enter the world? Not in a narratable coming, not by
that erstwhile king too cowardly to sustain the double bind of discrep-

ant laws. Evil comes in an untold move, when singularization is cut off from one's constituted world, when one blinds oneself against it; when in the name of a jealous fantasm capable of subsuming everything that can become phenomenal one "comes down on one side" of the discrepant binds; when such a fantasm is made to command exclusive allegiance; when it integrates doing, acting, and knowing in a frame that can be mastered and in this sense appropriates the world; when expropriation from that world is denied.

Was sacrificing Iphigenia right or wrong? It is more instructive to see that it is the battery of values that makes one commit acts of that kind. The primal scene does not allow "the problem of evil" to be confined within "morals" because, from the point of view of ultimacy, evil cannot be a matter of *mores,* of conduct and habit, or of inner disposition and intention. It therefore does not reveal itself to a theory one might juxtapose, for instance, to a political theory, thus rendering conduct and intention accessible to investigation or speculation. Theorizing evil—saying "Morally he was wrong," "Politically he was right"—amounts to passing off classifying for explaining. From the bird's eye view on secondary types of discourse, types not grounded in themselves, how is one to adjudicate what is good, what is evil, if not by recourse to some primary discourse, which treats of one grounding principle? Such principles, however, in the name of which issues fall into kinds, are the ones that owe their sovereignty to an act of tragic denial.

A metaphysical discourse about ultimates differs from a phenomenological one, as negation (Verneinung) differs from denial (Verleugnung). Negating standards is a metaphysical operation since it depends on a prior positing of the standards negated. Denying a knowledge, on the other hand, involves no such theticism. Its analysis devolves on a phenomenology.

As suggested by the primal scene of the doctrine of principles, the pull dispossessing us of any given phenomenality remains systematically operative in every positing of a law, which is thus in advance suspended, struck with interdiction. Such is the dubious charm of theticism: to argue positions amounts inevitably, forcibly, to both recognizing and silencing the dispossession that always pulls on phenomena as an undertow, always depriving them of their world.

In order to think evil one is left with, one the surface, a host of questions to which everyone keeps returning: What is the good life? What are proper conduct and right intention? . . . as well as, in depth, a dispossessing which keeps returning. Are death and evil then to be charged to that dispossessing? At first sight, nothing would seem more plausible. Both death and evil disown us of the good life, love and the like. In ordinary experience we do know better than to exalt now this, now that colossal referent, and like dwarfs to put our trust in it. We know better than to rank evil among the special issues dealt with in a special branch of philosophy, itself one branch of the human sciences in the shadow of the modern hegemonic referent—subjectivity⁴—posited to integrate (at least by right) knowledge claims as it is to integrate life worlds.

As to the deep answer, it is hardly more enlightening than the superficial one. Something in us, to be sure, applauds when with resignation we are told: evil is a special problem indeed. Were it not, it would be everywhere—a thought more difficult still to resign oneself to, unbearable. But something in us agrees as well that the "problem" in question does not belong in any discipline of knowledge, as the problem of motion belongs in physics and as the study of insects does in entomology. Indeed, we possess a prior knowing, but no clear knowledge of it. Deep etiologies have this superficiality about them that they promise they will consummate prior knowing in actual knowledge—a promise impossible to keep. Instead of fulfilling what they promise, causal accounts end up postulating some appellate jurisdiction. They have had to enlist into that service a breathtaking parade of names and standards.

Insight, then, is to be expected neither from surveys nor from deep burrowings. I see little else but a phenomenology of ultimates, conjoined with an historical topology of normative double binds, that may help one toward it. To carry out such a conjunction, the irreducible traits of maximization and singularization need to be gathered from everydayness and then put to historical-topological tests. Borrowing from Hannah Arendt (who on this point corrected, not without irony, Heidegger), one may call the traits of ultimacy "natality" and "mortality."⁵ The first, the archic trait prompts us toward new commencings and sovereign commandings. It makes us magnify standards. The second always pulls us back from the world of such archic referents. It is a singularizing, dispersing, desolating, evicting, dephenomenalizing, exclusory trait. The two do not pair off. They are originary, yet not binary traits. They are not jointly exhaustive of one genus. In other words, they do not divide one first posit that would yield to one encompassing discourse (*oppositorum eadem est scientia*).⁶ As incongruent, they derail experience. There exists therefore no better heuristics than the daydreamy wonderings about how I can ever have come to be and how it is possible that I shall cease to be. The larger the design of these traits, however, the more legible will they be. This is why a topology of the normative double binds[7] by which the West has actually lived needs to turn to the pages where the impulse of natality appears colossal: the pages in which bastions against temporality have been erected, greater than which nothing can be desired. Those bastions never failed, however, to crumble under the return of the denied.

As to good and evil, they cannot parallel those phenomenologically originary traits gathered from everydayness. How could natality equal the good pure and simple? The fantasmic maximizations, to which it incites imagination and thought, kill. Nor can mortality, which ties us back to singulars,[8] be equated with evil. That those equations, tempting though they may be to the natural metaphysician in us, would be wrong is suggested by the primal scene; it is confirmed by the fate of the hegemonies, illustrated by the exhaustion of certain ideologies; and it is proven by ordinary ambivalences toward death. The last decade of this millennium has its own peculiar way of calling us back to the senseless that we know, namely, that a meaning is not something one posits or composes; but that it comes about as a world phenomenalizes itself, and that we always receive it only to find ourselves in advance expelled from it.

As if the lesson of those institutions of which nothing more magnificent can be conceived and which for a while go without saying before collapsing under the return of the denied—as if that lesson from history were not crass enough, the twentieth century has indeed outperformed previous ages. It has incurred a voidance of standards such that one cannot help wondering if in the end it will not suffice to pull us from denial and teach us the Yes to dispossession. Who, "us"? There has been no lack of moments in history in which a Yes to the universalizing-singularizing double bind was lived by all.[9] Who then still needs to learn that of which he possesses a prior knowing? The thetic metaphysician in us will have to learn tragic thinking.

To the thetic impulse of natality we owe our normative referents. It is the tie that sets us free. Is it not a bit hasty, then, to assert that this impulse does not amount to the good as such? It is the impulse that unifies life. Correlatively, is singularization—the retraction, subtraction, by which we incur loss of love, of home and country, of health and life—not the most plausible candidate for evil as such? These correlations fed the gigantomachia concerning ultimacy when, in the nineteenth century, normative argumentation began to savor of desire's labor. The young Nietzsche still held keenly that out of unification comes the good and out of individuation, evil. We must consider, he wrote, "the state of individuation as the source and the originary ground of all suffering. . . . The *mystery doctrine of tragedy:* the fundamental knowledge that all that there is is one; the consideration of individuation as the originary ground of evil." [10]

Evil would equal being dispossessed of some fundamental unity that allows for communication. The equation also fits all too well with the common opinion held in each of the linguistic eras of philosophy. For the Greeks, evil meant to be dispossessed of the good, at the very bottom of the ladder crowned by the one; for the Latins, it meant the dispossession of telic continuity which whoever acts against nature brings upon himself; for the moderns, it meant a dispossession of enlightenment which turns one radically away from self-consciousness. Each time the good posits itself, which is why it determines what holds as law. So long as otherness remains conceived as negation and denial itself is denied, evil can only stand opposed to such self-positing. It arises when the one, nature, or self-consciousness are deprived of their full normative presence. It is nothing but a misuse of those principal foci which life's first sufferings should have taught us to let shine in their splendid evidence. "Evil is to evilly use the good." [11]

A historical topology of normative double binds (which this is not the place to develop) teaches one something altogether different. Philosophers cannot think in our place. They can show us ways of thinking that we did not anticipate. Is it not thetic desire yet again which speaks through the wish that self-positing, hence normative evidence, may shine? Such desire has posited all *single binds*. The simplicity of singly binding referents proved however to be not given, but rather made by a bold stroke—the stroke of an ax. Concerning the non-simplicity of the good, there is therefore a truth that we know but which we do not fully understand. It teaches us that by its very positedness the law extenuates its subsumptive power (inasmuch as *das Gesetz* is always *das Gesetzte*). Such knowing should prevent us from fidgeting if the good shows an affinity with double binds. Let us therefore bracket the popularity of good and evil. It is about evil that a phenomenology of ultimates can teach us something.

The first, perhaps, who in the nineteenth century thought differently than in homage to a form of "unitary ground" (although to render homage to ethics instead), and who thought otherness differently than as determinate negation, was Kierkegaard. "Any discourse about a superior unity that would reconcile absolute contradictions is a metaphysical assault on ethics." [12] Instead of metaphysical grounding, there is to be ethical seriousness. Now "seriousness is: the singular." [13] The good is no longer met anywhere on the subsumptive scale—neither at the top, to be beheld universally, nor particularized at the bottom. Instead of the good's evidence, there remains "the dread of the good." [14] Dread, since the serious good demands of me that I singularize myself, just as Abraham singularized himself sacrificing Isaac. Who, then, is speaking when individuation is treated as evil? The natural metaphysician is speaking again, dreaded this time but hushing dread promptly by desire's megalomaniacal therapy. Desire cannot bear seriousness. It cannot but deny such inversion of the primal scene. Still, from one sacrifice to the other, from Iphigenia's to Isaac's, the function of simple ultimacy passes from the common to the singular.

With that translocation, now, the wherefrom of evil becomes difficult to fathom: does it arise as universal principles get obfuscated in their simple evidence, or rather as singularizing dread gets muzzled—like Iphigenia gagged—by tragic denial? A narrator of epochal hegemonies might arbitrate without metaphysical hardship. He might say: until normative self-consciousness began to wane (roughly, until the deaths of Hegel and Goethe), singularization and individuation smacked of evil. Then, with the destitution of the modern referent, masters of suspicion appeared who inverted everything. Not unlike Kierkegaard, they placed the singular at the top of the ladder of values and the universal, the one, every fantasm of unity, at the bottom. Yet the hegemonies cannot be recounted as one recounts periods in factual history. They do not stretch time into duration. Theirs is not the historian's history. Here again, therefore, what intelligibility concerning ultimate conditions of evil would be gained with the piece of information about normative inversion in the last century? None.

In truth, if natality and morality are phenomenologically originary, we do know what to make of the inversion thesis (a thesis it is). To report that after about 1830 values got inverted, the bottom of the ladder now counting for the top and the top, for the bottom—such storytelling is not exactly free of any interest. It allows one to classify one's neighbor, if he locates high what is ultimate, as "still a metaphysician": for two centuries now, the *ultimate* insult. But the interest in simple ultimacy makes this verdict, "still an X," in its turn a thoroughly metaphysical insult. Let us rather say that, in Kierkegaard's words, the voice of dread beneath that of desire then made itself heard. Discordant voices became listened to, voices by which it is useful to let us be instructed. Through their discordance speaks tragic knowing. They testify to the *orietur* which always attracts us toward some focal meaning, as well as to the *morietur* subtracting us from it.

The two incongruent functional clusters, attraction-natality-maximization-appropriation and subtraction-mortality-singularization-expropriation, then the denial of this whole second cluster as well as the exaltation of attractive, maximally normative, theses: these then are conditions of evil other than ethical, moral, or onto-theological.

There are to be sure others, and more that we do not understand than ones we do. At least for a phenomenology of ultimates, *the* condition of evil does indeed not exist. No more, one may add, than exists *the* way of demonstration or *the* method in phenomenology. It would therefore be non-pertinent to object: You set out from the premises of natality-mortality, only to step from the descriptive to the prescriptive and so end up with normative double binds. The objection is beside the point. First, philosophy's point consists in submitting to rigorous thinking elements of experience of which we do have prior knowing; an argumentative circle is thus not vicious if it allows one to understand conditions better. Furthermore, it would be one thing to state first propositions held to be true, but it is quite another to begin from originary traits with which everyone is familiar; natality and mortality are thus not premises for deductive reasoning. Lastly, those traits cannot be described like givens; the conditions of evil just mentioned thus do not result out of a metabasis from the describable.

Kierkegaard can help one undo entanglements, knitted by a long tradition, which tie evil back to the singular: to individuation, and also to one single condition which would account for evil. But in order to descry the originary dissension that ruins from within any normative posit, an analytic is needed that brings an historical topology to bear on daily knowing.

OF IMPOSSIBLE NORMATIVE SIMPLICITY

That analytic, varied according to the natural languages and the epochs on which each put its stamp, can be schematized here only by a few pointers. Firstly, singulars and singularities follow phenomenologically from singulariz*ation* (from the pull of mortality). Furthermore, as originary, singularization works on normative posits from within, thus depriving us of any appellate jurisdiction. Also, recognizing the singular as irreducible to the particular and hence to subsumption—a recognition that remains oblique under the hegemonies and has shown to provoke either dread or elation at their limits—in no way means that one can somehow escape from under norms, depos-

ited though they are in advance by their singular extraction even as
they are posited as sovereign. Lastly, simple focal meanings are not
evil-gotten (their positing follows from the very attraction of natality),
but the equation "the ultimate is simple" kills, since it decrees as if
singularization were not. Of these pointers the first directs attention
to the to-come; the second to a certain anarchy; the third to the tragic
double bind that persists throughout historical dispositions; and the
last to the tragic hubris of simple sways.

"Develop your singularities," one was told not long ago in Paris as
well as in California. The exhortation entailed and entails analytically: "Respect singularities." Yet here is what was not said and is
however needed if philosophy's task remains to render explicit the
prior knowing that we have of conditions: Whence such an imperative? What renders it possible? Accordingly, no time was lost in Frank-
furt to retort: "In the name of what? Spell out your validity arguments." Now names and values, as well as the subjective (or
intersubjective) competency on which critical theorists rest such arguments, under topological inspection turn out as products, brought
into being by theticism.[15] Just as any other thetic referent, the one
invoked in the name of consensus through discursive rationality, or
through communicative action, can be posited only at the cost of denying the foreignness of singular references. These references enter
enabling strategies that are entirely other than subjectivist. They can
be detected, provided one ceases maximizing self-consciousness, be it
for the sake of a universal pragmatics. In order to reach an origin
other than posited and positive, there is no abundance of methods. I
need to return to what I always know, though poorly: namely, my
singularization *to come.*[16]

Polymorphous singularities constitute themselves,[17] and monomor-
phous theses get destituted, not to be sure by time as such. That would
amount to declaring yet another magnitude rather than gathering a
trait. Only the expropriating retraction toward my death, hence time
as *contretemps,* corners singularity. The singular I implies therefore
neither fullness nor ownness. It is not the achievement of autonomous
freedom, not the self. Rather it comes about with the dephenomenalizing strategy in ordinary experience: with expropriation from the
world as mine. Social theorists have always acknowledged such constitutive disownment, albeit indirectly, when they say that the world—
community or collectivity, family, civil society, state—does not come
about through accumulation and that, in all idealist rigor, the individual has no being. For a thinking that recognizes originary time in expropriation to come, there are singularities only as dispossessed. They

are nothing to flaunt since, inasmuch as my world is always about to expel me, they owe their being to the temporality of imminence. I am I, singularly dispossessed.

As differing ultimates, natality and mortality bear thus unequally on futurity. Death as dealt—this is not a popular thought, as from all sides norms and values are clamored for—results from the impulse of natality, at least when dealt "in the name of . . ." It has been said that there was an aspect of banality to exterminations. One may add: evil becomes banal, once a common focalization is posited and singularization denied. The other's death turns out to be easy as soon as a fantasm has carried the day and has come to obsess everyone's visual expanse. From the trait of mortality, on the other hand, results only death as suffered, presently imminent.[18] Maximizations will never stop being invested in, unless philosophy is trusted in its ability to dissolve the *hubris* behind any simple normative meaning: that is, to analyze it, decompose it into its elements, detect the denial, and thus beneath the prestige of names rehabilitate the temporality by singularization.

In philosophy, indeed, one may just as well put one's pens away if inquiring into ultimate conditions of experience is to be renounced. But one ceases to so inquire if some *a priori* is posited by maximizing one or the other representation that happens to enjoy prevalence. Such theticism meets one's wishes, which makes it essentially gratifying. It crowns one's fantasmic investments with a paramount guaranty, not unlike the way the FDIC guarantees bank investments. There exists today a whole philosophical industry, administered by the "functionaries of mankind" (Husserl), to sanction institutions and usages. But something unsteady remains about gratifications, since for the interval they last they require that I blind myself against negative experience. Such is the secret that accounts for the ascendancy of archic posits: they condense the true, the beautiful, the good to their extreme. And how could desire not find its fulfillment—its pleasure and climax—in such compactness? It would be hard to imagine an exaltation literally more marvelous than the ascent to ideals, including of course the ideal of undistorted intersubjective communication.

Yet it is concerning just such marvels that in everydayness we do know better. If pleasure demands that I deny negative experience, then this kind of experience has already been recognized. Otherwise there could be no denying it. In addition, everyone knows that it will have, and therefore already has, the last word. But then the platform from which fantasmic maximizations take off, and from which ascend therefore normative arguments, has in advance been cut out to serve more and less magnificent—because more and less magnifiable—interests.

Last century's Objective Idealism recognized the systematic need to trace the conditions of negative experience back to the "ground" (for Schelling, freedom). However, it is not difficult to see that by splitting the sovereign principle into originary ground and non-ground (*Urgrund* and *Ungrund*), one only applies to evil the same subsumptive exaltation to which we owe all hegemonic fantasms. Evil gets in turn maximized and introduced into the master referent. Thus, in Schelling, the absolute will universalizes ends and reasons, while also singularizing itself in original sin. Coupling evil absolutely with the good, one has hardly found a way out of theticism. For that it is necessary to remain faithful to the irreducible phenomena: the traits of natality and mortality. With such faithfulness, however, the ultimate condition can no longer be absolutely simple and in that sense archic.

Whether explicitly or tacitly and whatever its variant, a doctrine of principles cannot do without a concept of anarchy. In such a doctrine, this concept only sums up the axiom that forbids stepping back indefinitely towards more and more primitive conditions. Within theticism, the first *arché* will have to be anarchic, since it would no longer be first if in turn it had its *arché*.

Quite different is the anarchy that appears as one tries to unlearn truncating the phenomenologically originary conditions. Then singularization shows itself to impair any normative posit from within. The call to remain faithful to singularization jars with the call of simple principles establishing the law. Such ultimate dissonance deprives us, and has always deprived us, of any appellate jurisdiction. The origin thus proves *anarchic because in dissension with itself*.

The eras of philosophy, set apart by the languages in which it has been spoken, can best be described through fantasmic theticism. A thetic fantasm always regulates a given epochal array. The way these arrays are articulated on their regulatory posits mutates ceaselessly. Just as varying in every epoch is the destabilizing undertow by which singularization to come brings these normative arrays into disarray.

The topologist does, however, more than describe shifting territories and the breaks between them. Were he to stay content with descriptions, the very search for conditions would be blocked. Now if these conditions are not simple, how are they to be understood and told? It seems to me that they are most easily read in the elementary functions of maximization and singularization that traverse the history of referential theses. I have suggested that these functions reproduce in large script the traits of everyday experience. If that is so, then—whether the counterstrategies issuing from morality are recognized or denied—we remain faithful to the *polemos* of ultimates in everything we do and can do. Whatever the epochal order it conditions, the originary condition thus proves to be polemically turned against itself. There is more at stake than recognizing "beneath the rule: abuse" (Bertole Brecht). Rather transgression occurs at the very heart of legislation, in its essence and its instances. Not that agents always abuse the rule, but always, as it regulates, the rule abuses itself. To rule and regulate is to speak in the name of the common. It is to simplify the manifold, produce evidence, and thereby make oneself understood. The tragic authors saw an unruliness as part and parcel of the rule, a "dark light" (Hölderlin) at the core of evidence. They tell us: *You cannot understand. You must understand.* What? That any name laying down the law contains in it its own forces of abandon. That we always inhabit a fugued world, one about to withdraw even while it shelters us, a world escaping. The ultimates that are at the beginning of thought stay incomprehensible as they comprehend *it*. But what one cannot speak about, that alone the tragics have said, and it remains what wing all must be said.

The ceaseless rearrangements within any given language epoch appear only to a pre-understanding of ultimates. The same is true of the breaks when, instead of Greek, Latin—and later, one or the other modern vernacular—becomes philosophy's *lingua franca*. The originary double bind can be verified as it is put to the test of these historical loci. Its pre-understanding provides, not to be sure a fixed grid, but the dynamics of allocations and dislocations opening each time an epoch. Outside the epochal articulations, these traits remain indeed untreatable. They could solidify into theoretical objects, only at the cost of erasing the language breaks so as to decree some philosophical *volapük*. How could the refigurations and breaks even be investigated as such, unless one possessed a prior knowing that allows one to read both the trait that welds a world together and the one that tears it?

Now if we know ourselves to be so incongruously bound, there is something comical about the urge to force an exit from the ultimate double bind. Comical, inasmuch as that urge looks very much the same whether one seeks to rise to some speculative belvedere towering above one or the other metaphysical terrains, or whether one seeks on the contrary to escape all such terrains on which to speculate so as to gain private consolation and public consolation. This is also why "anarchy" does not mean and cannot mean to relegate all *archai* among obsolete philosophical tools and to go and settle happily in a place deprived of principles.[19] The phenomenology of ultimates adds an epilogue to hegemonic fantasms, but an epilogue to fantasms as such would be unthinkable. It would be no less unthinkable than not putting universals into the service of some consoling and consolidating name. All common names are capable of so consoling the soul and consolidating the city, inasmuch as we think and speak under the fantasmogenic impetus of natality. It is however possible to enlarge one's way of thinking[20] beyond the common so generated. In our languages, verbs in the middle voice always lead their speaker out of simple nominative rule governance. It is then possible to think for itself the double bind of which we have a prior knowing. After hubristic sufferings—not unlike Oedipus who at Colonus wants his eyes open, wants himself open-eyed—it is possible to love differing ultimates. This, I submit, would be expanding the limits of imagination.

Natality gives and regives us a world in which to dwell. It does this by extolling names or "general ideas" under which to rally. Of these, the best would be the most general, hence also the most simple. It would give us the best of all worlds. As a consequence of its simple bind however—and the West has witnessed those consequences—such a world kills. The thetic thrust mutilates thinking. Just as desire, of which it is the public agent, theticism has no use of remaining faithful to phenomena, which faithfulness is called thinking. It singles out some square meaning, augments it, institutes it as an authority, bestows hegemony on it. Such squaring of thought produces fantasms that are mortal not only in that they perish, but also in that make perish.

The metaphysician in us is recalcitrant against the insight that the ultimate is not—nor can be—simple; that it becomes so squared, only under blows of thetic denial. The tragics on the other hand did not fear what they knew. Beneath the profusion of plots they show one and the same nomic differing, first cut down for the sake of institutions, then suffered, recognized, accepted, embraced. For them, some blinding meaning was instituted only as a result of a different blinding: of *hubris*.

Thinking becomes urgent, one would like to say easy, once *hubris* has been committed. Then Antigone all of a sudden speaks in the voice of Creon and Creon, in Antigone's.[21] The Furies, avengeresses according to the terrible heroic code, suddenly plead the democratic order; and Athena, the city's tutelary, advocates the *deinon* in institutions.[22] This discursive permutation has been praised as the moment of dialectical reconciliation. But not so, since the opposition does not amount to a determinate negation. Rather thinking here stays faithful to disparate ultimates. In the aftermath of *hubris* committed (totalitarianisms lying behind us in Europe, it seems), new questions get a chance such as: how could thoughtlessness ever go so far? Concerning these aftermaths, we enjoy today an indisputable prerogative. At the end of this century in the West, we are rather well stationed to recover—if that were possible—from denial and thoughtlessness. Looking back from *hubris* toward tragic knowing, expanded imagination may indeed see singulars jar incongruously with their the world:

> No one was able to remember when and how long ago Akaky Akakievich had entered the ministry, nor who had given him the job. The directors, department heads, division managers and other administrators came and went; he was always seen in the same place, in the same position, at the very same duty of a copying clerk. No respect was shown him in the office. The porters, far from getting up from their seats when he came in, took no more notice of him than if a fly had flown across the room. The head clerk's assistant would throw papers under his nose without even bothering to say "Copy this." The younger clerks jeered and made jokes at him to the best of their clerkly wit. They would scatter bits of paper on his head and exclaim "Snow falling!" Akaky Akakievich, however, remained impassive. Only when one of them jolted his arm and hindered him from doing his work, he simply said:
> "Leave me alone. What have I done to you?"
> There was something strange in these words. He uttered them in such a poignant tone that one young man, new to the office and who, following the example of the rest, had allowed himself to tease him, suddenly stopped as though cut to the heart. From that moment on, the world appeared to him in a different light.[23]

NOTES

1. This paper was originally delivered at the Cardozo School of Law in New York City in September 1991, at a conference on "The Politics of Transformation and the Limit of the Imagination".

2. Goethe, spokesman in this for the natural metaphysician in us, has Mephistopheles describe himself as "that spirit which always negates" (*ich bin der Geist, der stets verneint, Faust,* First Part, l. 1338). That spirit negates the good, whereby evil not only becomes knowable but also proves akin to the good: "As the opposite of the good, evil pertains to the order of the knowable as well as of the good" (*malum ex hoc ipso quod bono opponitur habet rationem cognoscibilis et boni,* Thomas Aquinas, *On Truth,* q. 2, art. 15, 2nd reply). In metaphysical theticism (a pleonastic phrase anyway), the other is always the other *of* some primary posit.

3. There is no equivalent in modern English for the distinction between *wissen* and *kennen* (or *erkennen*); in French *savoir* and *connaître*. Whenever the context is

not clear, one has to supply a distinction such as between "prior knowing" and "actual knowledge."

4. Concerning hegemonic referents, I can only refer to the work in progress from which, with minor modifications, this paper is excerpted. In that work, a topology of normative binds will be attempted.

5. H. Arendt, The Human Condition 246f (1958).

6. The axiom is current in scholasticism (e.g. Meister Eckhart, *Die lateinischen Werke*, vol. I, 149 (Konrad Weiß ed. 1937). "Actual knowledge" results from recourse to one such generic science or discursive type. "Prior knowing," we will see, seizes disparate opposites, without a genus. To step from *Wissen* to *Wissenschaft*, the ultimates of tragic knowing need to be subjected to the principles of non-contradiction, of identity, and of the excluded middle.

7. See supra note 4.

8. An argument relating evil to good as mortality relates to natality, would do no more than disguise phenomenologically a metaphysics of identity. If evil amounts to a singularization that is equi-originary with the good, then how is one to avoid relapsing into some gnostic dialectic? That such a dialectic would be non-viable appears from singulars' *differing* with particulars. Singulars remain impossible to dialecticize. They are opposed to universals, neither contradictorily nor contrarily, but rather incongruently.

9. Cf. the enumeration of "the rare moments of freedom" according to Hannah Arendt (H. Arendt, The Origins of Totalitarianism 497 and elsewhere [1958]).

10. F. Nietzsche, The Birth of Tragedy, § 10.

11. *"Malum est male muti bono,"* Augustine, On the Nature of the Good bk. I, ch. 36 (PL vol. 42, col. 562).

12. Søren Kierkegaard, Diary, entry dated August 1, 1835.

13. S. Kierkegaard, Gesammelte Werke, vol. 30, 9 (E. Hirsch ed. 1958).

14. S. Kierkegaard, Der Begriff Angst 117ff. and 135ff (1923).

15. The words "value," *Wert, valeur* pass from the vocabulary of political economy into that of philosophy, about the times of Hume and Kant. That idiom is not only contemporaneous with the institution of the modern hegemony, it is one of that institution's immediate effects. Values come into being, in valuations performed by the originarily spontaneous subject. Trying to develop "arguments of validity" from communication, one does therefore not cease turning in circles in the arena of hegemonic self-consciousness. With such arguments, it is still subjectivity that sniffs its own traces, i.e. the values it has posited with the transcendental turn.

16. This phrase is used here to underline in what Heidegger called being-towards-death the temporal pull of imminence, as well as the subtraction from the world induced by that pull.

17. It would be no less a thetic operation top speculate on *the* sexual difference, as if singularities were safe as long as one proves capable of counting up to two and posits no longer the (male) one, but the (female) other. In speaking of sexualities, common names such as "feminism" can only perpetuate binary models and hence the most crudely metaphysical antitheses.

18. On the discrepancy between death about to be dealt on a large scale, banal as a

consequence of a common belief, and death as imminently suffered, see the novel by Christa Wolf, *Cassandra* (trans. J. van Heurck, 1984). Nothing I know illustrates better the two incongruent kinds of futurity.

19. Jacques Derrida gives an example of anarchy as characterizing an "outside" on which to settle in a resolute "decision." He describes a strategy of "changing terrains, in a discontinuous and irruptive fashion, by brutally placing oneself outside and by asserting an absolute break and difference." Margins of Philosophy 135 (A. Bass trans. 1982). I read these lines as a description of events in France at the time the essay was finished ("May 12, 1968," *ibid.*, p. 136).

20. In Kant, the "expanded way of thinking" (*die erweiterte Denkungsart*) consists in a judgment that takes singulars into account, cf. *Critique of Judgment*, § 40, 77.

21. Sophocles, *Antigone,* lines 504–09 and 734–41.

22. Aeschylus, *The Eumenides,* lines 517, 696ff.

23. N. Gogol, "The Overcoat," in *The Collected Tales and Plays* 564f (C. Garnett trans., L. J. Kent rev. 1964) (translation slightly modified and abbreviated).

Index

Contributors

DAVID GRAY CARLSON is Professor of Law at the Benjamin N. Cardozo School of Law, Yeshiva University. He teaches in the areas of commercial law and bankruptcy, and is co-editor of *Hegel and Legal Theory* (Routledge 1991).

DRUCILLA CORNELL is Professor of Law at the Benjamin N. Cardozo School of Law, Yeshiva University. She is the author of *Beyond Accommodation* (Routledge 1991) and *The Philosophy of the Limit* (Routledge 1992) and co-editor of *Hegel and Legal Theory* (Routledge 1991).

FRED DALLMAYR is the Dee Professor of Government at the University of Notre Dame. He is the author of numerous books, which include *Twilight of Subjectivity* (1981), *Polis and Praxis* (1984), *Language and Politics* (1984), *Critical Encounters* (1987), *Margins of Political Discourse* (1989), and *Life-World Modernity and Critique* (1991).

JACQUES DERRIDA currently teaches at l'Ecole des Hautes Etudes en Sciences Sociales in Paris. He is also a regular Visiting Professor at the Benjamin N. Cardozo School of Law, Yeshiva University, the New School for Social Research, New York University, and at the University of California at Irvine. His principal texts include *Speech and Phenomena* (1973), *Writing and Difference* (1978), *Of Grammatology* (1974), *Dissemination* (1981), *Margins of Philosophy* (1982), *Mémoires: For Paul De Man* (1986), *Spurs* (1979), *Truth in Painting* (1987), *The Post Card* (1979), and *Limited Inc., ABC* (1988).

HENRY LOUIS GATES is the W.E.B. Du Bois Professor of the Humanities, Director of the W.E.B. Du Bois Institute and Chairman of the Afro-American Studies Department at Harvard University. Some of his recent books include *Loose Canons: Notes on the Culture Wars* (1992), *The Signifying Monkey: Towards a Theory of Afro-American Literary Criticism* (1988), and *Figures in Black: Words, Signs, and the Racial Self* (1987).

AGNES HELLER is the Hannah Arendt Professor of Philosophy and Political Science, the New School for Social Research, New York City. Among her many books are *General Ethics* (1988), *Beyond Justice* (1987), *The Power of Shame* (1986), and *Radical Philosophy* (1984).

BARBARA HERRNSTEIN SMITH is the Braxton Craven Professor of Comparative Literature and English at Duke University. Her books include *Contingencies of Value: Alternative Perspectives for Critical Theory* (1988) and *Shakespeare's Sonnets* (1969). She is recently the co-editor of *The Politics of Liberal Education* (1991).

ARTHUR J. JACOBSON is the Max Freund Professor of Litigation and Advocacy at the Benjamin N. Cardozo School of Law, Yeshiva University. He is an editor of "Philosophy, Social Theory and the Rule of Law," a series published by the University of California Press. His *Dynamic Jurisprudence* will appear in the series, along with *Weimar Jurisprudence,* a collection of translations of leading works of Weimar legal theory, which he is editing with Bernhard Schlink.

MICHEL ROSENFELD is Professor of Law at the Benjamin N. Cardozo School of Law, Yeshiva University. He is the author of *Affirmative Action and Justice: A Philosophical and Constitutional Inquiry* and co-editor of *Hegel and Legal Theory* (Routledge 1991). He is an editor of "Philosophy, Social Theory and the Rule of Law," a series published by the University of California Press, and is currently working on a book entitled *Contract as Justice* for that series.

J. HILLIS MILLER is Distinguished Professor of English and Comparative Literature at the University of California at Irvine and is the author of ten books, including *Versions of Pygmalion* (1990), *Ariadne's Thread* (1992), and *Illustration* (1992).

REINER SCHÜRMANN is Professor of Philosophy at the New School for Social Research, New York. He is the editor of *The Public Realm: Essays on Discursive Types in Political Philosophy* (1988), and the author of *Heidegger on Being and Acting: From Principals to Anarchy* (1986) and *Meister Eckhart, Mystic and Philosopher* (1978).

SAMUEL WEBER is Professor of English and Comparative Literature at the University of California at Los Angeles. His recent books include *Return to Freud: Jacques Lacan's Dislocation of Psychoanalysis* (1991).

ALAN WOLFE is Dean of the Graduate Faculty and Michael E. Gellert Professor of Sociology and Political Science, the New School for Social Research, New York City. His recent works include *Whose Keeper?: Social Science and Moral Obligation* (1989) and *Sociology and the Human Subject* (forthcoming 1992). He is also the editor of *America at Century's End* (1991).

CHARLES M. YABLON is Professor of Law at the Benjamin N. Cardozo School of Law, Yeshiva University. He is the author of *Cases and Materials on Civl Procedure* (Foundation Press 1992), along with A. Leo Levin and Phillip Shuchman.